# Asian Advantage

# Also by George S. Yip

*Total Global Strategy: Managing for Worldwide Competitive Advantage*

# ASIAN ADVANTAGE

## Key Strategies for Winning in the Asia-Pacific Region

GEORGE S. YIP

ADDISON-WESLEY

Reading, Massachusetts

*To our families*

---

Many of the designations used by manufacturers and sellers to distinguish their products are claimed as trademarks. Where those designations appear in this book and Addison-Wesley was aware of a trademark claim, the designations have been printed in initial capital letters.

*Library of Congress Cataloging-in-Publication Data*
Yip, George S.
    Asian advantage : key strategies for winning in the Asia-Pacific
region / George S. Yip.
        p.   cm.
    Includes bibliographical references and index.
    ISBN 0-201-33978-1 (alk. paper)
    1. Asia—Economic conditions.   2. Pacific Area—Economic
conditions.   3. International business enterprises—Asia.
    4. International business enterprises—Pacific Area.   I. Title.
    HC412.Y55   1998
330.95'0429—dc21                                    97-36580
                                                       CIP

Addison-Wesley is an imprint of Addison Wesley Longman, Inc.

Jacket design by Suzanne Heiser
Text design by David C. denBoer
Set in 10pt New Baskerville by Nighthawk Design

123456789-MA-0201009998
First printing, March 1998

Addison-Wesley books are available at special discounts for bulk purchases in the U.S. by corporations, institutions, and other organizations. For more information, please contact the Corporate, Government, and Special Sales Department at Addison Wesley Longman, Inc., One Jacob Way, Reading, MA 01867, or call 1-800-238-9682.

Find us on the World Wide Web at
http://www.aw.com/gb/

# Contents

# List of Figures

# List of Tables

# Preface

THIS BOOK IS THE culmination of a nearly three-year effort by a team of sixteen coauthors spread across thirteen Asia-Pacific countries plus the United States. We have met as a group in both Hong Kong and Manila, individually in different parts of the world, and electronically frequently.

I have lived what I teach: global strategic alliances. I wish to thank all of my coauthors, first for joining the team and, second, for all the effort they have put in. My coauthors have contributed not just to their respective country chapters but to other chapters in the book and to the overall framework. I also value their friendship.

I wish to thank all of the assistants who have worked with my coauthors. I also wish to thank the many research assistants who have helped me: Lynda Bahaudin, Heather Berry, Bill Fink, Mark Junkunc, Jina Kang, Kate Kimball, Konstantina Kiousis, Avanish Sahai, Steve Valerie, Don Wong, and Vitus Wong; all were UCLA Anderson MBA or doctoral students. Mohan Sankaran and Tal Simchoni skillfully produced the exhibits used in this book. Randy O'Toole of the Federal Reserve Bank of San Francisco helped with economic data. I also wish to thank a number of support staff, especially Allen Nepsa, Susan Wu, and Carolyn Tutas.

I wish to thank José de la Torre and the Center for International Business Education and Research, Anderson School at UCLA, for partial funding of this project. Danny Stern of the Leigh Bureau arranged talks that funded my frequent trips to Asia.

We are also very grateful to the many executives who read the manuscript to check and comment on what we wrote about their own or competing companies. These include: Beiersdorf—Ralph Gusko and Wolfgang Wunsche; Matsushita Electric Industrial—Norio Gomi; Motorola—Larry Ohlrogge and C. D. Tam; Philips—Nigel Freedman; Procter and Gamble—Don Johnson, V. Bali, Ed Imperial, Peter Laing, Esmond Mok, Paul Nix, J. D. Weedman, James Wei, and Carol Yang; Toyota—Toshiaki Taguchi; and Unilever—R. H. P. Markham and André van Heemstra. Ruy Moreno of Arthur Andersen, Ho Chi Minh City, helped with information about Vietnam.

A very special thanks is due to Nick Philipson of Addison Wesley Longman. He has enthusiastically and capably supported this project since its inception. I also thank Maria and David denBoer of Nighthawk Design for their editorial and production help.

Lastly, I thank my wife Moira and my children, Andrew and Sarah, for coping with my absences on trips or while working in my study.

*November 1997*

# CHAPTER 1

# Evaluating the
# Asia-Pacific Opportunity

THE ASIA-PACIFIC REGION should provide the most profitable prospects for business activity over the next several decades, although shaken by the financial crises that began in 1997. The third millennium will still begin with the "Pacific Century." While other regions, such as Latin America, the countries of the former Soviet bloc, the Middle East, or even sub-Saharan Africa, may offer spectacular growth in the future, it is the countries of Asia-Pacific that have already achieved economic takeoff and can be of immediate profit for multinational companies both as markets and as sources of production—and increasingly as sources of innovation. The economies in the triangle bounded by Japan, India, and New Zealand already account for a third of the world's gross national product (GNP), and have enjoyed most of the fastest growth rates in recent years (Table 1.1).[1] Using purchasing power parity (PPP) measures (i.e., adjusting for differing price levels in each country) of gross domestic product (GDP), the economic strength of most Asia-Pacific countries looks even greater (see columns four and six of Table 1.1). Furthermore, these economies attract a great deal of foreign direct investment, and many of these Asian economies also make significant investments in other countries (Tables 1.2, 1.3, and 1.4).

So managers in multinational companies (MNCs), whether from North America, Western Europe, Asia, or other parts of the world, need to develop effective strategies for the Asia-Pacific region—for individual countries, for the region as a whole, and for how the region fits into an overall global strategy. We have written this book to help managers develop these strategies, and, for those already in the region, to improve their strategies.

To succeed with an Asian (or any regional) strategy, a company needs to work on four levels:

1. overall global strategy
2. regional strategy
3. country strategy
4. country operations

Table 1.1

**Key Statistics of Asia-Pacific and Other Economies**

| | Population 1995 (millions) | Population 2020 (millions) | GNP 1995 (U.S.$ billions) | GNP (PPP[a]) 1995 (U.S.$ billions) | Per Capita GNP 1995 (U.S.$) | PPP[a] Per Capita GNP 1995 (U.S.$) | Avg. GDP Growth 1995-1997 (%)[b] |
|---|---|---|---|---|---|---|---|
| *Asia-Pacific* | | | | | | | |
| Japan | 125.5 | 130.9 | 4,975 | 2,775 | 39,640 | 22,110 | 2.8 |
| South Korea | 44.9 | 57.5 | 436 | 514 | 9,700 | 11,450 | 7.7 |
| China | 1,200.2 | 1,489.0 | 744 | 3,505 | 620 | 2,920 | 10.5 |
| Taiwan | 22.0 | 27.5 | 246 | 279 | 12,265 | 14,295[c] | 6.0 |
| Hong Kong | 6.2 | 7.0 | 144 | 142 | 23,200 | 22,950 | 4.9 |
| Singapore | 3.0 | 3.2 | 80 | 68 | 26,730 | 22,770 | 7.2 |
| Malaysia | 20.1 | 26.3 | 78 | 181 | 3,890 | 9,020 | 8.3 |
| Thailand | 58.2 | 81.0 | 159 | 439 | 2,740 | 7,540 | 7.2 |
| Indonesia | 193.3 | 269.6 | 189 | 735 | 980 | 3,800 | 7.5 |
| Philippines | 66.6 | 99.9 | 72 | 196 | 1,050 | 2,850 | 5.5 |
| India | 929.4 | 1,252.8 | 316 | 1,301 | 340 | 1,400 | 5.9 |
| Vietnam | 73.5 | 119.1 | 18 | 96[c] | 240 | 1,310[c] | 9.0 |
| Australia | 16.1 | 19.9 | 339 | 343 | 18,720 | 18,940 | 3.3 |
| New Zealand | 3.6 | 3.9 | 52 | 59 | 14,340 | 16,360 | 3.5 |
| *Other* | | | | | | | |
| United States | 263.1 | 282.3 | 7,098 | 7,098 | 26,980 | 26,980 | 3.2 |
| Germany | 81.9 | 70.7 | 2,253 | 1,644 | 27,510 | 20,070 | 2.9 |
| Mexico | 91.8 | 145.6 | 305 | 588 | 3,320 | 6,400 | 2.0 |
| Poland | 61.1 | 44.4 | 170 | 330 | 2,790 | 5,400[d] | 6.4 |

*Sources:* International Economics Department, The World Bank; *Asiaweek*, March 28, 1997, p. 72.

[a]*Purchasing Power Parity*

[b]*Includes estimates for 1997.*

[c]*GDP*

[d]*For 1994*

## Table 1.2
### Foreign Direct Investment Inflows, 1990–1996

| | 1990 | 1991 | 1992 | 1993 | 1994 | 1995 | 1996 |
|---|---|---|---|---|---|---|---|
| | (U.S.$ millions) | | | | | | |
| *Asia-Pacific* | | | | | | | |
| Japan | 1,753 | 1,730 | 3,490 | 234 | 908 | 39 | 220 |
| South Korea | 788 | 1,180 | 727 | 588 | 809 | 1,500 | 2,308 |
| China | 3,487 | 4,366 | 11,156 | 27,515 | 33,787 | 37,500 | 42,300 |
| Taiwan | 1,330 | 1,271 | 879 | 917 | 1,375 | 1,470 | 1,402 |
| Hong Kong | 1,728 | 538 | 2,051 | 1,667 | 2,000 | 2,100 | 2,500 |
| Singapore | 5,575 | 4,879 | 2,351 | 5,016 | 5,588 | 5,302 | 9,400 |
| Malaysia | 2,333 | 3,998 | 5,183 | 5,006 | 4,348 | 5,800 | 5,300 |
| Thailand | 2,444 | 2,014 | 2,116 | 1,726 | 640 | 2,300 | 2,426 |
| Indonesia | 1,093 | 1,482 | 1,777 | 2,004 | 2,109 | 4,500 | 7,960 |
| Philippines | 530 | 544 | 228 | 1,025 | 1,457 | 1,500 | 1,408 |
| India | 162 | 141 | 151 | 273 | 620 | 1,750 | 2,587 |
| Vietnam | 16 | 32 | 24 | 25 | 100 | 150 | 156 |
| Australia | 7,077 | 4,903 | 4,912 | 2,687 | 4,423 | 13,094 | 6,043 |
| New Zealand | 1,686 | 1,698 | 1,090 | 2,200 | 2,796 | 2,483 | 2,528 |
| *Other* | | | | | | | |
| United States | 47,918 | 22,020 | 17,580 | 41,128 | 49,760 | 60,236 | 84,629 |
| Germany | 2,689 | 4,071 | 2,370 | 277 | -2,993 | 8,996 | 20,809 |
| Mexico | 2,549 | 4,742 | 4,393 | 4,389 | 7,978 | 6,984 | 7,535 |
| Poland | 89 | 291 | 678 | 1,715 | 1,875 | 2,510 | 5,196 |

*Source:* United Nations Conference on Trade and Development, *World Investment Report 1997: Investment, Trade and International Policy Arrangements,* Annex Table 1, 227–232

*Overall global strategy.* Before deciding whether and how to do business in Asia, or any other region of the world, a company needs to have a clear global strategy. Key elements of this strategy include the core business strategy, the competitive objectives for the business, and the extent to which the business will be operated as a single integrated business or as a looser collection of geographically independent units.

*Regional strategy.* Next, a company needs to decide on the overall role of Asia within the global strategy. Should Asia be a source of growth, or profit, or both? Should Asia be primarily a source of supply or a locus of markets? Or should different countries play differing roles? In which countries in Asia should the company do business?

*Country strategy.* Having selected the countries in which to be involved, the company should develop a country strategy that includes the mode of entry, partner selection, the usual elements of a business strategy, (including what activities to conduct and what parts of the value chain to locate in the country), and how activities in the country will relate to those in the rest of the region and the world.

**Table 1.3**
**Foreign Direct Investment Outflows, 1990–1996**

| | 1990 | 1991 | 1992 | 1993 | 1994 | 1995 | 1996 |
|---|---|---|---|---|---|---|---|
| | | | (U.S.$ millions) | | | | |
| *Asia-Pacific* | | | | | | | |
| Japan | 48,024 | 42,619 | 21,916 | 15,471 | 18,521 | 21,286 | 23,440 |
| South Korea | 1,056 | 1,500 | 1,208 | 1,361 | 2,524 | 3,000 | 4,188 |
| China | 830 | 913 | 4,000 | 4,400 | 2,000 | 3,467 | 2,200 |
| Taiwan | 5,243 | 1,854 | 1,869 | 2,451 | 2,460 | 3,822 | 3,096 |
| Hong Kong | 2,448 | 2,825 | 8,254 | 17,713 | 21,437 | 25,000 | 27,000 |
| Singapore | 2,034 | 1,024 | 1,317 | 1,784 | 2,177 | 2,799 | 4,800 |
| Malaysia | 532 | 389 | 514 | 1,325 | 1,817 | 2,575 | 1,906 |
| Thailand | 140 | 167 | 147 | 221 | 493 | 904 | 1,740 |
| Indonesia | −11 | 13 | 52 | −31 | 15 | 12 | 512 |
| Philippines | −5 | −26 | 5 | −7 | 28 | 9 | 182 |
| India | 6 | −11 | 24 | 41 | 49 | 38 | 43 |
| Vietnam | 0 | 0 | 0 | 0 | 0 | 0 | 0 |
| Australia | 186 | 3,126 | 113 | 1,611 | 5,842 | 5,372 | 1,343 |
| New Zealand | 2,365 | 1,475 | 392 | −1,370 | 2,041 | 1,310 | −157 |
| | | | | | | | |
| *Other* | | | | | | | |
| United States | 27,175 | 33,456 | 38,978 | 68,978 | 45,640 | 95,509 | 84,902 |
| Germany | 24,214 | 23,723 | 19,698 | 13,176 | 14,653 | 35,302 | 28,652 |
| Mexico | 224 | 167 | 730 | 16 | 1,045 | 597 | 553 |
| Poland | 0 | −7 | 13 | 18 | 29 | 20 | 30 |

*Source:* United Nations Conference on Trade and Development, *World Investment Report 1996: Investment, Trade and International Policy Arrangements,* Annex Table 1, 233–37.

*Country operations.* Lastly, the company has to be concerned with implementation at the operational level. Here the company has to deal with detailed matters such as how to adapt to local culture and business practices, how to develop the right kinds of contacts, how to find customers, and how to cope with the country's written and unwritten regulations.

As illustrated in Figure 1.1, this book focuses on the issues in levels 2 and 3. My previous book, *Total Global Strategy,* deals with level 1. Books of the genre, "How to do business in Country *X,*" and more general social commentaries, help with level 4.[2]

## Asia-Pacific as a Region

Regions can be defined in many ways, depending on the purpose of the definition. For multinational companies, geographic proximity is usually the default basis of definition, if only because of the extensive travel involved in running a global business. A region defined for strategic reasons is also easier to administer if it has geographic coherence or even just spans the same band of time zones. But, in addition, a region defined for

*Table 1.4*
**Cumulative and Net Foreign Direct Investment, 1990–1995**

| | (U.S.$ millions) | | |
|---|---|---|---|
| | Cumulative Inflow | Cumulative Outflow | Net Cumulative Inflow |
| *Asia-Pacific* | | | |
| Japan | 8,154 | 167,837 | −159,683 |
| South Korea | 5,592 | 10,649 | −5,057 |
| China | 117,811 | 15,610 | 102,201 |
| Taiwan | 7,242 | 17,699 | −10,457 |
| Hong Kong | 10,084 | 77,677 | −67,593 |
| Singapore | 23,142 | 11,135 | 12,007 |
| Malaysia | 26,668 | 7,152 | 19,516 |
| Thailand | 11,240 | 2,072 | 9,168 |
| Indonesia | 12,965 | 50 | 12,915 |
| Philippines | 5,284 | 4 | 5,280 |
| India | 3,097 | 147 | 2,950 |
| Vietnam | 347 | 0 | 347 |
| Australia | 37,096 | 16,250 | 20,846 |
| New Zealand | 11,953 | 6,213 | 5,740 |
| *Other* | | | |
| United States | 238,642 | 309,736 | −71,094 |
| Germany | 15,410 | 130,766 | −115,356 |
| Mexico | 31,035 | 2,779 | 28,256 |
| Poland | 7,158 | 73 | 7,085 |

*Source:* United Nations Conference on Trade and Development, *World Investment Report 1996: Investment, Trade and International Policy Arrangements,* Annex Table 1, 227–37.

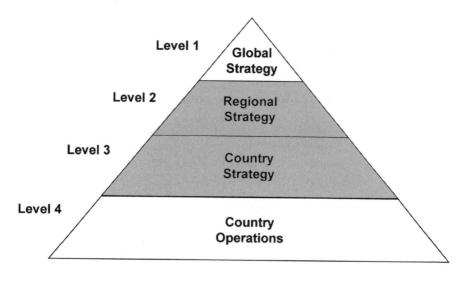

**Figure 1.1** Geographic Levels of Strategy

purposes of business strategy should have a high degree of commonality and mobility in as many as possible of the following characteristics:

- culture
- history
- language
- way of doing business
- form of government
- institutional arrangements
- cross-investment
- intraregional trade
- trade policies and agreements
- economic performance and prospects
- infrastructure, such as airline connections

Using these characteristics, we define Asia-Pacific as that area compris-
ing the countries and economies in the triangle from Japan to India to
New Zealand. Within this region we provide in-depth analysis of Japan,
South Korea, China, Taiwan, Hong Kong, Malaysia, Singapore, Thailand,
Indonesia, the Philippines, India, Australia, New Zealand, and Vietnam
(the latter to a lesser extent because it has much less history of MNC involvement) (Figure 1.2). Regardless of their political status, Taiwan and
Hong Kong have sufficiently strong and distinctive economies to join our
list. So we exclude all the countries from the former Soviet Union, Pakistan, and the Middle East. These excluded countries share few of our
defining characteristics and do not have the economic prospects of Asia-
Pacific. Perhaps most important, the following two characteristics dominate and distinguish the nature of business in the excluded countries.

First, the countries of the former Soviet Union struggle under both the
legacy of the Soviet system and the aftermath of its collapse. While part of
it lies in Asia, Russia is not an Asian country. The Central Asian states of
the former Soviet Union have perhaps more Asian characteristics, but
their recent history and current outlook further differentiate these countries from the rest of Asia. In contrast, China, although still a communist
country, is making a very successful and rapid transformation to a market
economy. Furthermore, China cannot, for economic purposes, be sepa-
rated from the nonnation of overseas Chinese, whose money, skills, and
connections are playing such a huge role in the transformation of their
mother country. Similarly, Vietnam, although still very dominated by its
communist political and economic system, is poised for takeoff and has
joined (in 1995) the most important Asian institution, the Association of
South-East Asian Nations (ASEAN).

Second, for Pakistan and the states of the Middle East or West Asia, Islamic institutions and culture play a far more dominant political, social,
and business role than they do in the Muslim countries of Asia-Pacific
(Malaysia, Indonesia, and Brunei). Furthermore, the focus of Pakistan
and other West Asian states is much more within the Middle East region
than on the Pacific region. And again, the prevalence in business of over-

**Figure 1.2**   Map of Countries and Economies Studied

seas Chinese in Malaysia and Indonesia helps integrate those countries into the rest of the region. In addition, the economies of the West Asian states still depend primarily on the export of oil and gas, and have not yet become significant production sites for MNCs outside the energy sector.

India, while not bordering the Pacific, has ties both with Asia-Pacific and the Middle East, not least because of ethnic Indians living overseas. Furthermore, MNCs increasingly look to India as a substitute location for activities in Asia. Including Australia and New Zealand is somewhat of a stretch, but they exhibit a number of qualifying characteristics. Both have now deemphasized their British heritage and have committed themselves to becoming part of Asia. Most important, they have opened their borders to immigration from Asia. One of the ASEAN leaders, the prime minister of Singapore, has extended an open invitation to Australia to join ASEAN. So the links northward will continue to strengthen. Many Hong Kong entrepreneurs have emigrated to Australia and New Zealand, bringing these countries into the overseas Chinese network. In addition, a large number of Australian nationals, and to a lesser extent, New Zealanders, have spread throughout Asia in the role of expatriate managers.

Lastly, as the objective of this book is to help multinational companies develop strategies for the most important economies in the region, we focus on those countries and economies in which MNCs have already participated in major ways. While they are part of the Asia-Pacific region, we exclude from our analysis smaller countries such as Brunei, Sikkim, Bhutan, and the Pacific island nations; the barely emerging economies of Sri Lanka, Myanmar (formerly Burma), Cambodia, and Laos; and the closed economy of North Korea. Macao (spelled "Macau" locally), the Portuguese colony that will be returned to China in 1999, has become increasingly important to MNCs but, with a population of under 500,000 it is dwarfed in significance by its immediate neighbor, Hong Kong.

## Role of Integrating Factors for Business in Asia-Pacific

Each of the regional integrating factors listed earlier can potentially affect the strategies of MNCs. We provide here a brief analysis of each factor in turn.

### Culture

Vast amounts have been written about the cultures of Asian countries. While each country has many unique aspects to its culture, features common to most of the countries in the region from the viewpoint of business include the following:[3]

- an enthusiasm for business, exceeding perhaps even that in the United States
- a very strong work ethic, including the Confucian work ethic (an important part of Asia's version of the West's Protestant work ethic)
- respect for authority
- importance of family relationships and other connections and cooperation

### History

Most of the countries have some common historical experiences:

- colonization for all except China, Japan, and Thailand. But China has been colonized at its edges (Macao, Hong Kong, Taiwan by Japan, and the Shanghai and Canton concessions), and Japan's occupation and restructuring by the United States produced a quasi-colonial experience.
- occupation by Japan or threat of such occupation during World War II.

These experiences have made countries in the region comfortable with absorbing new ideas and practices, including those introduced by foreigners, which can be a very significant factor for Western MNCs seeking to transfer their approaches to these countries.

## Language

Although the countries in Asia-Pacific mostly have different native languages, and often more than one in each country, they all share English as the language of international business. But English in Asia is, of course, less prevalent than Spanish in Latin America, Arabic in the Middle East, or Russian in the former Soviet bloc.

## Way of Doing Business

Three, rather than one, modes of doing business prevail in Asia-Pacific. The first mode is represented by the large, diversified companies of Japan and South Korea with their extensive linkages with group members (the *keiretsus* of Japan and the *chaebols* of South Korea). The second mode is the family-oriented, entrepreneurial concerns of Hong Kong, Indonesia, Taiwan, and Thailand. As these latter concerns have expanded, many have become conglomerates, as typified by firms such as Salim Group in Indonesia and Charoen Pokphand in Thailand. The third mode is the standard Western professional manager approach typical in Australia and New Zealand. Some Asian firms, such as Acer, the Taiwanese computer producer, are shifting from the family mode to the managerial mode. Stan Shih, the CEO of Acer, has over the past ten years eased out relatives and installed an American professional manager as president. In the face of tough economic conditions, the companies at the center of the Japanese *keiretsus* face increasing pressures to weaken their ties to group members. The South Korean *chaebols* are being weakened by the anticorruption probes begun in late 1995, probes reflecting in part public dissatisfaction with the dominance of these few companies.

## Form of Government

With the exception of China, Vietnam, and Hong Kong, the countries covered in this book all have increasingly democratic forms of government, although some face problems of leadership succession and sharing or transfer of power. As of 1997, China, Vietnam, Hong Kong, Indonesia, Thailand, Singapore, and Malaysia have faced these issues to varying extents.

## Institutional Arrangements

The Asia-Pacific region has relatively few institutional arrangements that foster mixing of the citizens of its different countries. But increasing intraregional tourism and business dealings do create extensive informal tions. Perhaps most important, the smartest and most affluent Asians go to the same universities for their college or advanced education, not in Asia, but primarily in the United States and, to a lesser extent, Australia and Britain. The rise of Asian business schools is also helping create institutionally based networks. There also exist many professional organizations and national industry associations.

## Cross-Investment

The region now exhibits a very high level of intraregional investment. Most notably, about 80% of the investment in China from the mid-1980s to the mid-1990s came from, or through, Asian countries (see Table 4.2). An increasing number of cross-border mergers and acquisitions within Asia-Pacific provide further glue.

## Japanese and Other Multinational Companies

Japanese multinational companies have also played, and continue to play, a major role in regional integration through their production and marketing systems. As costs have risen in Japan, Japanese companies have dispersed production and sourcing activities throughout Asia (we give many examples in the country chapters). But the production sites do not operate independently; they form part of the companies' integrated networks. Similarly, Japanese companies have extended integrated marketing networks across the region. South Korean companies are beginning to play such an integrating role also, as will MNCs from other countries in the region.

## Intraregional Trade

The growth of Asian economies has depended a great deal on trade with the rest of the world. Now, intra-Asian trade is playing a bigger role. In 1994, Asia accounted for 27.0% of world exports (U.S.$4.1 trillion) and 24.3% of world imports (U.S.$4.2 trillion) but intra-Asia exports accounted for 48.5% of total Asian exports.[4] Thus, Asia now trades as much internally as externally. At the same time, it needs to be recognized that a large portion of this intra-Asian trade constitutes intermediate goods that depend on Western end markets.

## Trade Policies and Agreements

Trade policies in the region vary tremendously, from nearly totally open markets, such as in Hong Kong and Singapore, to heavily controlled ones, such as in Vietnam. But all these economies are moving in the direction of greater openness, except for Japan. Table 1.5 shows how average tariff rates have fallen in almost all cases from 1988 to 1996. Furthermore, we have the rapid growth of many intraregional mechanisms to reduce trade barriers. Several regional institutions, particularly ASEAN, its ASEAN Free Trade Area (AFTA) program, the Asia-Pacific Economic Cooperation (APEC) forum, and "growth triangles" or "growth polygons"

### Table 1.5
### Average Tariff Rates, 1988–1996

| Asia-Pacific | 1988 % | 1993 % | 1996 % |
|---|---|---|---|
| Japan | 7.2 | 6.5 | 9.0 |
| South Korea | 19.2 | 11.6 | 7.9 |
| China | 40.3 | 37.3 | 23.0 |
| Taiwan | 12.6 | 8.9 | 8.6 |
| Hong Kong | 0.0 | 0.0 | 0.0 |
| Singapore | 0.4 | 0.4 | 0.0 |
| Malaysia | 13.0 | 12.8 | 9.0 |
| Thailand | 40.8 | 37.8 | 17.0 |
| Indonesia | 20.3 | 17.0 | 13.1 |
| Philippines | 27.9 | 23.5 | 15.6 |
| India | n.a | n.a | n.a |
| Vietnam | n.a | n.a | n.a |
| Australia | 15.6 | 9.0 | 6.1 |
| New Zealand | 15.0 | 8.0 | 7.0 |
| | | | |
| *Others* | | | |
| United States | 6.6 | 6.6 | 6.4 |
| Germany | n.a | n.a | n.a |
| Mexico | 10.6 | 12.8 | 12.5 |
| Poland | n.a | n.a | n.a |

*Sources:* PECC, UNCTAD and APEC

play increasingly important roles in fostering regional trade, although APEC includes countries on the other side of the Pacific. (Chapter 16 will deal with the roles of these and other regional institutions.)

## Economic Performance and Prospects

Most of the economies discussed in this book have performed well economically and continue to have favorable economic prospects. We believe that the economic turmoil that hit the region in 1997 will be of limited duration. The fundamentals are still sound. Furthermore, the fall in exchange rates in many of the ASEAN countries from mid-1997 to late-1997 (South Korea about 40%, Thailand nearly 40%, Indonesia over 40%, Malaysia nearly 30%, the Philippines about 25%, Singapore about 10%, and Hong Kong still holding out at the time of writing) can increase the attractiveness of these countries as production sites even as their markets become correspondingly less attractive. These economic prospects help create a shared vision of mutual prosperity and dependence. More specifically, each economy is eager to invest in other economies in the region. While Australia's economic performance has lagged behind that of the rest of the region, it constitutes an attractive haven of political stability for those wishing to diversify their risks within the region.

## *Infrastructure*

The distances in Asia-Pacific are vast. The airline distance from Tokyo to Singapore is 5,318 kilometers (3,303 miles), almost the same as the distance between New York and London. And the 8,815 kilometers (5,475 miles) from Tokyo to Auckland exceeds the 8,300 kilometers (5,155 miles) from San Francisco to Tokyo. Furthermore, land transport is not possible in most cases. But the region enjoys excellent shipping and air transportation services. Furthermore, being mostly in a small band of time zones allows business travelers to fly long distances overnight and not lose any part of the working day. An executive can fly from Tokyo to Sydney overnight, work all day there, and return on another overnight flight.

## Objective of This Book

This book describes and analyzes the role of key Asian countries in the global strategies of multinational companies. We take a systematic and practical approach that will provide managers in multinational companies with

- an evaluation of each Asian country in terms of its potential role in the global strategies of multinational companies. The evaluation will include each country's prospects both as a market and as a production or supply site.
- a diagnosis of the extent to which multinational companies will have to adapt their global strategies to each Asian country.
- evidence and examples of how multinational and local companies use these countries in their global strategies.
- a framework and techniques for developing a customized Asian strategy analysis for individual industries and businesses.

Previous books have typically stressed the unique aspects of each country. *Asian Advantage* focuses instead on commonalities these countries have with each other and with the developed economies that are the home bases of Western multinational companies (i.e., the United States and Western Europe). *Our objective is to help managers find ways to include Asian countries in their global strategies, rather than to find reasons they cannot.*

This book is not about "how to do business" in each country. Plenty of such guides exist (see Bibliography). This book also does not emphasize the economic and political prospects of each country, although these will be discussed.

## Relation of This Book to Others

No one who is serious about doing business in Asia should read just one book. A number of books have been written about Asian countries from a macroeconomic or social viewpoint. A good example of the latter is *Man-*

*agement: Asian Context,* edited by Joseph Putti,[5] a collection of se]
authored chapters on management in twelve Asian countries. Min
*Asian Management Systems* provides a more theoretical approach
SarDesai's *Southeast Asia: Past and Present* presents a survey history of many
countries in that region, providing important background for understanding the cultures and sociopolitical systems in Asia.[7] M. S. Dobbs-
Higginson's *Asia-Pacific* provides a popular overview of Asian history and
culture.[8] There have also been many books at the very micro level of the
genre of "How to Do Business in Country *X*," or general guides about
doing business in Asia.[9] Philippe Lasserre's and Helmut Schutte's *Strategies for Asia Pacific*[10] provides a useful and interesting general survey of issues for developing strategies. Jim Rohwer's *Asia Rising* provides an in-
sightful view of how national development policies contributed to the
growth of Asian economies.[11] James Abegglen's *Sea Change: Pacific Asia as
the New World Industrial Center*[12] takes the most strategic perspective to
date, emphasizing what companies *have* done in Asia and the economic
and political prospects for each country.

There have been many books about business in individual countries,
especially Japan, such as Abegglen and Stalk's *Kaisha.*[13] Books about
China include N. T. Wang's *China's Modernization and Transnational Corporations,*[14] books about Hong Kong include Enright, Scott, and Dodwell's
*The Hong Kong Advantage,*[15] and books about South Korea include T. W.
Kang's *Is Korea the Next Japan?*[16] The *Economist Intelligence Unit* and multinational accounting firms produce excellent, up-to-date guides on investment and tax regulations, as well as legal aspects of doing business.[17]

This book provides a strategic analysis of Asia from the viewpoint of
the managers of multinational companies. It describes and analyzes the
role of the fourteen most important Asia-Pacific countries and economies
in the global strategies of multinational companies. By using a common,
systematic framework of analysis, based on my previous book, *Total Global
Strategy,*[18] we aim to provide readers with a methodology for developing
their own regional and country strategies for Asia-Pacific. And, given the
rapid pace of change in the region, our approach emphasizes potential,
as much as current, strategies. Our team approach of multiple co-authors
using a common framework is unique, and parallels the appropriate strategy in Asia for MNCs. We have a team of local partners to provide local
expertise; the team, in turn, is guided by a central partner, and we have
worked with a joint strategy to achieve an optimal overall result.

## Methodology

This book applies a common framework for analyzing each country (Figure 1.3). The framework begins with industry analysis of globalization drivers. These *industry globalization drivers* (market, cost, government, and
competitive) create the potential for a worldwide business to achieve the
benefits of global strategy. Analysis of these drivers indicates the potential
role for MNCs of each country and its industries. Globalization drivers

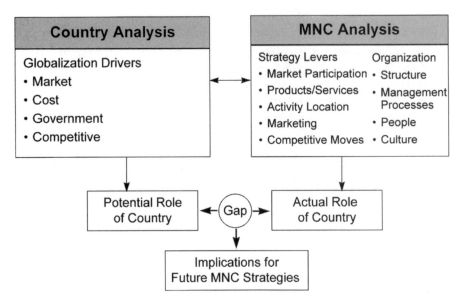

**Figure 1.3**    Conceptual Framework

also indicate what opportunities an MNC's overall global, regional, and local strategies and organization should exploit. An MNC needs to set its *global strategy levers* (e.g., use of globally standardized products) appropriately relative to the industry drivers. *Organization* factors affect how well the formulated global strategy can be implemented. Analysis of the strategies and organization of MNCs in each country then indicates the actual role played by each country and its industries. Lastly, we examine the gap between the potential and actual country and industry roles in order to draw implications for future MNC strategies.

## Approach to Industry Analysis

For industry globalization drivers, our end objective is that readers should be able to conduct an analysis of drivers for their own industry in the Asian country of interest. To reach this objective we take a pyramid approach, going from the general to the more specific. First, we provide an overview analysis of globalization drivers in the entire region (this chapter). Second, in each individual country chapter, we provide an overall analysis of globalization drivers for that country. Third, for a few countries we analyze key industries that have become globalized through MNC participation. We do so for China because of its central importance; for Singapore, because it constitutes the case of the greatest MNC involvement in an Asia-Pacific economy; and for a few other selected cases. Clearly, a few industries cannot represent an entire country. But our analysis of them should provide readers with a guide to how they can analyze the globalization potential of industries and countries in which they are interested.

## Diagnosing Globalization Drivers in the Asia-Pacific Region

We use four sets of industry globalization drivers (listed in Figure 1.3), diagnosing the *current* and *potential* situation of each economy. In this section, we describe each driver and provide examples of how they apply in Asia. The appendix to this book provides a technical definition of each driver. In the country chapters we evaluate these drivers qualitatively. In the concluding chapter we provide a quantitative rating of each driver to allow for cross-country comparisons.

### Market Globalization Drivers

Market globalization drivers—common customer needs, global/regional customers, global/regional channels, transferable marketing, and lead countries—particularly affect whether and how MNCs should participate in Asian markets, the types of products and services they should offer, and the marketing approaches they should use.

*Common customer needs.* Common customer needs represent the extent to which customers in different countries have the same needs in the product or service category that defines an industry. Many factors affect whether customer needs are similar in different countries. These factors include whether differences in economic development, climate, physical environment, and culture affect needs in the particular product or service category, as well as whether the countries are at the same stage of the product life cycle.[19] Some highly Westernized Asian countries, such as Hong Kong and Singapore, typically have needs and tastes that are very similar to those in the United States and Europe. Other countries, such as India and China, have very distinctive cultures and much lower per capita incomes, combining to make their needs and tastes different in many cases from the global norm.

*Global/regional customers or channels.* Global/regional customers or channels of distribution buy on a centralized or coordinated basis for decentralized use, or at the very least select vendors centrally. For this factor to be significant, a country needs to have the global/regional headquarters of MNCs located there. Only Japan, and to a lesser extent, South Korea, are home to a significant number of global MNCs, although many Asia-Pacific MNCs are now achieving global prominence. But more Asia-Pacific countries host the regional headquarters of MNCs. Japan, Hong Kong, and Singapore lead this list, but Taiwan is now making a major effort with its Asia-Pacific Regional Operation Center (APROC) initiative, as is Manila, and some MNCs also have regional head offices in Australia.

*Transferable marketing.* The nature of the buying decision may be such that marketing elements, such as brand names and advertising, require little local adaptation (i.e., brand names and advertising are readily transferable). The degree of familiarity with the English language plays a major role in the need to standardize or adapt marketing. For example, more thought needs to go into adapting marketing for China. In contrast,

countries in the Asia-Pacific region have large segments of the pop-
n with good knowledge of English. For example, India has the third
largest number of English-speakers in the world (after the United States
and the United Kingdom), and the Philippines has the fourth.

Countries with tonal languages, particularly Chinese (and also Thai,
Punjabi in India, and Vietnamese among the countries covered in this
book), pose special difficulties. To maximize recognition of their brand
names, most Western companies choose transliteration[20] rather than translation of their brand names. But such an approach has sometimes resulted in unfortunate connotations or errors.

The transferability of marketing also depends on the availability of
media, which varies greatly by country. An important development has
been the creation of Asia's first regional satellite television service, Star
TV, by Hong Kong's Hutchison Whampoa (controlled by Li Ka Shing),
since sold in 1994 to Australia's News Corporation. Star TV broadcasts
throughout the region in Mandarin Chinese, English, and French.

*Lead countries.* Innovation in products or markets may be concentrated in
one or a few countries because of the presence of innovative competitors,
demanding customers, or both. Japan stands out, of course, as a major
source of innovation, and indeed, on a patent count surpasses even the
United States. In Asia-Pacific only the more advanced economies play any
significant role at this time.

## Cost Globalization Drivers

Cost globalization drivers—global/regional scale economies, sourcing
efficiencies, favorable logistics, good infrastructure, favorable country
costs, and technology role—primarily affect where MNCs should locate
their activities and in which countries.

*Global/regional scale economies.* Global/regional scale economies or scope
economies apply when single-country markets are not large enough to
allow competitors to achieve optimum scale. The issue concerns the extent to which a country has markets that can contribute sales volume to
MNCs needing to achieve global or regional scale economies. Alternatively, is the local market large enough to support a minimum efficient
scale plant? If not, are there sufficient exports to support such a plant?
The countries with the largest GNPs or populations obviously offer the
best prospects for scale and scope economies. In Asia-Pacific these countries are Japan, China, Indonesia, India, the Philippines, Thailand, and
South Korea.

*Sourcing efficiencies.* A country may be able to provide critical factors of
production in efficient volumes. Which country depends on the factor
being supplied. In Asia, plentiful low-cost labor can be found in all of the
populous countries except Japan. Raw materials obviously vary: Australia
and Indonesia are sources of many minerals; Indonesia, Malaysia, China,
and increasingly Vietnam are sources of oil; and so on. Many Asia-Pacific
countries are also becoming sources of skilled technical workers.

*Favorable logistics.* A favorable ratio of sales value to transportation cost enhances the ability of MNCs to concentrate production. For countries, location near major markets or suppliers makes for favorable logistics. In Asia-Pacific, Singapore, for example, has highly favorable logistics both as a production site and as a distribution center, while New Zealand is poorly located for both.

*Good infrastructure.* The quality of a country's infrastructure—roads, power, communications, and so on—very much affects the cost and effectiveness of MNC operations. For our purposes, infrastructure differs from logistics. Infrastructure concerns primarily internal conditions, while logistics primarily involves shipments to and from the outside world. So, for example, New Zealand has excellent internal infrastructure, but its location at the edge of the populated world gives it poor logistics. In contrast, Thailand has a somewhat overwhelmed infrastructure, but is well placed from a logistics viewpoint within Southeast Asia, particularly relative to the emerging markets of Indochina.

*Favorable country costs.* Countries vary in their production costs, taking into account not just labor wage costs, but also overhead costs as well as exchange rates. While there can be important variations by industry, average labor rates and productivity are fairly good indicators. In Asia-Pacific, Japan has higher labor costs than even the United States. At the other end of the scale, China, Indonesia, India, and Vietnam have typical labor costs in the range of 25 to 40 U.S. cents per hour (Table 1.6). In addition, MNCs might wish to look to other parts of the world, such as Latin America (represented in Table 1.6 by Mexico) or Eastern Europe (represented in Table 1.6 by Poland). But MNCs need to worry about more than costs. Other factors such as the quality of the workforce, its availability, and its rate of turnover also matter. A re-cent survey of these factors and cost together suggest that India has the best overall skilled labor attributes while Hong Kong has the worst (Table 1.7), and the United States scores rather well.

Universities

*Technology role.* Countries vary in the extent to which they can be used as a base for developing technology. Japan obviously leads, as evidenced by its ranking in worldwide patent filings. But other Asian countries are making progress. Singapore's government has committed the state to becoming the region's high-technology center outside Japan. Hong Kong's government has set up the new Hong Kong University of Science and Technology with the ambition of it becoming "the M.I.T. of Asia." Thailand has its Asian Institute of Technology (a regional institute with master's and doctoral programs). Since the early 1980s, South Korea has had a priority science and technology program to develop a pool of over two thousand world-class engineers and R&D personnel. Large populations and a facility for technical learning increasingly make India and China serious players in technology development. In spite of their much smaller populations, both South Korea and Taiwan are also well down that path.

*Table 1.6*
**Labor Costs[a] in Asia-Pacific and Other Economies**

| Asia-Pacific | U.S.$ 1985 | U.S.$ 1995 |
|---|---|---|
| Japan | 6.34 | 23.66 |
| South Korea | 1.23 | 7.40 |
| China | 0.19 | 0.25[b] |
| Taiwan | 1.50 | 5.82 |
| Hong Kong | 1.73 | 4.82 |
| Singapore | 2.47 | 7.28 |
| Malaysia | 1.08 | 1.59 |
| Thailand | 0.49 | 0.46 |
| Indonesia | 0.22 | 0.30 |
| Philippines | 0.64 | 0.71 |
| Vietnam | n.a. | 0.25[c] |
| India | 0.35 | 0.25 |
| Australia | 8.20 | 14.40 |
| New Zealand | n.a. | 9.36[c] |
| | | |
| *Other* | | |
| United States | 13.01 | 17.20 |
| Germany | 9.60 | 31.88 |
| Mexico | 1.59 | 1.51 |
| Poland | n.a. | 2.09 |

*Source:* Morgan Stanley study, reported in *The Economist*, November 2, 1996, 77.
[a]Hourly labor costs in manufacturing (including benefits).
[b]Closer to $1.00 for urban, coastal areas.
[c]Authors' estimates.

## Government Globalization Drivers

Government globalization drivers—favorable trade policies, favorable investment rules, participation in trade blocs, absence of government intervention, absence of state-owned competitors, legal protection, compatible technical standards, and common marketing regulations—affect whether MNCs can participate in a country and in what ways. Governments typically intervene more in business in developing countries and where the political and social culture favors a strong role for the state. Both these conditions apply in most countries in the Asia-Pacific region. So governments in the region usually play a very strong, sometimes dominant, role in the affairs of business. An unfortunate effect is often a high level of corruption. The 1995 *World Competitiveness Report,* produced by the World Economic Forum and the International Institute for Management Development (IMD), provides evidence on this point.[21] This report ranked forty-eight countries based on a survey of three thousand business executives. On the measures of "absence of state control of enterprise" and "absence of bribery in the public sphere," many Asian countries ranked near the bottom of the list (Table 1.8).

### Table 1.7
#### Comparison of Skilled Labor Attributes[a]

| | Quality | Cost | Availability | Turnover | Average Grade |
|---|---|---|---|---|---|
| India | 4.29 | 2.14 | 2.57 | 3.71 | 2.80 |
| Australia | 2.00 | 4.71 | 2.29 | 3.14 | 3.39 |
| BRITAIN | 2.75 | 4.25 | 2.88 | 3.83 | 3.50 |
| Philippines | 4.65 | 3.24 | 4.12 | 4.50 | 3.55 |
| UNITED STATES | 2.22 | 5.06 | 3.67 | 3.94 | 3.70 |
| SWITZERLAND | 1.20 | 8.00 | 2.75 | 1.75 | 3.76 |
| Vietnam | 6.82 | 3.30 | 7.00 | 5.80 | 4.08 |
| China | 6.12 | 3.40 | 6.12 | 4.83 | 4.22 |
| Indonesia | 6.42 | 4.46 | 6.27 | 4.83 | 4.28 |
| Japan | 2.92 | 8.08 | 5.33 | 2.08 | 4.40 |
| Taiwan | 3.28 | 5.44 | 4.50 | 5.05 | 4.41 |
| Thailand | 5.61 | 5.00 | 6.39 | 5.18 | 4.41 |
| South Korea | 3.82 | 5.88 | 4.94 | 4.76 | 4.58 |
| Singapore | 2.45 | 6.41 | 4.86 | 5.29 | 4.67 |
| Malaysia | 4.83 | 5.06 | 5.95 | 5.35 | 4.77 |
| Hong Kong | 3.32 | 6.32 | 5.42 | 5.77 | 4.92 |

*Source:* Political and Economic Risk Consultancy, Hong Kong, reported in "Asia's Costly Labour Problems," *The Economist*, September 21, 1996, 62.
[a]Results of survey of managers: 0 = best, 10 = worst.

### Table 1.8
#### State Control of Enterprise and Bribery

| | Absence of State Control of Enterprise[a] | Absence of Bribery in the Public Sphere[a] |
|---|---|---|
| Hong Kong | 1 | 17 |
| New Zealand | 4 | 1 |
| UNITED STATES | 6 | 15 |
| Singapore | 10 | 2 |
| Taiwan | 21 | 28 |
| Australia | 22 | 5 |
| Malaysia | 23 | 23 |
| Thailand | 28 | 37 |
| Philippines | 33 | 45 |
| South Korea | 35 | 26 |
| Indonesia | 37 | 43 |
| Japan | 38 | 20 |
| China | 41 | 41 |
| India | 42 | 46 |

*Source:* World Economic Forum and International Institute of Management (IMD), *The World Competitiveness Report*, 1995, Lausanne, Switzerland.
[a]Ranking out of forty-eight countries.

*Favorable trade policies.* With a few exceptions, notably Hong Kong, Singapore, New Zealand, and Australia, most countries in the region have less open trade policies than the United States and Western Europe. Many of these countries have particularly restrictive nontariff barriers, both official and unofficial. For example, in both Japan and South Korea the authorities sometimes audit the tax returns of those who buy a foreign car! But most of these countries are gradually opening up their markets. In some cases, we see a struggle between the national government favoring more open markets and local or special interests resisting, as in the agricultural sector in Japan. The percentage of exports and imports provides an overall indicator of the openness of each country to trade (Table 1.9). Singapore and Hong Kong clearly lead on this dimension, with both exports and imports exceeding 100% of GNP for both economies. In contrast, both India and Japan (the lowest on our list) import less than 10% of GNP.

*Favorable investment rules.* Rules on foreign direct investment vary greatly and continue to change, mostly in a more open direction. Again, Japan and South Korea have severe official and unofficial restrictions, while most other economies eagerly seek foreign investment. We recommend that readers check current country guides for specific rules by industry, such as those published by the multinational accounting firms.

*Participation in trade blocs.*  Participation in regional trade blocs (such as AFTA), "growth triangles," and free trade zones helps open up an economy for MNC activity. The countries in Asia-Pacific vary greatly in the extent of their participation. Hong Kong, already totally open in trade, does not participate in official trade blocs, although its heavy involvement with China easily constitutes an unofficial trade grouping. The ASEAN nations are the most active in formal groupings; Japan and South Korea are standouts for having little involvement; Taiwan is excluded for political reasons; and Australia and New Zealand would like to join Asian groupings.

*Absence of government intervention.* Most governments are sensitive to foreign dominance of, or even participation in, key industries, and hence intervene. Typically such industries include defense, infrastructure such as telecommunications, and media. Asian governments are no exception, although these industries, except for defense, are beginning to be deregulated. In addition, some are sensitive to industries that affect their citizens' lifestyles and culture. So in India, some socialist provincial governments oppose foreign fast-food chains for their spread of Western lifestyles, and also because they want to see foreign investment in "microchips" rather than "potato chips." We will use the analyses of individual industries to show how government sensitivity and intervention manifest themselves in each country.

*Absence of state-owned competitors.* Government-owned competitors (and customers as well) have extra leverage in dealing with foreign MNCs. Furthermore, their presence in an industry greatly influences government policy toward foreign MNCs. On the other hand, state enterprises also

**Table 1.9**
**Dependence on Trade**

| Asia-Pacific | Exports[a] | Imports[a] |
|---|---|---|
| Singapore | 147.5 | 155.3 |
| Hong Kong | 120.8 | 134.0 |
| Malaysia | 94.7 | 99.4 |
| Taiwan | 37.8[b] | 34.7[b] |
| Thailand | 35.4 | 44.4 |
| South Korea | 28.7 | 31.0 |
| Vietnam | 28.5 | 41.2 |
| New Zealand | 26.6 | 27.0 |
| Philippines | 24.3 | 39.3 |
| Indonesia | 24.0 | 21.6 |
| China | 20.0 | 17.4 |
| Australia | 15.6 | 18.1 |
| India | 9.7 | 10.9 |
| Japan | 8.9 | 6.8 |
| *Others* | | |
| United States | 8.2 | 10.9 |
| Germany | 23.3 | 20.6 |
| Mexico | 26.1 | 23.8 |
| Poland | 12.7 | 21.0 |

*Source:* The World Bank, International Economics Department, Development Data Group.
[a]As % of GNP, 1995.
[b]For 1994.

suffer the usual disadvantages of government ownership. In Asia, government involvement in business is generally far more prevalent than in the West. We discuss in each country chapter how state enterprises interact with foreign companies.

*Legal protection.* A major concern in Asia is the poor protection of contracts, trademarks, and intellectual property. A combination of undeveloped legal systems, lax enforcement, involvement of state officials or their relatives in pirating activities, and general corruption can make these problems severe in some countries. As a consequence, many MNCs are reluctant to market or produce in many Asian countries. Nike, the American shoe company, depends entirely on production by subcontractors in Asia, and with its highly valued brand name is very vulnerable to illegal imitations. Its solution has been to keep ahead of the imitators by changing its designs every six months, the approximate lead time needed by would-be pirates.

*Compatible technical standards.* Differences in technical standards among countries affect the extent to which products can be standardized. Government restrictions in terms of technical standards can make or break efforts at product standardization and be used to restrict imports. Japan has been a master at using such restrictions, such as its attempts to keep out

Swiss-made skis on the grounds that they were not suitable for Japanese snow, or its claim that American rice is unsuitable for Japanese stomachs. Other Asian countries have used some of these tactics. Technical standards vary by both country and industry. We analyze them in the context of individual industries in each country.

In addition to differences in technical standards, MNCs need to worry about each country's ability to maintain the highest international technical standards in, for example, maintenance, operating procedures, and safety issues. The Bhopal disaster in India in 1984 may have been caused by local staff who were unable to operate under Union Carbide's standards. The spate of airline crashes in China during the early 1990s arose mainly from not following maintenance and safety procedures.

*Common marketing regulations.* The marketing environment of individual countries affects the extent to which uniform global marketing approaches can be used. Certain types of media may not be allowed or may have restrictions on their use. For example, television advertising is still highly restricted in both coverage and content in China. As a general rule, most Asian countries are much more restrictive than Western countries about the use of sex appeal in advertising.

## Competitive Globalization Drivers

Competitive globalization drivers—global/regional strategic importance of a country, globalized domestic competitors, the presence of foreign competitors, and the interdependence of countries—all spur MNCs to participate in a country and also affect the kinds of strategies they should adopt.

*Global/regional strategic importance.* The global/regional strategic importance of a country affects what role each country should play in the portfolio of an MNC. Global/regional strategic importance differs by industry, and is defined in terms of the country being a

- large source of revenues or profits
- significant market of global competitors
- major source of industry innovation
- home market of global customers
- home market of global competitors

In terms of being a large source of revenues or profits, or being a significant market of global competitors, obviously the countries with the largest GNPs and populations, as well as rapidly rising incomes, may play such a role in many industries (Japan, China, Indonesia, India, the Philippines, South Korea, and Thailand). We discussed the role of technology and innovation earlier in this section.

In terms of being the home market of global competitors or global customers, only the most advanced economies, particularly Japan (141 companies in the *Fortune* "Global 500" in 1995),[22] and to a much lesser extent South Korea (12 companies), Australia (4), Hong Kong (1), India (1), and Taiwan (1), are home to global companies. But most countries have some global leaders among their companies. For example, Singapore boasts Singapore Airlines, the world's most highly rated and most profitable air carrier. Hong Kong has world leaders in banking (Hong Kong and Shanghai Bank [HSBC Holdings]) with the most capital in the world as of 1996, hotels (Peninsula Group, Mandarin, and the Regent [now part of British Trust Houses Forte]), and airlines (Cathay Pacific). Australia has mining companies such as RTZ, media such as News Corporation, and a leader in package delivery (TNT). New Zealand has Fletcher Challenge, one of the world's largest forest products concerns. In the Philippines, San Miguel, which partners with global giant Nestlé, has world-class beer, food products, and packaging. On a smaller scale, Malaysia has Royal Selangor in the pewter products industry. As regional leaders, we see many more examples: the Hong Kong trading companies Jardine Matheson, Swire, and Hutchison Whampoa; Indonesia's Pertamina in petroleum production, Hero in grocery distribution, and Lippo in financial services; and Australia's David's in grocery distribution.

Another aspect of a country's global strategic importance is the extent to which the country has a "competitive" economy. Participation in such economies will bring MNCs both direct benefits from sharing in the success of the economy and indirect benefits from being exposed to the practices of institutions and companies in the economy. Several Asia-Pacific economies rank highly in the annual surveys of country competitiveness, particularly Singapore, Hong Kong, and New Zealand (Table 1.10).

*Internationalized domestic competitors.* Local competitors that are internationalized, with significant foreign activities, usually pose a greater challenge for foreign MNCs. These internationalized competitors can learn from their other markets, leverage activities across their international network, and launch counterattacks in other countries. Again, Japan has predominantly the most internationalized, even globalized, domestic competitors. But most of the other countries have competitors that have internationalized at least within the region. So MNCs interested in Asia need to systematically evaluate the capabilities and intentions of domestic competitors, particularly those that have internationalized.

*Presence of foreign competitors.* The presence in a country of foreign competitors, particularly other rival MNCs, can pose greater challenges for those companies seeking to enter the country. At the same time, such presence can also be a signal that MNCs have good prospects there. Or such presence may merely indicate lemming-like imitative behavior with potentially disastrous consequences. The rush of many MNCs to enter China during the past ten years may, in some cases, have followed this latter pattern. So managers need to carefully analyze what the presence of other foreign competitors may mean for their own strategies.

*Interdependence via MNC value chains.* MNCs create strategic interdependence between a country and others through sharing of activities such

*Table 1.10*
**Ranking of Competitiveness[a] of World's Economies, 1996**

| Economy | Ranking | Economy | Ranking |
|---|---|---|---|
| *Singapore* | 1 | Egypt | 28 |
| *Hong Kong* | 2 | *China* | 29 |
| United States | 3 | Portugal | 30 |
| Canada | 4 | Belgium | 31 |
| *New Zealand* | 5 | Czech Republic | 32 |
| Switzerland | 6 | Mexico | 33 |
| United Kingdom | 7 | *Philippines* | 34 |
| *Taiwan* | 8 | Slovak Republic | 35 |
| *Malaysia* | 9 | Turkey | 36 |
| Norway | 10 | Argentina | 37 |
| Luxembourg | 11 | Iceland | 38 |
| Netherlands | 12 | Italy | 39 |
| Chile | 13 | Peru | 40 |
| *Japan* | 14 | Colombia | 41 |
| *Indonesia* | 15 | Brazil | 42 |
| Ireland | 16 | Jordan | 43 |
| *Australia* | 17 | South Africa | 44 |
| *Thailand* | 18 | *India* | 45 |
| Finland | 19 | Hungary | 46 |
| Denmark | 20 | Venezuela | 47 |
| *Korea* | 21 | Greece | 48 |
| Sweden | 22 | *Vietnam* | 49 |
| France | 23 | Poland | 50 |
| Israel | 24 | Zimbabwe | 51 |
| Germany | 25 | Ukraine | 52 |
| Spain | 26 | Russia | 53 |
| Austria | 27 | | |

*Source:* World Economic Forum, *Global Competitiveness Report, 1997,* Lausanne, Switzerland.
[a]The World Economic Forum (Geneva, Switzerland) defines competitiveness as the ability of a country to achieve sustained high rates of growth in GDP per capita, and uses eight factors:

- openness of an economy to international trade and finance
- role of the government budget and regulation
- development of financial markets
- quality of infrastructure
- quality of technology
- quality of business management
- labor market flexibility
- quality of judicial and political institutions

as factories or other parts of the value chain. Many Asian countries are already part of such interdependent networks in many industries—Hong Kong in watches and consumer electronics, China in toys and clothing, Singapore in hard disk drives, Malaysia in telephone sets, Thailand in automobile components, Taiwan in personal computers, Indonesia in electronics, and the Philippines in semiconductors and other electronic parts.

# Developing Global/Regional Strategies in the Asia-Pacific Region

The types of global/regional strategies that MNCs can develop can be grouped under five major categories or global/regional strategy levers: global/regional market participation, global/regional products and services, global/regional location of activities, global/regional marketing, and global/regional competitive moves. In this section we explain each of these strategies and provide some Asian examples. But as these strategies are specific to individual companies, there are few generalizations that we can make here. In the country chapters we do so for each country as a whole and for individual industries. *The reader should use our frameworks, analyses, and examples as a guide to develop his or her own best strategies, remembering also the need to continually monitor and change if necessary.*

## Global/Regional Market Participation Strategies

MNCs need to choose the country-markets in which to conduct business, as well as the nature and level of activity, particularly in terms of target market share. Managers need to select country-markets not just on the basis of stand-alone attractiveness, but also on the basis of how participation in a particular country will contribute to globalization benefits and the global/regional competitive position of the business. Furthermore, different countries can play different strategic roles as markets.

Participating in markets outside the home country acts as a lever for both internationalization (the geographic expansion of activities) and globalization (the global integration of strategy). But in the internationalization mode managers select countries based on stand-alone attractiveness. In contrast, when used as a global strategy lever, market participation involves selecting countries on the basis of their potential contribution to globalization benefits, and to the global competitive position of the business. The same considerations also apply to determining the level at which to participate (primarily the target market share) and to determining the nature of participation (building a plant, setting up a joint venture, and so on).

For an Asian strategy companies need to determine first the overall role that Asia-Pacific should play in the global portfolio, and second, the role of individual countries within the Asia portfolio. Typically, these roles depend on a combination of the country-market characteristics and of the company's history and position in that country-market. For example, most U.S. companies are relatively new to China, so that country tends to be assigned an investment role supported by cash from outside Asia or from other Asian countries.

## Global/Regional Product and Service Strategies

MNCs need to decide which products and services to offer in each country, and whether and how much to adapt them to the local markets.

The conventional wisdom has been to adapt as much as possible to local needs and tastes. But global thinking now recognizes the costs of adaptation and product proliferation and emphasizes instead the potential benefits from maximizing standardization. Furthermore, regardless of cost, overadaptation can reduce the appeal of an MNC's offerings, particularly when the MNC comes from a more developed country. In most Asian countries, customers want their products to be clearly Western or Japanese in origin. Chinese go to Kentucky Fried Chicken because the taste and overall experience are different and American. After all, Chinese cuisine knows many ways of cooking chicken tastily. This preference for foreignness can produce surprising results. In Japan many buyers of foreign luxury automobiles want the steering wheel to be on the wrong side, so that everyone will know their car is foreign. In some countries, consumers have a "blue seal" mentality—for decades, imported cigarettes in many countries have had a blue seal, and this connection has transferred to other products. Conversely, there have been countless examples of failures from insufficient adaptation—appliances too large for Japanese kitchens, full packages of sanitary napkins too expensive for China's consumers, and the ink of ballpoint pens not flowing well in hot and humid climates.

The challenge for MNCs is to find the right balance between standardization and adaptation. In the country chapters we provide many examples of what companies have done in each country.

## Global/Regional Activity Location Strategies

MNCs have the opportunity and challenge to optimally configure and locate their entire value-added chain—research, development, procurement, raw material processing, intermediate production/subassembly, final production/assembly, marketing, selling, distribution, customer service, management, and support activities.[23] A global approach to activity location means deploying one integrated, but globally dispersed, value chain or network that serves the entire worldwide business, rather than separate country value chains or one home-based value chain. Asian countries have played an increasing role in the value chains of Western and Japanese firms, as the latter seek lower production costs.

The role of most countries is evolving. For example, Malaysia moved from being a source of rubber to becoming a location for subassembly and final production of automobiles. As the technical skills of Asian countries increase, MNCs are beginning to locate research and development activities there, not just production. Many MNCs now conduct R&D in Japan, of course. But many do so also in Singapore and other countries. Texas Instruments set up in the late 1980s a software design subsidiary in Bangalore, India, in order to access the low-cost, but highly skilled technical workers available there. This subsidiary communicates with Texas Instruments' R&D center in the United States via satellite each day, thus operating very much as part of a global network. This location strategy, and the resulting benefit of high-quality design work at low cost, is made possible by the strength of the industry globalization driver, favorable country costs.

MNCs need to think creatively about activity location, and may find surprising solutions. American Express has centralized all billing functions for Asia-Pacific in one city in the region—Sydney, Australia. That may not seem an obvious choice, but total Australian costs are now low relative to some Asian countries and, because of extensive immigration, Sydney has inhabitants speaking every Asian language. So American Express can have its bills processed in Asian languages by native speakers.

In the country chapters we discuss the location strategies of many MNCs and the likely role of each country in the overall regional and global value chains of MNCs.

## Global/Regional Marketing Strategies

MNCs need to decide on the extent to which they adapt their marketing in each country for each element of the marketing mix: positioning, brand names, packaging, labeling, advertising, promotion, distribution and selling methods, sales representatives, and service personnel. They also need to identify the special aspects of marketing success factors needed in each country. As discussed under market globalization drivers, many Asian countries have distinctive cultural and behavioral aspects that require marketing adaptation. As with product adaptation, MNCs need to strike the right balance. And, again, overadaptation can be as wrong as underadaptation. In most product categories, Asians prefer Western brand names. Even in Japan, with its high per capita incomes, Western brand names play well, and some Japanese companies use Western brand names, such as "My First Sony" (a children's recorder/player), "Pocari Sweat" (a health soft drink), and "Soup-Career Woman" (an instant soup). Two leading Hong Kong clothing companies use Italian brand names—Giordano for clothing and Bossini for shoes. In Indonesia, local fast-food chains adopt Western names such as California Fried Chicken (on the other hand, U.S.-based Church's Fried Chicken changed its name to Texas Fried Chicken to avoid undesirable connotations for Indonesia's mostly Muslim population). So each element of the marketing mix needs careful analysis. If any general rule can be made, it is that more strategic elements of the marketing mix such as brand names, packaging appearance, and advertising themes should tend toward being global or regional. With increasing travel within and outside the region and with increasing exposure to regional and global media, cross-country spillovers become increasingly common. For example, between the southern Philippines and eastern Malaysia, and between Japan and China, television viewers can tune into the other country's television shows and advertising. So companies need to maintain uniformity to avoid contradictions and lost opportunities for recognition and purchase. On the other hand, more tactical elements of the marketing mix—selling, promotion, and distribution—usually need to be adapted to local conditions. In a nice example of such adaptation, Procter and Gamble has maintained in China one of its core sales approaches—promotional sampling—but adapted its implementation. Capitalist P&G uses the older women of the Communist Party's "neighborhood committees" to hand out detergent samples.[24]

### Global/Regional Competitive Move Strategies

MNCs make competitive moves in individual countries as part of a successful global competitive strategy. So for individual countries, the issue concerns the extent to which MNCs should include the country when they make global/regional competitive moves, as opposed to making competitive moves in the country independent of moves in other countries. The competitive globalization drivers of global strategic importance of a country, globalized domestic competitors, presence of foreign competitors, and interdependence of countries affect whether and how to make such moves. Because of the global strength of its companies, Japan is now widely recognized by MNCs as an essential part of their competitive planning. South Korea and Taiwan are beginning to be recognized in the same way. As companies from other Asian countries gain global competitiveness, MNCs will have to take these countries into account also. One of the future pressing competitive issues for Western/Japanese MNCs will be how to respond to the rise of tough Chinese global competitors, and further out, perhaps Indian competitors.

## Overall Global Organization and Management Issues

Organization factors affect both what the nature of global strategy should be and the effectiveness of its implementation. The nature of the organization—its structure, management processes, people, and culture—significantly affects the ability to implement global strategy. The more centralized, integrated, and uniform are the organization elements, the easier it is to formulate and implement global strategy. The appropriate degree of integration also depends on the company's history. On the other hand, local characteristics, such as culture and work style, require MNCs to tailor their organizations to each country. In Asia, these local characteristics often demand significant modification of global/regional organizational approaches.

We do not attempt in this book to address all the issues in regard to organizing and managing global companies or managing in Asia. For detailed coverage of these topics, we recommend some of the books cited earlier.[25] For Asia there are, however, some common issues that we can address as background to the more specific organizational issues that we will discuss for each country.

### Organization Structure

Two critical issues arise in terms of organization structure in Asia: the need of partners and the autonomy of subsidiaries.

*Do not need local partners.* In most Asian countries, a critical issue in organization structure is whether the foreign company can go it alone or needs a local partner. Such partners can provide the right to operate at all, access to factors of production, access to markets and customers, government contacts, and local expertise. Depending on the country, the right type of partner will vary. But in most Asian countries, partners with direct or indirect ties to the authorities are usually needed. And given the strong Asian emphasis on family ties, what might seem to a Westerner a remote relationship, like a second cousin or a sister-in-law, can be a strong bond. MNCs may also get involved in tiers of partnerships. For example, their Hong Kong or Singapore joint venture may set up further partnerships or joint ventures in other countries, such as Indonesia or China.

*Give significant autonomy.* MNCs need to decide how much autonomy each country operation should have. While this decision depends on the subsidiary's level of experience, managers, and role, it can also depend on country characteristics. In particular, countries with less business experience, a weaker work ethic, or a higher degree of corruption generally need tighter control. On the other hand, Bausch and Lomb's problems in the early 1990s with financial fraud in Asia surfaced in Hong Kong. Barings Bank's demise came from giving too much autonomy in Singapore to its securities dealer there. Daiwa Bank's trading problems occurred in the United States. So operations in any country can suffer from too much autonomy, and of course, from too little autonomy also.

## Management Processes

Management processes comprise the activities such as planning and budgeting that make the business run. These processes include strategic planning, budgeting, cross-country coordination, motivation, performance review and compensation, human resource management (including career planning and employment terms, e.g., lifetime employment), and information systems.

*Use global management processes.* MNCs need to decide for each country whether and how to adapt management processes and which ones. A key determinant here is the level of experience that the country has with modern management techniques. MNCs usually find themselves in the position of having to "push the envelope" in changing and upgrading practice. We provide in the country chapters examples of what individual companies have done.

*Participate in global processes.* A second issue concerns the extent to which MNCs can expect subsidiaries and partners in a country to participate in global management processes. For Asia, geographic distance from America and Europe can pose a practical barrier to involving Asia-based executives in global forums.

## People

People issues can be summarized in three categories: (1) using and developing locally capable managers and staff; (2) using nonlocal managers (i.e., expatriates); and (3) using Asia as a training ground or a source of global managers.

*Can use local managers.* A shortage of local management talent has been a significant constraint in many Asian countries. Many MNCs have relied on some combination of expatriates, returning nationals, or local people. The need for local language capability and knowledge varies by country, from vital in China to unimportant in Singapore. An increasingly good source of younger management talent is business schools in and outside Asia—many of their graduates now want to return to Asia. Particularly in the United States, with its huge numbers of Asian college students, both American and foreign, MNCs have the opportunity to build up language capability through entry-level hiring. But few American or European companies do that. Instead, they lament their current lack of executives who can speak Asian languages. They should have been filling up the pipeline these past ten years.

*Can use nonlocal managers.* As with other regions, many Asians hold various prejudices about which foreign managers are acceptable in their respective countries. MNCs need to be bold about appointing the best executives, without being held hostage by national prejudices.

*Source global managers.* The strategic importance of Asia and the distinctiveness of business culture and practices there make the region an important source of global managers. MNCs need to develop career plans that rotate high-potential executives in and out of the region. Any MNC doing significant business in Asia needs to ask how many top executives and board directors they have from that region. The answer in most cases is "none or far too few"!

## Culture

Culture comprises the values and rules that guide behavior in a corporation. National cultures clearly affect how managers behave and how they fit into the corporate culture. Asian countries have very strong and distinctive cultures and they can be viewed at different levels of aggregation, from Asian culture in general to individual country and subcountry cultures. The larger countries, in particular, China, India, and Australia, exhibit wide differences in culture between regions—the Cantonese are known as the "Italians of China" and Queenslanders as the "Texans of Australia." We can also see groupings, such as the North Asian/Oriental cultures of Japan, South Korea, China, and Taiwan; the mixed international cultures of Hong Kong and Singapore; the Malay/Islamic cultures of Indonesia and Malaysia; the American/Hispanic/Southeast Asian culture of the Philippines; the quintessentially Southeast Asian cultures of

Thailand and Vietnam; the Anglo-Indian culture of India; and the British cultures of Australia and New Zealand.

MNCs need to take all these cultural differences into account, but again must strive to go beyond them. As Percy Barnevik, the former CEO of Asea Brown Boveri, put it, "We must be sensitive to national cultures but not be paralyzed by them."[26] In some cases, though, MNCs would be wise to build on certain aspects of existing national cultures.

*Instill global culture.* Overall, MNCs need to decide how far they can go in instilling their global corporate culture, and how much they need to adapt to local culture.

## Companies Analyzed

To illustrate the types of global and regional strategies that MNCs can use in these countries, we focus on six MNCs that are present in most of these countries: Motorola and Procter and Gamble from the United States, Philips and Unilever from Europe, and Matsushita and Toyota from Japan. Using the same set of MNCs also has the benefit of providing commonality across the countries to enable comparisons of the roles played by each country in the strategies of these MNCs. While we selected these companies on the basis of having activities in as many as possible of the countries being studied, in some cases we had to use substitutes.

## Guide to The Book

After this introductory chapter, Chapters 2 to 15 cover each economy in turn. Chapter 16 reviews trade and other institutional groupings such as ASEAN, AFTA, and APEC. This review provides critical background for understanding how each country relates economically to others in the Asia-Pacific region. The closing chapter provides a quantitative summary of our evaluations of each economy and an interpretative review with lessons and implications for multinational companies.

### NOTES

1. Paul Krugman, "The Myth of Asia's Miracle," *Foreign Affairs* 73, no. 6 (November–December 1994): 62–78, has argued that the high growth rates of Asian economies can be entirely attributed to the movement of labor from agriculture into industry and by high savings rates. He predicts that the growth of Asian economics will slow in the same way as did that of the former Soviet Union. Nevertheless, the already developed economies of Asia—in particular, Japan and to a lesser extent the "four dragons" (South Korea, Taiwan, Hong Kong, and Singapore)— have reached economic levels far above those ever achieved by the former Soviet Union. Critics, of which there are many, of Krugman's view argue that Asian economies are now poised to greatly increase productivity and are in a far different condition than the Soviet economy was. On the other hand, the region's economic turmoil that started in 1997 may yet prove Krugman right.

2. See, for example, Sanjyot P. Dunung, *Doing Business in Asia: The Complete Guide* (Lexington, Mass.: Lexington Books, 1995), as a current example of a book on how to do business in Asia; and John Naisbitt, *Megatrends Asia* (New York: Simon & Schuster, 1996), as an example of social commentary.

3. These features are among those identified in Hofstede's seminal work on differences in national culture within one multinational company. See Geert Hofstede, *Culture's Consequences: International Differences in Work Related Values* (Beverly Hills, Calif.: Sage, 1984).

4. World Trade Organization, *1995 International Trade: Trends and Statistics* (Geneva, Switzerland: World Trade Organization, 1995).

5. Joseph M. Putti, ed., *Management: Asian Context* (Singapore: McGraw-Hill, 1991).

6. Min Chen, *Asian Management Systems: Chinese, Japanese and Korean Style of Business* (London and New York: Routledge, 1995). See also Tan Jing Hee and You Poh Seng, eds., *Developing Managers in Asia* (Singapore: Addison Wesley, 1987).

7. D. R. SarDesai, *Southeast Asia: Past and Present,* 3rd ed. (Boulder, Colo.: Westview, 1994).

8. M. S. Dobbs-Higginson, *Asia-Pacific: Its Role in the New World Disorder* (Hong Kong: Longman Group [Far East], 1994; London: Mandarin Paperbacks, Reed Consumer Books, 1995).

9. For a recent example, see Dunung, *Doing Business in Asia.* For China, see Arne J. de Keijzer, *China: Business Strategies for the '90s* (Berkeley, Calif.: Pacific View, 1992).

10. Philippe Lasserre and Helmut Schütte, *Strategies for Asia Pacific* (New York: New York University Press, 1995).

11. Jim Rohwer, *Asia Rising: Why America Will Prosper as Asia's Economies Boom* (New York: Simon & Schuster, 1995).

12. James C. Abegglen, *Sea Change: Pacific Asia as the New World Industrial Center* (New York: Free Press, 1994).

13. James C. Abegglen and George Stalk Jr., *Kaisha: The Japanese Corporation* (New York: Basic, 1985).

14. N. T. Wang, *China's Modernization and Transnational Corporations* (Lexington, Mass.: Lexington Books, 1984). See also Ezra Vogel, *One Step Ahead in China, Guangdong under Reform* (Cambridge, Mass.: Harvard University Press, 1989).

15. Michael J. Enright, Edith E. Scott, and David Dodwell, *The Hong Kong Advantage* (Hong Kong: Oxford University Press [China] Ltd., 1997).

16. T. W. Kang, *Is Korea the Next Japan?* (New York: Free Press, 1989).

17. See, for example, Price Waterhouse, *Doing Business in Indonesia* (Jakarta: Price Waterhouse, 1990), and others in this series; or Arthur Andersen, *Doing Business in Vietnam* (Ho Chi Minh City, Arthur Andersen, 1995), and others in this series; or Citibank, *Indonesia: An Investment Guide,* APEC ed. (Jakarta: Citibank N.A. and Ida Sudoyo & Associates, 1994).

18. George S. Yip, *Total Global Strategy: Managing for Worldwide Competitive Advantage* (Englewood Cliffs, N.J.: Prentice Hall, 1992); and Business School ed. (paperback) 1995; Indonesian ed. (Gramedia Pustaka Utama, Jakarta, 1998), Japanese ed. (Japan Times, Tokyo, 1995), and Korean ed. (Gimm Young, Seoul, 1994). See also Christopher J. Lovelock and George S. Yip, "Global Strategies for Service Business," *California Management Review* 38, no. 2 (Winter 1996): 64–86.

19. See also Pradeep A. Rau and John F. Preble, "Standardization of Marketing Strategy by Multinationals," *International Marketing Review* (Autumn 1987): 18–28.

20. Transliteration involves conversion into foreign words that sound like the original name, but may not have the same meaning as in the original language.

21. *The World Competitiveness Report 1995* (Geneva, Switzerland: The World Economic Forum, 1995).

22. "Fortune's Global 500 Ranked within Countries," *Fortune,* August 5, 1996, F30–F40.

23. See Michael E. Porter, *Competitive Advantage* (New York: Free Press, 1985); and idem, "Changing Patterns of International Competition," *California Management Review* 28, no. 2 (Winter 1986): 9–40.

24. "How and Why to Survive Chinese Tax Torture," *The Economist,* December 2, 1995, 63–64.

25. For management in Asia, see, in particular, Min Chen, *Asian Management Systems,* and Putti, *Management.* For management of global corporations see, particularly, C. K. Prahalad and Yves L. Doz, *The Multinational Mission: Balancing Local Demands and Global Vision* (New York: Free Press, 1987); and Christopher A. Bartlett and Sumantra Ghoshal, *Managing across Borders: The Transnational Solution* (Boston: Harvard Business School Press, 1989).

26. Speech at Academy of International Business Conference, Toronto, October 1990.

# CHAPTER 2

# Japan—Still Bubbling?

*Yoko Ishikura and George S. Yip*

THE VERY RAPIDLY grown and long-sustained economic performance of Japan has been the envy of the rest of the world. After decades of stellar growth, however, Japan's economy is beginning to stumble through a period of slow, almost zero, growth. Nevertheless, Japan's GNP is currently over 1.5 times greater than the combination of all the other Asia-Pacific economies in this book. As we approach the twenty-first century, the questions for MNCs in regard to Japan continue to be: "How can we succeed in Japan?" and, increasingly, "Do we need to be in Japan?"

## Economic Prospects

The appreciation of the yen held up progress toward economic recovery and spread fears of deflation throughout the business world. The exchange rate, which peaked at U.S.$1 = 79 yen in April 1995, together with overemployment, particularly of white collar middle management, dealt a double blow to many large Japanese companies. In addition, there are concerns regarding the future of the Japanese financial system, characterized by huge bad debt, and punctuated by the 1996 Daiwa Bank trading scandal and the exposure of Sumitomo's copper trading on the London Metal Exchange, and the 1997 bankruptcy of Yamaichi Securities. The yen's falling back to the 125 level (versus the U.S. dollar) in 1997 may help. On the other hand, Japan's economy will undoubtedly be hurt by the current troubles of South Korea and of many ASEAN economies, now key markets for Japanese companies.

Noneconomic problems have also shaken Japan. During 1995, several unusual events undermined the confidence of the Japanese people. First, the Kobe earthquake claimed more than five thousand lives; then the Aum Shinrikyo cult released deadly nerve gas in the Tokyo subway and other sites. The former tragedy exposed the local and central governments' ineffectual response to crises; the latter shattered the long-held belief that Japan was one of the safest industrialized countries. This public confidence, along with economic prosperity, had characterized the nation for fifty years. On top of this came the food poisoning outbreak of 1996, centered on Sakai City.

The year 1995 was also a difficult one in politics as forty years of Liberal Democratic Party rule came to an end. Voter discontent climaxed during the gubernatorial elections when voters chose two so-called independents, both theatrical comedians by profession, as governors in Tokyo and Osaka. The upset of established political parties and politicians derives from the public frustration over politicians who merely react to economic problems and are unable to take effective action.

Economically, socially, and politically, Japan is now faced with unprecedented uncertainties, for which it is not well equipped to respond. Bad debt continues to plague many financial institutions. Furthermore, it is becoming clearer that the success of many Japanese companies has masked the weakness of many others, and that success in blue collar productivity has masked very low levels of white collar productivity as evidenced by overstaffing and the low usage of computers. During the four-year recession, following the "bubble" burst of the late 1980s, Japan spent 16 trillion yen on public works over the years 1992–1994, just to keep the economy afloat.[1]

In the summer of 1996, the economy finally began showing a slow, but steady recovery. Corporate after-tax profits of over one thousand listed companies (excluding financial services such as banks, securities, and insurance) almost doubled in the fiscal year ending in March 1996.[2] The yen moved back to the level of 105–109 yen to the U.S. dollar and consumption is finally rising, following the "price destruction" that occurred in many sectors, such as consumer electronics, foods and beverages, and apparel, among others. Imports showed sharp increases. Even during the downturn in fiscal year 1993, Japan's fiscal deficit was only 1.7% of GNP, still lower than that of the United States (4%) and Germany (2.4%). The budget deficit in 1994 was 2.9% of the nominal GDP for Japan, just about the same level as the 3.01% for the United States.[3] Japan's economic recovery seemed real for the first time in five years and there appeared to be some optimism in the summer of 1996. Concerns remain, as a large portion of investment has been made outside Japan, companies continue to seek ways to reduce their work forces, and unemployment is rising. The rate of recovery is projected to be very slow and the restructuring of industries will continue.

In early 1997, the positive sentiment of the Japanese business community and public waned, in contrast to the hope for economic recovery held in late 1996. This was due to several reasons: the plunge of the stock market, weak consumption, and concerns about employment. Headlines such as, "End of Japan," "Japan Passing," "Will Japan Survive in the 21st Century?" became commonplace in Japanese business periodicals. Under these circumstances, deregulation became a top priority for the Japanese economy. Though there are some differences in scope and among areas in government proposals, the most discussed and notable is the "Big Bang" in financial markets, which will liberalize trading commissions and tear down the walls separating compartmentalized financial industries, as well as deregulation in industries such as telecommunications, insurance, domestic air, energy, retail distribution, trucking, and shipping. The need for deregulation has been made even more urgent by the troubles in Japan's ASEAN markets and by the threats to the Korean economy, another major market for Japan.

Will deregulation actually take place according to plan? If so, what will be the magnitude and pace? There are divided opinions regarding these key questions. *The Economist* offered a more optimistic view in early 1997, although with some qualifications, pointing out that (1) once deregulation starts, it will be difficult to limit its scope, (2) there is consensus for deregulation among politicians, bureaucrats, the business community, and the public, and (3) there is no other choice in sight for the recovery of the economy.[4] On the other hand, some doubt whether deregulation will proceed as planned since current Prime Minister Hashimoto's cabinet has such limited power. Also, the private sector, particularly banks, may not be quite prepared for free competition, while the Japanese public tends to have a "fad" mentality, forgetting about such topics after a while.

Although it is still too early to predict with confidence, deregulation will certainly open up part of the Japanese market to foreign MNCs and domestic entrants, notably insurance and retail distribution. Further, it will push formerly regulated industries such as telecommunications so they more closely align with global standards, and affect labor management practices through elimination of the existing ban on holding companies, further restructuring parts of the Japanese economy. On the other hand, deregulation may bring bad news to some foreign MNCs. Price reduction will reduce profitability in industries, such as energy, making it difficult for new entrants that lack efficient cost structures.

Deregulation in Japan may not take the same pattern as that in the United States or the United Kingdom in terms of thoroughness, transparency, and pace. Hesitancy to let the market economy take care of losers, persistent objections from vested interest groups, and interest in maintaining employment levels will remain strong, resulting in evolutionary—rather than revolutionary—restructuring of industries.

Another effect of the economic stagnation in 1997 was to create greater opportunities for alliances. MNCs, such as Toyota, Matsushita, Sony, and Toshiba have performed well despite the overall slowdown of the Japanese economy, while Japanese oil companies and other protected companies have struggled to survive. These internationally competitive companies are now willing to break from a "closed-system," conducting value chain activities on their own, to an "open system" with more possibilities for alliances. Gone are the days when the desire to maintain employment and respect for past relationships dominated. In the increasing competition for a de facto standard in high technology, and the accelerating pace of development in information technology and systems (ITS), more Japanese companies are realizing that they will not be internationally competitive with high administrative costs. They are now willing to be flexible in their supplier relationships and use alliances as viable strategies. The relationship web in multimedia, for example, is so complex that a single company can be a supplier, competitor, customer, and cooperator at the same time.

This change in mentality of Japanese corporations will bring good opportunities for foreign MNCs that are seeking partnerships with Japanese corporations not only for the Japanese market, but for the Asia region as a whole. Foreign MNCs may learn from Cisco Systems, a major U.S. information systems company, which, under the initiatives of Masayoshi Son (founder of Softbank) formed a strategic alliance with fourteen Japanese companies, including NEC, Fujitsu, Toshiba, and NTT Data, to help Cisco Systems Japan penetrate the Japanese market.

## Japan's Trade

Japan's economic success of the last thirty years has been matched by continuing frustration on the part of multinational companies. Imports constituted U.S.$275 billion in 1994, or 5.9% of GDP versus U.S.$396 billion in exports, 8.6% of GDP. Similar percentages based on GNP, listed in Table 1.9 in Chapter 1, show that Japan has the lowest import ratio of any country in Asia-Pacific. For example, although Japan has a GNP about sixty-two times that of Singapore, the latter economy has an import ratio to GNP that is twenty-two times that of Japan. In other words, as a market for imports Japan is barely four times the size of tiny Singapore. The trade gap appears even more dramatic when we compare the sectors in which Japan exports to those in which it imports. The largest export sectors are in industries, such as automobiles and electrical goods, in which many foreign MNCs compete. In contrast, most of the largest import sectors are in industries that contain few significant Japanese firms.[5] In other words, Japanese companies compete successfully in export markets of the world's largest MNCs, while Japan imports primarily raw materials and foodstuffs that are not of interest to domestic companies except for processing.

This is changing, however. In 1995, manufactured goods accounted for 59% of Japanese imports (versus 23% in 1980).[6] Imports included automobiles, apparel, consumer durables such as color television sets, toasters, and clocks, office automation products such as computers, components for automobiles, consumer electronics products, electronic devices including semiconductors, and even machinery.[7] Asian goods accounted for 61% of Japan's imports of color televisions and 55% of hair dryers.[8]

This sharp increase in imports of manufactured products came from the exchange rate rise and from greater global integration on the part of Japanese MNCs. Advanced means of communication and transportation, via direct mail marketing, fax, Internet, and express parcel services, supported by ten million overseas travellers a year, have boosted parallel imports. Such products as cosmetics and alcoholic beverages, private brands of beer, dairy products, orange juice, and some household products such as detergents have shown sharp increases in imports in the 1990s.

## Foreign MNCs in Japan

Foreign MNCs have long been active in Japan's economy, but most of them have experienced great difficulty and little profit.

### History of Foreign Involvement in Japan[9]

Since 1945 there have been several phases of involvement in Japan by foreign MNCs. The first phase, from the late 1960s through the 1970s, was triggered by the liberalization of foreign direct investment in Japan and Japan's joining the OECD. Consumer goods, chemical, and pharmaceutical companies that entered the Japanese market during this period included Du Pont, Dow Chemical, Monsanto, Merck and Pfizer from the United States; ICI and Beecham from Britain; Bayer, BASF, and Hoechst from Germany; and Ciba Geigy, Sandoz, and Hoffman la Roche from Switzerland. Successful companies focused on new product and technology development (as in pharmaceuticals) and brand marketing techniques (in consumer packaged goods). Prevention of foreign control and the extraction of foreign know-how were priorities of the Japanese government during this period.

The second phase, during the 1980s, was characterized by increasing deregulation of industries formerly classified by the government as important or critical to the nation. Multinationals that expanded into Japan in the 1980s were Unisys, DEC, Hewlett Packard, Texas Instruments, Motorola, and Intel in the computer, electronics, and semiconductor industries. Most of these companies appeared to view Japan not only as a market, but also as a production site for world and/or Asian markets or even as a site for R&D activities. Joint ventures, such as Unisys with Mitsui, and Hewlett-Packard with Yokogawa, were formed. On the other hand, very few companies in these industries entered from Europe—Philips being the exception.

In service industries, U.S. companies were aggressive, capitalizing on uniquely developed systems and business practices; for example, McDonald's, American International Underwriters Insurance Company (a member of the American International Group), American Family Life Insurance, and Manpower. Caterpillar, Xerox, 3M, and Michelin are successful joint ventures that established themselves in the Japanese market during the 1980s.

Some failures were Colgate-Palmolive from the United States and Henkel of Germany in household products; Chrysler and Ford in automobiles; and Sears Roebuck and Woolworth in retailing. No significant European examples of success existed in this early period. In the automobile industry, Germany's BMW, which was established in Japan in 1981 as a sales company, marked the turning point. Until then, foreign auto companies had entered Japan in the form of equity participation. BMW's success was followed by the establishment of Volkswagen Audi Japan in 1983, Mercedes Benz in 1986, and General Motors Japan in 1991.[10] During this period Asian companies began exporting products to Japan, but so far, few have invested in Japan. Still, there are a number of potential candidates for significant exports to Japan. Among them are Samsung, Hyundai, Lucky-Goldstar, and Daewoo of Korea; several companies such as Acer Computer International from Taiwan; Quok Industry of Malaysia; and Salim Industry of Indonesia.

## Present Status of Foreign MNCs in Japan

Foreign MNCs still play a very small role in Japan. As of 1996, foreign MNCs accounted for a minuscule 2.6% of assets, 2.8% of sales, and 1.5% of employees.[11] The number of foreign MNCs in Japan has stayed at the level of about three thousand since 1989.[12] An examination of the MNCs that are typically cited as examples of foreign companies that have succeeded in Japan reveals two patterns. The first pattern shows that most exports are in sectors that have few Japanese companies. Boeing's jet aircraft and Weyerhauser's lumber exports fall into this category, and, until the advent of Japanese luxury automobile divisions (Honda's Acura, Toyota's Lexus, and Nissan's Infiniti), so did BMW and Mercedes.

The second pattern has companies that do not export to Japan but produce there. Examples of such foreign successes in Japan include IBM, Coca-Cola, McDonalds, and Procter and Gamble. IBM is often praised for being Japanized, which in itself tells a story of what it takes to succeed in Japan. In contrast, Motorola provides one of the few, but increasing, examples of an emerging third pattern: a foreign company that successfully exports to Japan against strong domestic competition. Service companies such as Toys 'Я Us and Tower Records are beginning to contribute to this third pattern. Indeed, in 1993, less than 20% of entrants were manufacturers, the majority being information service and sales companies.[13] Computer-related companies have entered Japan since the mid-1980s, triggered by the establishment of Microsoft in 1986. Recent entrants into Japan include Acer Computer in 1988; Dell Computer in 1989; Novell and Compaq in 1990; Cisco Systems and SAP Japan in 1992; 3Com in 1993; Informix in 1994; and Gateway 2000 in 1995.

Recent entries are characterized by larger capital investment—those with over 1 billion yen (U.S.$8 million at the exchange rate of 125 yen), accounting for 12.4% of the capital from 3,055 foreign ventures in 1996.[14] On the other hand, the number of exits is increasing rapidly, for several reasons. The major movement into the Japanese market of foreign MNCs took place in the 1980s, with the peak occurring in 1987 and 1988, during the "bubble" economy. By the mid-1990s, many of these MNCs reviewed their operations in Japan, and the recession of the mid-1990s led a number of companies to exit. Some companies have exited completely. Some large foreign MNCs have merged smaller subsidiaries (e.g., Nestlé's combining of its Nesfit and Buitoni Japan units, and IBM's merging of its Japanese operations). Other MNCs have sold their shares to Japanese joint venture partners.

In contrast, in 1996, Ford increased its equity-holding in Mazda to 33.4%, crossing the threshold under Japanese law to gain management control. Ford announced the appointment of one of its American executives as the new president of Mazda in Japan—the first time a foreigner has held the top spot in a significant Japanese company.

Table 2.1 lists the largest foreign MNCs operating in Japan, mostly American and mostly in consumer products.

## Role of Japanese MNCs

The success of many Japanese MNCs has been well documented.[15] By 1995, Japanese companies accounted for 141 of the Fortune Global 500, second only to the United States (Table 2.2). Of the top transnational corporations (TNCs) ranked by foreign assets in 1993, twenty-one were Japanese.[16] In this chapter, we focus on the foreign direct investment activities of these companies, particularly in Asia.

*Table 2.1*
**Largest Foreign Multinational Companies in Japan**[a]

| Rank | Company | Nationality | Main Business in Japan | Taxable Income 1995 U.S.$ million |
|------|---------|-------------|------------------------|-----------------------------------|
| 1 | Coca-Cola Japan | U.S. | beverages | 567 |
| 2 | Amway Japan | U.S. | household goods | 432 |
| 3 | Tonen | U.S. | petroleum products | 405 |
| 4 | Fuji Xerox | U.S. | office equipment | 382 |
| 5 | General Sekiyu | U.S. | petroleum products | 304 |
| 6 | American Family | U.S. | insurance | 300 |
| 7 | Esso Sekiyu | U.S. | petroleum products | 275 |
| 8 | Banyu Pharma | U.S. | pharmaceuticals | 222 |
| 9 | Alico Japan | U.S. | insurance | 190 |
| 10 | Mobil Sekiyu | U.S. | petroleum products | 183 |
| 11 | Nippon Petroleum Refining | U.S. | petroleum products | 178 |
| 12 | Bayer | Germany | pharmaceuticals | 142 |
| 13 | AIU Insurance | U.S. | insurance | 140 |
| 14 | Hewlett Packard | U.S. | computers | 133 |
| 15 | McDonald's Japan | U.S. | restaurants | 130 |
| 16 | Nippon Berlinger Ingelheim | Germany | pharmaceuticals | 120 |
| 17 | Nippon Motorola | U.S. | electronics | 119 |
| 18 | Mercedes Benz Japan | Germany | automobiles | 111 |
| 19 | BMW Japan | Germany | automobiles | 110 |
| 20 | Louis Vuitton Japan | France | apparel | 104 |

*Source: Toyo Keizai Shinposha,* "Status of Foreign MNCs 1996."
[a]Based on taxable income in 1995.

**Table 2.2**
**Largest Japanese Company Groups**[a]

| Rank in Japan | Global Rank | Company | Major Businesses | Revenues 1995 U.S.$ billions |
|---|---|---|---|---|
| 1 | 1 | Mitsubishi | trading/diversified | 184.4 |
| 2 | 2 | Mitsui | trading/diversified | 181.5 |
| 3 | 3 | Itochu | trading/diversified | 169.2 |
| 4 | 4 | Sumitomo | trading/diversified | 167.5 |
| 5 | 6 | Marubeni | trading/diversified | 161.1 |
| 6 | 8 | Toyota Motor | automotive | 111.5 |
| 7 | 11 | Nissho Iwai | trading/diversified | 97.9 |
| 8 | 13 | Hitachi | electrical | 84.2 |
| 9 | 14 | Nippon Life Insurance | insurance | 83.2 |
| 10 | 15 | Nippon Telegraph and Telephone | telecommunications | 81.9 |
| 11 | 19 | Matsushita Electric Industrial | electrical | 70.4 |
| 12 | 21 | Tomen | trading/diversified | 67.8 |
| 13 | 23 | Nissan Motor | automotive | 62.6 |
| 14 | 26 | Dai-ichi Mutual Life | insurance | 58.1 |
| 15 | 32 | Toshiba | electronics | 53.0 |
| 16 | 33 | Tokyo Electric Power | utility | 52.4 |
| 17 | 35 | Nichimen | trading | 50.8 |
| 18 | 36 | Sumitomo Life Insurance | insurance | 50.7 |
| 19 | 37 | Kanematsu | trading | 49.8 |
| 20 | 40 | Sony | consumer electronics | 47.6 |

*Source:* "Fortune's Global 500 Ranked within Countries," *Fortune,* August 5, 1996, F30–F40.
[a]Based on revenues on consolidated basis in 1995.

## Foreign Direct Investment by Japanese Companies

As the yen strengthened to record highs, the pace of Japanese firms expanding their investment overseas accelerated. In fiscal 1994, North America accounted for 42.4% (U.S.$15.3 billion) of Japanese foreign direct investment, followed by Europe with 22% (U.S.$7.9 billion), Asia with 18.4% (U.S.$6.6 billion), Central and South America with 9.4%, and Oceania at 5.6%. In fiscal 1995, Asia accounted for 24% and North America 44%.[17] As of October 1995, there were 10,715 subsidiaries of Japanese corporations throughout the world, double that in 1985.[18]

Japanese firms still appear to be motivated more by aspirations to increase market share than to maximization of their profits, even over the long term. Increasingly their production will be based outside Japan to be near local markets, or in newly industrialized countries where labor costs are low. In 1995, there were 938 cases of Japanese corporations establishing overseas subsidiaries (including by merger or acquisition), showing the first growth in the number of incidents since 1989. Manufacturing accounted for 515, showing a 30% rise. Asia accounted for 72%

(677), followed by North America (98), and Europe (97) at 10% respectively. Japanese direct investment in Asian manufacturing increased from an annual average of 355 to 938 in 1995. Asia and North America will grow even further as sites of Japanese foreign direct investment.[19]

In Asia, China had the largest number (364) in 1994, but was expected to decline in 1995. Rapid increase is expected to come from ASEAN countries, including Vietnam. Manufacturing has shown a rapid increase, while nonmanufacturing declined. By industries, the rapid growth is in auto, component parts, and chemicals. Expansion into Asia is also characterized by a low level of exits.

In the mid-1990s, imports of manufactured goods back to Japan showed rapid increase. According to a survey by the Ministry of International Trade and Industry (MITI), Asian subsidiaries of Japanese corporations exported 19.1% of their output from abroad back to Japan in 1994.[20] The expansion of East Asian economies offers a vast market for the goods and services of advanced economies. In the development of Pacific Asia generally, Japanese firms are exploiting their geographic and cultural advantages relative to Western firms.

The evolving structure of comparative advantage in Japan has led to important changes in the composition of its exports and imports from low skill-intensive products to more advanced technology- and skill-intensive manufactured goods. Japan is also exhibiting a growing disadvantage in goods that are natural resource-intensive and unskilled labor-intensive, typically supplied by developing countries. In the future, Japan is likely to continue to lose market share to the lower cost East Asian economies in such standardized, mass-production industries as steel, automobiles, and even consumer electronics.

Overall, Japanese companies are taking further steps toward global coordination, by balancing production between Japan and overseas, and marketing in growing Asian markets in their effort to recover international competitiveness.

### Shift to Asia

Recent overseas operations by Japanese companies exhibit very aggressive investments in Asia both to capture markets as well as to create production centers for the world market. The shift of production from Japan to Asia, which was spurred by the astonishing level of U.S.$1 = 80 yen in the summer of 1995, has continued even after the rate stabilized above the 100-yen level. Japanese companies are also making production shifts among Asian locations. Sony was a late entrant into the Asian region relative to other global consumer electronics companies, but has been aggressively expanding its production and marketing there since the late 1980s. It began production in Singapore in 1987, followed by Malaysia and Thailand in 1988. Since 1994, Sony has been exporting products manufactured in Asia to North America and Europe. For example, Sony Malaysia produces Sony's state-of-the-art high definition TV for export to

Japan. Starting in 1995, Sony began focusing on the large emerging markets, including China, India, Vietnam, Mexico, Argentina, Russia, and South Africa. In the same year, Sony began coordinating its procurement within ASEAN countries through four centers in Asia, including Singapore and Hong Kong, controlled from Singapore by its SONIS unit.

Aiwa, Sony's subsidiary and manufacturer of audio video products, provides another example of Japanese companies capitalizing on the Asian production network. Since the mid-1980s, when it suffered a loss, Aiwa shifted not only production, but also its corporate function to Asia. Design, parts approval, procurement (overseas procurement accounted for 80% of the total in 1994), and logistics functions have been performed at Aiwa's Singapore plants since 1988. Probably one third of Aiwa's products are designed in Asia. Overseas production accounts for over 80% of Aiwa's total, 50% of which was in Singapore and Malaysia in fiscal year 1994, with OEM production accounting for 13%. Sales in Asia and Oceania on a consolidated basis reached 25% in fiscal year 1995.

Electronics companies such as NEC, Fujitsu, and Toshiba shifted assembly of their semiconductor production to Asia, to take advantage of low labor costs. It is likely that the wafer fabrication phase of production will be moved to Asia in the near future, as the components-supply infrastructure is being established. NEC procured 90% of its components overseas, and Toshiba plans to increase procurement of parts in Asia for use in Japan from ¥50 billion in 1994 to ¥200 billion in 1998.[21]

Most consumer electronics companies have shifted, or are in the process of shifting, production of color TVs and VCRs to Asia. They keep only high value-added models such as wide-screen TV in Japan, simply to maintain their work force there. Toshiba and Mitsubishi went so far as to transfer their product division headquarters to Singapore from Japan. This was done to recover profitability of the products and, at the same time, to capitalize on the high-growth potential of Asian markets.

Auto manufacturers such as Toyota and Honda are now designing "Asian cars" specifically for the region. Toyota launched its Soluna model at the end of 1996. Kao began marketing its Sifone brand shampoo, developed and produced in Taiwan specifically for Asia, against global competitors such as Procter and Gamble, and Unilever. Its success remains to be seen. Japanese MNCs in consumer electronics and other branded products see Asia as the market both for low-priced standardized products and for the most up-to-date, premium products.

## Overall Globalization Drivers for Japan

The Japanese market has been a strong attraction for foreign MNCs, while at the same time, a source of formidable obstacles. According to a 1994, MITI survey,[22] motivations behind expansion into Japan include

the growth of the Japanese market (79.3%)
the appeal of Japan as a base for Asian strategy (33.8%)

the high technological level in Japan (25.4%)
the good supply of Japanese raw materials and parts (10.8%)
the fact that there are few competitors in Japan and Asia (8.8%)
the abundant financial capital (7.6%)

On the other hand, according to a survey of foreign MNCs in Japan,[23] obstacles to Japanese operations include

high cost of land and rent (73%)
high prices of goods (52%)
too many government regulations (40%)
difficulty of finding good personnel (38%)
standards are more complex than other countries (34%)
corporate and income tax too high (32%)
the existence of *keiretsus* (25%)

According to a 1994 study by the American Chamber of Commerce, the Council of the European Business Community, and A. T. Kearney (a management consulting firm), the challenges faced by foreign MNCs in Japan are price and asset deflation, rise in the value of the yen, increasing foreign competitiveness in pharmaceuticals, computers, semiconductors, and some consumer product categories, unstable political leadership, a deflationary and restructuring environment, value-based consumerism, the problem of massive underemployment, and soaring welfare costs.[24]

So there are many obstacles for MNCs. At the same time, some globalization drivers provide significant opportunities for MNCs to participate in or source from Japan.

## Market Globalization Drivers

Japan's market globalization drivers have increasingly moved in favor of foreign MNCs. The sharp increase in the income of Japanese consumers, from the 1980s on, and the concurrent reduction of trade barriers to foreign imports have created favorable opportunities for foreign businesses in Japan. The modernization and westernization of Japanese preferences and consumption patterns have also led to a significant increase in Japanese imports of manufactured goods. The younger, more affluent, and internationally oriented generation of Japanese consumers has been particularly influenced by changes in lifestyle and outlook. It is they who are more likely to increase their purchases of imported apparel, sporting goods, recreational vehicles, and the like. At the same time, the majority of Japanese consumers may have increased their propensity to consume imports because there is no longer any social stigma attached to the purchase of foreign goods. A greater familiarity with imported products may have led to the lowering of what has been dubbed the "cultural barrier" against foreign imports. Even so, understanding the rapidly changing pattern of Japanese consumer spending habits and preferences, good marketing skills, and up-to-date product design and development are critical to success for foreign companies in the Japanese market.

Japanese business and industrial customers, particularly MNCs, are increasingly behaving as regional or global customers. For highly globalized industries such as consumer electronics, semiconductors, personal computers, and telecommunications, Japanese customers are becoming increasingly global and regional. Spurred partly by the appreciation of the yen, rising skills, and engineering capabilities in some Asian countries such as Singapore and Malaysia, and rapid growth of Asian markets, an increasing number of Japanese companies are procuring electronic components on a global scale. For some industries, such as consumer electronics and personal computers, they are buying regionally now that so many global suppliers are producing in Asia.

For consumer packaged goods and groceries, regional and global channels of distribution are emerging, such as the strategic alliances among Ito-Yokado of Japan, Wal-Mart of the United States, and the Metropolitan group in Europe.[25] Japanese consumers increasingly accept American and European brand names, packaging, and advertising, indicating the success of U.S. and European "brand marketing" techniques in Japan. Indeed, many brand names in Japan use English words (e.g., My First Sony, and Pocari Sweat). Advertising, by both Japanese and foreign companies, also makes extensive use of foreign celebrities, such as athlete Carl Lewis and boxer Mike Tyson in the late 1980s; then basketball player Michael Jordan, actor Harrison Ford, and American supermodels in the mid-1990s. Equity participation by Rupert Murdoch's News Corporation (of Australia) in one of Japan's TV networks, through a joint venture in the summer of 1996, is expected to affect the formerly regulated mass communications industry, opening up more opportunities for marketing transfer.

Because Japanese consumers are very demanding, success in Japan can be transferred to other countries. Japan's ability to play a lead market role for other countries is often cited as a reason for the success of Japanese companies in quality-salient industries such as automobiles and consumer electronics.

A negative market globalization driver is the unique Japanese distribution system and its deep relationships—these present a formidable barrier to new entrants, whether foreign or domestic. Japanese companies often form long-term contracts and lasting personal relationships with their suppliers and subcontractors. So new entrants may be at a disadvantage when attempting to conduct business with Japanese wholesalers or retailers, even if their products or services carry a lower price or are of superior quality. Manufacturers often form their own distribution systems that carry only their own brand. The vertical integration of Japanese companies, combined with regulatory delays, makes penetration of the Japanese market difficult for foreign firms. New entrants may find it necessary to establish their own distribution networks. This can involve considerable risk and heavy up-front costs.

In the mid-1990s, however, new opportunities seem to have opened up for foreign MNCs, particularly as related to channels of distribution. Bypassing existing distribution systems—as in the cases of Monsanto,

Philips, General Electric, Electrolux, and South Korea's Lucky-Goldstar Group (for consumer electronics and white goods such as refrigerators and washing machines)—and the merging of wholesalers by Yukijirushi are some examples of innovative approaches.[26] Direct marketing by personal computer manufacturers, such as Dell Computer, and by apparel manufacturers such as L. L. Bean and Land's End has increased sharply. Cooperative or "team merchandising" by manufacturers and large retail chains such as the Ito Yokado group (which owns U.S.-based convenience store, 7-Eleven) and Daiei, in the area of apparel, household products, and food, has increased in the mid 1990s in the move toward rationalized distribution.[27] Toys 'Я Us, the U.S. toy discounter, was able to break into Japan in the early 1990s with elimination of the rule allowing neighborhood retailers to veto the opening of large, new stores. Foreign car manufacturers such as Ford, Mercedes, and Chrysler are now using the dealer networks of Japanese auto manufacturers. In apparel retailing, The GAP, Limited, and others have successfully entered the Japanese market through alliances with local department stores.

## Cost Globalization Drivers

Most cost globalization drivers for Japan are unfavorable for foreign MNCs, stemming from the very high prices of all factors of production, and from Japan's geographic location at the northeast corner of the Asia-Pacific region. Furthermore, the unpredictable yen increases the financial risk for MNCs setting up Japanese subsidiaries, but may also lower the cost of importing goods and supplies into Japan. Japan's one favorable cost globalization driver lies in its potential contribution to MNCs' global and regional economies of scale and scope. For most industries, Japan, with its large purchasing power and population, can contribute quite large sales volumes to MNCs, particularly in the industries that have recently been deregulated, such as cellular phones and PHSs (Personal Handy-phone Systems). In the case of personal computers, Japan now provides the second largest market after the United States, spurred partly by the country's craze for Internet access beginning in late 1995.

Japan holds limited attraction as a site for value chain activities other than R&D. The strong yen makes direct investment in Japan more costly, in addition to the already high cost of land, buildings, and labor. Some MNCs have moved their regional headquarters from Tokyo to Singapore or Hong Kong, and more will do so.

Even among Japanese corporations, investment in Japan was low in the early 1990s, due in part to active investment during the "bubble" economy of the mid-1980s, and in part to the relatively high cost of doing business in Japan. Investment in plant and equipment began growing again in fiscal 1996, after four years of decline for Japanese manufacturers. However, increase in investment is found mainly overseas with foreign investment up 28.1% in fiscal 1995, and 1.8% in fiscal 1996. For fiscal 1996, overseas investment was estimated to account for 28.4% of total investment in property, plants, and equipment.[28]

For some industries, such as cellular phones, which are relatively new, Japan serves as a potential source for faster movement down the experience curve, because of its large market size and rapid diffusion of products. On the other hand, the mature stage of the Japanese market for a majority of industries, including consumer packaged goods and cars, makes it difficult to provide much volume for advancing.

Not having low-cost labor or raw materials, Japan does not provide much in the way of global sourcing efficiencies. The high cost of land, utilities, and personnel has also eliminated the potential for Japan to serve as a production center for components, with the exception of those having very high technological content, as in the case of manufacturing equipment for semiconductors. Nor is Japan attractive as a gateway to Asia in terms of logistics, because of its geographical position and high operation costs.

Japan remains an R&D center for some industries, such as consumer packaged goods and electronics, but is losing its position in high technology industries such as semiconductors. Despite the advanced stage of its technology and engineering and the fast pace of technological change in digital imaging, high administrative and personnel costs have led some companies, such as Intel, to move their R&D centers to other Asian countries, such as Singapore, and/or to consolidate within the United States, as in the case of Motorola.

## Government Globalization Drivers

Japan's formal and informal government policies have often been cited as being very unhelpful to foreign businesses.[29] Certainly, the very low share of GNP that imports have provides bottom-line evidence of high trade barriers, and the very low level of foreign direct investment strongly suggests barriers in that area. Trade policies continue to be somewhat protective, although formal trade barriers in Japan are not exceptionally high and, indeed, have been reduced since 1977. However, one leading survey of international business rates Japan below average among eleven Asian economies. It is ranked low in the areas of equal treatment of foreigners (score of 4.2 on a scale of 0–10) and employment of foreigners, due to the immigration law (score of 4.1). Japan is also ranked below average in terms of transaction cost-related barriers to foreign direct investment. And it is ranked low in terms of state control, transparency, bureaucracy, and lobbying.[30]

Substantive deregulation began in 1994 but varies among industries. In a 1995 survey of Japanese companies, more than 53%, both listed and unlisted, responded that deregulation has made inroads in their industries.[31] In the construction and real estate industries, however, deregulation is perceived not to have progressed. The Japanese government has also used technical standards unique to Japan as one way of protecting the market, as in the case of skis and cosmetics. The long and complicated approval process for pharmaceuticals and medical equipment is another example. In high technology industries, the government approach

has been mixed. For cellular phones and PHSs, Japan has unique technical standards, although they are being quickly transformed to de facto
global standards, thanks to the lobbying of U.S. manufacturers and
Japanese MNCs who need large volume to be internationally competitive.
For high definition TV, it still remains to be seen whether the standard
will be compatible with the U.S. or European standard.

Japan's marketing regulations do not particularly inhibit foreign companies. Japan is not restrictive in advertising, unlike some other Asian
countries. For example, TV ads are allowed for cigarettes and hard
liquor. For cosmetics, which are often cited as protected products whose
prices in Japan are much higher than those overseas, certification to indicate ingredients in detail were required for approval to sell cosmetics in
Japan. Because of this procedure, parallel imports were near to impossible. The procedure was revised in 1996, making it possible for large retail
chains and discounters to import and market foreign cosmetics. The effects of this deregulation have yet to be felt.

Overall, the Japanese government is in a dilemma. On the one hand, it
is sensitive to foreign dominance of key industries such as telecommunications and construction of public works, while on the other hand, it is
also sensitive to foreigners' claims that Japan plays by a different set of
rules from those of other industrialized countries, such as in the cases of
semiconductors and photographic film. It is quite difficult to predict how
the government will react in various industries, because it is now under
multiple pressures. For one, it faces pressure from the Japanese elec-
torate to make the public bidding and approval process more transparent, as in the case of pharmaceuticals (such as for AIDS treatments), and
for public bidding by general contractors in construction industries. It
also feels pressure from Japanese MNCs to make Japan part of the global
market so they can compete in the de facto standards battle taking place
in many industries such as digital video discs and others.

### Competitive Globalization Drivers

Despite the many difficulties, Japan still has several compelling competitive globalization drivers. First, among Asian countries, Japan has the
largest number of global competitors. For some industries such as consumer electronics, Japan is the home of many global competitors and is,
therefore, a "must" for foreign MNCs interested in global competition
for intelligence purposes. In addition to the globally well-known companies such as Sony and Canon, Japan has some emerging global leaders in
selected industries, (e.g., Nintendo and Sega Enterprises in the video
game industry). On the other hand, consumer packaged goods have
been, and still are, dominated by foreign MNCs, such as Coca Cola and
Nestlé; household products and personal care products by P&G and
Unilever, and recently, Amway. The pharmaceutical industry is another
example dominated by foreign MNCs.

Second, the market potential, if successful, is enormous. Particularly
for the industries that are being deregulated—such as health care,

telecommunications, and financial services—Japan's potential for rapid growth cannot be understated for foreign MNCs. High technology industries such as telecommunications routing and networking, computer software and retailing, are the potential battlefields for global competitors, as few Japanese MNCs compete successfully. Among the foreign MNCs newly active in Japan are Cisco Systems, Oracle, Toys 'Я Us, GAP, and Levi Strauss. In electronic components foreign MNCs are competing fiercely in Japan against Japanese MNCs. In the mid-1990s, entry into Japan through private labels has proven successful for some products such as photographic film.

## Overall Global Strategies for Japan

As discussed earlier, many foreign MNCs have struggled to succeed in Japan. Japan's potential as a market depends, first, on whether the foreign MNC seeks to export directly into Japan, or second, whether it seeks to produce and sell locally, with the latter strategy having a far higher chance of success. The four non-Japanese MNCs—Unilever, Procter and Gamble, Philips, and Motorola—on which this book focuses, have all experienced both failure and success in Japan.

### Market Participation Strategies

The low margins on products, the presence of a dominant local brand, and the critical nature of consumers have prevented some multinationals from succeeding in Japan on a large scale. On the other hand, increasing acceptance by Japanese consumers of Western-style marketing techniques and of functionally superior products could allow foreign MNCs to achieve greater inroads in the future.

The case of Procter and Gamble is particularly salutary.[32] The company entered Japan in 1972 as P&G Sunhome, a 50-50 joint venture with N. S. H. Sunhome, a local chemical producer. In 1978, P&G Sunhome became a wholly owned subsidiary after the joint venture partners sold their shares. P&G's first decade in Japan was characterized by the straight introduction of U.S. products and marketing into the Japanese market. Though it met with some initial success for laundry detergent and disposable diapers, the company failed miserably in this period. In 1973, P&G launched *Cheer*, a laundry detergent that was superior in performance to Japanese products at that time. Aggressive TV advertising and the huge sampling that was characteristic of P&G's marketing were introduced in Japan. But although the brand attained a 20% share, it continued to lose money because of high marketing investment. The launch of *Pampers* disposable diapers in 1977 provides another example of huge initial success followed by failure. When *Pampers* was introduced, it almost created a new market. Total market size, which was ¥1.5 billion in 1977, grew to ¥4.5 billion in 1978, and ¥11.1 billion in 1979. In this rapidly growing market, P&G enjoyed a near monopoly share of 90%. But its share plummeted to less than 10% when a Japanese company, Uni

Charm, introduced its product, *Moonie,* in 1981, and when Kao, Japan's dominant consumer products company, entered this market in 1983. P&G also tried to introduce *Pringles* potato chips in alliance with Japanese brewer, Suntory, in 1977, but withdrew later (although it has since reentered with *Pringles* quite successfully, but with a small market share).

There are several reasons for P&G's failure during its first decade in Japan: straight transfer of marketing from the United States to Japan (without due consideration for the characteristics of the Japanese market, including customer acceptance, needs, and competitive behavior); lack of communication between the expatriate top management and Japanese employees; strict control over information (as was practiced in the United States); aggressive price discounting causing loss of consumer confidence and low margins for the trade; and lack of control over management, due to the 50-50 joint venture structure.

The second decade was one of recovery, reflected in P&G's share recovery in disposable diapers, sanitary napkins, and laundry detergents. What made the difference was P&G's awareness of the characteristics of the Japanese market and of Japanese business practices, which was gained mainly by interviewing people in the field and identifying problems. The company also began to recognize the strategic importance of the Japanese market. In addition, P&G instituted in 1985, a three-year "Quantum Leap Program": new product development to meet the needs of the Japanese market; pricing higher than the competition to match superior product performance, a departure from P&G's traditional discounting; sales promotion to avoid price discounting at the retail level; and changes in the distribution system through "strategic alliances" with selected wholesalers (50 core companies). This program ended in 1988, with tripling of sales in three years. P&G's position concerning nontariff barriers to the Japanese market has also changed. The company used to claim its low share in Japan was due to nontariff barriers. Currently, it views the Japanese market to be strategically important, because "we can succeed anywhere if we succeed in Japan," as one senior P&G executive noted.

Unilever began operation in Japan in 1964, as Honen Lever, a joint venture with Honen Oil. It began production and sales of margarine and other fat products in 1966. After the liberalization of the soap market in 1970, Honen Lever entered this business in the form of a 70-30 joint venture. The company expanded its operations to other food products in 1975, and to toiletries in 1976. In hair care products, Unilever became famous for its successful introduction of the *Timotei* line in 1984. During a short period following the launch, *Timotei* took 15% of the Japanese hair care products market. Its share declined, however, after response by strong Japanese competitors, such as Kao and Shiseido. In 1993, Unilever bought the *Marina* margarine brand trademark from Ajinomoto, when this major local company decided to withdraw from the category in the face of flat growth and fierce competition, including from Unilever itself, which now holds the number two position. So it appears that Unilever considers the Japanese market important for its large size and sophistication. In January 1994, the company announced the introduction of a new "Corporate Identity." In marking its thirtieth anniversary in Japan, it targeted sales of ¥200 billion for the early twenty-first century in the context of its "Vision 2000" program. On the other hand, in its annual review of 1994, Unilever stated that its growth in the Japanese market has been modest, compared with that in China.

Philips was just about the only European electronics manufacturer to enter Japan in the early years, perhaps initially for the purpose of market monitoring. Philips began operation in Japan in 1952, as Matsushita Electronics, a joint venture with Matsushita, then adding in 1953, Philips Japan, Ltd. as a wholly owned subsidiary. Philips's joint venture with the Matsushita group appears to have benefitted both Matsushita and Philips. But in 1993, Matsushita acquired Philips's equity in Matsushita Electronics for ¥185 billion. Discussions regarding the acquisition took quite some time, as there were several areas of disagreement concerning Philips' and Matsushita's operations outside of Japan. The joint venture production of color TV sets in Beijing, which began in 1989, was one source of disagreement; semiconductor manufacturing in the United States was another. Finally, under President Morishita of Matsushita, a clear decision to acquire was made.

Philips has had mixed results from other Japanese alliances. The company's alliance with Sony in development and commercialization of the compact disk for music, or for CD-I (compact disc interactive—which can retrieve not only voice, but also pictures interactively) has not translated into tangible success for Philips. For the digital video disk, Philips joined with Sony in the battle for the de facto standard. The results are not yet clear, as Philips' brand awareness in Japan is associated more with small electric appliances, such as coffee makers and electric shavers, than with electronics products. For example, its share of the Japanese color TV market is less than 1%. Nevertheless, the company considers Japan to be a key market for its leading high technology products such as the DCC (digital compact cassette) and CD-I. The head of the Consumer Electronics Pacific Division maintains that "Unless we succeed in Japan, we will be behind in product development of the new generation."[33]

As argued earlier, Motorola provides perhaps the best example of any U.S. or European company that has established itself in Japan in the face of fierce local competition. Motorola began operations in Japan in 1962, initially to purchase components. In the early 1980s, Motorola found itself under attack in its home market by Japanese competitors in both its semiconductor and communication businesses. At the same time, Motorola faced seemingly insuperable barriers protecting its rivals' home markets. Undeterred, Motorola mounted a sustained effort to both defend its U.S. markets and invade markets in Japan. This effort included soliciting the threat of U.S. congressional action. Motorola's reward has been the gradual yielding of barriers in Japan and an increasing number of contracts won. Perhaps more important, Motorola has been able to preserve its market leadership at home.[34] In 1986, the company was able to enter the pager business in Japan by acquiring the equity of Tokyo Tele Message. In 1987, Market-Oriented Sector Selective (MOSS) talks between the United States and Japan concluded with the decision to separate car phone systems into two major regions. Motorola was awarded the right to serve the Kansai region by selling its Total Area Communication System (TACS) to DDI, a new Japanese competitor to NTT. It was later allowed to expand into the Tohoku and Hokkaido regions. In 1987, Motorola established Tohoku Semiconductor Ltd. as a 50-50 joint venture with Toshiba. In 1990, the Japanese Ministry of Post and Telecommunications even selected a Motorola design for a digital cellular telephone component as a national standard. Today, Nippon Motorola sells in Japan microcomputers, semiconductors, cellular and car phones, communications equipment, data communications equipment, pagers, and personal computers.

## Product and Service Strategies

Japanese consumers used to be less price sensitive than those in almost all other countries and more insistent upon high quality products. Consequently, marketing strategies that have proved successful elsewhere may not yield the same results in Japan. Specifically, a strategy of product differentiation, with premium pricing and emphasis on after-sales service, can be more appropriate for Japan, compared to a low-cost, low-quality strategy. Cosmetics was formerly an example of this, although it is now showing some signs of change. In the mid-1990s, Japanese consumers began showing "value-consciousness." This was due in part to increasing awareness of the comparatively high costs of living in Japan; to their own experiences of overseas travel; and to the availability of information through satellite television. Thus, private label and generic products have found a considerable following among the Japanese. Examples include film (manufactured by Germany's Agfa Gevaert and sold by the local Daiei GMS chain), dairy products (imported from Australia and New Zealand), household products including detergents (manufactured in South Korea), and imported beer. In apparel, private label basic goods have found a niche in the market.

White goods, such as refrigerators, manufactured by General Electric, and distributed by mass merchandiser, Kojima, have made some inroads into the Japanese market. Imports of refrigerators increased by 71% in 1995, to reach close to 400,000 units. These imports are priced at one-half to one-third of the comparable Japanese products, and target young dual-income or single-person households.

In consumer packaged goods, some regional products are emerging such as Kao's *Sifone* brand hair care products designed particularly for Asian markets. "Asian cars" are being developed by Toyota and Honda, specifically for the Asian market. For neither of these categories, however, is Japan included as a part of the "regional market" for regional products. Few such regional products, like P&G's potato chips with labels in different languages, have made significant inroads as yet.

P&G coordinates product development and marketing globally. For example, new products have been launched in ninety countries within a year of their U.S. launch. The company's successful recovery of market share in disposable diapers illustrates how P&G responded to the unique characteristics of the Japanese market. When its share plummeted, P&G began thorough research of Japanese customers, finding that Japanese mothers are extremely demanding concerning leakage and, therefore, require a tight fit and high absorbency; that they have more time for child care and, therefore, change diapers more frequently; and that Japanese apartments have little space for bulky products. In response, P&G introduced in 1985, *New Pampers Compact,* a denser product, and in 1987, relaunched *New Pampers* to respond to further customer complaints. By 1988, P&G had regained the top share position. Share change is very quick in this category—Uni Charm captured the top share in 1992, by launching a pants-type diapers.

P&G's design and marketing of the sanitary napkin, *Whisper,* indicates well its use of coordinated product design and marketing on a global scale. *Whisper* was originally launched as *Always* in the United States in 1983. For three years, P&G Far East researched in detail the use of sanitary napkins by 10,000 Japanese women. The company found that Japanese women are smaller; they use twice as many napkins as do American women; and they want little sound from breaking the bag, because they do not want others to know that they are menstruating. Based upon these findings, P&G revised the product, making *Whisper* smaller and more compact and the package easier to break open.

At the same time, both P&G and Unilever, as well as other multinational consumer products companies, seek as much as possible to market global products with minimal adaptation even for Japan. For example, in 1995, Unilever launched in Japan its new global "natural" hair care product, *Organics.* Unilever already holds a 9% share of the hair care market in Japan with its product, *Lux. Organic* is a strategic product expected to become a major driver to increase the company's market share to 15%.

Philips appears to transfer products for the European and/or U.S. market to Japan. Though there are some indications that Philips has finally begun an effort to develop products specifically for the Japanese market, their overall strategy is still very much focused on Europe and the United States. One example of a product developed specifically for the Japanese market, however, is a color TV with a built-in broadcasting satellite tuner. Philips can also interpret product strategy differently from its Japanese partners. Philips developed the CD-I product in conjunction with Sony and Matsushita, launching it in October 1991, in the United States and in April 1992, in Japan. Philips appears to be transferring its European and North American marketing strategy for this product to Japan, where it is targeting both institutional and home markets. Sony and Matsushita, however, decided on a different strategy from that of Philips because of the low profit potential of the product. Sony is focusing on institutional use, while Matsushita is taking a "wait and see" approach to introduction in the home market. Some observers believe that

Philips has little understanding of the difference in software development between the United States and Japan. In the United States there are many software houses ready to develop software for home use. In Japan they are reluctant to enter the CD-I business because it requires such heavy investment.

Motorola has found ways to make its products superior to those of its Japanese rivals. For example, its cellular phone terminals (TACS systems) are recognized as superior to those of NTT in technology and costs. Motorola also provides more choices to customers as its technological information is disclosed, compared with the NTT system for which such data is not generally divulged. In contrast, Motorola's primary Japanese competitor, IDO, is limited in its choice of products in terms of price and performance, because it has to buy NTT system cellular phone terminals from manufacturers who have contracts with NTT.

The bottom line for product strategy in Japan is that, more than anywhere else, foreign companies have to find a balance between the benefits of global standardization and those of local customization. Typically, successful foreign products need to offer both, which is why there are so few of them.

## Activity Location Strategies

As discussed earlier, rising costs are driving both Japanese and foreign MNCs to reconsider the need for production in Japan. A number of foreign firms have been forced to shift their production overseas and have either downsized or dissolved their Japanese subsidiaries. The desire to avoid the adverse effects of the strong yen, combined with the reduction of trade restrictions, has lessened the need for foreign MNCs to have production facilities in Japan. Unilever has been cautious about setting up production of its *Lipton* products, relying instead on local contract manufacture. The production of *Lipton Ice,* a newly introduced product, was intially contracted out to Pepsi Cola Japan, with Unilever playing a more important role in product planning, market research, and advertising than before. Nevertheless, Nippon Lever does operate factories in three locations. Such production flexibility is now turning into a strength for Unilever. P&G has found it worthwhile to invest further in local production. The Tochigi factory where sanitary napkins and diapers are produced was expanded at an investment of ¥12 billion in 1992. Nippon Motorola has production facilities for semiconductors located in Aizu Wakamatsu and Sendai. In December 1993, Motorola began construction of a semiconductor design center in Sendai. It also built a 16-MDRAM factory that began operations in 1995.

Foreign MNCs increasingly recognize the need to locate some R&D facilities in Japan, in order to gain access to technical and market developments there. P&G opened a technical center in Kobe in 1993, following the establishment of such centers in Belgium, the United Kingdom, Germany, and Venezuela. It appears that Japan is the base location for P&G

in Asia. The company is now in the position of transferring its product development capabilities at the technical center in Japan back to corporate headquarters. Unilever has had more success in Japan with its locally developed products such as *Lux* than with its global products, such as *Organics*. The company has now located a regional innovation center for hair care products in Japan. Motorola has a special research division with units in the United States, Japan, the United Kingdom, and Germany. Motorola also maintains an educational institute located in Yokohama, with branches in Beijing, Singapore, and Seoul.

Other parts of MNCs' value chains seldom get located in Japan, because of the high costs and geographic inconvenience.

## Marketing Strategies

As with product and service strategies, foreign MNCs need to develop marketing for Japan that is leveraged by global strengths, such as brand names, and local adaptation, such as in advertising. While Japanese consumers or businesses may exhibit strong preferences for domestic products, it is possible to market manufactured products successfully in Japan if foreign managers can understand Japanese culture, lifestyle, and consumer behavior.

One commonly successful strategy for foreign marketers is to maintain a price premium. Japanese consumers' association of high prices with good product performance makes them suspicious of price discounting. P&G, for example, had to revise its traditional discounting strategy when it entered the Japanese market. In the 1970s, P&G tried to bolster sagging sales of its new introduction, *Cheer* laundry detergent, by aggressively discounting the price. But instead of attracting new customers, the detergent's market share plummeted. Following the *Cheer* debacle, P&G replaced price discounting with sales promotions and has seen its market position improve. *Vidal Sassoon* hair care products provide another example of the successful positioning of premium-priced products in the mid-1990s. There is also the famous instance of *Chivas Regal Scotch* whiskey losing sales when it cut prices, thereby reducing its status as a prestigious gift.

As the ratio of private brand products has increased in the mid-1990s, "value pricing" has become increasingly important. On the other hand, unclear positioning (being "stuck in the middle" of the value map for price and quality) does not work well in this highly competitive and fluctuating market, as was shown by P&G's aborted national rollout of its *Oil of Olay* line in 1995.

Using uniform global brand or corporate names has worked very well for Japanese companies around the world. Developing one strong brand name for the product category appears to be very effective, not only in Japan, but also in Asia. Well-established brands such as Unilever's *Jif* household cleaner and *Domestos* toilet cleaner helped the company achieve a dominant position against local competition in these product categories.

Alternative distribution channels are starting to emerge. Mass merchandisers and discounters are becoming more powerful at the expense of the manufacturer-controlled networks of small retailers. Deregulation in the laws governing large retail outlets, coupled with plunging commercial rents, have accelerated store openings by large foreign retailers such as Toys 'Я Us. Music retailers in particular are making inroads into Japan's distribution system. Virgin has a megastore in Japan and Tower Records has opened the world's largest music store in Tokyo. As mentioned earlier, direct mail has been successful for apparel, providing opportunities for foreign MNCs.

As in most of Asia, MNCs also need to heavily "market" to government officials and regulators. Motorola is particularly shrewd at educating and leading government agencies, capitalizing on its global position in frontier technology. Its negotiations with NTT and the Ministry of Post and Telecommunications are managed well. In Japan, NTT and the Ministry play significant roles. But Japanese manufacturers take a more passive stance than those in Europe and the United States in influencing government regulations. Motorola, being a global competitor, capitalizes on its knowledge of deregulation and the shift to the market economy in emerging markets.

## Competitive Move Strategies

As discussed earlier, Japan's competitive globalization drivers—being the site of many global competitors and a source of innovation in some important high-technology industries—make it very strategic for monitoring competition and coordinating competitive moves. These imperatives must be balanced against the cost of being in Japan. Companies in the same industries have taken different approaches. For example, Motorola includes Japan as a part of its global value chain, while Intel does not. As noted earlier, Motorola very much includes Japan in its global competitive moves.

P&G clearly sees the importance of being in Japan for its demanding customers and for global intelligence. That P&G positions the Japanese market as a strategically important one is apparent from its regional and global moves. Competition with Kao, a strong Japanese competitor, and Unilever is intense in Asia. P&G's acquisition of the Japanese subsidiary of Max Factor appears to be a move against Unilever, which bought Elizabeth Arden, and also against Kao which has *Sofina* brand cosmetics. It may also be aimed at Shiseido.

Unilever also appears to include Japan as an important component of its regional and global moves. For example, its entry into detergents in 1990, did not seem solely for the sake of the Japanese market. This also seems to have been a move against P&G and Kao, two major global competitors operating in Japan with strong positions in detergents. For food products, which now account for 30% of its total sales, Nippon Lever is seeking strategic alliances with manufacturers in Japan.

Lastly, strategic alliances with local partners continue to be an important competitive play in Japan. This need applies particularly in high technology industries. To meet requirements of short cycle times and huge investments, many strategic alliances have been formed. Motorola has had a very strong and successful alliance with Toshiba. Intel's alliance with Sharp in flash memories is another example. In addition, Japanese manufacturers are allying themselves with Asian companies, in a form that moves beyond the traditional technical licensing and OEM supply, to engage in joint development of the next generation of semiconductor memories.

## Overall Organization and Management Approaches for Japan

Because of the differences between Japanese and foreign MNCs in overall organization and management approaches, we describe both for some of the topics discussed below. Many Japanese MNCs, who compete globally, adopted a four-region structure in the mid-1990s. Corporate headquarters are, in the majority of cases, located in Japan, with regional headquarters in North America, Europe, and elsewhere in Asia. Examples include Sony and Matsushita. For some products, such as videocassette recorders, a few Japanese companies have moved their *business unit* headquarters to Singapore, and a few Japanese companies have moved their *corporate* headquarters to locations outside Japan, such as Yaohan to Hong Kong. Some foreign MNCs, such as P&G, have located their regional headquarters in Japan, while others are relocating their Asian regional headquarters elsewhere because of high costs and the decreasing importance they place on Japan.

Many Japanese subsidiaries of foreign MNCs operate quite autonomously, due to the size of the market and the unique characteristics of the customers and competitive patterns in Japan. Some foreign MNCs, such as IBM, merged their subsidiaries during the 1990s in order to improve operational efficiency. Traditionally, many MNCs have entered via joint ventures with local companies. Unlike most Asian countries this was not because of government requirements (there being no significant government or other constraints on a firm's choices in the matter of foreign ownership, equity position, or organizational structure) but in order to gain market access. At the same time, many foreign MNCs have found such joint ventures to lead to global competitive threats from their partners.[35] Still, in industries such as multimedia and semiconductors, strategic alliances are unavoidable, these being formed and dissolved weekly, if not daily.

Human resource management is an area in which many changes are taking place in Japan, beginning in the mid-1990s. The traditional strength of the so-called "Japanese management style," characterized by lifetime employment and the seniority system, are now under pressure and being scrutinized, because overstaffing at the middle management level has damaged the international competitiveness of Japanese MNCs. The progress of information technology and systems and the increasing use of e-mail, Internet, and Intranet have reduced the power of middle management, once called the "hidden asset" of Japanese corporate strength. Many large Japanese corporations have taken countermeasures, cutting new recruits, adopting a voluntary retirement system, and transferring people from corporate headquarters to sales and subsidiaries. The traditional importance attached to the lifetime employment system and the social infrastructure, including tax incentives, which has supported the system in the past, may be difficult to abolish openly and officially. Many approaches are now being taken to dismantle this system, but the results are still uncertain.

As to compensation, many more Japanese companies are adopting meritocracy and the annual renewal of contracts, but the outcome here also is still uncertain. Foreign MNCs, which formerly faced difficulties and challenges in the area of human resource management, because of the unique characteristics of Japanese human resource practices, are finding the changes to be a double-edged sword. Some companies have gone a long way to Japanize their human resource management systems, only to find that Japanese companies are now taking a new approach. Others are wondering whether this is a good opportunity to make the human resource practices of their Japanese subsidiaries globally compatible.

Because of the strong Japanese preference for working with other Japanese, more than in any other Asian country, MNCs need native managers. So one of the issues most cited by foreign MNCs in Japan is the difficulty in recruiting capable local people. This difficulty stems from several causes: the fixed nature of the recruiting process (limited duration of the annual recruiting period and the inflexible link with university professors for hiring new engineers), and the stereotyped image of the harsh and competitive personnel evaluation systems of foreign MNCs. From the mid-1990s, however, an increasing number of managers became attracted to the positions offered by foreign MNCs, as shown by the increasing use of professional recruiters to find top management for foreign automobile companies from among Japanese automobile manufacturers. Japan has become a major market for international recruiting firms. Overstaffing at the large Japanese corporations and little hope for promotions may have encouraged this movement. In addition, in high technology industries, the younger generation, including new recruits, finds refreshing the performance evaluation system of the foreign MNCs, based upon output rather than seniority. The recent popularity of entrepreneurship and ventures in Japan also may be helping foreign MNCs to attract young people.

Lastly, corporate culture continues to be highly Japanese, even in the subsidiaries of foreign MNCs. Despite almost five decades of a market economy and internationalization, the culture in Japanese corporations still remains rather unique and incomprehensible to outsiders. IBM Japan, often cited for its success in Japan, provides a prime example of a foreign company that has gone almost totally "native." American and

European management consulting firms, accounting firms, investment banks, and other professional service companies find it almost impossible to field non-Japanese in client contact positions. However, there are signs that this is changing in some new, emerging Japanese corporations where technology change is quick and global. Increasing exposure to global business practices, products and services, through Internet and other means, together with the increasing number of younger Japanese traveling and studying overseas, may change the culture of Japanese corporations and corporate working life in the future.

## Conclusions

Japan is still economically a huge part of Asia-Pacific. Its companies play very large roles in most of the region. But Japan, itself, offers mixed globalization drivers for foreign MNCs. It still provides a huge market for new products in high technology and emerging industries such as personal computers, cellular phones, and other multimedia products. It is a home country of significant global competitors and, thus, an important place for honing strategic advantages and for monitoring purposes. At the same time, its very low import ratio greatly reduces its potential importance relative to smaller but much more receptive economies elsewhere in Asia. In addition, the economy is maturing despite a slight recovery from 1996, particularly as compared with other Asian economies. The cost of doing business is very high and not expected to come down in the near future. It is less and less cost effective to manufacture in Japan, as its own companies are recognizing. Complex and difficult to understand administrative mechanisms and channels of distribution still present significant obstacles, so MNCs may increasingly choose to bypass Japan. On the other hand, Japan's increasing role in technology in many industries obligates foreign MNCs in those industries to find some way to tap into Japan's new knowledge. One approach may be to make more use of alliances with Japanese companies, despite past poor experiences many foreign MNCs have had.

MNC managers should note, however, that Japan is in the process of change for some industries such as retailing, software, and health care. The traditional inflexible system has been attacked and bypassed not only by innovative foreign MNCs but also by some unconventional Japanese challengers. The scene—regulations, technology, and markets—is changing very quickly. MNCs that are willing to invest energy for in-depth analysis by industry, and are at the same time quick enough to exploit the "windows of opportunity," can have the best of both worlds in Japan.[36]

## NOTES

1. Nomura Research Institute.
2. *Nihon Keizai Shimbun,* June 30, 1996.
3. Comparative Economic and Financial Statistics 1995, Bank of Japan.

4. "Changing Japan—Whispering Reform," *The Economist,* January 11–17, 1997, pp. 19–21.

5. Foreign Trade Statistics, Ministry of Finance, *White Paper on International Trade with Japan 1995,* Ministry of International Trade and Industry, Tokyo Japan.

6. "The Sun also Rises," *Far Eastern Economic Review,* June 20, 1996, pp. 62–66.

7. Tokei Geppo, "Import Penetration of Machineries," *Toyo Keizai Shinposha,* October 1995, pp. 18–27.

8. "The Sun Also Rises."

9. This section is drawn from Ryuichiro Inoue, "Motivations behind Direct Investment in Japan by Foreign MNCs," *Gaishikei Kigyo Soran 1995, Toyo Keizai Shinposha,* pp. 102–7.

10. Tokei Geppo, "Performance of 3,200 Foreign Affiliated Companies in Japan," *Toyo Keizai Shinposha,* July 1996, pp. 10–15.

11. Tokei Geppo, "FAC's Share in Japan Less Than 3%," *Toyo Keizai Shinposha,* July 1997, pp. 10–13.

12. "Performance of 3,200 Foreign Affiliated Companies in Japan."

13. *Gaishikei Kigyo Soran 1997.*

14. "Performance of 3,200 Foreign Affiliated Companies in Japan."

15. For a review of these sources of success, see George S. Yip, "Global Strategy as a Factor in Japanese Success," *The International Executive,* Special Issue on Japan, 38, no. 1 (January–February 1996): 145–67.

16. *The World Investment Report 1995: Transnational Corporations and Competitiveness,* UNCTAD Division on Transnational Corporations and Competitiveness, New York and Geneva.

17. "Gaishikei Kigyo no Doko" (Status of FACs), Ministry of International Trade and Industry, August 1995.

18. Tokei Geppo, "Rapid Shift of Investment to Asia by Japanese Manufacturers," *Toyo Keizai Shinposha,* May 1996, pp. 19–23.

19. Ibid.

20. "Overseas Activities of Japanese Companies," Ministry of International Trade and Industry, July 1995, pp. 90–91.

21. "The Sun also Rises."

22. "Gaishikei Kigyo no Doko," pp. 41–42.

23. "Japanese Market Barriers," *Nikkei Business,* June 6, 1994, pp. 126–29.

24. "Japan in Revolution: An Assessment of Investment Performance by Foreign Firms in Japan, 1995," American Chamber of Commerce in Japan, the Council of the European Business Community, and A. T. Kearney.

25. "Hurry Up Optimal Purchasing" *Nikkei Business,* June 24, 1996, pp. 44–46.

26. Walter E. Shill, Todd Guild, and Yumiko Yamaguchi, "Cracking Japanese Markets," *McKinsey Quarterly* no. 3 (1995): 32–40; Tokei Geppo, "Price Destruction in Household Appliances," *Toyo Keizai Shinposha,* June 1996; *Nihon Keizai Shimbun,* September 28, 1995.

27. Tatsuo Ohbora, Kanoko Oishi, and Hirokazu Yamanashi, "The Emperor's New Stores," *McKinsey Quarterly* no. 2 (1994), 75–82

28. Tokkei Geppo, "Cautious Approach to Investment," May 1996, *Toyo Keizai Shinposha,* May 1996.

29. See, for example, Clyde V. Prestowitz, *Trading Places* (New York: Basic, 1988); and a more general review in Yip, "Global Strategy as a Factor in Japanese Success."

30. *The World Competitiveness Report 1995,* The World Economic Forum, Geneva.

31. Tokei Geppo, "Reexamination of Deregulation," *Toyo Keizai Shinposha,* Januaary 1996.

32. This section is based on M. Y. Yoshino and P. H. Stoneham, "Procter & Gamble in Japan (A), (B), (C), and (D)," cases 9–391–003, 9–391–005, 9–391–005, 9–391–054 (Boston: Harvard Business School Press).

33. Philips, Annual Report, 1994.

34. See David B. Yoffie and John Coleman, "Motorola and Japan (A), (A) Supplement, and (B)," cases 9–388–056, 9–388–057, and 9–389–008 (Boston: Harvard Business School Press, 1988–89).

35. See Gary Hamel, Yves L. Doz, and C. K. Prahalad, "Collaborate with Your Competitors and Win," *Harvard Business Review* (January–February 1989): 133–39.

36. Some industries attractive for foreign companies include recreational vehicles; products and services targeting Japan's aging population such as health care, housing, furniture, and food; both hardware and software in multimedia industries; and many sorts of luxury goods.

# CHAPTER 3

# South Korea— New Prosperity and Agony

## *Yongwook Jun and George S. Yip*

THE SOUTH KOREAN ECONOMY is undergoing fundamental restructuring. After a successful economic transformation from an agricultural base to a global manufacturing center for major industries such as textiles, shipbuilding, steel, consumer electronics, automobiles, and semiconductors since the end of the Korean War, the South Korean economy now faces serious challenges. Given the drastic changes in national factor costs such as wages, land, and interest, South Korean industries are facing competitive threats from Asian neighbors, such as China and ASEAN nations, that enjoy much lower factor costs. So South Korean industries are no longer competitive in low-value-added goods. For example, the share of all South Korean goods in the U.S. market has declined from 3.7% in 1990, to 2.6% in 1996, while that of Chinese goods went up from 3.2% to 6.4% in the same period.[1]

In order to make up for the losses in low-end goods and traditional industries, South Korea has to catch up with developed countries in high-end goods and in high-tech industries. The transition to this new economic level is, however, painful due to the significant gap in technological capabilities and marketing skills. Furthermore, there is unwillingness on the part of developed countries to transfer technologies for fear of the possible "boomerang" effect (building a new competitor). In a sense, the South Korean economy is stuck in the middle of global competition. The agony is that South Korea does not seem to be catching up with developed economy competitors in high-end products or new industries fast enough relative to the speed with which it is losing ground in low-end goods and traditional industries. In this aspect, South Korea will have to accept a larger role for foreign multinational companies to help their economy make this transition. So the South Korean economy will depend more, in the future, on foreign companies for technology and soft skills.

We will see more interaction among foreign multinationals, indigenous South Korean firms, and the South Korean government in the future. The quality of such interaction will have significant ramifications for the Korean economy in the globalized world. But South Korea has a long way to go to attract foreign companies. According to a *Far Eastern Economic Review* survey of top Asian executives,[2] South Korea ranked last out of eleven major Asian economies as the most attractive country in which to invest. South Korea did not get any nomination at all. (The Philippines received the most votes followed by Malaysia.) The major reason for this poor ranking was possible social disorder and political instability.

## Economic Performance

The economic performance of South Korea in the thirty years since it started its first five-year economic development plan in 1962, was quite phenomenal. It has become a model for what developing countries can achieve. By 1995, South Korea was the eleventh largest country in the world in terms of GNP and thirteenth in international trade volume. South Korea has become a major trade partner of world economic power groups. It also jumped the $10,000 per capita income hurdle and successfully joined the club of wealthy nations, namely the Organization for Economic Cooperation and Development (OECD), as the twenty-ninth member in 1996. South Korea is the largest producer of Dynamic Random Access Memory (DRAMs), a key computer component, third largest in consumer electronics and shipbuilding, and sixth largest in steel production in the world. But South Korea's economic growth rate slowed from 9% in 1995, to 7% in 1996, and a rate of 5% is expected in 1997,[3] the major culprit being the weakened trade sector. The current deficit of South Korea has sharply risen from $8 billion in 1995, to $23 billion in 1996. In 1996, South Korea was the second largest current account deficit country in the world, after the United States whose deficit amounted to $149 billion.[4] The poor performance of major export industries, strong consumer demand for luxury goods imports, and the overseas tourism boom have contributed to this heavy deficit. The export volume of South Korean semiconductor, shipbuilding, steel, and consumer electronics industries slumped in 1996. Besides the fundamental weakness of South Korean industries, the mid-1990s devaluation of the Japanese yen vis-a-vis the U.S. dollar (from 80 yen to 120 yen) has played a big role. In contrast, the South Korean won has been devalued only 18% against the U.S. dollar in the same period. As South Korean products compete with Japanese products in major global industries such as semiconductors, shipbuilding, steel, consumer electronics, and automobiles, this efective devaluation of the Japanese yen directly hurts the competitiveness of South Korean products in the global market. In addition, South Korea's newly affluent consumers started in the 1990s to travel overseas and enjoyed their new income by spending on foreign goods and services. The current economic condition of South Korea does not seem to be a transitory phenomenon. Rather, South Korea is suffering from structural problems. The formula that led to the economic miracle does not seem to work anymore in the changed national and global environment. The issue for the country is how fundamentally to strengthen national competitiveness now that the society is a high cost, low efficiency one and the market is being opened to global competition.

South Korea's major forte was a cost leadership strategy that focused on selected industries. South Korean companies, with some government direction, selected a few strategic industries and made heavy investments in global scale operations to take advantage of significant economies of scale. Combined with the low cost of direct labor, this strategy enabled South Korean firms to dash the global market with big volume export. This export-based strategy worked quite well in the past. It is, however, quite vulnerable to changes in the environment: factor costs of South Korea, import policies of consuming countries, and exchange rates. Furthermore, the industry structure (mainly big-scale/high fixed-cost operations) has its own structural rigidity. South Korean firms have to maintain volume production despite external changes such as economic cycles and factor costs.

Despite these changes in the environment, South Korea has not restructured its economy fast enough and, hence, now suffers from high cost and low efficiency. This restructuring will now be accelerated by the economic crisis triggered in late 1997. As South Korea became the latest Asian domino to fall, its currency devalued 40% relative to the U.S. dollar amid recognition of its debt and deficit problems. The nation had to accept the world's largest ever international rescue—U.S.$57 billion from the International Monetary Fund, the World Bank, and others. The nation faces the tall order of transforming its economy once again to be globally competitive.

## Foreign MNCs in South Korea

Unlike Singapore and Malaysia, which have depended heavily on foreign multinationals for capital and new technology, the South Korean government preferred the channel of borrowing from international banks and foreign government institutions. For technology transfer, South Korea utilized the market mechanism, namely technology licensing, mostly from the United States and Japan. In the 1960s and 1970s, this mode of technology access was quite available because South Korea was not, then, perceived as an economic threat. Because of this national policy, the presence of multinational companies and their contribution to the South Korean economy has been minimal. Furthermore, the strong presence of South Korean conglomerates in the national economy, as well as protective government policies, were major deterrents to the entry of foreign multinationals into South Korea. As the economy expanded and the access to foreign technology became more limited, the restrictive policy toward foreign investment softened over time. In the 1980s, a negative system was adopted replacing the positive system for the categories of investment approval. In the 1990s, the policy was further deregulated and the approval system has been changed to a reporting system. As a result, approvals of foreign investment in South Korea increased from $803 million in 1990, to $1.04 billion in 1993, $1.94 billion in 1995, and $3.2 billion in 1996 (although actual investments have been lower). By the end of 1996, cumulative foreign investment in South Korea reached $14 billion, compared with cumulative overseas investment by South Korean firms of $10.2 billion. In terms of sources of investment, the United States has, since 1995, replaced Japan as the top investor.[5] One major change in recent foreign investment in South Korea is that the motivation has become more to penetrate the expanding domestic market rather than to use South Korea as a regional or global sourcing center. Examples include the entry of Ford and BMW for the direct marketing of their automobiles, and the establishment of mass retailing facilities by global players such as Price Club, Tower Records, and Carrefour. Table 3.1 lists the largest foreign investors in South Korea.

## South Korean Multinational Companies

Partly because foreign firms have been kept out, the South Korean economy is dominated by a small number of very large multinational companies—the *chaebols*. Twelve of these ranked in the *Fortune Global 500* list for 1995. These South Korean multinational companies have achieved significant global successes. The Samsung, Daewoo, LG (formerly Lucky-Goldstar), and Hyundai groups have become global household names. Samsung Electronics, a flagship company of Samsung Group, is the world's largest producer of memory chips and color monitors, and the second largest maker of microwave ovens with global market shares of 15%, 17%, and 18% respectively as of 1995. It is also the company that in 1996 acquired U.S.-based AST Research, then the fifth largest personal computer maker in the world. Daewoo Electronics is the company that tried to become the largest color television producer in the world by acquiring Thomson Multimedia of France, but was blocked by French nationalist resistance. Hyundai Automobile is the twelfth largest automaker in the world and the biggest player from a developing country. LG Electronics became a force in multimedia by purchasing Zenith of the United States. These companies also hold oligopoly power in many domestic South Korean industries: Samsung, LG, and Hyundai in semiconductors; Hyundai, Samsung, and Daewoo in shipbuilding; Hyundai, Daewoo, and Kia in automobiles; Samsung, LG, and Daewoo in consumer electronics. These South Korean multinationals have become even more active in globalization in recent years, a response to the changing domestic and foreign market environment: deteriorating factor cost conditions in South Korea, emergence of regional economic blocs such as the European Union, pressures for domestic market opening, and the rise of

*Table 3.1*
**Largest Foreign Investors in South Korea**

| Rank | Company | Nationality | Main Business | Investment to date (end 1996) U.S.$millions |
|------|---------|-------------|---------------|---------------------------|
| 1 | Lotte Shoji | Japan | hotel | 669 |
| 2 | Aramco Overseas | Saudi Arabia/ Netherlands | oil refinery, trading | 470 |
| 3 | Lotte Transportation Service | Japan | hotel | 310 |
| 4 | Lotte | Japan | hotel, construction | 293 |
| 5 | Pan Pacific Industrial Investment | Ireland | chemicals | 291 |
| 6 | Procter & Gamble Far East | U.S. | packaged goods | 251 |
| 7 | Carrefour | France | mass retailing | 245 |
| 8 | Amalgamated Technologies | Ireland | oil refinery | 215 |
| 9 | Ford Motor Company | U.S. | auto distribution | 209 |
| 10 | Artec | Malaysia | engines, cars | 200 |
| 11 | Caltex Overseas | U.S. | refinery | 184 |
| 12 | E.I. Du Pont de Nemours | U.S. | chemicals | 145 |
| 13 | Duracell | U.S. | battery | 140 |
| 14 | Unilever | U.K./Netherlands | food | 126 |
| 15 | Nestlé | Switzerland | food | 125 |
| 16 | Coors Brewing | U.S. | beer manufacturing | 121 |
| 17 | 3M | U.S. | electrical products | 118 |
| 18 | Pacific Investment Capital | Malaysia | mass retailing | 100 |
| 19 | Vetrotex Finance | France | glass fiber, trading | 99 |
| 20 | Airtouch Communications | U.S. | telecommunications | 93 |

emerging markets such as China and India. Table 3.2 lists the largest domestic companies in South Korea.

We should note some new trends in the globalization of South Korean multinationals. One is that their major motivation for investing overseas has shifted from low-cost seeking or trade-barrier bypassing to active local-market seeking behavior. Given the formation of major economic blocs and the rise of newly emerging markets, it is getting more important to be an insider in these markets. They are trying to build a total business system covering R&D, manufacturing, marketing, and after-sales service instead of conducting piecemeal operations. Samsung and LG have set up regional headquarters in five regions of the world: North America, Europe, Southeast Asia, China, and Japan. Another trend is the diversification of investment locations. South Korean firms are shifting

*Table 3.2*
**Largest South Korean Companies**

| Rank | Company | Main Business | 1996 Revenues U.S.$millions |
|------|---------|---------------|------------------------------|
| 1 | Samsung | trading, investment | 25,005 |
| 2 | Hyundai | trading, investment | 21,743 |
| 3 | Samsung Electronics | trading, investment | 21,026 |
| 4 | Daewoo | electronics, appliances | 19,513 |
| 5 | LG | trading, investment | 13,569 |
| 6 | Hyundai Motor | automotive | 13,428 |
| 7 | Korea Electric Power | power generation | 13,006 |
| 8 | Pohang Iron & Steel | steel | 10,674 |
| 9 | Yukong | oil refining, exploration | 8,563 |
| 10 | LG Electronics | consumer electronics | 8,561 |
| 11 | Kia Motors | automotive | 7,647 |
| 12 | Hyundai Motor Service | car dealership | 6,884 |
| 13 | Ssangyong | general trading | 6,811 |
| 14 | LG Caltex Oil Refinery | oil refining | 5,787 |
| 15 | Sunkyong | general trading, oil | 5,255 |
| 16 | Daewoo Heavy Industries | shipbuilding | 5,147 |
| 17 | Hyundai Heavy Industries | shipbuilding | 5,079 |
| 18 | Hyundai Electronics | consumer electronics | 5,068 |
| 19 | Hyundai Engineering & Construction | engineering and construction | 4,996 |
| 20 | Ssangyong Oil Refining | oil refining | 4,512 |

their investment weight from developed countries to newly emerging markets. Daewoo has invested heavily in Eastern European and Central Asian countries for automobile manufacturing. Samsung and LG went massively into China to produce consumer electronics products ranging from color televisions to refrigerators. Hyundai and Kia went to India and Indonesia respectively to produce automobiles for domestic markets. A third trend is the increasing networking among scattered operations within a region. By integrating multiple operations into a cohesive web, the South Korean firms are trying to achieve economies of scope.

## Overall Globalization Drivers for South Korea

From the viewpoint of foreign MNCs, South Korea has increasingly favorable market globalization drivers, deteriorating cost drivers, previously unfavorable government globalization drivers becoming less so, and strengthening competitive globalization drivers.

### Market Globalization Drivers

With a per capita income of U.S.$10,000 in 1996, South Korean consumers have seen a considerable increase in disposable income and an upswing in discretionary spending that is likely to continue. For example, South Korean consumers' demand for automobiles is changing. First, replacement purchases are exceeding new purchases. In 1996, the replacement demand portion was 55%, whereas the new demand was only 39%. Second, cars are increasingly used for leisure and less for commuting. In comparison to 1995, when leisure demand took only 13% and commuting demand 48%, the former demand went up to 19% and the latter down to 37% in 1996.[6] Due to expanded opportunities for education, overseas travel, and multicultural contacts, South Koreans have had greater exposure to foreign cultures than ever before. As such, South Korean consumers, especially the younger generation, are moving in favor of high-quality, Western goods. Of those who responded to an Electronics Industry Association of South Korea study, 29.6% preferred South Korean products and only 6.6% bought foreign products. However, 63.8% of the respondents indicated they were undecided, suggesting that there remain favorable opportunities for foreign goods to penetrate the South Korean market. In fact, many imported goods and services have already made inroads into the South Korean market. For example, the total turnover of the eight largest fast food companies, including Kentucky Fried Chicken and Pizza Hut in 1996, increased by 63% compared to the previous year, and the sales of big department stores have recorded a growth rate of 20%, while general retail stores have shown an increase of only 10%.[7] Two cars out of five sold in 1996, were middle-sized or above, and large foreign-made home appliances sold better. Moreover, more than 80% of the market for small home appliances, such as shavers or coffee makers, went to foreign companies like Philips and Moulinex despite the presence of domestic manufacturers such as Samsung, Daewoo, and LG Electronics. Since the government started deregulating distribution channels in July 1993, more than one hundred distribution-related foreign businesses have commenced operation in South Korea, particularly in the areas of dining, retail, wholesale, and services, including: Amway and Nuskin in multilayered distribution, Tower Records and Museum Company in specialty distribution, and Sharper Image in catalog retailing. Price Club (warehouse shopping) of the United States has already landed in South Korea through a joint venture with Shinsegye Department Store. France's Carrefour hypermarket chain and the Netherlands' Makro distribution chain already operate in the country. Japanese distributors of consumer electronics that have been less active in the South Korean market will now promote more aggressively their operations in line with the market opening of the distribution industry. Foreign manufacturers such as Philips, General Electric, Siemens, Whirlpool, and Westinghouse are busy building up their market presence by expanding distribution networks, their professional sales workforce, customer service networks, and stores. These companies are also expected to act as global customers and distribution channels.

## Cost Globalization Drivers

The unfavorable increase in South Korea's factor costs is being offset by the rapid domestic market expansion that makes it much easier for firms to achieve economies of scale in production and marketing. For example, the demand for consumer electronics in South Korea is the second largest in Asia, after only Japan. Particularly in the newly emerging business areas such as telecommunication services, new demand is skyrocketing. In the case of paging services, subscribers jumped to 12.5 million in just three years since the inception of service in 1994.[8] From 1983 to 1996, nominal manufacturing wages increased six times, a rate significantly higher than the wage increase in competing countries: South Korean manufacturers recorded an average annual nominal wage increase of 14.3% between 1980 and 1993, while Taiwan recorded an increase of 10.2%, Singapore 6.3%, France 6%, the U.S. 4.1%, Germany 4%, and Japan 3.3%. Inflation-adjusted real wage increases in South Korea during the period 1990–95 totaled 40.8%, higher than the 2.1% wage increase of Canada, 4% of France, and 3.2% of Japan.[9] Interest rates in South Korea are about three or four times as expensive as those of other competing countries. The inflation-adjusted real interest rate of South Korea was 7.6% in 1996, which compares quite unfavorably with the 2.9% of Japan, 3.5% of Taiwan, 1.2% of Singapore, and 2.3% of Malaysia.[10] Consequently, South Korea is no longer attractive as a low-labor-cost production site. On the other hand, South Korea has a well-educated, highly trained workforce that can offset higher labor costs through operational efficiencies and production improvements for high value-added products. Production in South Korea no longer means assembly that involves multistage handling by large numbers of workers with minimum or no skills. Instead, production involves new features such as a minimal number of assembly stages, a high degree of automation, electronically controlled testing and inspection, and development of new parts and components. South Korea also offers, as an important source of comparative advantage, the ability for MNCs to adopt and deploy new technologies. South Korea's technology level is estimated around 70% to 90% of world leaders such as the United States and Japan, especially in the areas of memory chips, pagers, satellite broadcasting receivers, automobiles, and ultrasound medical equipment.[11]

To enhance South Korea as an attractive location for business as well as to assist its own industries, the government has been continuously upgrading its infrastructure. In manufacturing industries, MNCs competing in the global market will increasingly require excellent transport, power, and communications. In an effort to keep pace with the demand for new infrastructures, the South Korean government has initiated a number of large-scale public works to remove bottlenecks and improve logistics within the country, such as the construction of Yongjong-do New International Airport and the expansion of port capacity at Kadok-do and Kwangyang. The completion of the West Coast Freeway and the Seoul-Pusan High Speed Railway will also expedite traffic flow. Furthermore, the government plans to develop Yongjong-do into an international free city that will serve as a hub of international trade, banking, finance, and transportation with an eye to capture some of Hong Kong's business after its return to China in 1997.

## Government Globalization Drivers

The South Korean government is slowly changing its longtime discouragement of foreign participation in the South Korean economy. Liberalization and deregulation is slowly opening the economy to foreign investors, especially in the areas of construction, telecommunications, distribution, and finance. The constraint on the foreign equity ceiling in the telecommunications industry has been loosened a great deal from 10% to 33%. The key to South Korea's future industrial policy lies in the reform of the financial sector and deregulation of foreign capital. With the changes in the economic environment, the government has replaced the Foreign Capital Inducement Act of the 1960s with the new Foreign Investment Promotion Act to attract foreign investors. According to this step-by-step capital liberalization plan, the South Korean capital market will be opened to foreigners to invest in stocks and bonds and to issue securities.

The High-Tech Industry Cooperation Act of 1995 has been implemented to bring about tangible benefits for direct foreign investors in terms of taxation and financing. Taxation benefits include waivers of up to 100% for the first five years, and a 50% exemption of corporate, income, and local taxes for the following three years. Commercial loans for the importation of equipment are allowed up to 100% of the amount invested. Priority is given to investors who build production facilities in industrial zones where land can be leased at an annual interest rate of 1% for twenty years.

In order to respond more proactively to the globalization trend, the government has also revised its market-opening schedule to the year 2000, adding thirty-six industries such as distribution, communications, and services for further market-opening. Only forty-four industries will remain restricted to foreigners' investment in South Korea.

Restrictive trade barriers in South Korea are also in the process of being reduced and eventually dismantled. In response to the growing complexity of the economy, the South Korean government promoted the use of market mechanisms to improve the competitiveness of South Korean firms, and gradually lowered tariffs and loosened regulations. For example, one of the major trade barriers against Japanese imports was the import diversification regulation. This regulation was intended to block Japanese imports that might have direct negative impact on South Korean products such as consumer electronics and automobiles. Because of this regulation, Japanese-made Toyotas or Hondas cannot be imported to South Korea while American and German cars are freely imported. The only Japanese cars that can bypass this import diversification rule are those made in the United States by Japanese transplants. The number of items designated for import diversification will be reduced by 10% every year to leave only 129 items by 1998, or half that of 1993 (258 items). The abolition of the system itself will be considered after 1999. Lastly, many MNCs perceive that the level of intellectual property protection in South Korea is lower than in other developing countries. As a result, some foreign companies from the United States, Japan, and Germany have been reluctant to invest capital or transfer technology to South Korea. In order to protect intellectual property rights, the government plans to enact a series of laws related to intellectual property protection between January 1996, and the end of 1997. Under the new patent law, the patent life has been extended from fifteen to twenty years from the announced registration date. The life of utility model patents has also been extended from ten years after the announcement of registration to fifteen years after the application date. By doing so, South Korea hopes to attract foreign investment and acquire high technology.

## Competitive Globalization Drivers

South Korea is becoming a strategically more important country not only at the regional level, but, more importantly, at the global level. South Korea has already nurtured many global players active in key global industries: automobiles, semiconductors, consumer electronics, shipbuilding, and steel. For example, POSCO, one of the largest and most efficient steel mills in the world, has helped U.S. Steel in renovating the latter's California plant. Samsung, Hyundai, and LG together take more than 26% of market share in the global memory chip industry. Hyundai, Daewoo, and Kia are three very aggressive automakers with a strong presence in emerging markets. South Korea is also a country whose domestic market is expanding quite fast as per capita national incomes rise. The penetration of new information appliances is amazingly fast. The cellular phone market started at almost nil in 1993, but the total demand reached 2.4 million units in 1996, and is expected to increase to 75 million in the year 2000.[12] The personal computer penetration increased to ninety-five per 1,000 persons in 1995, approaching the level of Singapore (116 per 1000 persons). Many global players have developed a keen interest in the South Korean PC industry. An example is the LG-IBM alliance in South Korea to produce and sell PCs together locally. IBM provides key components and design know-how, and LG provides the distribution network and production facilities. They share a common brand name, LG-IBM. A similar deal is being discussed between Compaq and a South Korean PC giant, Sambo Computer. Lastly, South Korea is becoming a center of industrial innovation. As mentioned before, South Korea is generating many new innovations in DRAM, LCDs, satellite receivers, and ultrasound diagnosis technologies. The increasing strategic importance of South Korea seems to make it mandatory for foreign MNCs to have a presence in South Korea. Indeed, many new foreign firms are entering major industries, especially in the high-technology and service sector.

## Overall Global Strategies for South Korea

MNCs can, and in many cases, should, increasingly make South Korea part of their global and regional strategies. (As South Korea does not allow Japanese automobile companies to participate in its market, we have substituted Mercedes Benz for Toyota among the foreign MNCs that we examine in this section.)

## Market Participation Strategies

Like Japan, the recent and increasing affluence of South Korean consumers poses a strong attraction for foreign MNC participation. Philips entered South Korea by establishing a marketing company, Philips Industries Korea Limited (PIKL), in 1976. Philips' continuous presence in the market has given the company a very strong position in small electronic products. As a result, Philips accounts for a 40% share in coffee makers and 27% in electric irons. In contrast, Philips possesses less than a 1% share of bigger appliances such as TVs and VCRs. Such an extreme situation derives from the distinct competitive structure of the South Korean consumer electronics industry. Philips has to face local giants such as Samsung, Daewoo, and LG in the brown goods market segment, but in small appliances it competes with technologically weak, small and medium-sized firms. The three major South Korean firms do not make the small appliances themselves. Philips has started to promote its *Match* line of television sets very aggressively in recent years in direct competition with local giants.

Mercedes Benz was one of the first foreign automobile manufacturers to enter the South Korean market. As soon as the South Korean government permitted the import of foreign passenger cars in 1987, Mercedes established an exclusive dealership with Hansung Motors to sell passenger cars in South Korea. In its first year, Mercedes sold only ten units. In 1996, however, Mercedes sold 1,121 units, which accounted for 12.6% of the import car market share. Of course, Mercedes' share in dollar terms is much higher since it only sells luxury cars. Mercedes also entered into a joint venture with Ssangyong in 1991, to produce engines for trucks and jeeps, and later expanded operations to develop family vans.

Procter and Gamble entered South Korea through a joint venture in 1989, with Seotong; P&G later acquired Seotong's equity in the venture in 1992. Following the acquisition, P&G divided its South Korean operation into three separate companies to accelerate its local business activities: P&G Manufacturing for production, P&G FED for importing, and P&G Korea for marketing. P&G later combined the production and marketing companies. P&G enjoys a very strong market position. One of its leading brands in disposable diapers, *Pampers,* holds a market share of 20%, and another brand, *Whisper,* in women's sanitary napkins, holds 52% of the South Korean market.

Unilever commenced its South Korean operations in 1982, through a series of joint ventures. The company entered its first joint venture with Pacific Chemical Company to produce *Close Up* toothpaste, followed by a venture with Aekyong to produce shampoos and soaps (a venture that ended in a breakup), and with Dong Bang Corporation to gain distribution and expertise in the South Korean food business.[13] Unilever also started to produce *Lipton Ice Tea,* through a technology tie-up and joint investment with Maeil Dairy Company in 1993. All Unilever products are distributed through the Haepyo Unilever distribution network. Maeil will continue to manufacture and distribute *Lipton Ice Tea* until they run out of existing packaging material stock, but their contract has formally expired and will not be renewed.

Motorola commenced its South Korean operation in 1967, to take advantage of low wages to assemble semiconductors, by establishing a 100%-owned manufacturing subsidiary, Motorola Korea Industry (MKI). Motorola expanded its business line in the 1980s to include communications equipment, which is sold through its second subsidiary Motorola Electronics and Communications Incorporated (MECI). Motorola enjoys a strong domestic market position in the South Korean communications business. For cellular phones, its market share reached 80% in the late 1980s, making the South Korean government nervous about its dominance. However, with the advent of strong local competitors such as Samsung, LG, and Hyundai, as well as other foreign brands such as Nokia and Ericsson, Motorola's market share tumbled to 56% in 1995 and 19% in 1996. Furthermore, as the South Korean government adopted the CDMA system (initiated by Qualcom of the USA) as the national standard for its cellular phone service, Motorola had difficulty introducing its digital phones on time for the new system. Motorola is currently a follower in this segment.

## Product and Service Strategies

MNCs have discovered that their products and services are eagerly sought after in South Korea. Since consumers are beginning to increase their consumption of Western goods, MNCs can offer a wide range of product and services. Consequently, MNCs can introduce their global brands with little adaptation to the local market.

The products that are sold in South Korea by Philips are all produced overseas and imported, not localized for South Korean markets. Sampling in advance products that are somewhat new or unfamiliar to South Koreans even creates demand, as was the case with coffee makers and electric shavers for women. Philips is well accepted in South Korea with its prestigious brand image, good design, and advanced technology. Worldwide after-sales service is available for all products, whether bought inside or outside South Korea, although weakness in after-market parts still puts considerable limits on Philips's business activities.

Mercedes adopts a global product strategy under which premium cars produced with full options in Germany are imported and sold in South Korea. At the same time, Mercedes has jointly developed with Ssangyong a full-sized passenger car with engine displacement of over 3000cc named *Chairman* for introduction in 1997, to the domestic market. Mercedes introduced its C-class, E-class, S-class, and SE-class models in the passenger car category, and G-class model in the jeep category, to the South Korean market. In the van category, Mercedes developed an Asian regional model together with Ssangyong. The van, named *Istana* for the local market and *MB 100* for the regional market, will be distributed to the South Korean market through the Ssangyong network and through the Mercedes network in Asia. Mercedes is expecting to sell about 15,000 units of these vans annually in Asia.

Both P&G and Unilever have achieved success by offering a wide range of global products with little or no local adaptation, although they have found some need to reformulate or adapt to local regulations or preferences. P&G produces locally *Pampers, Whisper,* and three kinds of shampoos, but imports *Ivory, Blendax, Vidal Sassoon, Pringles,* and *Old Spice.* Raw materials for locally produced goods are all imported from the United States, Canada, China, Australia, and the Philippines. The imported goods are consolidated by P&G Korea, but are distributed by different local companies under different marketing strategies. Unilever, however, is also developing products for the local market. Among the goods produced locally by Unilever are soaps like *Dove Cream Shower* and *Cream Bath.* However, products such as the *Dove* bar, *Lux* skin care bar, *Pounds* capsule, and *Close Up* are imported from the United States and New Zealand. Unilever-Haepyo was established jointly with Dong Bang Corporation in 1993, to produce the *Yofresh* series that includes *Yogonaise* (mayonaise), *Yogodressing* (salad dressing), and *Yogospread* (sandwich spread). As is the case with several items, including *Ponds Cleansing Cream,* localization has been made in accordance with a regional strategy for Asian markets. A global product concept of "same products, same quality" applies basically to every Unilever (and P&G) product, although regional versions occasionally are made to the specific characteristics of the region.

Motorola offers a global line of products and services in wireless communications and nonmemory semiconductors and adapts to the local market condition as necessary. Wireless communications equipment is generally imported as finished product and are highly standardized. The only localization involves adjusting the frequency for personal cellular phones and converting English expressions into South Korean letters on pagers. In the case of nonmemory semiconductors, however, Motorola also meets the custom orders of major clients like LG, Samsung, and Hyundai. For most of its business, Motorola's product strategy involves high-quality service and technical excellence. As major competitors have entered the South Korean market for nonmemory semiconductors and communications equipment, Motorola is trying to protect its competitive position by enhancing its customer satisfaction through more close counseling and technological assistance.

## Activity Location Strategies

Recognizing that South Korea is no longer a site for low-cost production, most foreign MNCs have shifted toward high value-added activities.

Although most of its products are produced overseas and imported to South Korea in finished form, Philips has two manufacturing companies that were jointly established with South Korean companies to produce automobile lamps and compact fluorescent lamps for homes. PIKL, a marketing company, assumes all the marketing activities in South Korea and is now expanding its service network to eleven cities in order to cope with the full opening of the distribution industry, and to compete with other distributors including Japanese companies.

Mercedes Benz uses South Korea as part of its regional strategy. As a luxury car maker, Mercedes does not have sufficient local or regional volume to fully achieve economies of scale or scope on its own, so it must rely on local partners to share costs. Hansong Motors, for example, provides support in marketing and customer services for passenger cars. Ssangyong, by contrast, cooperates with Mercedes for family vans in development, subassembly, and final production. In 1995, the facility produced 60,000 units, two-thirds of which were sold locally by Ssangyong and the rest through the Mercedes network in the Southeast Asian market, including Taiwan, the Philippines, Vietnam, Malaysia, and Thailand. This venture also provided a good starting point for Mercedes to enter the Southeast Asian market since it had been undergoing difficulties in reducing costs and attracting customers in European markets. Furthermore, Ssangyong has completed a component parts distribution center to carry 50,000 after-market items while Hansong Motors runs two service centers in Seoul with the support of Mercedes.

P&G and Unilever, too, use South Korea as part of their regional activity strategies. The bulk of P&G operations in South Korea revolves around marketing efforts including distribution and after-sale service. Local production is limited to shampoos, *Whisper* feminine products, and *Pampers* diapers. Among these, shampoos are for domestic sale while *Whisper* and *Pampers* are exported to Singapore, Hong Kong, Thailand, the Philippines, Indonesia, Malaysia, Vietnam, and Taiwan. Raw materials for local production are directly imported from the United States, Canada, China, Australia, and the Philippines; soaps and cosmetic goods are imported from overseas plants. There are no R&D facilities in South Korea, but the regional R&D headquarters in Japan takes charge of developing local versions for the South Korean market. Conversely, Unilever places more emphasis on South Korea as a production site. Unilever plans to increase local production up to 97% for all daily commodities at its Taejon plant. Initially, Unilever alleviated its weakness in marketing, as compared to P&G, by utilizing different distribution networks of local partners. Now Unilever distributes all its products through one network, Haepyo Unilever. Both P&G and Unilever have found that tie-ups with local companies, which also sell their own products, lead to conflicts in priorities or emphasis.

Motorola has a full range of activities in South Korea although the nature and composition of its activities have changed. For example, Motorola South Korea continues to export 90% of its output to the global Motorola network, but the plant size in terms of manpower was halved from 5,000 in the mid-1980s to 2,700 in 1995. This occurred because South Korea is no longer a site for labor-intensive production. Motorola will expand its production operation in South Korea in a phased fashion from a production center for discrete devices, to components, modular parts, and finally finished systems. It will get into a limited R&D operation in the form of an application lab.

## Marketing Strategies

MNCs have found that global marketing strategies can be transferred to South Korea. In general, U.S. and European brand marketing techniques are used with great success, as are globally standardized marketing and advertising.

Philips has achieved a strong market position by being one of the first MNCs in South Korea. With a brand image second only to Sony, Philips can set the price of its products 10% to 15% higher than comparable South Korean-made products. At the same time, Philips's success in small consumer electronic products has prepared a beachhead from which it can expand its product line to larger general electronic goods. Small consumer appliances are sold through its own PIKI, while the larger items, such as TVs and VCRs, are sold through the distribution network of Tongyang Magic. In order to reposition itself as a producer of advanced general electronic products, Philips has increased its advertising expenditure quite significantly. Mercedes Benz adopts a consistent marketing mix including brand name, positioning, product design, pricing strategy, and advertising. In South Korea, Mercedes positions itself as a premium passenger car maker and targets high-income customers through its high-price strategy. It has adopted a skimming strategy and targets specific groups of potential customers through newspapers and magazines rather than broader media. With the deregulation of advertising for imported goods, however, Mercedes has increased its advertising efforts through television, spending more than 2 billion won (over U.S.$2 million) in 1995, which was the highest among foreign car companies in South Korea.

As it does elsewhere, P&G focuses on marketing its brand names rather than the company name. In addition to utilizing a global marketing strategy, P&G has had great success in transferring its promotional activities. For example, P&G supplies quantities of free samples of its new products to attract South Korean customers who have a propensity for foreign goods and free distributions. One marketing element that P&G has altered is pricing. Although P&G previously priced goods slightly higher than those of its competitors, the company has begun to lower the price of its locally produced goods. It plans to continue to supply high-quality products at lower prices by minimizing margins.

Unilever uses a similar marketing approach as P&G and implements a marketing strategy centered around brand names rather than the company name. Unilever uses mostly the same brand names in South Korea as it does worldwide. This has allowed the company to reduce marketing and advertising expenses.

In contrast to P&G and Unilever, Motorola advertising strategy promotes the corporate image rather than specific products. To promote the company image, Motorola has opened Motorola Brand Shops, which carry all of its product lines and provide quality after-sale service. Due to its early entry into South Korea, Motorola enjoys a perception of quality and excellence and has been able to position itself as a technological leader in South Korea. As a result, Motorola has gained substantial market share for its products despite higher prices compared to other local competitors, and has enjoyed the boom in pagers and mobile phones. Motorola has been strong in its market position both in the semiconductor and mobile communications business. But from 1995 they started to lose their market leadership in the cellular phone business. Motorola yielded its top position to Samsung whose *Anycall* brand topped their *Microtech* series. There are two reasons for this failure. First, Motorola emphasized too much its technology leadership when the technology itself was no longer the best. Especially when the Korean industry went into COMA technology, Motorola was late in introducing coma phases on time. Second, Motorola's advertising copy was not appealing to the South Korean audience in comparison to that of Samsung's. Samsung's *Any Call* advertisement emphasized that its phone was more attuned to South Korea's mountainous conditions while Motorola's advertisement was generic, not specific to South Korea, "a world everybody dreamed of." In fact, South Korea is a country with 80% of its land being mountainous and, hence, quite difficult for cellular phone transmission. The case of Motorola provides a lesson for foreign multinationals marketing in South Korea: marketing tactics are not transferable for all products. Depending on the stage of product technologies and local market peculiarities, marketing tactics need to be localized to a certain extent.

## *Competitive Move Strategies*

MNCs would do well to include South Korea in their global competitive moves, especially in those industries with significant South Korean players. Philips has adopted a very active localization strategy through technology transfer, arranging for imports of key parts, and assisting in exports for small and medium-sized South Korean firms. In the past, Philips benefited from the import diversification policies of the South Korean government against Japan and had to compete with local companies only. Now that the import diversification policy is to be abolished, Philips is working out measures to cope with Japanese consumer electronics makers in South Korea. Philips is optimistic that it can compete with Japanese makers mainly for two reasons. First, younger South Koreans under the age of thirty-five generally prefer good design and European style. Second, Philips has advantages over Japanese firms in terms of distribution and selling networks. As the Dutch company entered the

South Korean market much earlier than have Japanese firms, Philips has established a marketing infrastructure that its Japanese rivals are building only now. Furthermore, Philips has some strong alliance networks with South Korean firms: with Tongyang Magic for product swaps; with Yongyang, which supplies thermal rice cookers to Philips under OEM arrangements for both domestic and international (mostly Asia) markets, as well as importing Philips consumer electronics products for domestic sales; and with Samsung Electronics to jointly develop multimedia systems. As with the consumer electronics industry, the recent affluence of South Korean consumers gives the nation strategic importance to manufacturers of luxury goods. Mercedes, for example, has developed its own niche in the South Korean market. While South Korean automobile manufacturers focus on producing affordable small cars, Mercedes offers South Korean customers technologically advanced products at a premium price. The entry of Mercedes into South Korea has to be understood in the context of its need for a foothold in the Asian market, one that has been showing the highest growth rate in the world. As Mercedes Benz is changing its global business strategy, it is expanding its production capacity outside of Germany into South America and Asia and trying to introduce more diverse models ranging from mini cars to full-size ones. Sticking to its premium strategy to attract customers willing to pay for its technology and high engineering, the firm has been expanding its production capacity to add small city cars (A-type), people carriers (vans), and sports utility vehicles.

## Overall Organizational and Management Approaches for South Korea

One of the major organizational issues that foreign MNCs face in doing business in South Korea is the selection of entry mode, especially among exporting, licensing, and direct investment. In the cases of exporting and licensing, MNCs can use many South Korean firms that provide services for MNCs in their exporting and licensing business. In the case of foreign direct investment, however, MNCs have to decide whether or not they will share business control and ownership with local South Korean partners. There is not any government regulation stipulating the equity mode. MNCs are free to choose between joint venture and 100% ownership in South Korea. Unlike in Japan, most foreign MNCs take a majority or 100% ownership position. For example, in the case of Motorola's semiconductor operation in South Korea, which has the global supply mission for certain types of semiconductors for its worldwide network, Motorola runs the factory as a 100%-owned subsidiary in order to secure full business control. In contrast, in the case of the Unilever operation in South Korea, which basically distributes consumer packaged goods for the local South Korean market, Unilever relies on South Korean joint venture partners for access to their distribution networks.

However, even in the case of local distribution, the general trend is toward 100% ownership by MNCs themselves as the South Korean local market expands and the South Korean government accelerates its market opening process for the retail and wholesaling business. Ford and BMW started their own marketing subsidiaries by terminating their former reliance on South Korean local firms for the distribution of their cars. In the past, Ford sold its Sable model through its South Korean partner's (Kia Motors) sales network. Likewise, BMW used Kolon group, another South Korean *chaebol,* as its exclusive dealer in the past, but both of them terminated the agreement with local South Korean firms last year and established their own distribution arms.

Another organizational issue foreign MNCs face in South Korea is whether to follow the same organizational structure of the parent firm for their South Korean operations. The case of Motorola is a good example. The organizational tradition of Motorola is a strong decentralized structure, allowing each sector full autonomy for business decisions. Motorola has five business sectors: semiconductors, communications, military electronics, automotive electronics, and computers. Though this decentralized structure ensures fast decisions and a clear line of command, there are a few critical drawbacks of this structure, such as duplication of scarce resources and confusion of company image from different strategic approaches being taken in the same market place. Such problems are worse for a country as small as South Korea. If every sector approached the South Korean government on its own, the clout of Motorola would be much less. Likewise, if each sector had its own public relations and advertisement program, there would be not only a waste of common resources, but also minimal impact of the Motorola image on the South Korean audience. An organizational innovation of Motorola South Korea was the formation of a few subject-based committees and councils that provide a forum to derive effective solutions for common interests of different sectors. A few examples are a public relations committee to develop a strong and consistent Motorola image in South Korea, and management board meetings to derive effective measures for responding to South Korean government policies that may work against Motorola's interests. The consolidation of different sectors under one roof in one downtown office was also the result of such efforts. In the past, Motorola offices were scattered around different parts of Seoul. The whole purpose of this kind of organizational design was to generate organizational synergy as much as possible while maintaining the autonomy of individual sectors. The Motorola case seems to suggest an effective approach or MNCs in small-market countries.

Human resource management poses another major management challenge for the South Korean operations of foreign MNCs. A major concern is to recruit the right personnel for the right positions. The recruiting pool is limited by the additional requirement of fluency in English for the job. Though English education starts from the junior high school years through college, oral and writing skills in English are very limited even among college graduates. Therefore, most of the job applicants for the positions of MNCs are not fresh college graduates. Instead, they are mostly experienced workers from major South Korean firms or other MNCs. In the 1960s and 1970s, foreign MNCs could recruit the best-quality personnel from the South Korean labor market. But with the emergence of many indigenous South Korean firms in the job market, the relative attractiveness of working for foreign MNCs is now declining. Many South Korean workers worry about career prospects in foreign firms. South Korean applicants for jobs with foreign firms typically weigh limited upward mobility against better pay and a more comfortable working environment. In this sense, it is imperative for foreign MNCs to provide career prospects to attract managers in South Korea. Given the strong peer group competition and the importance of "face" in South Korean culture, the appropriate job title and upward mobility potential will be important tools for recruiting high-quality local personnel.

Another important recruiting issue is the hiring of female college graduates. Many MNCs in South Korea discriminate much less against career women than do South Korean firms. Given the limited job opportunities for female college graduates, South Korean women often prefer to work for foreign companies. With the increasing supply of high-quality female college graduates and South Korean women's demand for more active social participation, women constitute a strong source of labor supply for MNCs in South Korea. Training opportunities offered by MNCs also attract workers. As South Korean employees working for MNCs basically value job mobility much more than do their peers in South Korean firms, they attribute much value to in-house job training that enhances their job skills and helps later job changes. Motorola operates its Motorola university program both in South Korea and in its Asian regional headquarters. In contrast to training opportunities, overseas job rotation is not widely sought by South Korean employees. Even though many MNCs are offering job rotation opportunities mostly within the regional boundary (i.e., Asia), not many South Korean employees are taking those opportunities. This is because South Korean employees are not yet fully globalized in their mind-set, feeling uncomfortable working in different cultural settings. Social constraints such as family support and educational disadvantages for their children (ill-preparation for entrance exams in high school and college), are also important impediments to their global mobility.

Another management issue of significant importance for foreign MNCs in South Korea is how much to localize their corporate culture and management process. It seems that most foreign MNCs are trying to transplant their unique management cultures to their South Korean operations. Some important tools for nurturing such corporate cultures are in-house training, social gatherings for business conferences, and the performance review process. In general, South Korean employees do not have any strong resistance to foreign corporate cultures. Unlike Japan, there is not any dominant South Korean management style per se in South Korea. As such, South Korean employees are more accommodating to foreign cultures and there is not any significant resistance in the organization. In a sense, South Korean employees in foreign MNCs are already much more internationalized than those in South Korean companies. For example, the safety-oriented culture of Du Pont and the people orientation of Motorola are well received and accepted in South Korea.

Nevertheless, the above does not mean that foreign MNCs can apply management practices without modification in South Korea. Even if South Korean employees accept the core value or rationale of the foreign management practice, they expect some flexible application of those concepts in the South Korean setting. An example is the application of meritocracy in the performance evaluation. Instead of strict application of meritocracy, the combination of performance review and seniority works better in South Korean culture.

## Conclusion

South Korea has been globalizing fast with strong pushes from market, government, competitive, and cost drivers. Overall market drivers have been favorable for globalization. South Korean consumers have had much purchasing power. At the same time, South Koreans are being exposed to global information for world-class products and services, thanks to the spread of the Internet and satellite broadcasting services. Moreover, South Koreans have become avid global tourists and shoppers. The major chilling factor in market globalization drivers is the current severe downturn of the South Korean economy, mostly due to sagging performance of the export sector and its consequent effect on the domestic spending of South Korean households. Government globalization drivers are very favorable. By joining the OECD in 1996, the South Korean government will have to adjust its regulatory and economic systems to international standards, which should eliminate much unnecessary government regulation. This will help create a much more favorable climate for foreign investors. Furthermore, the IMF and other loan backers are insisting that South Korea open up its economy for foreign participation. The South Korean government is also getting internal pressure to deregulate the economy. South Korean business firms are strongly pushing the government to reduce many restrictive regulations that impede their achieving international competitiveness. So the South Korean economy will be on the way to becoming more open and deregulated. South Korea will be an increasingly competitive battleground for major global firms in the future. Along with the favorably changing market and government drivers, a major competitive driver pushing South Korea to fast globalization is the rise of a significant number of indigenous multinationals. Foreign MNCs would be foolish to neglect these South Korean MNCs.

Unlike market, government, and competitive drivers, cost drivers do not favor the globalization of South Korea. Along with the geopolitical location of South Korea in Northeast Asia, squeezed between world political powers such as China, Russia, and Japan, factor costs in the South

Korean economy are so unfavorable that South Korea is no longer the right place for global or regional sourcing for low-end products. Even South Korean firms are trying to find overseas production sites for their products, contributing to the globalization of South Korean firms. The only offsetting cost factors are the increasing pool of high-caliber human resources and the potential achievement of economies of scale in certain product categories due to the expanding domestic market size.

Based on South Korea's globalization drivers, we can derive three major strategic implications for foreign MNCs. First, South Korea became much more attractive as a country market. Therefore, much more committed market participation is required from MNCs in order to benefit once market growth resumes. The control of key marketing channels is especially critical as channels become more accessible to foreign firms with the government's opening-up measures. We recommend acquiring a preemptive position before the market gets too crowded. Timing is critical.

Second, given the fast internationalization of South Korean customers, not much product adaptation is required to meet local conditions. What is more important is new image creation or differentiation rather than simple physical product adaptation. Considering that South Korean consumers are becoming international shoppers, what they expect from the products and services of foreign firms are not basic needs or functions, which domestic products can more than satisfy, but more sophisticated or differentiated needs that cannot be accommodated by local goods.

Third, the rise of South Korean multinationals creates not only threats to foreign MNCs, but also new business opportunities for joining forces with them. South Korean multinationals need business partners—on the one hand, to protect their own domestic markets and, on the other hand, to penetrate overseas markets more effectively. In this process, they need to form strategic alliance networks with leading MNCs. South Korean MNCs have their own unique competitive assets to offer, such as diversified business lines, a strong drive generated from single ownership-management, and local market power based on their domestic marketing infrastructure. From the viewpoint of established MNCs, South Korean MNCs can be a help not only in establishing a strong market position in the South Korean market, but more importantly, to penetrate emerging markets in Asia as well as in other parts of the world. South Korean companies can bring their strong adaptability (from recency of experience) and appropriate technology that fits the adverse conditions of developing countries. Lastly, the debt and other crises facing the *chaebols* should make them more receptive to foreign partners.

## NOTES

1. "Only Korean Firms Are Performing Badly in the U.S. Market," *Maeil Business Newspaper,* February 27, 1997.

2. "The Most Attractive Country to Invest in Asia," *Far Eastern Economic Review,* February 13, 1997.

3. "It's Time to Boost Up the Economy," *Maeil Business Newspaper,* February 10, 1997.

4. "The Sharply Rising Korean Debt," *Maekyung Business Weekly,* December 25, 1996.

5. Ministry of Trade Industry and Energy, 95 White Paper, 88.

6. "It Is Time to Change Cars," *Joongang Daily Newspaper,* March 9, 1997.

7. "Declining Economy Due to Consumer Behaviors," *Joongang Daily Newspaper,* March 9, 1996.

8. "Hot Competition in the Beeper Service Market," *Dong-A Daily Newspaper,* January 12, 1997.

9. "The Real Wage in the Manufacturing Industry Has Risen 40% for the Past 5 Years," *Joongang Daily Newspaper,* March 18, 1997.

10. "It's Time to Talk about Economy," *The Korea Economic Daily,* March 1, 1997.

11. "Korean Technology, Only 70–80% Level of Developed Countries," *Joongang Daily Newspaper,* March 11, 1997.

12. "Successful Development of Core Chip in Digital Cellular Phone," *Maeil Business Newspaper,* September 30, 1996.

13. "The Strong Power of Multinationals in the Domestic Consumer Packaged Goods Market," *The Korea Economic Daily,* June 28, 1995.

# CHAPTER 4

# China—Enter the Giant

## Kam-hon Lee and George S. Yip

NAPOLEON SAID OF CHINA, "Let China sleep, for when she wakes, she will shake the world." Not only has China woken from its sleep but the country is moving rapidly in its participation in the global economy. China's population size—nearly twice that of the United States, the European Union, and Japan combined—and its strong economic growth mean that few MNCs can avoid having a strategy for China. Many MNCs have entered China in the last fifteen years with the hope of exploiting its huge market potential. Some have succeeded while others have failed. With continuing dramatic growth prospects, the allure of China as a market will not fade soon. In addition, companies are finding China to be a source of production, products, and now even a source of research. Just as absence from Japan during the previous twenty years has caused major problems for multinational companies, absence from China in the next twenty years may cause its own problems. At the same time, China presents significant political uncertainties as power is transferred to a new generation from the last of the original leaders of the communist revolution. Also, ongoing political conflicts with the United States sometimes generate repercussions for trade and investment for MNCs from all nations.

## Background

Economic reform, the "open door" policy, and consequent dramatic growth characterize China's economy since 1978. Many of the world's most important MNCs have responded to the lure of the globe's potentially biggest market.

### The Process of Economic Reform

After the disaster of the Cultural Revolution (1966 to 1976), China's leaders have increasingly embraced the market economy as the mode of modernization. Since 1978, there have been four distinctive phases of development.[1] The first phase, from 1978 to 1984, focused on rural reform, with the intention of enriching the peasants first, in order to gain their support. The second phase, from 1985 to 1988, focused on urban reform. Individually owned enterprises and township enterprises became more and more active. Joint ventures began to take shape, especially in the Pearl River Delta area and Guangdong province in the south. Foreign direct investment came mainly from or via Hong Kong. State-owned enterprises played a decreasing role in economic activities. Some state-owned enterprises were sold to joint ventures, while some were reorganized in order to become competitive in the marketplace. The third phase, from 1989 to 1991, covered price reform of nonstaples, the opening of the stock exchanges in Shanghai and Shenzhen, and some reform of the money market.

The fourth phase, from 1992 to 1997, was marked by Deng Xiaopeng's visit to the south, confirming China's future as a "socialist market economy," (i.e., a market economy under the guidance of the Communist Party). The start of this phase was a turning point for MNCs, who became aggressive in investing in China. Foreign direct investment jumped from the U.S.$3 billion level in 1990,[2] to over $30 billion a year by 1994.[3] While initial development occurred primarily in the coastal provinces, especially Guangdong (opposite Hong Kong) and Fujian (opposite Taiwan), current efforts seek to channel economic activity to the inland provinces. For example, a structural change has begun in the textile industry in Shanghai. Factories there will move to Xinjiang (nearly three thousand miles inland). In turn, some female workers in the textile industry in Shanghai went through retraining programs to become airline flight attendants.

A fifth phase seems to have been initiated in September 1997, when President Jiang Zemin at the People's Party Congress announced that most state-owned enterprises (SOEs) would shift to "public ownership" (his deliberately ambiguous phrase that Western observers consider to mean privitization). This next phase will create huge opportunities and pitfalls for foreign MNCs, especially in terms of acquiring and restructuring these SOEs.

The pattern of economic development has been supported by the social and political culture. China's leaders have increasingly stressed the country's tradition of Confucianism with its ideology of obedience to authority, order, and stability.[4] The government has implemented reform cautiously and in a step-by-step fashion in an attempt to preserve order and stability. Some observers have described China today as a "cage economy," with the cage gradually becoming bigger over time.

## Economic Performance

China's economy has become more open and grown steadily over the years from the mid-1980s to the mid-1990s, and the projection into the future is very positive (Table 1.1 in Chapter 1). As discussed in Chapter 1, China's recent growth rate exceeds that of most other countries in the Asia-Pacific region. Its nominal GNP of U.S.$744 billion in 1995, is the second largest in Asia, but dwarfed by Japan's U.S.$4,975 billion. However, using Purchasing Power Parity measures, China's GNP of U.S.$3,506 billion is already larger than Japan's U.S.$2,775 billion, and second only to that of the United States' U.S.$7,098 billion (Table 1.1 in Chapter 1). As China continues its transformation toward a market economy, the resultant growth could eventually make China the single most important economy in Asia, and perhaps even the largest in the world, by the year 2020.

### Largest Domestic Companies

China's largest domestic companies are all state-owned and operate primarily in four industries—petroleum, petrochemical, steel, and automotive (Table 4.1). None of the top twenty state-owned manufacturing companies has significant foreign revenues. On the other hand, many are beginning to make investments outside, especially in Hong Kong (see Table 6.2 in Chapter 6) and the United States. Most of these state-owned enterprises are struggling with how to open themselves to market reform.[5] Many face real difficulties in competing with more efficient and nimble foreign MNCs.

China's oil industry typifies the complexities of Chinese state-owned businesses. To meet the challenge of globalization, China recently reorganized this industry (Figure 4.1). In this new structure, the China National Petroleum Corp. (CNPC) is China's major producer of crude oil. In a rationalization move, CNPC was formed when the former Ministry of

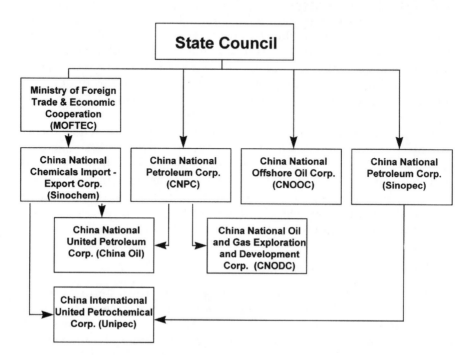

**Figure 4.1**  Organization of China's Oil Industry. *Source:* U.S. Government Accounting Office (GAO).

**Table 4.1**

**Largest State-Owned Manufacturing Companies in China**

| Rank | Company Name | Industry | 1994 Revenues U.S.$ millions |
|---|---|---|---|
| 1 | Daqing Petroleum Administration Bureau | petroleum | 3,127 |
| 2 | Anshan Steel Company | steel | 2,198 |
| 3 | Baoshan Iron Steel (Group) Corporation | steel | 2,110 |
| 4 | China Automobile Group Co. No. 1 | automobile | 1,947 |
| 5 | Capital Iron-Steel Company (General) | steel | 1,743 |
| 6 | Victory Petroleum Management Bureau | petroleum | 1,697 |
| 7 | Dangfeng Automobile Company | automobile | 1,574 |
| 8 | Wuhan Iron & Steel Group Company | steel | 1,331 |
| 9 | China Petrochemical Beijing Yanshan Petrochemical Company | petroleum | 1,324 |
| 10 | Liaohe Petroleum Exploration Administrative Bureau | oil & gas | 1,179 |
| 11 | Xinjiang Petroleum Administration Bureau | petroleum | 1,125 |
| 12 | China Petrochemical Qilu Petrochemical Corporation | petroleum | 1,108 |
| 13 | China Petroleum & Chemical Fushun Petroleum Chemical Corp. | petroleum | 1,098 |
| 14 | Shanghai Petrochemicals Co. Ltd.[a] | chemicals | 990 |
| 15 | China Petro-Chemical Daqing Petro-Chemical Fty (General) | petroleum | 969 |
| 16 | Shanghai Power Company | utilities | 942 |
| 17 | Maoming Petrochemcial Corp. of Chinese Petroleum Chemicals Co. | petroleum | 903 |
| 18 | Baotou Iron & Steel Rare-Earth Company | steel | 822 |
| 19 | Jinling Petrochemical Industry Co. of Chinese Petrochemical Industry (General) | petroleum | 804 |
| 20 | China Petrochemical, General Corp. Shanghai Gaoqiao Petrochemical Co. | petroleum | 774 |

*Source:* Rankings based on *China Leading Companies 1995.*
1994 data source from the *Directory of Key Manufacturing Companies in P.R. China 1995–96* (Hong Kong: Dun & Bradstreet Information Services, 1995).
[a]Share system

Petroleum was dissolved in 1988. The company accounted for 99% of crude oil output in 1990, and about 97% in 1992. It was expected that CNPC would account for more than 90% of crude oil output over the next decade and possibly beyond. When CNPC adopted a corporate structure, it became possible for it to form a wholly owned subsidiary, China National Oil and Gas Exploration and Development Corp. (CNODC), that could serve as the contracting agent for CNPC coopera-tion with foreign companies. CNPC would also be able to delegate au-thority to regional bureaus to operate as independent and responsible units. In the meantime, the CNPC president still holds ministerial rank and retains the prerogatives of a ministry. The China National Offshore Oil Corp. (CNOOC) was formed in 1982. CNOOC controls all offshore oil and gas fields in water more than five meters deep. CNOOC is a more commercial operation, having more cooperation with foreign compa-nies. But in reality, CNOOC is inferior to CNPC within the Chinese gov-ernment, with the CNOOC president holding the rank of a vice minister only. The China National Petrochemical Corporation (Sinopec) was formed in 1983, and is the major refiner and producer of petrochemical products, responsible for almost 90% of China's refinery products. An-other unit, Sinochem, a trading company under the Ministry of Foreign Trade and Economic Cooperation (MOFTEC) had been the only com-pany permitted to trade petroleum and petrochemical products from on-shore sources. But Sinochem had many conflicts with CNPC and Sinopec. To resolve the conflicts between these state corporations, China National United Petroleum Corporation (China Oil) and China Interna-tional United Petrochemical Corporation (Unipec) were formed in 1993, as 50-50 joint ventures between Sinochem on the one hand and CNPC and Sinopec on the other hand.

### Foreign Investment in China

Since the early 1980s, foreign companies have rushed to invest in China. Perhaps over U.S.$100 billion was invested between 1984 and 1993 (Table 4.2), of which most came from Hong Kong, Macau, and Japan. A further U.S.$100 billion was invested between 1994 and 1996 (Table 1.2 in chapter 1). It should be noted that a large part of the investments from Hong Kong and Macau have come from overseas Chinese using these two locales as conduits to China. Also, although the vast bulk of foreign direct investment into China comes via Hong Kong, in many cases the technol-ogy and market expertise comes from Japan, the United States, or Europe.

The United States and individual European countries lag well behind investments from Hong Kong, Macau, and Japan. But the list of the largest U.S. investors constitutes some of the most prominent American MNCs, with Motorola having the largest stake (Table 4.3).

### Largest Foreign Companies

The largest foreign-funded manufacturing companies in China oper-ate in similar industries to state companies (Table 4.4) with the addition

**Table 4.2**
**Foreign Investment in China**

| | Total U.S.$ billions | Share in percent | Equity U.S.$ billions | Loans U.S.$ billions |
|---|---|---|---|---|
| Hong Kong, Macau | 45.7 | 36.0 | 39.3 | 6.4 |
| Japan | 28.7 | 28.8 | 5.0 | 23.8 |
| United States | 6.7 | 5.5 | 5.2 | 1.6 |
| France | 4.8 | 3.8 | 0.4 | 4.4 |
| Taiwan[a] | 4.2 | 3.3 | 4.2 | — |
| United Kingdom | 3.2 | 2.5 | 0.6 | 2.6 |
| Germany | 2.8 | 2.2 | 0.7 | 2.1 |
| Italy | 1.6 | 1.2 | 0.3 | 1.3 |
| Singapore | 1.5 | 1.2 | 0.9 | 0.6 |
| Canada | 1.5 | 1.2 | 0.3 | 1.3 |

*Source:* MOFERT, China, reported in Kevin Hamlin, "Greater China's Future," *International Business,* May 1995, 31–37.
[a]Includes 1992–93 figures only for Taiwan
*Note:* Figures might not agree due to rounding

of some consumer packaged industries, such as soft drinks. Among the top twenty foreign-funded manufacturing companies, only the first is comparable in size to the top twenty state-owned manufacturing companies. The second to the fourth companies are smaller than the fiftieth largest state-owned companies. All other foreign-funded manufacturing companies in the table are smaller than even the one hundredth largest state-owned company. Among the top five foreign-funded manufacturing companies, four are in the automobile industry. Japanese companies participate directly in five of the top twenty foreign-funded ventures, American companies in three, and European companies in five.

Despite well-publicized problems, such as with the Guangzhou to Shenzhen super-highway toll-road built by Gordon Wu's Hopewell Holdings (a leading Hong Kong conglomerate), more MNCs have been successful than not in China. According to a survey conducted by the Economist Intelligence Unit and Andersen Consulting, the investment environment continues to become more favorable.[6] While companies in China more than 5 years would take 2.3 years to reach profitability and 7.1 years to pay back initial investment, companies in China less than 5 years would take 1.6 years to reach profitability and 4.7 years to pay back initial investment. Also, according to the same survey, MNCs reported that business basics matter more than connections (*guanxi*).[7] These MNCs identified the key success factors to be business strategy, human resources, cost controls, product quality, and building trust with their Chinese partners. They did not see that *guanxi* or business practices unique to China matter much. Among the more than seventy MNCs surveyed, about two-thirds were profitable, and one-third were not profitable. The single most important motivator for all the MNCs (both profitable and unprofitable) was the market potential of China. More than 25% of the profitable companies also regarded China as a base for the Asia-Pacific

*Table 4.3*
**U.S. Companies with Biggest Stakes in China**

| Company | Commitment U.S.$ millions | Activity |
|---|---|---|
| Motorola | 1,200 | The company's most recent commitments include several joint ventures and a $560 million semiconductor wafer fabrication plant in Tianjin. |
| Atlantic Richfield | 625 | ARCO has completed China's largest offshore natural gas project, a $1.13 billion pipeline half-owned by the Chinese government. |
| Coca-Cola | 500 | Coke, Fanta, Sprite, and Hi-C are bottled at 16 locations. Seven more facilities are being considered. |
| Amoco | 350 | Amoco started producing oil in March 1996, from a development project in the South China Sea. |
| Ford Motor | 250 | Ford has three factories making auto components, light trucks, and vans; two other plants are under construction. |
| United Technologies | 250 | UT's Otis subsidiary makes elevators and escalators; Carrier manufactures air-conditioning equipment. |
| Pepsico | 200 | Pepsi has 12 bottling plants, two joint ventures prduc-ducing Cheetos, 62 KFC franchises, and 19 Pizza Huts. |
| Lucent Technologies | 150 | The AT&T spinoff is involved in seven joint ventures, including a $70 million project to provide digital private-line service to Beijing. |
| General Electric | 150 | GE is part of 14 joint ventures, including those that make X-ray and other medical systems; it owns 80% of the largest lighting manufacturer in China. |
| General Motors | 130 | Delphi, a subsidiary, is a partner in three auto-parts facilities. Not counted, because the money is not committed, is GM's 50% partnership in a $1 billion project to build cars in Shanghai. |
| Hewlett-Packard | 100 | HP has been investing in China for 12 years and now manufactures computers, medical systems products, and analytical chemical equipment. |
| IBM | 100 | IBM has six joint ventures, producing computers, electronic cards, advanced workstations for the banking industry, and software. |

*Source:* Melanie Warner, "Motorola Bets Big on China," *Fortune,* May 27, 1996, 118.

region. About 25% of the nonprofitable companies saw limited market potential in the developed world, and also saw that all their competitors were in China. They did not want to be left out. It seems that for these MNCs, their moves to China were mainly market-driven, and to a lesser extent competition-driven.

## Overall Industry Globalization Drivers in China

China's globalization drivers are a mixed bag. The huge potential market size dwarfs the many difficulties posed by its unique and complex market

## Table 4.4
## Largest Foreign-Funded Manufacturing Ventures in China

| Rank | Company Name/Type of fund[a] | Foreign Partner | Nationality | Industry | 1994 Revenues U.S.$ millions |
|---|---|---|---|---|---|
| 1 | Shanghai Volkswagen Automobile Corp. Ltd.[b] | Volkswagen | Germany | automobile | 1,221 |
| 2 | Beijing Jeep Automobile Co. Ltd.[b] | Chrysler | U.S. | automobile | 384 |
| 3 | Shanghai Bell Telephone Equipment Corp. Ltd.[b] | Alcatel | Belgium/France | telecommunications | 328 |
| 4 | Peugeot Automobile Co. Ltd. of Guangzhou[b] | Peugeot | France | automobile | 297 |
| 5 | Guangzhou Steel & Iron Co. Ltd.[c] | Guangdong Enterprises (Holdings) | Hong Kong | steel | 272 |
| 6 | Chunlan (Group) Corp.[c] | Taizhou Chunguang Refrigerating | Hong Kong | machinery | 237 |
| 7 | Dazhong Automobile Co. Ltd. of Automobile Group Co. No. 11[b] | Volkswagen | Germany | automobile | 184 |
| 8 | Beijing Light-Duty Automobile Co. Ltd.[c] | Xiaodeji | Hong Kong | automobile | 184 |
| 9 | Beijing Matsushita Color Kinescope Co., Ltd.[b] | Matsushita Electric | Japan | optical | 174 |
| 10 | Fujian Hitachi Television Set Co. Ltd.[b] | Hitachi | Japan | television | 167 |
| 11 | Sanshui Jianlibao Drink Factory[c] | Huiyuan Investment | Hong Kong | beverage | 162 |
| 12 | Shanghai Mitsubishi Elevator Co. Ltd.[b] | Mitsubishi Mechanical & Electronic | Japan | elevator | 154 |
| 13 | Wuyang-Honda (Guangzhou) Motor Co. Ltd.[b] | Honda Technical Industrial | Japan | automobile | 151 |
| 14 | Shanghai-Yichu Auto Bikes Co. Ltd.[b] | Chiatai Group-Yichu | Thailand | bicycle | 150 |
| 15 | Huaneng Nantong Electricity Station[b] | Huaneng Enterprises | Hong Kong | utility | 134 |
| 16 | Baojie Co. Ltd. of Guangzhou[b] | P&G, Hutchison Whampoa | U.S. & Hong Kong | telecommunications | 134 |
| 17 | Beijing International Switching System Co. Ltd.[b] | Siemens | Germany | telecommunications | 128 |
| 18 | Tianjin Otis Elevator Co. Ltd.[b] | Otis Elevator | U.S. | elevator | 126 |
| 19 | Shenzhen Saige Rili Color Display Co. Ltd.[b] | Hitachi | Japan | optical | 124 |
| 20 | Shanghai Yongxin Color Kinescope Co. Ltd.[c] | Yongxin Technological Development | Hong Kong | television | 123 |

[a]Type of fund    [b]Chinese and foreign venture
[c]Chinese, Hong Kong, Macau, Taiwan joint venture

conditions. Many cost globalization drivers are unfavorable, but again dwarfed by the one very favorable driver of having the world's largest pool of low-cost labor in a functioning economy. Government globalization drivers make life very difficult for most MNCs. Lastly, strong competitive globalization drivers spur many MNCs to participate in order to stay abreast of competitors.

## Market Globalization Drivers

Most market globalization drivers favor integration of China into the global and regional strategies of MNCs. Economic growth and social changes are slowly moving China toward the consumption patterns of developed Western economies. During the 1970s, the four consumer "musts" or aspirations (*shi da zhen*—"four big things") were a bicycle, a black and white television set, a refrigerator, and a washing machine. Today, these "musts" have become a video camera, a CD hi-fi system, a personal computer, and an air conditioner. Particularly among the young and particularly in the major cities and coastal provinces, Western and Japanese consumer products hold great allure. Chinese consumers have embraced McDonald's, Kentucky Fried Chicken, and Sony. Only limited buying power and unavailability of infrastructure such as electricity and roads hold back more purchases of Western and Japanese products. Despite such limits, a significant market for luxury goods has also emerged.[8] Only government disapproval and strictures slow down the adoption of Western lifestyles.

MNCs increasingly include China in their global sourcing. Historically, such sourcing has been of low-value-added items such as nuts and bolts, cheap hand tools, toys, and apparel. A downside for global customers has been the accusation that China uses prison labor to produce some of the goods supplied to MNCs. Logistics within China pose so many problems that global and regional distributors have not used China as a base for the rest of the region.

Several factors can make it difficult to transfer marketing approaches from Western environments: the very strong and ancient Chinese culture with its emphasis on "face" and protocol, the tonal nature of the Chinese language, its many distinctive regional dialects that are almost languages in their own right, the low level of ownership of televisions, and government restrictions on advertising and promotion. On the other hand, much of the population has been exposed to foreign media. Hong Kong-based Star TV reaches much of Guangdong province in the south. Similarly, Beijing residents can receive Japanese television broadcasts. One of the world's best global advertising media, motor racing, now includes race sites in China. Visits by relatives and business executives from outside Mainland China also help spread tastes for foreign products. Overall, as the country becomes more developed, consumers should become very amenable to marketing strategies commonly used in other countries. On the other hand, for the foreseeable future, China is unlikely to be a lead country, even within Asia, in terms of setting market trends.

## Cost Globalization Drivers

Despite its enormous size, import barriers restrict China's cost role in mostly one direction—as an outbound, but not inbound, source of cost savings. Although China is a huge country, high barriers to imports mean that in most industries foreign MNCs have to produce locally. So while they may be able to achieve efficient scales on a local basis, China as a market can seldom contribute sales volume to production facilities outside China. Thus, China offers only limited potential for global and regional scale economies. But local production that supplies both China and external markets can achieve significant scale. For example, joint ventures of consumer packaged goods MNCs, such as Unilever, Procter and Gamble, and Nestlé, often produce goods in China and sell the same items there as well as exporting them to Hong Kong and nearby Asian countries.

Because of the scarcity or poor quality of most raw materials and because of poor transportation infrastructure, China offers limited scope as a source of production inputs. One increasing exception comes in technical staff. As education levels rise, from both domestic and foreign schooling, Chinese technicians are becoming cost-competitive. For example, Fourth Shift, an American-owned software concern, has all of its development work done by Chinese engineers in Tianjin (the industrial city and port near Beijing).

China has good outbound logistics, but poor logistics internally. Relatively efficient port facilities allow MNCs to ship effectively from China, and the country's location relative to regional and global markets is as good as any other in the Asia-Pacific region. In contrast, the inadequate internal transportation system operates way beyond capacity, causing long waits and delays for shipments. For distribution-intensive businesses, such as consumer products or even building materials, the end link can often be a man on a bicycle.

The big attraction of China as a production site lies, of course, in the very large supply of low-cost labor (among the lowest wage rates in Asia, as discussed in Chapter 1). Offsetting these low wages are low productivity, the high overhead of social costs, and the difficulty of discharging employees once hired or inherited. To date, most MNCs producing in China have operated in high labor-content, low-skill sectors. The automotive joint ventures provide a good test of China's ability to upgrade to more demanding products, as does China's increasing participation in Boeing's aircraft production system.

While limited today, China's role in technology development will increase rapidly because of education and technology transfer. The post-Cultural Revolution generation has demonstrated the ability to acquire the highest levels of technical education from the West, and increasingly from schools in Asia or China itself. For example, students from China now account for one of the largest national groups in the scientific/technical doctoral programs of U.S. universities. Furthermore, in some fields, especially defense-related ones, China's technology is globally competitive. For example, the country has adapted its missile program to use its Long March rockets in launches of commercial satellites, although with mixed success (the Long March having the highest launch failure rate in the industry). And with technology transfer as the government's top priority in dealings with MNCs, China's capabilities will accelerate. For example, Emerson Electric, a leading U.S. concern, is trying to establish an Asian engineering center in Shanghai to make use of local engineers to develop technology.

## Government Globalization Drivers

Perhaps more so than in any other country in the region, government in China plays the dominant role in the prospects of MNCs. Furthermore, with the current fragmentation of power, it is governments in the plural with whom MNCs need to deal—national, provincial, city, state enterprises, and the military being the primary ones. Combined with an uncertain legal system, both in terms of laws and enforcement, dealings with the state pose the greatest challenges for foreign companies. McDonalds's experience in Beijing in 1994, illustrates this problem. Only two years after signing a twenty-year lease in the center of Beijing, the company found itself about to have to close one of its largest stores in the world. Senior officials in the Beijing city government had made an agreement with a Hong Kong tycoon to redevelop the property in which the McDonald's store was located. But more than Big Macs were at stake. There was a power struggle underway between the national government and the Beijing authorities. Eventually, a deputy mayor of Beijing committed suicide in the face of corruption accusations. In the aftermath, McDonald's emerged with a better deal but still had to move out temporarily during redevelopment.[9]

Overall, government intervention is very high, as evidenced by China's ranking of 121st (tied with Congo and Mauritania) in the Heritage Foundation's 1995 Index of Economic Freedom. China continues to maintain strongly protectionist trade policies in many sectors, with tariff rates over 100% being common (e.g., 120% on beer brewed with malt, and 150% on tobacco products) although the weighted average duty is around 40%.[10] Many lucrative sectors, such as domestic banking and telecommunications services, remain closed to foreign participation. But President Jiang Zemin announced, at the Asia-Pacific Cooperation Council's 1995 summit in Osaka, a plan to cut import tariffs on four thousand items by 30%.

China's government is highly sensitive to possible foreign dominance in key industries, so it sets stringent rules on foreign direct investment. The bottom line is that everything has to be negotiated at great length and with many partners and government bodies. One observer has commented that the 1995 award to General Motors to build Buick model cars with Shanghai Automotive Industry Corporation merely gave GM the right to negotiate to make an investment.[11] GM was finally able to sign a $1.6 billion deal in 1997. Similarly, as of 1997, Mercedes-Benz was losing hope that it could finalize its U.S.$1 billion deal to build minivans in China.[12] National interests and policy dominate, although status as an old friend and a cordial relationship and track record also help.

For China, technology transfer is the critical factor in its dealings with foreign companies and governments. China's history plays a major role in this desire. The country remembers only too well its former role as the most advanced nation in the world. Furthermore, official ideology holds that the West and Japan conspired from the 1840s on to suppress China's economic development. Now it is China's chance to catch up. Once again, the Central Kingdom is demanding tribute from foreigners—this time, technology. China now uses its purchasing power to strongly negotiate for the transfer of both technology and jobs. For example, China's airlines have become among the largest customers of new aircraft from Boeing and its competitors, and China exerts pressure to swap jobs and technology for market access. So Boeing has shifted half of the tail-section production for its 737 jets from Wichita, Kansas, to Xian in China, along with other activities. Similarly, Europe's Airbus is under pressure to relocate some production work.[13]

China maintains stiff tax policies. In addition, the authorities find many indirect ways to add to the tax burden, such as in very high property rentals for foreign companies. In late 1995, China proposed changes that would burden foreign businesses even more. As these rules change continually, we recommend that readers consult more current guides such as those published by multinational accounting firms.

Perhaps the greatest source of uncertainty for MNCs in China lies in the lack of a business legal system. In turn, this lack exacerbates the common attitude among Chinese partners that the contract binds the foreign partner but not themselves. For example, about thirty Japanese and European joint-venture leasing companies have lost a total of $600 million, and have little chance of recovering the money because both repossession and secondary markets are nonexistent.[14] China is trying to build a legal system, so the situation will gradually improve.

China is notorious for its poor protection of trademarks and intellectual property. Furthermore, the participation of government officials, particularly local ones, in many of the businesses making violations, has made it almost impossible for the central government to improve the situation. For example, the United States has applied intense pressure from the early 1990s, with little success, to close down factories making counterfeit copies of compact discs and movies. Sometimes an MNC's own partner can be the source of pirating.[15] The U.S. government has made the protection of trademarks and intellectual property a major requirement for China's joining the World Trade Organization. Finding the right Chinese partner seems to be key for an MNC seeking to protect its rights.

As a socialist economy, most local competitors and many customers are government-owned. In consequence, such competitors and customers have extra leverage in dealing with foreign MNCs. On the other hand, they also suffer the usual disadvantages of government ownership. For example, in the beer industry, through poor management actions, state-owned Tsingtao has lost its lead to aggressive foreign brewers, notably America's Pabst and Holland's Heineken.[16]

Lastly, marketing regulations can be both restrictive and arbitrary, especially those affecting advertising. For example, the Chinese authorities have rejected one advertisement that depicted the Statue of Liberty and another that featured the word "Hollywood."

## Competitive Globalization Drivers

Because of import restrictions, China in most cases is not yet a globally strategic market. In most industries, China can qualify in only the first two items of the list of criteria for being a globally strategic market:[17]

- a large source of revenues or profits
- a significant market of global competitors
- a major source of industry innovation
- a home market of global customers
- a home market of global competitors

Exceptions are high-technology industries in which China is a major customer, such as commercial aircraft. On the other hand, China can be strategic as a source of production, particularly in labor-intensive industries.

More than for any other country in Asia, however, China has become the market in which MNC rivals imitate each other. The huge market potential makes companies fearful of allowing their competitors to steal a march. In addition, the glamour of the China market has encouraged CEOs to enter for the sake of bragging rights, although none will admit to such a motive. China is rapidly replacing Japan as the ultimate test, actual or perceived, of a company's international competitiveness.

# Overall Global Strategies for China

China has become such an attractive market and production site that MNCs face many choices when including China in their regional and global strategies.

## Market Participation Strategies

As mentioned earlier, many MNCs have rushed to enter China's markets, including the MNCs on which we focus in this book. China's huge population makes it particularly attractive for consumer products companies such as Unilever and Procter and Gamble. Unilever first entered China, starting a soap operation, in the 1920s, only to be driven out in 1953. After an absence of thirty-three years, Unilever returned to China in 1986. It spent the initial years after its return studying the new environment in China, accumulating experience from some smaller scale projects. Before 1992, Unilever had hired fewer than one thousand people in China. During the next three years, Unilever increased the hiring to five thousand people. The number of expatriates increased from four to eighty in the same period of time. Its China operation has become increasingly important for Unilever. In 1995, the company operated nine joint-venture operations in China—six in Shanghai, two in Beijing, and one in Guangzhou. In terms of global market participation, China is a country that Unilever cannot afford to ignore. However, the unpleasant experience in China in the 1950s left a question mark in the minds of senior executives. Thus, even when China adopted an open-door policy, Unilever wanted to move cautiously and studied the situation carefully. In 1992, when it was clear that the markets in Western Europe and North America offered little growth, and when it was confirmed that China would uphold the open-door policy, Unilever moved with full speed to launch new and larger-scale joint ventures.

Procter and Gamble teamed up with Hutchison Whampoa, a major Hong Kong trading company, and with a Chinese soap factory in Guangzhou to form Procter and Gamble (Guangzhou) in 1988. In addition, P&G used its Hong Kong organization to support this new venture. From the very beginning, P&G invested heavily in China.[18] Up to 1995, P&G had operations in more than two hundred out of five hundred cities in China. There were more than two hundred management executives and more than five thousand factory workers. In terms of global market participation, China is a must for P&G. The huge market potential is more than enough to justify early and significant actions. Also, P&G has achieved some significant successes. For example, in shampoo, P&G brands took more than 50% of the Chinese market in 1995.

Philips began operations in China in 1985, under the direction of its Hong Kong office, which was an important part of the Asia-Pacific operation. Philips executives now believe that they did not start soon enough in China. To date, the company has not gained leading market shares in its major business lines such as lighting or sound and vision. But Philips now clearly views China as a very significant future market. There are several clear indicators of this determination. First, in November 1995, Shanghai became the headquarters of the China/Hong Kong operation. The Vice-President of Corporate Human Resources moved to Shanghai first. Gradually, the whole management team will station there, so that the Shanghai office will be in full operation in early 1997. By so doing, Philips wants to show its commitment to China. Secondly, Philips is creating more and more joint-venture operations in China. At the end of 1995, there were a total of seventeen joint ventures—more than half in eastern China, investing in Shanghai, Nanjing, and Suzhou. Although quite a number of the joint ventures are not profitable, it is a nonissue for the time being. Philips is encouraged by the fact that production runs are becoming more satisfactory year after year. There is a total of close to thirteen thousand employees for all the operations in China. Lastly, in terms of market coverage, the Philips operation in China is even more comprehensive. Trading/marketing operations cover eastern China (Shanghai as the center), northern China (Beijing as the center), southern China (Guangzhou as the center), and even western China (Chengdu as the center). The marketing network operates in about fifty cities.

Motorola's participation in China provides a good example of why many MNCs believe they have to be there. Motorola is one of the leading players in the semiconductor industry—in 1994, it ranked after only Intel, NEC, and Toshiba. Computers and telecommunications are becoming increasingly important for China, a huge developing country, and semiconductors are key components for all computer and telecommunications products. So Motorola jumped at the China opportunity. After four to five years of hard work and negotiation Motorola was able to establish a 100% wholly owned subsidiary, Motorola China, in November 1993, in the Tianjin Economics and Technology Development Area. By the end of 1994, the company had invested U.S.$280 million in a factory to produce pagers and cellular phones. Motorola also maintains sales offices in Beijing, Shanghai, and Guangzhou. In October 1995, Motorola announced its next phase of investment, worth U.S.$720 million, bringing the total investment in China to over U.S.$1 billion. Out of the U.S.$720 million, more than U.S.$500 million is for a wafer fabrication manufacturing project—the high-technology part of semiconductor production.

## Product and Service Strategies

In many industries, MNCs have been able to sell products in China that have little local adaptation, including many consumer packaged goods and technically advanced products. In some other industries, particularly because of affordability and poor infrastructure, MNCs continue to need to make significant adaptations. Unilever finds that it needs to adapt products that are closely related to the physical and/or the cultural environment, such as toothpaste. Because of long-time consumption experience, a fruit-based aroma and taste for toothpaste is much preferred to the internationally accepted mint-based aroma and taste. In contrast, the company finds that it does not need to adapt products that are totally foreign to China. For example, despite China's extensive tea heritage, *Lipton Iced Tea* is a sufficiently foreign concept that it does not require adaptation to local expectations. Also, for its regional and global products, Unilever is able to maintain its worldwide quality standards in China.

P&G also finds that it can market global and regional products in China. The company's "Strategic Global Effectiveness" program implemented in 1993, cut down product offerings and simplified production. The program allowed limited choices for product formulas, and individual countries could choose among the limited available choices. But the program allowed more flexibility in packaging size to cater to the needs of a particular country. So P&G in China offers smaller packaging sizes so that the unit price will still be affordable for the general public. Thus, the product formula is standardized while the package size differs.

Philips's products and services are more or less standardized around the world, with a little localization and adaptation. For example, round television sets sell well in Europe, but do not in Asia despite promotion efforts. Philips finds it can sell only rectangular sets there. Within the region, there are also some differences. While in Hong Kong, the television box is either black or dark grey, in China it may be blue or red in order to appeal.

Since semiconductors are a highly standardized industrial product, local adaptation is a nonissue for Motorola. On the other hand, there is always a need to produce tailor-made chips to meet the needs of specific customers. Besides the standard chips, it has always been a challenge for semiconductor manufacturers to customize their products. However, the customized efforts are company-specific rather than region-specific. In the case of China, the real challenge lies in the percentage of localization in production rather than anything else. Motorola has a target to increase the percentage of locally made product to 50% by the year 2000, from about 30% in 1995.

## Activity Location Strategies

Many MNCs set up production in China to take advantage of its low cost-production factors and to export the goods produced there. For those companies selling within China, many have to produce there because of import restrictions. Because of technological backwardness, most companies conduct R&D elsewhere. Also, because of poor service attitudes, companies do not locate customer service functions in China unless absolutely necessary. So the typical value-chain strategy has been to locate only production and local distribution functions in China. Both Unilever and P&G take this approach. Furthermore, their typically bulky products cannot be economically shipped in from outside. In order to meet the requirement of government regulations, P&G also maintains an organization unit for conducting low-end research and development activities. Unilever expects that in the future China can be a source for product research and development, and also for more raw materials. Philips is still struggling to fine-tune its production operation, but plans to source engineers in China and set up an important center for research and development. Motorola, too, limits its activities to production for export and local markets, and selling, distribution, and customer service activities for northern China. Again, China may hold for Motorola a future role in R&D for wafer fabrication.

## Marketing Strategies

In many markets, China is open to global marketing approaches. Localization has usually involved finding the best transliteration of brand names, avoiding inauspicious names, numbers, and phrases. For example, it is well known that any model name should usually avoid the number "4," as the Chinese word for four sounds the same as that for death, while the number "8" has connotations of prosperity. So while hotels in the United States may avoid having a thirteenth floor, in China many avoid having fourth, fourteenth, twenty-fourth floors, and so on.

Most marketers in China, whether local or foreign, adopt the practice of not setting retail prices for the product (no resale price maintenance). So prices vary among different cities in China and can differ from the rest of the region and the world.

In China it is usually important to have heavy advertising before a company can promote a new product. In addition to creating awareness and good will, advertising plays two other particularly important functions in China. One, because of the popularity of counterfeit products, it is extremely important to have television advertising to assure consumers that a new product really comes from the advertiser rather than from fake goods manufacturers. Two, trade acceptance depends heavily on whether there is an advertising campaign. So consumer companies, such as Unilever, P&G, and Coca-Cola, all invest heavily in advertising.

Philips finds that its global marketing expertise generally applies to China as well. However, due to the environmental situation, the allocation of marketing budgets is quite different from a typical Philips operation in other countries. Since mass media are not that well developed, media advertising accounts for less than 30% of the marketing budget, which is quite small by Philips's standards. Among media advertising formats, signboards prove to be the most effective. More resources are invested in point-of-sale promotions, displays, and service centers. Distribution channels are quite intensive and comprehensive. Since state-owned enterprises, such as department stores, still constitute a major channel of distribution, it becomes important for Philips to hire promotion workers to station in those stores to help promote and sell the products, while all the profits will go to the stores. By so doing, Philips manages to overcome the problem of the lack of incentives given state employees.

## Competitive Move Strategies

The most common competitive move has been to buy out local competitors. Procter and Gamble, for example, has bought up some of the best Chinese brands. So in its toiletries and detergent markets, most of its competition now comes from its global rival, Unilever, rather than from locals.[19] As P&G moves from a country-based to a more regional concept of operation, China, as a significant country in this region, usually plays a leading role in the regional team. In turn, it becomes natural for China to participate as a member of the global team.

Many MNCs make moves in China on a stand-alone basis, mainly because of its large size and many unique aspects. But this is probably a mistake. In contrast, Philips recognizes that the leading competitors in all its major business lines have already established solid operations in China. In lighting, General Electric is already there. In sound and vision, Panasonic and Sony are already there. So Philips is very aware of how moves in China can affect its global competitive position.

# Overall Organization and
# Management Approaches for China

Each of the four sets of organization factors has distinctive aspects in China.

## *Organization Structure*

For China, undoubtedly the most important issue in organization structure is finding and working with the right partners. While local partners are important in most Asian countries, they have been essential in China. MNCs especially need to consider three types of partners: national government, local government or business, and overseas Chinese. With the heavy government involvement and intervention, having a national government partner is often essential, and having the right one even more so. Peregrine Investments, a Hong Kong-based investment bank and trading company, catapulted to prominence in a very short time based on its assiduous cultivation of the right relationships. The families of government officials are often a prime source of suitable partners. The children of the most senior communist officials—commonly known as the *tai-zhi* or "princelings"—are much sought after as business partners. There is even a Hong Kong consulting firm that specializes in investigating the families of Chinese officials to identify the best potential partners.[20]

Local business partners are often needed to provide a source of supply or additional government relationship. Kentucky Fried Chicken, for example, partnered in 1986 with the Beijing Tourist Bureau to obtain a site in Tiananmen Square for its first restaurant, and with Beijing Animal Production, a Beijing city government-controlled producer to obtain an assured source of chickens.[21] On the other hand, many foreign companies have experienced so many problems with their Chinese joint-venture partners that many are beginning to go it alone, and successfully doing so. Wilfried Vanhonacker argues that several ingredients now make foreign equity ventures less viable and favors wholly owned subsidiaries:[22]

- increasing competition in China's marketplace and more aggressive plans by foreign companies
- crumbling of traditional distribution channels
- more difficulty in finding buyers for a joint venture's output
- limited scope of Chinese partners' connections
- inability of Chinese companies to keep up with the speed and scope of change in China's markets
- differences between foreign and Chinese partners in time horizons and profit objectives

Many Western MNCs also benefit from adding an overseas Chinese partner. Such a partner may be based in Taiwan, Hong Kong, Singapore, some other Asia-Pacific country, or even in the MNC's home country.

These partners can bring their own relationships in China and also help bridge the gap between Western and Chinese business practices. In Hong Kong, trading companies, or *hongs,* such as Jardine Matheson, Swire Pacific, or Hutchison Whampoa now play such a role.

Each of Unilever's joint ventures in China have different partners, with each an independent legal entity. Unilever also established Unilever (China) Ltd., to coordinate among all the joint ventures operating in China. In turn, Unilever (China) reports to the Unilever North East Asia Business Group located in the United Kingdom. P&G typically organizes operations in China as autonomous subsidiaries. Philips does the same. Key decisions—setting up joint ventures, new product launches, and setting the minimum pricing levels for various products—have to be referred back to the Asia-Pacific headquarters or even to the Philips Group Management Committee. The subsidiaries are free to set prices higher than the minimum levels as appropriate. Asia-Pacific has been a growing and increasingly more important region for Motorola. Motorola Semiconductor operations in China reports to the Motorola Asia-Pacific Semiconductor Products Group in Hong Kong. Among various countries in this region, Motorola Asia-Pacific Semiconductor Products Group has identified Tianjian, Hong Kong, and Singapore as three key cities. Tianjian supports northern China, Hong Kong supports southern China, and Singapore supports Southeast Asia. In contrast, Motorola maintains only sales offices in Korea, Taiwan, Malaysia, India, Australia, and New Zealand.

## Management Processes

Western management practices are so alien to China that MNCs have taken a long time to both adapt their practices and to train their Chinese managers. With the rapid establishment of Western-style business schools, such as the new China-Europe International Business School in Shanghai, and increasing experience in Western companies, it will become easier to transplant professional management techniques.

## People

A shortage of local management talent has been the great constraint. Many MNCs find that, with their China operations continually expanding, there are just not enough executives. So they have been importing managers from Hong Kong, Singapore, the United States, and other countries. MNCs particularly like to hire expatriate overseas Chinese or returning mainlanders who have been educated abroad. But such executives are in such short supply that MNCs find it very difficult to hold onto them. One solution is to train local managers. Ingersoll-Rand, a U.S. engineering company, has recruited most of the managers of its air compressor business from its local joint-venture partner. After several years of training these managers, Ingersoll-Rand's venture sells more compressors with two hundred staff than the state-owned parent does with two thousand seven hundred.[23] It is too early, however, to gauge the potential for transferring local managers from China to other countries.

Philips in China has significant freedom in personnel policies: designing the compensation packages, deciding on hiring and firing, etc. At Philips, there is a belief in internation flow of managers among countries in the Asia-Pacific region. However, for the time being, the demand for competent managers is huge in China, such that practically all the qualified executives in China are fully occupied in the China operation. Philips has had to import more than 110 expatriates from Europe, North America, Singapore, Taiwan, and Hong Kong.

Motorola is a global company, opting for international integration of human resources. In practice, the challenge in the Asia-Pacific region is to nurture local managers to take up tasks in their respective countries. Ideally for Motorola, practically all local jobs should be taken up by local managers. In the case of the China operation in Tianjian, as a relatively new operation, they have to import expatriate managers from Hong Kong, Taiwan, Singapore, Malaysia, and the United States.

In general, employees in China accept expatriates, even though the latter receive much higher compensation and benefits than local managers. However, because of the changeover of Hong Kong in 1997, there has been an unhappiness among employees in China about accepting expatriates from Hong Kong. Many mainland employees consider it "unreasonable" that Hong Kong employees should enjoy expatriate terms.

## Culture

The key cultural issue for MNCs is to overcome the "iron rice bowl" work attitude (lifetime employment and care) and the aversion to providing service, both legacies of the communist system. The Chinese government itself has recognized these problems. In 1995, the authorities began a campaign to banish such customer-unfriendly phrases as the infamous *mei-you* or "we don't have it/don't bother me." Then, of course, there are the usual cultural issues of preserving "face" and the like.[24] So, for example, management should avoid open discussion of appraisal results.

## Globalization of Two Industries

For China we have selected the soft drink and automobile industries for in-depth analysis of the globalization process and MNC participation. The soft drink industry illustrates a situation in which foreign MNCs have been able to rapidly gain market share and achieve profitability. In contrast, the automobile industry provides a situation in which the government and foreign manufacturers have significantly opposing interests, with much less success for MNCs.

## Soft Drink Industry

The population of 1.2 billion in China presents an attractive market for any consumer product or service company. With its low unit price (between ten and fifteen U.S. cents per eight-ounce bottle, compared with an average hourly wage of forty-five U.S. cents in 1995) soft drinks constitute an early entry into the consumer market for the population of a developing country like China. Furthermore the experience of other countries suggests huge growth potential as per capita income rises. Industry analysts predict that China will become the largest soft drink market outside the United States within 15 years.[25]

The two major soft drink giants (Coca-Cola and Pepsi-Cola) entered the China market in the early 1980s within a year of each other. Both the market and their share of it grew rapidly over the next ten years. By 1992, *Coke* and *Pepsi* already dominated the market, with *Coke* having twice the share of the largest local competitor. More important, the two American companies were leading the development of the market in product and marketing innovation. The largest local player, Jianlibo, strictly speaking, is not even a soft drink producer, its honey-based carbonated drink being more a health drink than a soft drink. The once significant player in Shanghai, *Zhenguanghe,* became very minor by 1992. By 1995, the market shares of *Coke* and *Pepsi* had grown to 18%–19% and 9%–10% respectively.[26] Lastly, none of the local players have achieved significant sales internationally. How have foreign companies been able to achieve such success? Industry globalization drivers provide much of the answer.

## Industry Globalization Drivers

Soft drink industry globalization drivers turn out to be mostly favorable for foreign companies.

*Highly favorable market globalization drivers.* The most favorable market globalization drivers in China's soft drink industry concern common customer needs, global channels of distribution, and transferable marketing. In terms of common customer needs, as a relatively young category, soft drinks do not have distinctive local preferences and tastes. So consumers had little difficulty in switching from local products to the tastes of global products. Furthermore, soft drinks have strong lifestyle connotations and so constitute an easily affordable taste of the highly coveted American way of life.

Global hotel chains have acted as a channel of distribution, usually stocking *Coke* and *Pepsi* and other product items from these two companies to meet the needs of international hotel customers, and so helping to introduce the product to local customers.

Marketing approaches and assets have transferred very easily. The ultra-strong global brand names of *Coke* and *Pepsi* (numbers one and nine among all brands in the world)[27] created rapid recognition and acceptance. A 1995 poll of brand awareness in Beijing, Shanghai, and Guangzhou, the three largest cities, showed very high awareness levels for the three leading brands of the two giants:[28]

| Coca-Cola Co. | | Pepsi-Cola Co. | |
|---|---|---|---|
| Coke | 36% | Pepsi | 34% |
| Sprite | 30% | 7 Up | 5% |
| Fanta | 2% | Miranda | 3% |

The difference between *Sprite*'s and *7 Up*'s performance arises from the always present pitfall of Chinese translation and highlights the continuing need for careful local adaptation. The Chinese transliteration of *Sprite* carries the connotation of "snow jade." The brand's slogan, "crystally clear, thoroughly cool," also achieves a very positive effect. In contrast, *7 Up* in Shanghainese carries the connotation of "death from drinking."[29] Similarly, in the 1920s, Coca-Cola had to change its original transliteration from one meaning "dry mouth full of wax" to another signifying "happiness in the mouth."[30]

Distribution caused initial problems, because of the mandated ownership structure of bottling operations (cooperative joint venture rather than equity joint venture), and because retail distribution channels are largely through state-owned stores. American-style sales promotion has also gained acceptance. An obvious example can be found in Shanghai. The Oriental Pearl Broadcasting Tower was completed in 1995, as a key sightseeing spot in that city. Surrounding the spacious outer area inside the entrance, stand elegantly decorated open-area cafes offering only *Coke* and *Sprite*. Many standard point of purchase materials like banners and umbrella tents are nicely arranged. So soft drinks have rapidly achieved in China the famous "three As" of marketing—acceptable, affordable, and available.

*Very weak cost globalization drivers.* Cost globalization drivers are not at all strong in the soft drink industry. Because of high transportation costs and poor transportation infrastructure, bottlers and distributors are even more limited in their geographic scope in China than elsewhere. On the other hand, the high population density in the urban areas allows each bottling plant to easily achieve a large enough market to support its minimum-efficiency scale. So foreign soft drink producers can easily enter China in selected locales but cannot bring production-scale advantages that are shared from other countries. Instead they are forced to produce locally. This requirement for local production also eliminates possible global strategies in exploiting the experience curve or differences in country costs. On the other hand, the backwardness of domestic producers has allowed Coca-Cola and Pepsi-Cola to achieve major advantages in the deployment of their superior management expertise and production technology.

*Moderate government globalization drivers.* Compared with government intervention in other industries with foreign participation, the soft drink industry faces moderately favorable government globalization drivers. The key factor for a benign government approach is that production is local, even though some foreign exchange goes out to buy concentrate and pay licensing fees. On the one hand, the authorities tried to regulate joint-venture agreements with the aim of protecting the many domestic producers (in such a visible product category, sensitivity to foreign dominance is quite high). On the other hand, in order to have effective technology transfer, the authorities gradually loosened regulations over time. The government has sought to develop a win-win situation by encouraging the giants to help develop and renovate some of the local brands. Coca-Cola and Pepsi-Cola have also been quite disciplined in monitoring their share penetration. At the same time, the government has been careful to limit the competitive thrust of the two foreign giants. China allows both to compete in the economically more-developed cities, like Beijing, Shanghai, Guangzhou, and Harbin. In other cities, only one of the two giants is allowed. For example, Coca-Cola is operating in Chengdu, Hainan, Kunming, and Nanjing, while Pepsi-Cola is operating in Chongqing, Guiyang, and Guilin. Lastly, in this industry, the authorities have been serious in upholding international technical standards, adopting common marketing regulations, and protecting trademarks.

*Mixed competitive globalization drivers.* Competitive globalization drivers are mixed. China qualifies in the soft drink industry as a globally strategic market in two ways—as a potentially large source of revenues or profits, and as a potentially significant market of global competitors. In addition, what the giants learn from the China market will, to a large extent, be applicable to the situations in emerging markets like India (another huge market) and Vietnam (another communist country opening to the world). On the other hand, logistical constraints prevent significant exports from China. Nor is it likely that MNCs can develop any competitve advantages in China that can be transferred elsewhere. Furthermore, the size and diversity of the country will allow many niche producers to continue to thrive, and will allow even the global producers to offer purely local products (as Coca-Cola has done in Japan with *Georgia Coffee,* a hugely successful cold soft drink developed for that market only).

## Strategies of Soft Drink MNCs

Coca-Cola and Pepsi-Cola have made use of some global strategies but not others.

*Pursue participation in China.* The two companies have clearly identified China as being a strategic market for them and have pursued participation vigorously. The lure of one billion thirsty throats has been impossible to resist.

*Offer global products.* Both companies have realized that their appeal in China lies in the very fact that their products are American, foreign, and global. So product adaptation would have been a mistake, let alone unnecessary.

*Locate downstream activities locally.* Because of the severe limits in product transportability, both companies have applied their usual strategy of localizing downstream activities. In addition they have had to use local joint-venture partners.

*Use global marketing.* Coca-Cola and Pepsi-Cola have used primarily global marketing approaches and themes. Localization has come, first, in finding the best Chinese transliteration of their brand names and, second, in the development of some local promotions. When Coca-Cola was aggressively launching its advertising campaigns in China in the early 1990s, consumers were quite receptive to the ones prepared for *Sprite* and *Fanta*. The one for *Coke,* however, was not that effective, leading to the development of a new campaign. The new advertising has such favorite Chinese images as family ties, wedding ceremonies, Chinese New Year celebrations, and the great earth. A pop singer from Taiwan, who was the most popular in China, was commissioned to compose and sing for that commercial.

*Make local competitive moves.* Nontransportability of the product isolates geographic segments of the soft drink industry. Consequently, both companies have focused on making local competitive moves.

## Summary

The rapid success of foreign MNCs in the soft drink industry in China depended on strong market forces, particularly the widespread desire and ability to partake of an American lifestyle, the weak local competition, and limited government intervention. Coca-Cola and Pepsi-Cola have successfully applied highly standardized global strategies.

## Passenger Car Industry

In contrast to the soft drink industry, the Chinese government has strenuously limited foreign participation in the automobile industry, with the very obvious objectives of minimizing imports and maximizing technology transfer. So foreign imports accounted for less than 5% of 380,000 passenger cars sold in 1995.[31] In addition, foreign joint ventures account for over 90% of domestic production. The automobile industry is a key one in China. Quite a number of the top state-owned enterprises and foreign-funded enterprises belong to this industry (Tables 4.1 and 4.4 earlier). But the market is still very small, particularly for a country the size of China. China's total passenger car production of 230,000 units in 1993 (and 370,000 in 1995), is dwarfed by figures of 6 million for the United States, 8.5 million for Japan, and 3.8 million for Germany.[32] To date Japanese companies have dominated the import sector, with a 70% share of all vehicle imports in 1992, followed by Germany with 14%, France with 11%, and the United States with 3%. Of joint ventures producing in China, Volkswagen (German) and Daihatsu (Japanese) sell the most and have achieved excellent profitability of over 50% returns on investment (Table 4.5). But as of 1997, VW was having problems selling the *Jetta* models produced in its Changchun operation.[33]

While some joint ventures have been successful, others have been disastrous. General Motors launched a venture with Jinbei Automotive in 1992, to build trucks. Jinbei proved to be very inefficient, employing 50,000 workers to produce just 40,000 vehicles in 1994. In contrast, GM's *Saturn* division in the United States that year made 286,000 cars with 6,800 plant workers.[34]

*Table 4.5*

**Automotive Joint Ventures in China**

| Chinese Company | Foreign Partner | Nationality of Partner | Brand/ Model | 1995 Unit Sales |
|---|---|---|---|---|
| Shanghai Automotive Industry | Volkswagen | Germany | Santana | 160,000 |
| Tianjin Automotive | Daihatsu[a] | Japan | Charade | 65,000 |
| Beijing Jeep | Chrysler | U.S. | Cherokee | 30,000 |
| Dongfeng Motor | PSA | France | Citroen | 30,000 |
| Guangzhou Peugeot | PSA | France | Peugeot 505 | 20,000 |
| Changan Automobile | Suzuki | Japan | Alto | 20,000 |
| First Auto Works | Volkswagen | Germany | Jetta | 20,000 |
| First Auto Works | VW/Audi | Germany | Audi 100 | 20,000 |
| Shanghai Automotive Industry | General Motors[b] | U.S. | n.a. | 0 |

*Sources:* China National Auto Industry Corporation company reports; A. T. Kearney estimates, in "The Long Drive into the Middle Kingdom," *The Economist,* June 8, 1996, 64–65.

[a]Technology license

[b]Awaiting government approval

## Industry Globalization Drivers

China's industry globalization drivers are mixed in favorability for foreign companies.

*Market globalization drivers are strong.* Potential market size constitutes the most important market globalization driver. China represents one of the last large markets for automakers in the world, with enormous growth potential. There may be room for all of the world's major automakers to compete.

In terms of whether customer needs are common with the rest of the world, China's automotive market does not have distinctive Chinese characteristics but does have characteristics common with other developing countries. So basic reliability, durability, and economy are much more important than refinements such as power steering, handling, or safety features such as airbags.

*Cost globalization drivers are mixed.* Because of the government's emphasis on local production, and because of the need to design local models, foreign automakers will not be able to make much use of China to contribute to global or regional scale economies in production. Furthermore, the currently tiny passenger car market of under 400,000 units per year (trucks are a much larger market—over one million units) prevents operation on the most efficient scales using the most advanced technology. In contrast, the annual output of the highly efficient Honda plant in Marysville, Ohio, in the United States, was 350,000 units in 1992.[35] But the low costs in China provide hope that the country can become a competitive source of exports. Lastly, the country will be a recipient of technology rather than a source of innovation.

*Government globalization drivers create many obstacles.* Since China regards automobiles as a pillar industry, there is a high degree of sensitivity to foreign dominance. It has been quite clear that the government wants more production rather than more imports to meet the growing demand. So import tariffs have been set very high—180% for small cars and 220% for large cars in 1993, but reduced to 110% and 150% respectively in 1994.

China also allows only joint, rather than wholly owned, venture operations in this industry. Furthermore, the government requires high levels of local content, and foreign partners have had to work hard to increase such content. Among all the Sino-foreign joint ventures, Shanghai Volkswagen managed to achieve an 80% local content objective after seven years of operation. All other ventures could not achieve a local content percentage beyond 60%. The imported component reflects how much advanced technology (usually the most difficult part) the Chinese side of the venture still does not have.

China's government seems to be particularly willing to bring in political considerations when negotiating contracts in the automobile industry. For example, it was probably no coincidence that two American companies, Ford and Chrysler, lost a bid to form a major joint venture with the Nan-fang South China Motor Corporation in mid-1995 at a time of heightened Chinese unhappiness over the visit of Taiwan's president to the United States. Instead, China awarded the contract to Germany's Daimler-Benz. But only a few months later, another American company, General Motors, won a contract to partner with Shanghai Automotive Industry.

The Chinese government has committed to invest a lot to develop this pillar industry, and has set four specific objectives for future development: (1) putting emphasis on the development of passenger cars; (2) trying to learn from advanced countries through joint ventures, licensing, and putting emphasis on raising the percentage of localization content; (3) increasing production volume of the key factories and trying to enjoy the benefits of scale economies; and (4) trying to produce in China to meet the growing national demand.[36] It is also a national objective to raise funds from the capital market to develop technologically independent state-owned automobile manufacturers.[37]

*Competitive globalization drivers require participation.* As with the soft drink industry, the huge automotive potential gives China global strategic importance as a market. In addition, the opportunity to export from China makes participation even more important. Most of the major automakers are now in a race to establish positions in the country. At the same time, all foreign companies face a classic prisoner's dilemma. They know that China's primary interest is to extract as much technology transfer as possible in order to build up its own capabilities. The relative fragmentation of the world automobile industry is allowing China to play each competitor against the others. The end result will probably be the creation of Chinese global competitors in the automotive industry.

## Strategies of Automotive MNCs

Unlike in soft drinks, MNCs have had to tailor their strategies much more for China. Both government and market requirements are pushing MNCs to pursue full localization of production and to develop products tailored for China.

*Rush to participate, but not by all.* From 1985 to 1993, five foreign MNCs set up major joint ventures. These ventures included Beijing Jeep (already operating in 1985), Shanghai Volkswagen (1985), Guangzhou Peugeot (1986), Tianjin Daihatsu (1987), and Volkswagen Changchun (1992). They constituted 70% of total production in 1985, 80% of total production in 1987, and over 90% in 1989–92. The Beijing Jeep operation has not performed well. This joint venture with American Motors Corporation (now merged into Chrysler) promised to create a new model together with the Chinese partner and export to the world market. But so far, as of 1996, this venture sells only 30,000 units a year in China and none outside.

The leading player, Volkswagen, has joint-venture operations in both Shanghai and Changchun. The combined production output of these two Volkswagen ventures already constitute more than 50% of total production in China. That country has become very important to Volkswagen. In 1995, the company sold more cars in China (221,700 vehicles) than in all of North America, significant compared with Germany (945,000 vehicles).

None of the leading Japanese companies produce cars in China. They have been reluctant to form joint ventures in China that might nurture serious future competitors in the global export market.[38] Unlike American and European companies, they have been strong enough, to date, to resist the temptation of the Chinese apple. Instead, back in the 1980s the big Japanese companies declined to invest in China, and focused on selling components instead. In 1996, Toyota agreed to set up a joint venture to produce up to 150,000 engines a year with Tianjin Automotive, a Chinese company that already makes cars and vans licensed from Daihatsu, a Toyota affiliate.[39] Negotiations between China and Toyota are tough. There is an uncomfortable sentiment between the two parties because of the Second World War experience. Toyota fears that China may follow in the footsteps of South Korea, transferring Japanese technology while not buying Japanese cars. For a smaller country like South Korea, this may still be tolerable. For a huge country like China, the boomerang effect could be very significant. Yet, China is such a huge market, and all key competitors have already gone there. So Toyota, as the leading Japanese automobile company, feels compelled to enter also and build a significant presence.

*Design local products.* The high prices of automobiles relative to per capita incomes (the cheapest new car representing over ten times average annual wages in the manufacturing sector) requires MNCs to design simpler, cheaper cars for the Chinese market. (GM found that the *S-10* trucks in its venture with Jinbei were both too small and too costly.) Some companies are now seeking a regional solution. Toyota has developed an Asian compact car for the entire region—the *Soluna*, assembled in Thailand.

*Emphasize local production.* Because of tariffs, other government obstacles, and limited consumer purchasing power, MNCs have had little choice but to set up local production. Their main degrees of freedom have come from which partner to work with and where within China to locate plants. But even these decisions have major restrictions imposed by the authorities. Furthermore, automobile production places enormous demands on the labor force and on the country's infrastructure. Performance to date suggests a long way to go to reach world-class standards.

*Make local competitive moves in a global context.* The adage, "think global, act local," applies very much to competitive moves in the Chinese automobile industry. The wrong kind of moves can have serious long-term global consequences.

### Summary

Tempting market potential, heavy government involvement, and difficult market and operating conditions combine to make it hard to forecast the prospects for foreign MNCs. The automobile market in China could be an elixir for some and a poisoned chalice for others.

## Conclusions

In conclusion, opportunities and prospects for MNCs in China depend greatly on the type of industry and on the competitive structure of the foreign industry. In the case of soft drinks, foreign MNCs have prospered rapidly in an industry that sells easily affordable products and that is not viewed by the government as strategic. Also, the duopoly nature of the global industry has given the two foreign MNCs very strong bargaining positions relative to Chinese authorities and partners. Other consumer packaged goods companies, such as Procter and Gamble and Unilever, have also been successful in China. In contrast, the automotive industry is viewed as strategic by the government, and the global industry is relatively fragmented with up to twenty major players. In consequence, China has been able to set its own terms and extract concessions, particularly technology transfer, from the weaker industry players.

So success for foreign MNCs, and corresponding success in terms of China's own development, has come initially in less strategic, low-technology sectors, particularly consumer goods. But the real test of success from China's viewpoint will be the development of industries such as automobiles, petroleum, steel, and the like. If the experience in consumer goods industries can be reproduced in these "heavier" sectors, economic reform will be a resounding success. In addition, the challenge in the financial sector will be even more critical.

China's government seems to recognize the economic challenges faced by the country. In the Ninth Five-Year (1996–2000) Plan, the authorities make it clear that they know the difficult issues they are facing, and they also recommend clear measures to cope with those issues. For example, China wants to speed up banking and exchange rate reforms to strengthen the government's ability to exercise macroeconomic control. The government wants to set "hard" budgets for state-owned enterprises. Loss-making enterprises will be allowed to merge with profitable ones in order to rationalize their operations. In order to narrow the income gap between regions, the government has made pledges to give more financial support to the interior provinces. With these measures in place, the economic prospects of China seem to be brighter.

## NOTES

1. Xianchun Kao and Fulin Chi, *China: In Transition to a Market Economy* (series in Chinese) (Hainan, China: China Reform and Development Institute, 1993).

2. Stephen M. Shaw and Jonathan R. Woetzel, "A Fresh Look at China," *The McKinsey Quarterly,* no. 3 (1992): 37–51.

3. Joseph Kahn, "Multinationals Faring Well in China, Surveys Show," *Asian Wall Street Journal* (September 15–16, 1995): 1 and 5.

4. Tak-Sing Cheung, *Confucianism and the Orderly Complex, A Sociological Interpretation of Chinese Thought* (in Chinese) (Taipei: Great Waves Publisher, 1989).

5. Trevor MacMurray and Jonathan Woetzel, "The Challenge Facing China's State-owned Enterprises," *The McKinsey Quarterly,* no. 2 (1994): 61–74.

6. Kahn, *Multinationals . . .*

7. Dusty Clayton, "Business Basics Put Ends to Myths," *South China Morning Post,* September 22, 1995, 14.

8. "A New Taste for Quality," *Far Eastern Economic Review,* December 7, 1995, 52–56.

9. *The Economist,* December 1995.

10. Ibid.

11. "First Prize, One Contract in China; Second Prize, Two Contracts," *Fortune,* December 11, 1995, 28.

12. "GM's New Promised Land," *Business Week,* June 16, 1997, 34.

13. Lewis M. Simons, "High-Tech Jobs for Sale," *Time,* July 22, 1996, 59.

14. Andrew Marshall Hamer, "Cashing in on China's Burgeoning Middle Class," *Marketing Management* 4 no. 1 (Summer 1995): 9–21.

15. "How and Why To Survive Chinese Tax Torture," *The Economist,* December 2, 1995, 63–64.

16. Ibid.

17. See George S. Yip, *Total Global Strategy: Managing for Worldwide Competitive Advantage* (Englewood Cliffs, N.J.: Prentice Hall, 1992) 71.

18. For example, the company solicited the help of the Faculty of Business Administration at the Chinese University of Hong Kong to train executives recruited in China.

19. *The Economist,* op. cit.

20. Political & Economic Risk Consultancy Ltd., Hong Kong.

21. Allen J. Morrison and Paul Beamish, "Kentucky Fried Chicken in China (B)," case 9–90–G002, 1990 (London, Ontario: Western Business School).

22. See Wilfried Vanhonacker, "Entering China: An Unconventional Approach," *Harvard Business Review* (March–April 1997): 130–40.

23. *The Economist,* op. cit.

24. For guidance, see, for example, Sanjyot P. Dunung, *Doing Business in Asia: The Complete Guide* (Lexington, Mass.: Lexington Books, 1995).

25. Sharon Foley and David B. Yoffie, (1994), "Internationalizing the Cola Wars: The Battle for China and Asian Markets," case N9–794–146 (Cambridge, Mass.: Harvard Business School Press).

26. "The Market Share for Pepsi in the China Soft Drink Market Is about 10%," *Hong Kong Economic Journal* (in Chinese), September 19, 1995.

27. Survey by Landor Associates, San Francisco, 1990. See also a study by Interbrand, London, 1996.

28. Anita Mei Che Ip, *Pepsi-Cola's Challenge in China and Its Strategic Moves Into Equity Joint Venture* (Hong Kong: Chinese University of Hong Kong M.B.A. Project, 1995).

29. Foley and Yoffie, *Internationalizing the Cola Wars.*

30. David A. Ricks, *Blunders in International Business* (Cambridge, Mass.: Blackwell, 1993) 34.

31. "The Long Drive Into the Middle Kingdom," *The Economist,* June 8, 1996, 63–64.

32. China Automotive Technology and Research Center, and Ministry of Machinery-Automotive Industry, *China Automotive Industry Yearbook-1994* (Shandong: New China Publishers, 1994).

33. "GM's New Promised Land," *Business Week,* June 16, 1997, 34.

34. *Fortune,* December 11, 1995.

35. Victor Sun, *China Auto Sector: Putting It Together* (London: Peregrine Securities [U.K.] Ltd., 1995).

36. Zhou Jiahua's speech delivered to the working conference for the China automotive industry in 1993.

37. Ziangpin Hsu, "Reflection on the Development Strategies for Passenger Car Industry in China" (in Chinese), *China Industrial Economics,* no. 6, 41–45.

38. Eeric Harwit, *China's Automobile Industry, Policies, Problems, and Prospects* (Armonk, N.Y.: M. E. Sharpe, 1995).

39. *The Economist,* June 8, 1996.

## CHAPTER 5

# Taiwan—Coming Into Its Own

### *Ching-sung Wu and George S. Yip*

BUOYED BY MORE THAN a decade of strong economic growth and an increase in national pride and ambition, Taiwan (also known as the Republic of China on Taiwan) is searching for a new identity. The economy started out making cheap textiles and wood products, graduated into consumer electronics and sophisticated plastics, then glided into the computer industry. Currently, Taiwan ranks number nine in both world export and import trade volume. Both amounts are around U.S.$100 billion. Prior to 1995, Taiwan's international trade had been heavily concentrated, with the United States, Japan, and the European Union accounting for about 50% of the total export volume. By 1995, however, Hong Kong and Mainland China had replaced the industrialized countries as Taiwan's largest export trading partners.[1] Taiwan had accumulated U.S.$90 billion in foreign exchange reserves through trade surpluses by the end of 1996, second only to China's $100 billion. MNCs have located extensive manufacturing and sourcing activities in Taiwan. But increasing labor and other local costs are causing foreign firms to move out low-value activities. On the other hand, increasing technological capabilities are encouraging many MNCs to conduct more sophisticated activities there.

## Background

Any discussion of Taiwan has to consider its unique political situation. Taiwan's government views itself as the government of China in exile while China's government views Taiwan as a rebel province. No resolution is in sight. After Taiwan's martial law decrees were repealed in 1987, a more democratic political system arose, allowing for legalization of opposition parties, rights to staging of political demonstrations, broader press freedom, and a grass-roots electoral process. Direct elections for Taiwan's president were held in 1996, confirming the position of Taiwan's first native-born president, Lee Teng-hui (a very important contrast to his mainland-born, unelected predecessors).

Taiwan has, however, been excluded from participation in most world affairs. It has been banned or removed from many world-level organizations or forced to change its name from "Republic of China" to "Chinese Taipei," which is regarded as demeaning to the Taiwanese government and people. Around 12% of the population call for the independence of Taiwan to form a new political sovereignty that breaks away from its Mainland China mentality. Around 40% of the Taiwanese, however, support reunification with Mainland China, although the two have been together for only four years (from 1945–49) since China ceded Taiwan to Japan in 1895. The tensions created by the two alternatives for Taiwan are of great concern for both locals and foreigners interested in participating in Taiwan's economic growth. To maintain the status quo and the delicate relationships with China are the most demanding tasks for the government. The uncertainty of the succession in China itself engendered in the mid-1990s a more aggressive stance by the mainland regime, culminating with China's missile launches into the Taiwan Strait in early 1996.

During the first ten years of its existence, the Taiwan government had tried a number of growth-enhancing policies that would lay the foundation for Taiwan's future development. Initial policies focused on land reform to provide raw materials for export, followed by a policy of import substitution. During this period, the government invested heavily in infrastructure, erected high tariffs to shield domestic industry from foreign competition, and subsidized industry. Light industries such as furniture, bamboo-made products, pulp and paper, and textiles contributed to the increase in industrial production. But importing capital and intermediate goods while penalizing exports contributed to a growing trade deficit that the government financed through foreign loans.

In the early stages of Taiwan's development, U.S. aid was an important source of funding. Anticipating the end of foreign aid and a need to obtain foreign exchange, the government shifted to a policy of export promotion from 1958 to 1972. Tariff and import controls were gradually reduced and labor-intensive industries such as plastics, electronic components, and consumer electronics were promoted. As a result, foreign direct investment replaced U.S. aid as the main source of foreign capital. Moreover, this foreign investment facilitated technology and skill transfers that improved the quality of goods and led to a diversification in industry. Exports, which had averaged a 12% annual growth from 1953 to 1962, grew 28% a year from 1963 to 1972.

As the spectacular growth of the 1960s and early 1970s sputtered to just below 7% in the late 1970s, the government moved to restructure the economy. The rapid industrial growth strained Taiwan's transportation and communication systems, low-wage nations emerged to compete for Taiwan's manufacturing jobs, and the world shifted its attention, recognition, and investments to Mainland China at the expense of Taiwan. Meanwhile, many Taiwanese firms shifted their footwear, textile, electrical appliance, and sporting goods manufacturing to their less-developed neighbors in China and Southeast Asia.

To remain competitive, the government invested heavily in infrastructure and focused on the development of capital-intensive, high-technology industries including semiconductors, biotechnology, petro-chemical, and information services. In addition to improving the infra-structure, industry, and technology of the country, the government also sought to coordinate the human resources of Taiwan. In 1984, the gov-ernment revised the tax laws to provide incentives for manufacturers who contributed to a research and development fund. Other government measures included revising the school curriculum to strengthen science and math skills and providing incentives to industry to expand and diver-sify their production.

After the Plaza Accord in 1985 sent the yen and other East Asian cur-rencies skyward, intra-Asian investment and trade flows spiraled upward. Taiwan's exports faced a loss of competitiveness due to the appreciation of the New Taiwan dollar and the rise of manufacturing wages. To miti-gate the detrimental effects of the appreciated currency, while integrat-ing the financial sector into the industrial policy, the Taiwan government actively engaged in the deregulation of financial institutions both in the domestic and international areas. In 1991, fifteen private local banks were granted licenses. Foreign banks were also allowed broader opera-tional freedom and encouraged to increase investments.

The effect of this policy can be seen in the changing composition of the economy. During 1986–94, the percentage of the manufacturing sec-tor's contribution to GDP declined from 39% to 29%. The major growth came from the service sectors, particularly in wholesaling, retailing, and professional and financial services. During the period 1986–2000, the ser-vice sector's growth should reach 7.4% per year compared with the man-ufacturing sectors' 6%, and 1.5% for the agricultural sector.[2]

## Foreign Participation in Taiwan's Economy

There has always been a foreign presence in Taiwan's modern eco-nomic history. At first, the United States was Taiwan's major trading part-ner. In recent years, however, Taiwan has been placing more emphasis on building relationships with its neighbors, thereby reducing its reliance on Western nations. From 1979–85, Japanese companies accounted for 76% of all foreign establishments, followed by American companies (21%), and European (3%). However, from 1985–94, foreign direct investment in Taiwan was accounted for as follows: Japan (32.4%), United States (24%), Hong Kong (9.6%), and Europe (14.5%), with the Netherlands, the United Kingdom, Germany, and Switzerland being the major Euro-pean investors.[3] In general, European investors are concentrated in the chemical and service industries, while U.S. and Japanese investors are evenly distributed among basic metal products, electric and electronic appliances, machinery, and service industries. In the service industries, retailing (especially hypermarkets) is the most attractive for foreign in-vestors. The top ten reasons cited for foreign investors being in Taiwan are as follows: political stability, sound social order, adequate technical level, fast economic growth, good quality of operational personnel, sound industrial infrastructure, favorable government policies toward foreign investment and incentives, liberalized trade policies, low level of wages, and open foreign exchange policy. Table 5.1 lists the top twenty foreign-owned or joint ventures in Taiwan.

Taiwan's trade deficit with Japan grew to U.S.$14.5 billion in 1994. Japan has been the largest exporter for essential components, raw materials, and machinery needed by Taiwan. The unfavorable exchange rate has brought the household appliance, electric machinery, and automobile industries under severe cost pressures.

Due to the changing focus of the government's investment policy, Taiwan has experienced a boom in both foreign exports and manufactured exports. The average export ratio (exports as a percentage of sales) of all foreign investments rose from 37% in 1987, to 43% in 1990. Japanese firms in Taiwan have the highest export ratio (45% in 1990), followed by U.S. (42%), and European firms (35%). Moreover, the scale of foreign

**Table 5.1**

**Largest Foreign-Owned or Joint Venture Companies in Taiwan**

| Rank | Company | Nationality | Main Business in Taiwan | 1994 Revenues U.S.$ millions |
|---|---|---|---|---|
| 1 | Ford Lio Ho Motor | U.S. | automotive | 1,595 |
| 2 | Philips Electronics Industries | Netherlands | electronics | 1,088 |
| 3 | Philips Electronic Building Elements Industries | Netherlands | electronics | 1,057 |
| 4 | Matsushita Electric | Japan | electronics | 1,037 |
| 5 | Texas Instruments | U.S. | semiconductors | 788 |
| 6 | China American Petrochemical | U.S. | petrochemical | 718 |
| 7 | Yamaha Motor | Japan | automotive | 604 |
| 8 | Motorola Electronics | U.S. | electronics | 565 |
| 9 | Digital Equipment International | U.S. | computers | 540 |
| 10 | Imperial Chemical Industry | U.K. | chemicals | 375 |
| 11 | Hitachi | Japan | electronics | 347 |
| 12 | China Nikken | Japan | services | 313 |
| 13 | Sheng Yu Steel | Japan | steel | 300 |
| 14 | International Standard Electronics | U.S. | electronics | 282 |
| 15 | Procter & Gamble | U.S. | household/ personal care | 263 |
| 16 | Taiwan Futaba Electronics | Japan | electronics | 263 |
| 17 | China General Plastics | U.S. | plastics | 257 |
| 18 | TDK Electronic | Japan | electronics | 227 |
| 19 | Kao | Japan | household/ personal care | 199 |
| 20 | Du Pont | U.S. | chemicals | 195 |

direct investments has been increasing, with investment amounts up to U.S.$10 million or higher accounting for 46% of the cases.

The "China Factor" looms large for foreign firms operating in Taiwan. Currently, China sales as a percentage of their global sales averages only 10%. In the future, these MNCs will reinforce their base in Taiwan and, at the same time, actively engage in direct investments in China. For instance, the main target of Volkswagen's joint venture with the local Chin-Fon Group is the Mainland China market. But Taiwan will remain an attractive market, a training center for technical personnel, and a supplier of major components.

## Taiwan Companies

Both Japan and South Korea based their economic development on large conglomerates, but Taiwan has very few of these. Instead it chose to promote small, home-grown companies that develop their own technology. Many of these companies were set up by Taiwanese returning to the country after a stint with top technology companies in the United States. Some of these companies, such as Acer, are now multinationals in their own right.

For the most part, small to midsize enterprises (SMEs) spearheaded Taiwan's remarkable success in export-oriented growth. The 850,000 SMEs in Taiwan account for 97% of the number of firms, 62% of employment, 59% of the industrial output, and 55% of exports. However, a recent survey of the top one thousand firms in Taiwan shows that large corporate conglomerates accounted for 51% of the GDP (with combined sales of over U.S.$100 billion).[4] Information, telecommunications, and related electronics sectors are the largest industries in terms of sales and profit, followed by petrochemicals, transportation equipment, basic metals, man-made fiber, other kindred foods, plastic products, chemical materials, feedstocks, and cement.

Despite the contribution of private industry to the Taiwanese economy, many of the top one hundred Taiwanese companies in terms of sales are state-owned or province-owned enterprises (Table 5.2). Several such enterprises—China Petroleum, Monopoly Bureau of Taiwan Tobacco and Wines, China Steel (privatized with significant state holdings), China Shipbuilding, Taiwan Sugar, and Taiwan Fertilizer—still play important roles. The government plans to privatize most of them in the coming years.

With structural and institutional changes occurring in the operating environment in Taiwan, firms within the industry have begun to pursue a two-pronged internationalization strategy. One is to develop the U.S., Japanese, and European markets to maintain previous market share positions achieved through OEM production (supplying products to be branded by other companies). The major modes are to set up assembly plants and maintenance centers, or to establish research and design centers and sales offices in these developed countries to catch up on market and technological information.

**Table 5.2**
**Largest Taiwan Companies**

| Rank | Company | Main Business | 1995 Revenues U.S.$ millions |
|---|---|---|---|
| 1 | Chinese Petroleum Corporation | oil exploration, refining | 12,414 |
| 2 | Taiwan Power | power generation | 8,543 |
| 3 | Chunghwa Telecom | telecommunications | 5,937 |
| 4 | Acer | computers | 5,705 |
| 5 | Nan Ya Plastics | petrochemicals | 3,992 |
| 6 | Taiwan Tobacco & Wine | trading, distribution | 3,927 |
| 7 | China Steel | steel products | 3,356 |
| 8 | Hotai Motor | car dealership | 2,530 |
| 9 | President Enterprises | food and beverages | 2,338 |
| 10 | China Airlines | airline | 1,781 |
| 11 | Ford Lio Ho Motor | automotive | 1,777 |
| 12 | Formosa Plastics | plastics | 1,651 |
| 13 | Tatung | consumer electronics | 1,542 |
| 14 | China Motor | automotive | 1,529 |
| 15 | Formosa Chemicals & Fiber | textiles | 1,526 |
| 16 | Chi Mei Industrial | plastics | 1,478 |
| 17 | San Yang Industry | cars, motorcycles | 1,401 |
| 18 | Hualon | textiles | 1,301 |
| 19 | Far Eastern Textile | textiles | 1,293 |
| 20 | Taiwan Sugar Corporation | sugar | 1,201 |

*Source:* "Top Enterprise By Country," *Asiaweek*, November 22, 1996, 156.

The other alternative is to build new production bases in the developing countries and/or shift existing operations abroad for lower-end products. For example, the ratios of foreign production in Mainland China, Thailand, and Malaysia rose during 1992–93 for computer monitors (20% foreign production in 1993), mother boards (24%), keyboards (69%), and power supplies (41%).[5]

## Taiwan's Semiconductor Industry

Compared to other major international competitors in the semiconductor industry, Taiwanese firms are small with limited resources. As such, they have to develop innovative strategies in order to compete effectively in the global arena, generally pursuing niche strategies coupled with shared resources in a vertically unintegrated industry structure. Through extended alliances with related firms in various semiconductor sectors, major companies in Taiwan are able to survive the global pressure for low cost and high efficiency. Taiwan has become the fifth largest regional player in the microprocessor chips business, behind the United States, Japan, Europe, and South Korea. On the manufacturing side, Taiwan's eleven major semiconductor firms grew from a combined revenue of almost nil in 1989, to approximately U.S.$2.5 billion in 1993.

The phenomenal growth of the semiconductor industry in Taiwan can be attributed to the growth of the computer industry. By 1995, Taiwan was the most active area for worldwide integrated circuits (IC) vendors from around the world. Taiwanese IC design houses have become the major personal computer chipset suppliers worldwide. This has also attracted leading foreign companies (Motorola, Texas Instruments, National Semiconductor, Sharp, etc.) to establish production and R&D centers in Taiwan.

The examples of United Microelectronics Company (UMC) and Taiwan Semiconductor Manufacturing Company (TSMC) can be used to demonstrate the strategic characteristics of the Taiwanese semiconductor industry and its role in international competition. After being spun off from the government-backed Industrial Technology Research Institute (ITRI) with proven technology and product, UMC acquired well-trained engineers and researchers from ITRI and the nearby scientific community. UMC was able to take advantage of good timing in the volatile and short product life cycle within the semiconductor family. Its product development teams are backed with significant capital investment in modern manufacturing processes. It also formed joint ventures and strategic alliances with related suppliers and customers. UMC was, thus, able to reduce fixed costs and, at the same time, retain flexibility and speedy operation by concentrating on its core product development capabilities.

TSMC, however, pursued a different strategy by becoming an OEM-only manufacturer. Its corporate charter prohibited it from entering into product design or marketing to end users. Its fabrication-only strategy allowed it to serve as a manufacturing base for other design houses in Taiwan—a silicon foundry, so to speak. This strategy solved the diseconomies of scale in the foundry process within the chip production stages in Taiwan. Its just-in-time delivery also provided significant competitive advantages for its customers.

TSMC also formed domestic and international cooperative relationships in order to share critical financial and technological resources. A joint venture with Philips provides TSMC with international reputation, technology, and financial support. In the IC packaging industry, local companies are also strengthening their integrating relationships with the fabrication and system manufacturers. At the same time, foreign companies are expanding their assembly capability and strengthening their purchasing arms in Taiwan.

## Taiwan's Computer Industry

In less than two decades, Taiwan has emerged as a leading producer of peripherals for nearly every major computer vendor in the world, despite little previous experience in high-technology industries. By 1995, Taiwan ranked fourth in the world behind the United States, Japan, and Germany in computer hardware production and exports through its strategy of being a "fast follower."[6] Taiwan's computer companies have responded rapidly and effectively to continuing changes in the international market by emphasizing close supplier relationships with multinational computer companies all over the world, and have been helped by the government's strong support in promoting the manufacture and assembly of microprocessors and related electronic components. Coupled with lower labor cost advantages, compared with Japan and the United States, Taiwan became the powerhouse for PC production and computer peripherals during the 1980s. In 1994, Taiwan supplied 80% of the mother boards not made in-house by computer manufacturers, 80% of the mouse pointing devices, 61% of the scanners, 56% of monitors, 49% of keyboards, 34% of network cards, 31% of power supplies, and 28% of portable (laptop and notebook) computers.

Acer Group, the leading Taiwanese company in the computer industry, made good use of these measures. Acer's predecessor, Multitech (changed to Acer in 1987) was founded in 1976, with capitalization of NT$1 million with the main business of trading and designing microprocessors. Acer grew rapidly to become by 1995, a giant conglomerate with over U.S.$5.7 billion in revenues and fifteen thousand employees worldwide. The company grew at a dazzling pace by introducing PCs with more features and lower prices than comparable IBM machines. Fashioning original products, not just cheap clones, and selling them mostly under its own name, enabled Acer to distinguish itself from other Taiwanese manufacturers. Acer is already the leading PC brand in Southeast Asia, Mexico, and the former USSR, and second in Latin America. In 1995, it moved into the number ten spot in the United States.

As part of its marketing strategy, Acer chose to gain a foothold in less developed and less competitive markets first rather than to directly confront preeminent global competitors (e.g., HP, Compaq, and NEC). In the more developed markets, Acer preferred to be an OEM or original design manufacturer (ODM) supplier. The higher value-added, technology-intensive industrial sectors and professional service industries will be the core for the next stage of economic growth. Closer regional economic integration through complementary international division of labor among the Asia-Pacific regions will further sustain the future economic performance of Taiwan.

Acer's operations mirror the rationalization strategy of foreign MNCs. After suffering dramatic losses in 1991, Acer began to recognize the need for a more integrated manufacturing relationship structure and decided to move both upstream and downstream within the information industry through extensive alliances. Chip production, auxiliary products for PCs, and multimedia applications are all within the realm of Acer's related diversification programs. To streamline Acer's manufacturing process, its engineers have designed a standard housing model for all Acer models that can be snapped together in thirty seconds. One of the biggest users of modular manufacturing, Acer ships unfinished computers to some sixty distributors around the world, and receives price-sensitive components just-in-time for final assembly. In the American market, Acer saves

4% on tariff charges by shipping machines without their microprocessors and buying them in the United States from Intel. Acer believes that control of technology, volume production of key components, coupled with a global brand, extensive channels, and a sound and flexible organization will be key success factors for computer makers. So it puts more effort into the front-end and back-end of the value-added chain, while farming out the assembly portion to lower-cost countries.

## Foreign Investment By Taiwan Companies

From 1987, outward foreign investment from Taiwan began to grow at an unprecedented rate, despite a short decline during 1990–91. As Taiwan settled into its newly industrialized status, internal and external challenges threatened the continued growth of the economy. These challenges include: the rise in land costs, a shortage of low-skilled and unskilled workers, underutilization of transportation facilities, mounting pressures for environmental protection, and the possible accession to the GATT/WTO. The formation of NAFTA also encouraged those Taiwanese firms with a global perspective to set up beachheads in Canada, Mexico, and South American countries to take advantage of falling tariff and nontariff barriers. Last, and by no means least, Taiwanese companies want to hedge against the uncertainty in Taiwan's relationship with China.

The major regions for Taiwanese foreign investment have shifted from the United States to the Asia-Pacific region (mostly in Southeast Asia and Mainland China) and European countries. About half of these investments are in service-related sectors. Investment in Hong Kong serves both as an indirect route for moving capital into China and to support the trading of raw materials and semifinished assemblies. The volume of trading activity between Taiwan and China via Hong Kong as a percentage of Taiwan's total trade has grown from 1.5% in 1986, to 8.4% in 1994. During 1990–94, the accumulated investments in China by Taiwanese firms totaled U.S.$4.55 billion.[7] The sectoral distribution areas were as follows: electric and electronics components (14.7%), food processing (11.8%), plastic products (11.4%), basic metal products (8.1%), and precision instruments and equipment (7.8%). But from the mid-1990s, the Taiwan government began to try to cool down the business enthusiasm for investment in China, and to encourage more investment in Southeast Asian countries.

## Overall Globalization Drivers for Taiwan

Most of Taiwan's globalization drivers are highly favorable for the global and regional strategies of MNCs. The main negatives are its relatively small and aging population of twenty-two million, its increasing costs, and the risk of conflict with China. Newly industrialized nations are often quick to lure MNCs with lucrative tax incentives, duty-free processing zones, and the retransfer of capital and profits without permits, but many

MNCs also look closely at the quality and availability of the labor force, re-sulting operating costs, and the overall business climate. Taiwan offers both types of attractions.

## Market Globalization Drivers

With a per capita income of over U.S.$12,000 in 1995, Taiwan is among the richest Asian economies and exhibits many of the consumption patterns of a developed nation. Its GNP in 1994, of U.S.$246 billion compares favorably with India's U.S.$279 billion, and even China's U.S.$630 billion. While a formerly traditional society, Taiwan has exploded into the developed capitalist world and spawned a new middle class with a taste for high quality consumer goods and the means to indulge that taste.

At the same time, Taiwanese consumers are among the most exacting in the world. However, MNCs have discovered that if they can respond to the exacting demands of Taiwanese customers for advanced products, services, and account and customer service, they will be ready to compete in opening markets throughout the world.

Structural changes have also occurred in the channels of distribution in Taiwan. Except for the military- or school-affiliated networks, there are five major types of retail channels, most of them foreign-owned or franchised: personal stores (e.g., Hong Kong-based Watson's), cash-and-carry volume discount stores (e.g., Netherlands-based Makro), supermarket chains (e.g., Hong Kong-based Wellcome), convenience stores (e.g., U.S.-based and Japanese-owned 7-Eleven), and hypermarkets (e.g., France-based Carrefour). In the near future, the most competitive distributors will be the international franchising chains. They bring together the most advanced Point of Sales (P.O.S.) and Electronic Data Interchange (E.D.I.) technologies to streamline warehousing, selling, logistics, and financial control systems.

## Cost Globalization Drivers

As an industrially developed economy, Taiwan has one of the highest labor costs in the region. Cheap unskilled labor, however, is not a primary motivation for Taiwan's technology-intensive industries, being a very small portion of total cost. Taiwan's strong educational and communication infrastructures help make it an attractive location for high-technology MNCs. Both foreign and domestic companies rely on Taiwan's relatively inexpensive brainpower to increase operational efficiency and maximize costs. After years of preparing a well-educated workforce that is not afraid of change, Taiwan has developed a significant number of intelligent, young engineers who are quick to exploit technology obtained from abroad, but earn significantly less than their U.S. counterparts. Consequently, Taiwan can position itself between low-end, labor-intensive economies like China and the high-tech powerhouses of the United States and

Japan. So the high labor and land costs in Taiwan are offset by a work-force with high skills, high productivity, low absenteeism, and low turnover.

### Government Globalization Drivers

Government drivers were, and continue to be, important to Taiwan as the economy prepares for the next century. During the 1980s, the government was keenly aware that Taiwan could not compete much longer for labor-intensive manufacturing jobs with lower-wage Southeast Asian countries. To prepare for that day, the government worked with private industry to develop high-skill, capital-intensive high technology industries such as information, biotechnology, petrochemicals, and electronics.

Strategic alliances guided and formed by the government-supported institutions have important implications for the economic development of Taiwan. By 1996, more than twenty MNCs had signed "Strategic Alliance Memorandums" with the government.[8] Among them are global giants such as Northern Telecom, Hewlett-Packard, Du Pont, Olivetti, Siemens, Westinghouse, and Philips, in industries ranging from consumer electronics, nuclear power, medical equipment, petrochemicals, and aerospace, to transportation. These companies intend to take advantage of the national construction plans for Taiwan's infrastructure improvements (highways, high-speed rail, mass rapid transit, harbor, airport, and telecommunications projects), to form cooperative ventures for the lucrative domestic market potential, to build export platforms for nearby Asian markets, to speed up the entry process into Taiwan, and to enjoy various incentives provided for their investments.

Government drivers have also been used to develop Taiwan's industrial base. Taiwan's success in the computer industry, for example, has been due to a coordinated government strategy to support private entrepreneurship by a large number of small, flexible, innovative companies. The Industrial Technology Research Institute (ITRI) provides government-funded R&D and technology transfer/diffusion opportunities to help develop a sound infrastructure for nurturing high-tech start-ups. For example, the Computer and Communication Research Laboratories (CCL) unit of ITRI launched a joint project for laptop computers in 1989. At that time, the PC notebook industry in Taiwan showed great disparities in both technical capability and market sensitivity among participants. Though a handful of more advanced companies (e.g., Acer) had already invested in product development, most local manufacturers still had little understanding of the technology. Standard product specifications were yet to appear, and it was difficult to obtain key components (e.g., LCD, HHD, and keyboards) economically. The lack of proper task division further increased the investment capital of individual manufacturers. After careful evaluation, ITRI proposed the idea of a "common machine architecture" to lower the investment risks of manufacturers. ITRI pushed for industry standards and division of tasks to make certain that device suppliers were willing to join the development project. ITRI also developed the CMOS technology that it bought from RCA in 1976. ITRI's electronics arm, Electronics Research and Service Organization (ERSO), also engaged in setting up prototype production processes to test out laboratory-developed technology for business application potential. ERSO would then spin off these product lines to independent companies for mass production. Under these policies, four companies came into existence: United Microelectronics Company (UMC), Taiwan Semiconductor Manufacturing Company (TSMC), Vanguard International Semiconductor Corporation, and Winbond Electronics Corporation. In such a vein, ITRI has actively planned, organized, and guided the industry-wide cooperative projects aimed at promoting the speedy commercialization of existing technology and sharing of costs and risks in the development of next generation products or processes.

The government is also promoting a better tax structure by establishing bilateral tax treaties with foreign governments to avoid double taxation. Administrative measures, such as better foreign visa entry regulations, investment application processes, and free flows of capital are also being established. With the attempt to enter the World Trade Organization, Taiwan has been reducing its customs duties dramatically for imported goods across the board. Laws to protect trade secrets and intellectual property are also being promulgated. The government is making major efforts to strengthen Taiwan's infrastructure to better position the island as an Asian hub for international business. In order to maintain and renovate Taiwan's industrial structure for the next century, the government is promoting the Asia-Pacific Regional Operation Center (APROC) initiative. The ultimate objectives of this initiative are to establish Taiwan as the manufacturing center, sea transport center, air transport center, financial service center, telecommunications center, and media center of the Asia-Pacific region. A major component of the manufacturing center involves building twenty to thirty intelligent industrial parks for high value-added manufacturing for the Asian region. The program will use Taiwan's existing competitive advantages in the design and production of high-tech products and its vast pool of scientific and engineering talents to provide research for anyone who needs it. For the sea transport center, the program plans to establish Kaohsiung harbor in the south as the region's preeminent transshipment hub to take advantage of Taiwan's excellent port facilities and geographic location athwart major Asia-Pacific shipping routes. In the air transport center, the aim is to establish Taipei's Chiang Kai-Shek international airport as an express cargo hub, general cargo center, and passenger transit hub.

Taiwan also seeks to attract foreign investment through the lure of overseas funding. The government hopes that foreign manufacturers will consider moving into a country from which they have received funding. Taiwan aims to become a center for international financial institutions based on the strength of its economic performance, large foreign exchange reserves, and ample supply of investment capital. In order to achieve these ambitious plans, the government is making significant efforts to overhaul legal frameworks, remove administrative red tape, and reinforce incentives for MNCs from North America, Japan, and Europe. Taiwan has also established international standards for pollution control, environmental protection, and ecological control. The "green marketing" concept has become prevalent in business operations and consumers' product purchasing decisions.

## Competitive Globalization Drivers

The importance of Taiwan in an MNC's competitive strategy continues to increase. Taiwan has become an integral part of many MNCs' global and regional value chains. Taiwan's various advantages can contribute to a significantly competitive position. The presence of many global competitors heightens Taiwan's role in competitiveness. Its local companies are beginning to globalize. Also very important, Taiwan provides a strategic location from which to access the People's Republic of China.

# Overall Global Strategies for Taiwan

MNCs initially focused on locating production in Taiwan. Now they are finding many other activities, and higher-value-added ones, to perform there. They are also able to fully include Taiwan in nearly all aspects of their global strategies.

## Market Participation Strategies

Most MNCs have found it best to enter Taiwan through a joint venture with a local partner—for operating reasons (such as buyer-supplier relationships) or strategic reasons (such as gaining a local capital provider or partner to enter China), rather than because of investment barriers. The APROC initiative will definitely strengthen this trend.

Motorola established operations in Taiwan in 1985, with invested capital of NT$1 billion to engage in the packaging and testing of IC components. From 1994–96, Motorola invested over NT$650 million (about U.S.$20 million) in the automation of plant operations, computer integrated manufacturing, and other machinery automation projects. Moreover, Motorola will invest U.S.$3 million into alliances with several local computer manufacturers to establish a "Power PC Center," in order to reestablish its market position in the semiconductor field. In recognition of Taiwan's prowess in designing and producing high-technology products, Motorola has made its Taiwan operations one of its beachheads in the Asia-Pacific region.

Matsushita regained its marketing and distribution rights from its previous Taiwan partners in 1991, and rationalized its production-marketing operations under the new corporate umbrella of Matsushita Taiwan. It has since caught up both in sales and earnings with its competitors and is now one of the prominent foreign operation bases for Matsushita Japan in the Asia-Pacific region.

Philips was another early MNC manufacturer in Taiwan. The company established its Taiwan operation in 1966, with its black-and-white television set assembly lines. By 1996, Philips had six plants in Taiwan producing lighting, instruments, monitors, display components, integrated circuits, and passive components, making Philips the largest foreign-invested enterprise in Taiwan. Philips has expanded in Taiwan through a series of joint ventures. For example, Philips and Hwa-Shin Lien-Hwa Electronics formed a joint venture to obtain the technology to produce liquid crystal displays (LCDs). Lien-Hwa Electronics and several electric appliance manufacturers formed a new company to cooperate with the Japanese SEL company in producing STN-type LCDs. In joint production and marketing, mouse manufacturers joined in an OEM venture with a firm that possessed the technology for palm-top image scanners, to develop the global market together.

Since 1947, Toyota has worked with Taiwan's Ho-Tai Motor to sell auto parts and components. Although Toyota has had a presence in Taiwan for decades, Toyota did not have local production facilities until 1984, when it invested in Kuo-Zui Motor Company, a small local truck and bus producer. While Toyota entered the Taiwan market later than its multinational competitors, the company has achieved remarkable success based on its worldwide operating experiences. After three years of marketing efforts, Toyota ranked as the fourth largest car seller in Taiwan with a 14% market share in 1994.

Procter and Gamble has long recognized the importance of the Taiwan market. In 1985, P&G entered the Taiwan market as a joint venture, Modern Home Product Ltd., with a local company, Nan Chow Group. In 1990, P&G purchased the 50% holding of Modern Home Product owned by Nan Chow and restructured the operation to become a full subsidiary of P&G U.S.A. During the first four years of operation, P&G shifted its marketing strategy from a local focus to an increasingly global brand strategy. Although Modern Home Product was only barely profitable while a joint venture, P&G gained significant market knowledge, access to local manufacturing factories, a distribution network, and local contacts that proved vital to doing business in the Taiwan market.

In 1984, Unilever entered the Taiwan market through a 50-50 joint venture, Mavibel Taiwan Ltd., with FUIC Group, a local maker of bar soaps, detergents, and food products. Like P&G, Unilever was able to gain significant operating experience in marketing, production, financial, and R&D by working with a local company.

## Product and Service Strategies

As a newly industrialized country, Taiwan has seen an influx of foreign products vying for a share of the market. Consequently, Taiwan consumers have many choices and will buy from only those suppliers who can best market to them, sell to them, and support them if certain applications meet their needs.

Motorola supplies a global line of products and services that meet the needs of the Taiwan market. Motorola offers a full line of telecommunications-related products, such as two-way radios, paging equipment, digital communications, and information processing. The growth of the home PC market and the accompanying surge of interest in the global network of the Internet have contributed to a massive surge in demand for telecommunications products and services. Along with increasing use of local area networks (LANs), enterprise-wide networking, the explosion in the use of mobile phones, and a growing demand for services such as video-on-demand, the communications sector (like the rest of the technology market) is under immense pressure to innovate and deliver performance.

Matsushita is readjusting its strategic portfolio in Taiwan from an emphasis on the household appliance sector to major systems integration, production facilities, and equipment. The company has planned that its systems equipment sector will account for 10%, while the components and production materials sectors will account for another 40% of the sales portfolio for Matsushita Taiwan in the near future.

Of the MNCs being discussed, P&G best exemplifies the need to understand and adapt to local needs. P&G's first attempt to enter the Taiwan market was disastrous. In 1963, P&G tried to convince Taiwan consumers to buy its famous detergent brand, *Tide,* without familiarizing itself with local consumer behavior or the increasingly competitive detergent market. As a result, P&G failed and sold the plant to Kao of Japan, exiting the Taiwan market. P&G's second attempt to enter Taiwan proved more successful. Through intensive market research P&G has now achieved acceptance of its major global brands. Its major product lines, such as disposable diapers (*Pampers*), sanitary napkins (*Safe & Free*), and hair care products (*Pert Plus, Pantene, Vidal Sassoon,* and *Head & Shoulders*), are the market leaders in their relevant product categories. Moreover, P&G's global acquisition of Max Factor Cosmetics to complement its *Oil of Olay* line made the company a formidable new entrant into the fast-growing skin care market in Taiwan.

## Activity Location Strategies

To date, many MNCs have located manufacturing activities in Taiwan or sourced from local producers there. MNCs have taken advantage of the flexible manufacturing capability and innovative skills in product development accumulated by the Taiwanese to achieve regional and global economies of scale. Although many MNCs have recently chosen to move assembly and other labor-intensive activities to lower-cost countries, they have also transferred some higher-value-adding operations, some R&D, and some marketing activities to Taiwan.

Motorola uses Taiwan as part of its industry innovation strategy. In order to gain a foothold in the region of its Japanese competitors, Motorola began OEM sourcing of parts and components to take advantage of the abundant supplies of competent engineers and competitive wage levels in Taiwan. To meet these needs, Motorola set up two plants for the production of semiconductor components, telecommunications equipment, and subassemblies. The production capacity of these plants not only serves the internal demands of Motorola's downstream plants, they can also supply to other customers or even potential competitors. Despite labor costs that are three times as great as Malaysia's or seven times that of the Philippines, the technical capabilities and number of trained engineers have enabled Motorola to have a cost advantage of 30–50% lower than plants in less-developed countries in the region. In recognition of the quality of the workforce, Motorola has made Taiwan its IC design center in the region.

Matsushita follows an activity strategy similar to Motorola's. In order to take advantage of Taiwan's capabilities in machinery and system integration, Matsushita Japan will transfer its production facilities and computer-aided-manufacturing business to Taiwan. Matsushita's regard for Taiwan's capabilities has allowed its Taiwan operations to develop technologies and improve products without active supervision from Japan. For example, through its R&D efforts, Matsushita Taiwan has developed light-emitting diode (LED) panels, water-proof computerized sets, and a Chinese version of automobile guidance systems. Furthermore, Matsushita Taiwan will strengthen its reexports back to Japan and also diversify its sourcing of Japanese parts and components to take advantage of the strength of the yen relative to the New Taiwan dollar. Matsushita defines its sourcing goals as 60% from Taiwan, 20% from Japan, and 20% from other Asia-Pacific countries.

Due to the 40% appreciation of the New Taiwan dollar and the subsequent increase in the cost of labor, Philips restructured its Taiwan plants to produce advanced manufacturing technologies to improve the quality and efficiency of its operations. In 1986, Philips joined with the government of Taiwan to set up the Taiwan Semiconductor Manufacturing Corporation (TSMC) and to establish a design center for advanced chips in Taiwan. In addition to cost, there is also the issue of the breadth of technology. Through this and other alliances, Philips has gained access to research for a wider spectrum of technology innovation without bearing the entire cost.

Like many other MNCs, Toyota is considering Taiwan as a future site for R&D and design. Through its venture with Kuo-Zui Motor Co., Toyota can harness the experiences and abilities of Taiwan in the design of parts and components, and has begun to ship one hundred to two hundred sets of engines per month back to Japan. Toyota has also relocated and expanded its auto parts and components supply network in Asia by increasing purchasing from Taiwan.

In order to speed up its delivery and inventory control process, P&G Taiwan chose a local transshipment company to handle the logistics of 216 kinds of goods. Imported products are also packaged and delivered by the same company. P&G Taiwan has invested large amounts of capital and resources to help the shipment company reengineering the whole delivery process by using a computer-aided warehousing and delivery system. To further improve operational efficiency, all the goods of P&G

Taiwan, imported or made locally, are centrally located in a large warehouse located in a rural plant.

## Marketing Strategies

The keys to surviving the coming changes in Taiwan are customer focus and operational efficiency. MNCs must respond to the discriminating Taiwanese consumer with new customer service skills so that the technology choices shaping new products and services are based on identified customer needs. This company vision then needs to be implemented through competitive and aggressive marketing, sales, and proactive customer service organizations that are supported by business processes and associated systems designed to continuously improve quality and reduce operating costs (i.e., as in the most demanding markets in the world).

Toyota's marketing strategy in Taiwan includes a unified Corporate Identification System (CIS), aggressive promotion tactics, and a widespread after-service network. Event marketing has been the major marketing innovation strategy for Ho-Tai Motor. Toyota has had to adjust its marketing strategy to match lifestyle changes in Taiwan. Toyota has found that, unlike in Japan, it needs to be aware of the role of family decision-making in car purchasing as well as local sentiment against sales calls to the home. So Toyota works on attracting the entire family to come to the car showroom.

For P&G, globalization means marketing world brands, such as *Pampers* and *Oil of Olay*, with some adaptation of marketing programs to suit Taiwanese consumer needs. As P&G Taiwan grew in operational experience and P&G USA recognized Taiwan as home of some of the most discriminating consumers in the region, the country began to play an increasingly important role for the growing Far East business. For example, P&G designated Taiwan as the lead country for the launch of the *Pantene Pro-V* shampoo/conditioner line in 1990, as Taiwan was the country with the most in-market experience in Asia at that time. In the marketing process, P&G Taiwan's advertising group worked closely with its counterparts in Japan to create the marketing strategy for the rollout across Asia. At the same time, Taiwan's product development group worked closely with each of P&G's Far East businesses to coordinate packaging and production start-ups. Following the introduction of *Pantene* in Taiwan, P&G rolled out the product in other Asia-Pacific countries with great success.

Unilever, by contrast, has learned to follow a more localized approach to marketing. The company's first product introduction in Taiwan was *Timotei* shampoo. Due to gaps in the understanding of Taiwanese consumer behavior, however, *Timotei* did not reach its expected market objectives. The addition of the *Ponds* line created the need to restructure Unilever's product portfolio. The marketing of a traditional detergents line and modern health care product line contrasts the relative emphasis on volume and dollar amounts. Unilever's previous focus on volume for detergent products needed to be adjusted for the high value-added but small amounts of usage in the personal care lines.

## Competitive Move Strategies

Improved political and economic relationships between Taiwan and Mainland China have created significant flows in both trade and investment activities either directly or indirectly through holding companies in Hong Kong by Taiwanese firms. With a population of twenty-two million, Taiwan alone does not have a large enough market nor can it provide sufficient personnel to give an MNC genuine global reach. Instead, MNCs regard Taiwan as a strategic market due to the presence of global competitors, industry innovation, and access to the People's Republic of China.

Matsushita regards Taiwan as a source of industry innovation. Over the years, Matsushita Taiwan has been able to independently develop technologies and improve products without active supervision from Japan. Matsushita has also been working closely with other international competitors, such as Philips and General Electric in Taiwan, to absorb new technology and managerial experience. In terms of division of international labor in the Asia-Pacific region, Matsushita Taiwan and Singapore will produce high-end video product lines and move its lower-end line to Mainland China. Its Chinese joint venture, BMCC, will supply foreign plants in the region with TV CRTs. With China now a large market for Matsushita Japan, the company has set up close linkages and shuffled production facilities between Taiwan and China. The Matsushita plant in Xiamen in China was transshipped from Matsushita Taiwan's audio plant.

Philips incorporates Taiwan at every stage of its competitive strategy. In 1990, Philips Taiwan acquired a 59% share of Avnet (formerly a U.S.-owned company in Taiwan), renamed the venture Philips CD-ROM Technology Inc., set up a new business development center to integrate related technologies, hired staff to accelerate Philips' technology development, and set up sales offices to commercialize efforts in Taiwan and the region. The combination of the technological and marketing advantages of consumer electronics and computers will put Philips in a strong competitive position. Another project of Philips in Taiwan is the establishment of a CD-ROM multimedia laboratory to participate in the development of Chinese-version interactive CD titles to compete with Digital Video Interactive systems promoted by Apple, Intel, and IBM. In addition to Taiwan, the markets Philips will target include Singapore, Hong Kong, and other Chinese-speaking areas.

# Overall Organization and Management Approaches for Taiwan

MNCs allow their Taiwan operations a high degree of autonomy. They have utilized a number of organizational structures to meet the specific needs of their industry. Motorola, for example, follows a decentralized approach. As such, each individual division has complete autonomy in deciding when, and where, to engage in foreign investments. For example, Motorola's consumer electronics division had failed twice in attempts to enter the Taiwanese television market. But management did not prevent other divisions (semiconductor and telecommunications) from entering successfully.

The high level of education of Taiwanese executives and their familiarity with foreign practices allow most MNCs to apply global management processes to their Taiwan operations. For example, Philips is able to include Taiwan in its use of transnational teams—work groups composed of multinational members whose activities span multiple countries and enable the company to globalize or extend products and operations across international markets. Philips uses such teams primarily to help achieve global efficiency—to develop regional or worldwide cost advantages, to standardize designs and operations, and so forth. P&G, by contrast, uses transnational teams for organizational learning in order to be locally responsive. Unilever has created a transnational team charged with achieving efficiencies on a pan-Asian basis while simultaneously being responsive to the local requirements and preferences of each country. The team leader works with five marketing managers, each based in a different country, including Taiwan, to coordinate the marketing and sale of Unilever's personal care products across Asia. Much work is delegated to the team members who, after achieving consensus among themselves, propose their ideas and action plans to the leader for his review and guidance.

Projects that transnational teams generally tackle are highly complex and have considerable impact on company objectives at every level of the value chain. As such, MNCs require a strong motivation to achieve, demonstrated personal leadership, high levels of intelligence, creative flair, and strong communication skills from its members. The quality and capabilities of Taiwan's workforce has encouraged foreign MNCs to include Taiwan on their transnational teams to improve operational efficiency and expedite organizational learning.

Although the majority of employees are hired locally, the management teams of P&G Taiwan come from all around the world. Most recently, the localization of top management has been pursued aggressively. The chief executive officer for Philips Taiwan is a Taiwanese assigned in 1988. Toyota relies on its joint venture with Kuo-Zui Motor Co., to bring together consumer and operational knowledge from various parts of the company, transfer technology, and spread innovations throughout the firm.

The continued importance of Taiwan in the operations of MNCs can be attributed to the high skill level of people in Taiwan. Many of Taiwan's hottest new high-tech companies are led by Taiwanese engineers and scientists who have returned from working overseas, especially from America. P&G Taiwan has been able to attract top talented people from both the local and overseas Chinese communities. Following the P&G philosophy that people are its most important asset, P&G Taiwan has implemented a promotion-from-within system. The basic belief of Matsushita Taiwan is that people should be placed before production of goods. Continuous training until the employees leave the company is their major policy.

## Conclusion

In summary, Taiwan's competitive advantages for MNCs in the Asia-Pacific region lie in the following characteristics:

- strategic geographical location with extensive Chinese linkages within the Asia-Pacific region
- high-caliber technical expertise important for supporting high-quality production and technology transfer within the region
- hard-working and well-educated labor
- adequate market demand throughout the complete value-added chain in many industrial sectors
- a small but highly affluent consumer market

MNCs that have made use of these advantages have benefited greatly. For the future, Taiwan is an economy in transition toward developed status. MNCs need to adjust their activities accordingly.

### NOTES

1. "Situation Analysis of Bi-lateral Trade between Taiwan and Mainland China," (Taipei: Board of Foreign Trade, 1996). Data were collected from Taiwan and Hong Kong customs bureaus.

2. *Essential Economic Indicators* (Taipei: Council for Economic Planning and Development, 1997).

3. Various issues of "Annals of Overseas Chinese and Foreign Investments, Technical Cooperation, Direct Foreign Investment, and Outward Technical Cooperation," (Taipei: Investment Review Commission, Ministry of Economic Affairs).

4. "Taiwan 1000," Special Issue, *Common Wealth,* June 5, 1995.

5. *Asian-Oceanian Information Technology Industry Report,* (Taipei: Market Intelligence Center [MIC], Institute for Information Industry [III], 1996).

6. Ibid.

7. Various issues of "Annals of Indirect Investments Towards Mainland China, Technical Cooperation, Direct Foreign Investment, and Outward Technical Cooperation," (Taipei: Investment Review Commission, Ministry of Economic Affairs).

8. *Progress Report on APROC Initiative,* (Taipei: Bureau of Industrial Development, 1997).

# CHAPTER 6

# Hong Kong—A New Role

*Kam-hon Lee and George S. Yip*

"To see how the free market really works," said Milton Friedman, "Hong Kong is the place to come."[1] This is high praise for a spot that the British government considered a barren rock suitable only as a typhoon shelter. Although Hong Kong's fate after its return to China in 1997, remains uncertain, its prospects appear bright due to the resilience and pragmatism of the Hong Kong people, as well as its strategic importance in sustaining China's rapid economic development. On the other hand, as of late 1997, Hong Kong was reeling from the 40% drop in stock market values in October 1997 and the accompanying pressure on its fixed exchange rate. But Hong Kong has survived previous bouts of stock market volatility. Our analysis of Hong Kong, using the globalization framework of this book, shows that any negative changes in globalization drivers post-1997, are likely to be offset by the many other globalization drivers that will not change or even become more favorable from the viewpoint of multinational companies (MNCs). Furthermore, it is scarcely possible anymore to analyze Hong Kong independently of China given the former's high level of economic integration with the latter.[2]

## Background

The story of Hong Kong used to be entirely about economics. Indeed, one explanation of Hong Kong's economic success is that its inhabitants have not been able to spend any time on politics. Today, MNCs also need to consider politics in both Hong Kong and China.

### The Effects of 1997

China ceded Hong Kong to Britain in 1842. On July 1, 1997, Hong Kong ceased to be a Crown Colony of the United Kingdom but became a Special Administrative Region of the People's Republic of China. This change was arranged by the Joint Declaration of 1983. That agreement triggered a new phase of economic activity. The business community expected at least ten to fifteen years of stability until China assumed control, not counting China's promise to Hong Kong of fifty years of autonomous rule. Combined with China's commitment to an open-door policy, its low labor costs (about one-tenth of those in Hong Kong), and cheap land and rental charges, the economic optimism attracted Hong Kong investment dollars into the mainland. Hong Kong manufacturers relocated many production sites to special economic zones and the Pearl River Delta in China. Textile and clothing, electronics, and other labor-intensive industries all began to move their factories across the border. Despite infrastructure and other logistical problems, manufacturers benefited from relocating their production operations.

Despite China's promise of fifty years of autonomous rule, the cloud of uncertainty hovering over 1997 caused concern in Hong Kong. Although the general population counted on a long period of stability before 1997, many considered immigration in order to secure a future for their families. In general, the well-to-do were the first to move abroad. Canada and Australia were two popular destinations, while the United States was the only country in the world to discourage wealthy immigrants (e.g., even a U.S.$1 million investment did not automatically secure an immigration visa for a wealthy applicant).

Political development in Hong Kong became increasingly active after 1984. Encouraged by the British government, direct election activities rose, and the democracy movement was perceived as another form of guarantee against China's oppression following 1997. The democratic movement aggravated Sino-Anglo relations concerning Hong Kong. The Chinese government repeatedly refused to recognize political reforms suggested by Hong Kong without China's prior approval and input. China threatened to remove the entire political structure in Hong Kong after 1997, and replace it with a structure based on the Basic Law (written by China to serve as Hong Kong's post-1997 constitution). This stance generated substantial concern in the Hong Kong citizenry. On July 1, 1997, China replaced the popularly elected legislature with a new "provisional" legislature and chief executive, Tung Chee-hwa.

Despite the substantial economic benefits, there are also significant costs to Hong Kong from its relationship with China. Its open border with Guangdong Province has increased the flow of Chinese guns southward into what was once an almost gun-free city. Stolen cars from Hong Kong are quickly smuggled north as contraband. The incidence of corruption, commonplace in China, will rise in Hong Kong. Powerful Chinese political officials and businesspeople often extract fees and kickbacks in exchange for special favors and preferential treatment. These practices will increasingly migrate southward after 1997. The most critical concerns stem from China's repressive political system and heavy-handed control of information. It is this uncertainty about China's intentions for Hong Kong that clouds the horizon of this former "Jewel in the (British) Crown." What is certain, however, is that Hong Kong's fate is inextricably tied to the giant to the north, an entity whose own future remains to be seen.

## Economic Performance

Hong Kong is a vibrant economy driven by capitalism and the unabashed pursuit of material wealth. A recent *Fortune* magazine survey of more than five hundred international corporate executives ranked Hong Kong as the best city in the world for business, ahead of New York and London. In 1993, according to GATT, Hong Kong ranked fifth in total exports, after the European Union, the United States, Japan, and Canada. China ranked sixth. Economic development in Hong Kong was at its peak towards the end of the 1970s and the beginning of the 1980s. Driven by the accumulation of wealth and the influence of Hong Kong businesspeople over the years, combined with China's open-door policy, overwhelming optimism permeated the Hong Kong business community.

The per capita and total GNP in Hong Kong have maintained consistent growth, while population growth has been under control. While exports as a percentage of GDP has always exceeded 100%, exports and imports have approximated one another over the years. Hong Kong has been an active and effective participant in the world economy. Although Hong Kong lags behind Japan in terms of nominal per capita GNP, Hong Kong leads Japan in terms of purchasing power parity per capita GNP, and lags behind the United States (the richest country in the world) by less than 15%. In this respect, Hong Kong may be a crystal ball into the future development of affluent Asian countries. For example, a leading authority in retailing,[3] recently visiting the Pacific Place Shopping Mall in Hong Kong together with one of the coauthors, noted a twenty-first century retailing setting well ahead of what one could find in the United States.

From the 1950s to about 1980, Hong Kong was a prime location for low-cost manufacturing. The "Made in Hong Kong" label used to attach to cheap toys, plastic flowers, electrical goods, and the like. All this has migrated to China and the rest of Asia. But employment has continued to increase. Before the opening to China, Hong Kong firms never employed more than about nine hundred thousand industrial workers. In 1996, they employed an estimated five million. Hong Kong's manufacturing role has expanded almost fivefold, but the work has moved upstream to management, design, and finance. Today, Hong Kong imports labor: including blue collar workers from China, household workers from the Philippines, and even young waiters, bartenders, and construction laborers from underemployed Britain, as well as legions of American and European MBAs, bankers, and lawyers. But the continuing cost gap with China may soon cause some unemployment among less-skilled Hong Kong workers.

## Hong Kong As A Global Financial Center

A key feature of Hong Kong is the role it plays as a major global financial center, thereby making business much easier for foreign MNCs. Hong Kong is globally ranked in several financial areas: third by the number of banks present, fourth by the number of offshore loans originated, and fourth by the capitalization of its stock market. With its advanced communications infrastructure, lack of political repression and interference, lack of restrictive financial and information controls, Hong Kong is strongly positioned to maintain its role as a premier global financial center in Asia.[4] Given the Hong Kong economy's historical reliance on international trade, it is not surprising that its financial markets have also developed and grown to be global powerhouses. Hong Kong is a funding center and a financial intermediary, funneling funds from outside its market area toward regional uses. As an international banking center, nineteen of the twenty largest banks in the world maintained full-fledged licensed banks in Hong Kong in 1989 (most coming from the United States and Japan).

The Hong Kong government has made two key policy decisions that have spurred the growth of the financial markets. The first occurred in 1982, when the government abolished the withholding tax on interest earned from foreign currency deposits. This led to a dramatic increase in foreign currency deposits in the Hong Kong banking system. The percentage of currency deposits out of total deposits soared. From 1982–89, it grew over 650%.[5]

The second policy decision was the bold move to peg the Hong Kong dollar to the U.S. dollar in 1983. This effectively stripped any control the government might have over interest rates and levels of foreign reserves. The benefits were immediate, however: increased confidence in Hong Kong financial markets, and added stability and fixed-rate convertibility to the Hong Kong currency. This decision complemented the government's "hands-off" policy and maintained a certain level of confidence in the financial system during periods of political strain. Of course, the government's traditional policy of budgetary surpluses provided the resources to maintain the fixed exchange rate.[6] Together, these two policies increased both liquidity and confidence in the financial markets. As a result, funds from abroad flowed more easily into Hong Kong for investment in the rapidly growing Asia-Pacific region.

But the peg to the U.S. dollar has been under intense pressure ever since the summer 1997 collapse of many other Asian currencies. Both the Hong Kong and Chinese governments have pledged to defend the peg, using their combined foreign exchange reserves of over U.S.$200 billion. Nevertheless, speculators continue to circle the Hong Kong dollar, looking for signs of weakness or lack of government resolve.

Other Asian cities, however, like Bangkok, Taipei, and Singapore, are positioning their markets to challenge Hong Kong's dominance. What these rivals lack are Hong Kong's access to, and concentration of, bankers, accountants, lawyers, and computer services. Singapore, the most likely challenger, lacks the critical mass of such skills. The Singapore government's tight controls on the press and stringent business regulations make it less attractive to the information-intensive, freewheeling financial industries that headquarter in Hong Kong.[7] In addition, Hong Kong possesses a larger and more active gold and equity market, making it more attractive to foreign fund managers and investors.[8] China is also promoting Shanghai as an alternative financial center, but this development will take substantial time for the reasons mentioned above: tight government controls and lack of financial expertise. In addition, a giant like China will require more than just one financial center, just as Japan has Osaka and Tokyo, and the United States has New York and Chicago.[9] Furthermore, Singapore is a funding center, while Hong Kong is a lending center, since countries surrounding Singapore (e.g., Malaysia and Indonesia) are not able to absorb all the funds in the Asian dollar market. Hong Kong, therefore, channels funds from the Asian dollar market to countries like South Korea, Taiwan, Australia, and China.[10]

With its liberal government, low tax rate, simple tax structure, and proximity to the financially hungry Chinese market, Hong Kong has risen to become one of the four global financial centers (along with New York, London, and Tokyo). The freedom granted by the local government may not last, however, if China chooses to intervene. Another question concerns whether China will at some date take over Hong Kong's very large foreign currency reserves (about U.S.$70 billion at the handover in 1997) and eliminate the Hong Kong dollar. Key officials from the Hong Kong Monetary Authority and the People's Bank of China have made repeated efforts to reassure the international financial community.[11] Effectiveness of these efforts remains to be seen.

Hong Kong will also be at the mercy of political uncertainty in China. When the World Bank and foreign commercial banks suspended new loans to China after the Tiananmen uprising in 1989, Hong Kong's financial markets were badly shaken. Hong Kong will continue to be buffeted by future political crises (including rising inflation) in China, as the latter has become one of its (and Asia's) biggest borrowers. If the Chinese government allows the financial markets substantial autonomy, however, Hong Kong's financial market will likely continue to thrive.

## Foreign Participation in the Economy

Hong Kong has attracted a great deal of foreign manufacturing investment, and has been a strategic locale for MNCs to locate regional headquarters and offices. According to a 1994 Industry Department survey, the value of foreign investments in Hong Kong's manufacturing industries have increased steadily in the past ten years.[12] According to a separate survey in 1994, the Industry Department determined that there were 714 regional headquarters and 1,132 regional offices operating in Hong Kong. In terms of the number of regional headquarters, the leading countries of origin were the United States (50%), Japan (13%), and the United Kingdom (13%).

## Hong Kong Firms

The twenty largest Hong Kong-based companies are of significant international stature and operate primarily in the areas of real estate and development, telecommunications, utilities, and banking (Table 6.1). Ac-

**Table 6.1**
**Largest Hong Kong Companies**[a]

| Rank | Company | Main Business | 1994 Market Capitalization U.S.$ billions |
|------|---------|---------------|-------------------------------------------|
| 1 | HSBC Holdings | banking | 28.5 |
| 2 | Hong Kong Telecom | telecommunications | 23.7 |
| 3 | Hutchison Whampoa | diversified, telecommunications, ports | 14.5 |
| 4 | Sun Hung Ki Properties | property | 13.8 |
| 5 | Hang Seng Bank | banking | 13.7 |
| 6 | Swire Pacific | diversified, trading | 9.0 |
| 7 | Cheung Kong (Holdings) | property | 8.9 |
| 8 | China Light | utility | 8.4 |
| 9 | Henderson Land | property | 7.6 |
| 10 | Wharf (Holdings) | diversified, trading, shipping | 7.3 |
| 11 | Hongkong Electric | utility | 5.5 |
| 12 | Hongkong Land Holdings | property | 5.2 |
| 13 | Jardine Matheson Holdings | diversified, trading | 5.1 |
| 14 | CITIC Pacific | investments | 4.8 |
| 15 | New World Development | property | 4.2 |
| 16 | Cathay Pacific Airways | airline | 4.1 |
| 17 | Hopewell Holdings | infrastructure | 3.6 |
| 18 | Wheelock and Company | diversified, trading | 3.3 |
| 19 | Hong Kong & China Gas | utility | 3.3 |
| 20 | Jardine Strategic Holdings | property, hotels, retail | 3.1 |

*Source:* Hong Kong Stock Exchange, *The Stock Exchange Fact Book 1994.*
[a]Based on market capitalization in 1994.

cording to a 1995 Business Week survey, all of these companies rate in the Global 1,000. Some of the very largest Hong Kong-based firms have moved registrations and stock listings elsewhere. For example, Hong Kong Bank (HSBC Holdings) is listed in Britain, Hong Kong Land in Singapore, and Jardine Matheson in Bermuda. Their operational bases, however, remain in Hong Kong.

## Overall Globalization Drivers for Hong Kong

Hong Kong has highly favorable market, government, and competitive globalization drivers. Its government drivers will deteriorate somewhat post-1997. Hong Kong, on its own, has mostly unfavorable cost drivers, but these become highly favorable when southern China is added as Hong Kong's hinterland (similar to the relationship between Los Angeles and Mexico or Berlin and Poland). Hong Kong and Guangdong province together comprise an entity of seventy million people speaking a common language, Cantonese.

## Market Globalization Drivers

Although it has a small population of only six million, Hong Kong's GNP of U.S.$144 million in 1995 compares favorably with that of much larger countries—Thailand's U.S.$159 million and Indonesia's U.S.$189 million. Furthermore, Hong Kong's typical import ratio of about 130% of GNP makes it an even larger market. Indeed, Hong Kong is the second largest importer (and exporter) in Asia-Pacific, behind only Japan.

An affluent and Westernized customer base demands the latest Western goods and technology. Consumer trends are similar to those of Japan for fashion, electronics, packaged goods, and durable goods. Perhaps the best example of globally common customer needs is the rapid acceptance of the mobile telephone in Hong Kong. In one decade, Hong Kong has become the most competitive and demanding mobile phone market in the world. With its long history of exposure to Western culture and ideas, Hong Kong poses few limits to transferable marketing. Of course, MNCs must be sensitive to the local Chinese culture, especially in the transliteration of Western brand names and advertisements.

In some industries, Hong Kong has also become a lead market. Hong Kong has become a major fashion design center and, along with Japan, sets the standard for rapid adoption and adaptation of Western trends and fads. The latest movies and popular music from Hong Kong are readily consumed in other Asian countries. Perhaps most important, Hong Kong culture has a huge influence over the billion-person market in China.

Hong Kong's entwining with China also makes it a major regional and global sourcing center for MNCs seeking products made in China, particularly in the contiguous Chinese province of Guangdong. In itself, Hong Kong is a major sourcing and distribution center for the garment industry, and a major financial services center. Lastly, Hong Kong's superb transportation links attract many MNCs to set up regional and global distribution centers.

These favorable market globalization drivers can only improve after the 1997 change of regime.

## Cost Globalization Drivers

Hong Kong's cost globalization drivers are now its weak point. The cost of doing business in Hong Kong ranks among the highest in the world. Limited land combined with high demand for office space and housing has driven rent up to Tokyo and Manhattan levels. Low unemployment levels have driven up wages, and are not likely to go down anytime soon. As shown in Table 1.7 in Chapter 1, Hong Kong has the worst labor situation in Asia relative to cost, availability, and turnover. This is balanced, however, by a hard-working, productive, and educated work force. This labor situation makes Hong Kong more suited to performing high-value-added tasks and professional services.

Hong Kong, in itself, also offers very limited scope for sourcing efficiencies. Despite its developed transportation infrastructure, the scarcity of raw materials greatly limits Hong Kong's scope as a source of production inputs. One exception is Hong Kong's excellence in design, and its expertise in managing and financing the manufacturing and flow of goods. For example, Hong Kong is a global player in the sourcing and distribution of low-end apparel.

Logistics are Hong Kong's strong point in cost globalization drivers. Hong Kong is served by a highly efficient and modern transportation system, which is constantly upgraded to keep pace with economic development. Hong Kong is surpassed only by the United States and Japan in the volume of shipping container throughput handled in its port. With one of the best natural harbors in the world (its name means "fragrant harbor"), Hong Kong's shipping ports and distribution facilities are some of the best in the world. It is a major entrepôt and nexus for regional and global shipping. A new port is being built to augment the increasing flow of goods through Hong Kong. Its new airport at Chek Lap Kok, due to open in 1998, will alleviate the territory's one weak point in transportation. Inside Hong Kong, foreign executives may notice the heavy traffic jams, but the city's general population is well served by its public transportation system of subways, tunnels, ferries, and buses.

With a small population and lack of local high-technology industries, Hong Kong will continue to play a limited technological role. To help offset this problem, the government founded the new Hong Kong University of Science and Technology (HKUST), which opened in October 1991. HKUST has the mission to become "the M.I.T. of Asia."

The return to China in 1997 should not have any direct effect on these cost globalization drivers, other than making Hong Kong even more part of the China-Hong Kong "double diamond,"[13] giving it greater access to China's favorable cost globalization drivers.

## Government Globalization Drivers

Hong Kong's government globalization drivers have been the most favorable in the world for business in general and MNCs in particular. These drivers combine completely open trade, low taxes, and minimal government intervention in business on the one hand with a strong legal and social system (e.g., subsidized public housing, education, and medical care), a highly efficient civil service, and total political stability on the other. All of these drivers face some risk in the post-1997 regime.

Hong Kong's trade policies are extremely open. Its economy is heavily dependent on foreign trade—with both exports and imports exceeding 100% of GNP (Table 1.8 in Chapter 1). Hong Kong has a free-trade economy, with no tariffs imposed on imported goods. It is not a member of any trade groupings, but is a member of the World Trade Organization. With totally free trade, Hong Kong has not felt the need to join any of the Asian trade blocs.

Almost unique in the world, let alone in Asia, the government does not try to protect local industry from foreign competitors. With the possible exception of Hong Kong Telecom's monopoly on international telephone calls, and the Hong Kong Jockey Club's monopoly on legal gambling, the Hong Kong government does not guard particular sectors of the economy. For example, in mobile telephones, the government welcomes the entry of global players to maintain Hong Kong's competitive market. So Hong Kong lacks the problem of government-owned or sponsored competitors to foreign MNCs. But this will change post-1997. Government-owned or connected enterprises from China are increasingly setting up business or acquiring companies in Hong Kong. Indeed, China is actively encouraging its largest state-owned enterprises to invest in Hong Kong. Table 6.2 lists the Chinese concerns most active in Hong Kong.

The most worrying case of Chinese government intervention in Hong Kong business concerns what some observers believe to be the forced sale by Swire Pacific (one of Hong Kong's largest companies) to Chinese entities of equity in the two airlines that Swire controls.[14] In April 1996, Swire Pacific announced an agreement to sell to Citic Pacific, the Hong Kong arm of China's main investment vehicle, a further 15% of the equity of Cathay Pacific Airways, Hong Kong's global air carrier and one of the most successful in the world, raising Citic's stake to 35%, and reducing Swire's stake to 43.9%, from 52.6%. In addition, Swire and other owners agreed to sell 35.9% of Dragonair, Hong Kong's leading regional carrier, to China National Aviation Corporation (CNAC). Many believe this agreement was made to ward off CNAC's threat to set up a rival carrier, China Hong Kong Airlines. Furthermore, analysts believe the sales were at prices discounted 15% to 20% from the real values.

The Hong Kong government makes no distinction between local and foreign companies, and it welcomes investment from both. There are no exchange controls, capital and profits can be freely repatriated, and there are very few restrictions on foreign investment. Again, unlike most of the rest of Asia, the Hong Kong government has no formal program or agenda for technology transfer. As a developed economy with strong communications and distribution infrastructures, Hong Kong has ready access to the latest technological advances. In some cases, Hong Kong is the regional design center for high-technology firms, including Motorola. As there is no "Chinese standard" in most areas of technology, Hong Kong readily adopts standards developed elsewhere. In the case of mobile phones, Hong Kong has in place three competing technical standards developed in the United States and Europe.

Hong Kong has consistently practiced a stable tax policy. Taxation for individuals has to date been 15% and for corporations 16.5%. Furthermore, the same taxation rates apply for foreign as well as local individuals and corporations. And, of course, there are absolutely no restrictions on the movement of capital and currency.

Generally, the legal system of Hong Kong follows that of the United Kingdom and continues to do so. The application of English Law Ordinance provides that the common law of England and the rules of equity shall be in force in Hong Kong so far as they are applicable to the circumstances of Hong Kong or its inhabitants. Hong Kong has a long

*Table 6.2*

**Chinese State-Owned Companies Most Active in Hong Kong**

| Company | Structure | Activity in Hong Kong | Sector |
|---|---|---|---|
| Bank of China Group (HK) | 100%-owned by the Bank of China | No Hong Kong listing | banking, finance |
| China Travel Service (HK) | 100%-owned by the Overseas Chinese Affairs Office | Owns 75% of Hong Kong-listed China Travel International Investment (HK) | travel, property |
| China Merchants Holdings | 100%-owned by the Ministry of Communications | Owns 65% of Hong Kong-listed China Merchants Hai Nong | shipping, finance, property |
| China Resources (Holdings) | 100%-owned by the Ministry of Foreign Trade and Economic Cooperation | Owns 57% of Hong-Kong-listed China Resources Enterprises | import/export, property, retail |
| China Everbright Group | 100%-owned by China's State Council | Owns 24% of Hong Kong-listed China Everbright International | property, invest-ment, retail |
| Citic Hong Kong | 100%-owned by China International Trust & Investment Corporation | Owns 45% of Hong Kong-listed Citic Pacific | property, trading, transport |
| Shougang Holdings HK | 100%-owned by Beijing-based Capital Iron & Steel Corporation | Owns 5 Hong Kong-listed companies including 49%-owned Shougang Concord International Enterprises | property, ship-ping, metals trading |
| Shanghai Industrial Investment Holdings | 100%-owned by Shanghai municipal government | Plans for Hong Kong listing | highway projects, property invest-ment, packaging |
| China Overseas Holdings | 100%-owned by China State Construction & Engineering Corp. | Owns 75% of Hong Kong-listed China Overseas Land and Investment | residential and commercial property devel-oper and con-tractor |
| Guangdong Enterprises Holdings | 100%-owned by Guangdong government | Owns 45% of Hong Kong-listed Guangdong Investment | infrastructure, tourism, trans-port |

*Source:* Bruce Gilley, "Great Leap Southward," *Far Eastern Economic Review*, November 23, 1995, 60–61.

history of practicing and enforcing modern Western business laws and judicial ideals. The official language of the courts has been English. There is an intention to use Chinese more and more as the official language after 1997. Beginning in February 1996, district courts could use Chinese to conduct hearings. However, that would be possible only when the judge and the lawyers could all use Chinese. Thus, in reality, there were very few cases using Chinese as the medium to conduct a hearing. It is expected to take a long time before Chinese can become a commonly used official language of the courts. One key transition issue is that the court of final appeal will no longer be in Britain, but a local supreme court of five judges, of whom only one can be a foreign citizen. This issue caused one of the major disagreements between Britain and China in the transition phase, being settled in the latter's favor. So there are now concerns as to how independent this supreme court can be.

The Hong Kong government believes in the protection of copyrights, trademarks, and intellectual property. Although a black market exists for pirated software (a CD-ROM copy of Microsoft's Windows 97, complete with photocopied manual, can be purchased on the street for about U.S.$10), music, and videotapes, these abuses are not nearly so rampant as those in China and other countries with undeveloped legal and enforcement systems. Lastly, marketing regulations in Hong Kong are similar to those practiced in Western countries.

Clearly, it is Hong Kong's highly favorable government globalization drivers that may be affected by the 1997 change. Among these drivers, that of "absence of state-owned competitors" will definitely deteriorate. Others may not change, although most observers predict some gradual deterioration. One study by a group of political scientists at the Hoover Institution in the United States predicts a worsening of press freedom, judicial independence, and overall autonomy for Hong Kong.[15] In contrast, China's officials promote the view of no change: "the horses will continue running; the dancing will continue" (in Cantonese, *mah jiu paau; mouh jiu tiuh*).[16] A recent book by some Harvard-related authors also takes a very positive view of Hong Kong's prospects.[17]

## Competitive Globalization Drivers

One primary competitive globalization driver spurs MNCs to participate in Hong Kong: its global and regional strategic importance. Although not a significant market by itself, Hong Kong is a major node within the Asian trading network. With an enormous market to its north, commitment to free trade, highly developed communications infrastructure, and strong financial market, Hong Kong is a strategic staging area for doing business in Asia. The 1997 change will make this driver stronger. The only weakening may come from some MNCs moving their regional headquarters out of Hong Kong (discussed below), thereby reducing the quality and atmosphere of world-class competition.

# Overall Global Strategies for Hong Kong

Perhaps more than for any other Asia-Pacific economy, the appropriate MNC strategies for Hong Kong are fairly clear cut. MNCs should participate in this small but lucrative market by selling globally standardized products and services, treat Hong Kong as a gateway to China, and locate management there rather than production activities.

## Market Participation Strategies

Although small in population, Hong Kong can provide quite a lucrative market in itself, given its very high per capita GNP, and its very high propensity to import. Thus, many MNCs eagerly market their products and services in the territory, particularly given the little adaptation they need to undertake. Also, with one of the world's highest proportions of millionaires to population, Hong Kong is a highly attractive market for most purveyors of luxury goods and services—as companies like Rolls Royce, Mercedes Benz, Rolex, Rémy Martin, and Louis Vuitton have found. In financial services, the combination of affluence and fear of the future also makes Hong Kong a prime market for overseas banking and investment services. As a market, Hong Kong also plays a role as a gateway to China. Many foreign products make their way into China from Hong Kong, first indirectly by being carried in by visitors from Hong Kong, then directly after demand has been created by the first route.

A good strategy for MNCs is to become the local leader to compete regionally. As an affluent and educated Chinese society, Hong Kong is the trendsetter for many East Asian countries. MNCs have leveraged success and leadership in the Hong Kong market to increase product exposure in nearby countries. Quite often, acceptance and success in Hong Kong boosts overall regional sales. For this reason, Toyota seeks to dominate the Hong Kong car market. Despite its wealth and developed economy, Hong Kong has only five cars per one hundred people, far lower than that in the United States (ninety-five cars), Japan (fifty cars), and many other countries (twenty-five to thirty-five cars). This is due to its lack of space and dense residential development. In consequence, car registrations in 1995 were only about 300,000. Nevertheless, Hong Kong is Toyota's showroom for many countries in Asia. Toyota's annual car sales in Hong Kong has ranged only from ten thousand to twenty thousand negligible figures relative to its annual worldwide sales of forty to fifty million cars. As the leading automaker in Hong Kong, however, its market share is approximately 29%, a superb performance within the Toyota family. It is the high market share that pleases Toyota's top executives and places Toyota in the limelight of this affluent, trendsetting market. As a lead market, Hong Kong can also be useful for testing and introducing new products. Toyota finds that new cars introduced and accepted in Hong Kong tend to succeed in other Asian countries as well.

Participation in Hong Kong also provides a gateway to China. Foreign companies pursuing business in China depend on Hong Kong to provide or channel technology, capital, management know-how, and ideas. Hong Kong investment dollars dominate China's special economic zones, and China's major ports are heavily staffed by Hong Kong managers. China's open-door policy has only increased relations with foreigners and, therefore, increased the need for Hong Kong as a gateway between East and West.[18]

## Product and Service Strategies

MNCs can clearly sell global products and services in Hong Kong with little adaptation. MNCs have successfully sold products there developed for Western markets, including consumer packaged goods and high-technology products. Hong Kong's affluent consumer base and exposure to Western culture minimizes the need to make local adaptations. For example, both Procter and Gamble and Unilever sell global products in Hong Kong. Neither company considers Hong Kong to be a globally significant market and do not adapt their products specifically for Hong Kong. But both companies typically use Asian formulas and products sourced within the region. Furthermore, as a small market, Hong Kong's unit advertising costs are high relative to larger markets, and there exists limited incentive to perform major product launches just for this small, mature market. On the other end, many companies introduce new products already launched elsewhere. Philips performs only minor product adaptations for the Hong Kong market and finds global products to be readily accepted. Toyota does not make adaptations to its automobile models for the Hong Kong market. In general, Hong Kong is quite receptive to globally standardized products and services, but with some exceptions. For example, television sets in Hong Kong are primarily black or gray while those in other countries may be quite colorful.

## Activity Location Strategies

Due to its limited market potential and high costs, most MNCs maintain only limited operations in Hong Kong to support the local market. Hong Kong's real role in MNCs' activity value chains is to be the manager of manufacturing in southern China and elsewhere in Asia. Motorola's manufacturing base in Hong Kong has shifted to support the southern Chinese market. Electronics is the second most important industry in Hong Kong, and although a market for semiconductors exists, saturation is a problem. The Hong Kong market pales in comparison with the market to the north. For Motorola, Hong Kong is a technological gateway to the vast Chinese market.

The Silicon Harbour Center, established in 1990, is the Asia-Pacific Headquarters for Motorola Semiconductor Products Group. Semiconductors are its primary business line in Hong Kong, employing about three thousand people. Motorola's other business lines employ a total of approximately five hundred people. Motorola also uses Hong Kong as its regional design center. The Silicon Harbor Center supports other centers in Singapore and Taiwan, and is the heart of the Asia-Pacific region in design expertise. Hong Kong is also important for intermediate and final production, assembly, marketing, sales, distribution, and customer service. In terms of Motorola's manufacturing activities, however, Hong Kong is most important for design. Engineers, professionals, and technical support staff comprise approximately 70% of Motorola's Hong Kong personnel. Hong Kong's expensive land, rental prices, and salary levels will continue to force local manufacturing activities to become more high-value-added.

Both P&G and Unilever have limited operations in Hong Kong. These two companies maintain only marketing, selling, and distribution operations there to support the local market. On the other hand, until its China operations were fully established, P&G used Hong Kong as a training ground for China. In addition, executives often commute north from Hong Kong to provide marketing support to the Chinese operations. P&G does not manufacture in Hong Kong, and sources products from other countries (China, Taiwan, Japan, etc.). P&G chooses its suppliers depending on exchange rates, delivery schedules, and other factors. P&G Hong Kong has sourced from China in the past, but currently sources from many other countries: Japan, South Korea, Taiwan, Thailand, Australia, France, and the United States. P&G Hong Kong may be integrated as part of the overall China operation after 1997. For Unilever, China has become increasingly open, its Hong Kong operation has been integrated into the larger Chinese market and may play a prominent role servicing the southern Chinese market.

Toyota does not manufacture in Hong Kong. Toyota cars sold in Hong Kong are all Japanese-made, but are widely accepted there. Since its Hong Kong operations are basically for distribution, global activities include only marketing, selling, distribution, and customer service. The high quality and success of its distribution operation has led Toyota to single out Hong Kong as its leading market and regional showroom in Asia.

With the rise of China as a manufacturing base and market, Hong Kong may one day be able to support world-class firms. Until now, the Hong Kong market was too small to support the kinds of world-class firms that characterize Japan (such as Sony or Fujitsu) and South Korea (such as Hyundai or Lucky-Goldstar). Hong Kong-based firms, such as Cheung Kong (real estate), Hutchison (satellite television, ports, mobile phone systems), and Hopewell (builder of infrastructure) are rapidly becoming world-class firms in their industries. As China-based companies set up international operations in Hong Kong and leverage it as a center to commercialize their broad base of scientific research, Hong Kong may grow into a center of globally recognized firms and brand names.[19]

Many MNCs also use Hong Kong as an Asian regional center (discussed in the organization section below). Some MNCs utilize Hong

Kong as a regional center for both product design and technical support for China and the Asian region.

## Marketing Strategies

Hong Kong is very open to global marketing. So MNCs make few adjustments to their marketing techniques and procedures from other markets. They do this for two reasons: they must for economic reasons—Hong Kong is a small market, and because they can—and Hong Kong consumers have readily adopted many Western goods and services. In addition, Hong Kong is well served by marketing support companies such as advertising agencies and market researchers.

P&G maintains a local marketing staff that reapplies global or regional marketing success models to Hong Kong. There are two primary determinants of success for P&G in Hong Kong. First, the company depends on a relatively small number of key retail chains (including Wellcome, Park 'n Shop, Watson's and Manning). As a result, P&G has less control over product pricing than in the United States where multiple retailers compete. Secondly, P&G has to source from other countries such as Japan and South Korea. So P&G also has less control over its cost of goods sold. Philips considers Hong Kong a developed market. For Philips, the marketing environment in Hong Kong is similar to other developed economies.

Hong Kong's markets have been dominated by foreign brands. Almost no local brands have achieved recognition outside Hong Kong, with the exception of the airline Cathay Pacific. One Hong Kong entrepreneur, David Tang, is seeking to build a premium Hong Kong-based brand that is, paradoxically, named "Shanghai Tang." This brand applies to Tang's department stores, lines of apparel, and related items. David Tang has also created a new type of "Made in" label. Instead of "Made in Hong Kong" or "Made in China," the Shanghai Tang labels say "Made by Chinese."

## Competitive Move Strategies

With a relatively small market, Hong Kong does not play a major role for competitive moves by MNCs. The Chinese market, however, makes Hong Kong significant in the areas of financing, human resources, and routing of trade (sourcing, shipping, etc.). Where MNCs do strive to compete in the local market, they typically strive to offer the very best in products or services. For example, Motorola's local design center ranks among the very best in the Asia-Pacific region and enables Motorola to work closely with its customers to meet specifications. Toyota excels in customer service and post-sales service. It offers a one-stop shopping experience where customers can obtain in-house financing, insurance, and motor club memberships. Perhaps most important, success in Hong Kong brings significant "bragging rights" in China.

# Overall Organization and Management Approaches for Hong Kong

Befitting this territory's history, management and organizational processes in Hong Kong are an amalgam of British, American, Chinese, and Japanese approaches. More than in other Asian countries, MNCs have found it relatively easy to implement their style of management. Indeed, it is local companies, with their tradition of autocratic entrepreneurialism that are finding it difficult to make the transition to professional management. An exception is Li and Fung, now headed by second-generation brothers, one of whom is a former Harvard Business School professor. The traditional British firms are also changing. Jardine Matheson, the British company that more or less founded Hong Kong, now has an American heading its most important sector, Jardine Pacific.

## Organization Structures

With few constraints on organizational structures from the government or the local work force, most MNCs maintain a global corporate culture in Hong Kong. Local managers take pride in embracing the company-specific culture and implement it as fully as possible in Hong Kong. Since Hong Kong is known for its flexible and friendly position toward different cultures, there is little need to adapt the corporate culture to the Hong Kong work force.

Increasingly, MNCs have integrated or shifted their Hong Kong operations to support growth in China. For those companies who have not done so, their Hong Kong operations will likely play a decreasing role in the overall regional corporate organization, perhaps in anticipation of unification in 1997.

Hong Kong has played a key role as a regional headquarters for MNCs. Most major firms require one headquarters in Tokyo and another in non-Japan Asia. As well as being major financial centers, Hong Kong and Singapore have tax and other incentives that attract businesses: Hong Kong with its cultural and entertainment opportunities, and Singapore with its peaceful physical and social environment. The most recent regional survey indicated that Hong Kong held 51% of Pacific Asia's regional headquarters, Singapore 29%, and Tokyo 20%.[20]

One factor that may hinder Hong Kong's continuing attraction as a regional headquarters for MNCs is China's possible rejection of Hong Kong's tradition of allowing foreigners to work in Hong Kong. China may force foreigners who wish to work in Hong Kong (and Hong Kong citizens holding foreign passports) to apply for permanent resident status in Hong Kong, and hence fully subjecting them to local laws. If this policy is enacted, Hong Kong will likely suffer a massive "brain drain" of some of its finest professionals. As discussed in other chapters, cities like Taipei, Singapore, and Manila are all seeking to capture some of Hong Kong's corporate regional head offices. But full-scale flight has not occurred. A few MNCs have moved out of Hong Kong, including Compaq and Levi Strauss, who have relocated their regional headquarters to Singapore, and Asea Brown Boveri to Beijing. In contrast, Castrol (a major British oil company) and MCA (a major American entertainment concern) selected Hong Kong in 1995.[21]

Motorola has remade its Hong Kong operations to support expansion in south China. Initially in 1967, Motorola's Hong Kong operations were independent of operations in other countries. By 1990, Hong Kong was remade into a base for the Asia-Pacific region and used to support the south China market. As the regional headquarters, Hong Kong oversees manufacturing and design operations in Tianjian and Singapore. All Asia-Pacific sales and marketing offices, including China and Singapore, report to Hong Kong.

Philips uses Hong Kong to service China and the local market. Among the more than one hundred ten expatriates working in China, seventy are from Hong Kong. The Hong Kong operations include marketing, sales, distribution, and trading. In the past, Hong Kong operated as an autonomous unit. With its central geographical location, employees in Hong Kong have been influential in framing regional competitive moves in the Asia-Pacific region. However, Philips recently relocated its China/Hong Kong headquarters to Shanghai and will move the Asia-Pacific headquarters to Singapore in 1997. As a result, the role of Hong Kong will be diminished. Operations in Hong Kong will probably be scaled down, and eventually, Hong Kong will be gradually integrated under Chinese operations.

P&G's and Unilever's Hong Kong operations once operated as entirely autonomous units but have been partly integrated into the overall China operation. P&G established its Hong Kong office in 1987. As of 1995, not including beauty advisers and merchandisers, the company had about one hundred fifty people working in the Hong Kong operation. P&G Hong Kong and P&G China share a common Regional Vice President, and the two Hong Kong general managers also have responsibilities for China. Unilever began its Hong Kong operations in the 1960s. It started as a trading company that also served China, with no local manufacturing, and focused on marketing and sales. Currently, Unilever employs more than one hundred people in Hong Kong.

Toyota has taken a different approach in Hong Kong, depending heavily on a local partner. Inchcape, a large British trading company, is Toyota's sole distributor in Hong Kong, a relationship that has been mutually rewarding since Toyota entered Hong Kong in 1966. So Toyota's presence in Hong Kong is basically a dealer operation that enjoys substantial autonomy and has no mandate to apply Toyota's management system locally. Toyota dictates only product and price, with Inchcape controlling all other marketing activities. Inchcape's success has led other Asian Toyota subsidiaries in Indonesia, Malaysia, and Thailand, to learn and apply marketing systems developed in Hong Kong. These are facilitated by special regional seminars arranged by Toyota for Asia.

## Management Processes

More than in other Asian countries, MNCs have found it relatively easy to implement their style of management. P&G and Unilever now use the regional team concept to manage their Asian brands. Since the Hong Kong operation has been profitable but is not a significant market on a global basis, there is less opportunity for local managers to take part in the regional/global management process. However, for those Hong Kong managers who are relocated to head up the Chinese operation, they have ample opportunities.

For Motorola, Hong Kong has been the most influential operation for the Semiconductor Group in the Asia-Pacific region. There is no sign of change even after 1997. For Philips, since Hong Kong has been the regional headquarters up to now, there is a lot of influence from Hong Kong in regional and even global management processes. Since a significant number of Hong Kong managers are now playing a key role at the Chinese national level or the Asia-Pacific regional level, there are real opportunities for local managers to take part in the regional/global management process.

## Human Resources

The very high levels of education in Hong Kong mean that MNCs can easily run their local operations with entirely local managers. Those who still use large numbers of expatriates probably do so for reasons of tradition, and are typically old-line Hong Kong firms, such as the Hong Kong & Shanghai Bank or Jardine Matheson. On the other hand, fear of 1997 led many professionals to emigrate, to be replaced by non-Chinese or by overseas Chinese such as American-born second- or third-generation Chinese. The real issue in human resources today is the relocation of Hong Kong managers to China and the increasing scarcity of experienced Chinese-speaking, but Western-skilled, executives with resultant high levels of job-hopping and inflating salaries.

Many MNCs (and local companies too) now maintain management offices in Hong Kong to supervise operations across the border. A major reason is the shortage of professional managers in China, especially those with experience in MNCs. Thousands of Hong Kong-based executives commute to China on a weekly or even daily basis. This phenomenon could be short-lived, as larger numbers of experienced Chinese managers should become available, for example, within ten years of the 1996 opening of China's first full-scale Western-style graduate business school—the China-Europe International Business School in Shanghai. Some young mainland Chinese executives already complain that they are really more qualified than their Hong Kong and overseas Chinese colleagues who are being paid multiples of mainlanders' salaries.

Motorola employs fewer than twenty expatriates in Hong Kong, and all have managerial positions. In 1993, some Hong Kong managers were relocated to Tianjian in China to aid the newly established plant. For Philips, Hong Kong has been the primary supplier of expatriate executives to China. Hong Kong has managers (marketing, human resources, finance, and accounting executives) important to the Chinese operation. Despite Philips's policy of encouraging a crossnational flow of executives in the Asia-Pacific region, the huge demand in China for experienced managers has captured the majority of available Hong Kong executives. In contrast, P&G is reducing the role of Hong Kong managers for China. Its operations in Hong Kong were an important support base for China in the early years. At one time, among the expatriates working in China, 80% were from Hong Kong. But by 1995, only 6% were commuters based in Hong Kong. Unilever has sought to identify suitable managers for its Chinese operations. With their greater understanding of the Chinese market, managers from Hong Kong, Singapore, and Taiwan will be the primary sources of talent for such critical functions as marketing. What is true for these MNCs has also been true for most MNCs operating in Hong Kong.

The flow of people also goes in the other direction—many business visitors come to Hong Kong from China. MNCs transfer promising executives from China to receive exposure and training in Hong Kong. State-owned enterprises, government agencies, universities, and other organizations in China also have been sending their employees to different organizations in Hong Kong to receive various kinds of training. Business firms, universities, government agencies, and other organizations in Hong Kong are also inviting their venture partners in China to come and visit. All these activities reinforce each other. It firmly glues the status of Hong Kong as the training ground and service center for China. The challenge to Hong Kong is whether its people can continue to work hard and learn faster to preserve its leading status. Equally important is whether Hong Kong can continue to be open-minded to those from different parts of the world (including from China), and absorb the best talents possible to take up different tasks in Hong Kong. If so, MNCs can continue to make use of Hong Kong as a nerve center to manage operations in Hong Kong, China, and possibly Taiwan, or even the whole of Asia-Pacific.

## Culture

Most MNCs can maintain a global corporate culture in Hong Kong. Motorola, Philips, P&G, and Unilever do not adapt their corporate cultures for Hong Kong's Westernized work force. Philips has exposed its Hong Kong staff to its global management culture for a long time. Employees in Hong Kong are receptive to executives from different countries. In formulating global strategies, Philips does not make special adaptations for Hong Kong. The same is true for P&G and Unilever and practically all other MNCs. Local managers take pride in embracing the specific company culture and implement it as fully as possible in Hong Kong. Since Hong Kong is known for its flexible and friendly attitude toward different cultures, it is almost unheard of that there is a need to adapt the corporate culture to Hong Kong.

## Conclusions

After Japan, Hong Kong is probably the most developed economy in Asia. The competitive advantages of Hong Kong include its central location in Asia, its well-developed communications network, solid infrastructure, low tax rate and simple taxation system, free port status, globally acceptable legal system, efficient support services, general efficiency of doing business, and availability of skilled labor. Practically all these advantages are sustainable. For a long time Hong Kong has positioned itself as the business gateway to China, and China's business gateway to the world. It has been quite clear that MNCs have been using Hong Kong as the stepping stone to understanding Chinese practices, and to chart their China strategies. The risks of the 1997 change are far less for MNCs than for Hong Kong's citizens. As we concluded in the chapter on China, that giant is a "must" play for most MNCs. Participating in Hong Kong will make that play easier in many ways.

### NOTES

1. Remark made on the television program, "The Power of the Market," part 1 of the ten-part PBS *Free to Choose* series, broadcast for ten consecutive weeks in 1980.

2. This integration provides another example of Alan Rugman's "double diamond" effect in analyzing country competitiveness, contrasting with Michael Porter's single diamond model. See Alan M. Rugman and Joseph R. D'Cruz, "The Double Diamond Model of International Competitiveness: Canada's Experience," *Management International Review,* (1993): 33 no. 2, 17–39; and Michael E. Porter, *The Competitive Advantage of Nations* (New York: Free Press, 1990); and idem, "The Competitive Advantages of Nations," *Harvard Business Review* (March–April 1990): 73–93.

3. Remark by Charles Ingene, editor, *Journal of Retailing* (1992–96).

4. William H. Overholt, "Hong Kong after 1997, The Question of Sovereignty," *Columbia Journal of World Business,* 30, no. 2 (Summer 1995): 23–25.

5. Richard Yan-Ki Ho, et al., eds., *The Hong Kong Financial System* (Hong Kong: Oxford University Press, 1991): 394–95.

6. Ibid.

7. Overholt, "Hong Kong after 1997."

8. Ho, *The Hong Kong Financial System.*

9. Overholt, op. cit.

10. Ho, op. cit.

11. For example, on September 10, 1996, Mr. Joseph Yam (Chief Executive of the Hong Kong Monetary Authority), and Mr. Chen Yuan, (Deputy Governor of the People's Bank of China), gave lengthy and detailed expositions on these issues in London and assured the international financial community that these were all unfounded worries. See *Ming-Pao* (in Chinese), September 11, 1996, D-11.

12. The survey identified a total of 433 MNCs in Hong Kong. In terms of total dollar investments, the leading countries of origin were Japan (34%), the United States (28%), China (11%), and the Netherlands (4%).

13. See note 2 above.

14. Michael Westlake, "A Wing and a Prayer: More Cathay Pacific Shares Change Hands," *Far Eastern Economic Review,* May 9, 1996.

15. Bruce Bueno de Mesquita, David Newman, and Alvin Rabushka, *Red Flag Over Hong Kong* (Chatham, N.J.: Chatham House, 1996).

16. *Far Eastern Economic Review,* June 27, 1996, 23.

17. Michael J. Enright, Edith E. Scott, and David Dodwell, *The Hong Kong Advantage* (Hong Kong: Oxford Press [China] Ltd., 1997).

18. Overholt, op. cit.

19. Ibid.

20. Ibid.

21. Bruce Gilley and Murray Hiebert, "The Lion's Share," *Far Eastern Economic Review,* November 9, 1995, 76–80.

# CHAPTER 7

# Singapore—Regional Hub

## *Kulwant Singh, Joseph Putti, and George S. Yip*

SINGAPORE'S CONSISTENTLY HIGH rates of economic growth since the middle-1960s have transformed the city-state from an underdeveloped country to among the richest in the world. Among many other accolades, Singapore has repeatedly been classified as one of the two most competitive economies in the world and as the best international city for business.[1] This success has been achieved despite the almost total absence of natural resources, severe constraints in land, capital, and human resources, and limited technological abilities.

## Background

### Steady Economic Growth

Singapore's rapid economic growth—8.25% real GDP growth per year between 1960 and 1991 (and about 7% per year in the 1990s)—has been attributed, to a large degree, to astute management by its government. In addition to actively participating in many sectors of the economy, the government has focused on providing a strong infrastructure to support Singapore's development into an efficient manufacturing base for foreign corporations. The key feature of Singapore's development strategy has been the attraction of multinational companies (MNCs) to undertake manufacturing and service operations for regional and world markets. As the domestic market was and is constrained by its small population (approximately three million) and land area (six hundred fifty square kilometers), Singapore's attraction for MNCs has been to serve as an efficient and, until recent years, low-cost center for manufacturing and service activities.

The success of Singapore's industrialization policy and the importance of MNC participation in the economy is reflected in the fact that approximately three thousand five hundred MNCs currently operate in Singapore. The total stock of foreign direct equity investment amounted to U.S.$35 billion in 1992, with European countries (28.9% of total foreign investments), Japan (23.3%), and the United States (17%) being the largest investors.[2] A further U.S.$5 billion a year was invested from 1993–95. This has resulted in high levels of foreign trade and activity in the economy, with Singapore having the highest ratio of foreign trade to GNP (approximately three to one) in the world.

## Foreign Participation in Economy

MNC investments have been broad-based, though the electronics, light manufacturing, and finance and banking industries have attracted especially significant foreign investment. Table 7.1 lists the twenty largest MNCs in Singapore ranked by sales. This list suggests that U.S. and Japanese MNCs have played a disproportionately important role in the economy, despite the diverse origins of the multinationals that have invested in Singapore.

The heavy MNC investments, Singapore's rapid development, and land and labor scarcity have, in recent years, made Singapore a relatively

*Table 7.1*

**Largest Foreign Multinational Companies in Singapore**

| Rank | Company | Nationality | Main Business | 1995 Revenues US$ millions |
|---|---|---|---|---|
| 1 | Caltex Trading | U.S. | petroleum | 7,566 |
| 2 | Asia Matsushita Electric (S) | Japan | electrical goods | 4,153 |
| 3 | Hewlett-Packard (S) | U.S. | computer products | 3,922 |
| 4 | Texas Instruments (S) | U.S. | semiconductors | 3,267 |
| 5 | Nissho Iwai Petroleum (S) | Japan | petroleum | 3,233 |
| 6 | Sumitomo | Japan | import/export | 3,183 |
| 7 | Yukong International (S) | South Korea | petroleum | 2,751 |
| 8 | BP Singapore | U.K. | petroleum | 2,353 |
| 9 | Mobil Oil (S) | U.S. | petroleum | 2,323 |
| 10 | Itochu Petroleum (S) | Japan | petroleum | 2,216 |
| 11 | Hitachi Asia | Japan | electronics | 2,049 |
| 12 | Toshiba Electronics Asia (S) | Japan | electronics | 1,636 |
| 13 | Samsung Asia | South Korea | electronics | 1,602 |
| 14 | Western Digital (S) | U.S. | computer products | 1,547 |
| 15 | Marubeni International Petroleum (S) | Japan | petroleum | 1,399 |
| 16 | Hewlett-Packard FE | U.S. | computers | 1,379 |
| 17 | Thomson Multimedia Asia | France | electronics | 1,293 |
| 18 | SGS-Thomson Microelectronics | Netherlands | electronics | 1,202 |
| 19 | Cosmo Oil International | Japan | electronics | 1,067 |
| 20 | Aiwa (S) | Japan | electronics | 1,042 |

*Source: Singapore 1000.* Datapool: Singapore, 1996.

high-cost location. In many respects Singapore has been found to be among the most expensive cities in the world for foreign businesses. Nevertheless, it remains attractive to MNCs and continues to draw heavy foreign investments. The primary advantages of investing in Singapore have shifted to its skilled work force, a world-class infrastructure, its status as a communications hub that provides ready access to the region, and for some industries, government financial incentives. Consequently, MNCs continue to play a major role in the Singapore economy, which is, possibly, the most global of any in the world.

## Domestic Companies

Singapore firms have played a relatively minor role in the economy, though there are signs that this may be changing. Most local firms tend to be small- or medium-sized, and concentrated in service or component manufacturing businesses. Though these small- and medium-sized firms comprise approximately 90% of firms in the country, they account for only 25% of the economy. Relative to Taiwan, South Korea, and Hong Kong, Singapore's growth has been driven to a larger degree by foreign firms, with local entrepreneurs playing a smaller role in the economy's growth. Nevertheless, a growing number of Singapore firms have become competitive in regional markets, and a few in global markets. Table 7.2 shows that the successful local firms are generally smaller than MNCs operating in Singapore. An important characteristic of many leading Singapore MNCs is that they are government linked corporations (GLCs), being owned and controlled in significant part by the government. Eight of the twenty largest and six of the twenty most profitable Singapore firms are GLCs. Somewhat unusually, these GLCs have been able to meet or exceed world benchmarks in operating and financial performance. More generally, the government has been estimated to account for more than 60% of the economy.[3] This heavy economic role reflects the importance that the government has placed on economic development and the active part it has played in directing the economy, making Singapore, arguably, the best example of the successful application of industrial policy.

Singapore's limitations and strengths in globalization have had a major effect on local industries and firms as well as on MNCs operating in the country. The more successful Singapore firms have become multinationals in their own right, with some having developed to the extent of becoming significant global players. Prominent among these are Singapore Airlines; Singapore Telecom; soundcard manufacturers Creative Technologies and Aztech Computers, who collectively account for approximately 70% of world soundcard production; and ship repairers Keppel Corporation and Sembawang Corporation. These firms demonstrate that at least some Singapore businesses have been able to develop the managerial and operating skills to compete in the global market.

These and other Singapore firms have, since 1993, been strongly encouraged by the government to expand their operations in the region.

*Table 7.2*
**Largest Singapore Companies**

| Rank | Company | Main Business | 1995 Revenues U.S.$ millions |
|---|---|---|---|
| 1 | Singapore Airlines[a] | airline | 4,635 |
| 2 | Kuok Oils & Grains | commodity trading | 3,013 |
| 3 | Singapore Telecoms[a] | telecommunications | 2,486 |
| 4 | United Overseas Bank | banking | 1,892 |
| 5 | DBS[a] | banking | 1,832 |
| 6 | Fraser & Neave | investment | 1,791 |
| 7 | Keppel Corporation[a] | investment | 1,700 |
| 8 | NatSteel[a] | steel | 1,465 |
| 9 | Great Eastern Life Assurance Company | insurance | 1,403 |
| 10 | City Development | property | 1,394 |
| 11 | Neptune Orient Lines[a] | shipping | 1,320 |
| 12 | Singapore Petroleum Company[a] | petroleum | 1,278 |
| 13 | OUB | banking | 1,218 |
| 14 | Creative Technology | computers | 1,188 |
| 15 | IPC Corporation | computers | 1,091 |
| 16 | STIC | industrial | 954 |
| 17 | Asia Pacific Breweries | beverage | 927 |
| 18 | Sembawang Corporation | investment | 847 |
| 19 | Cycle & Carriage Industries | motor vehicles | 847 |
| 20 | Hong Leong Corporation | general trading | 836 |

*Source: Singapore 1000.* Datapool: Singapore, 1996.
[a]Government-linked corporations.

The major motive for regionalization is the government's drive to develop a "second external wing" for the economy. Regionalization is viewed as a means for local firms to overcome the limitations imposed by the small domestic market and as a means for Singapore to participate in the rapid economic growth of the region. The government has supported this expansion with fiscal and other less-direct measures. In one program, the Economic Development Board has targeted approximately two hundred local firms, with the aim of helping one hundred of these grow to more than S$100 (U.S.$70) million in annual sales by the year 2005.

Singapore firms have responded to this challenge, with direct investments abroad rising from S$7.8 (U.S.$4.3) billion in 1990, to S$13.1 (U.S.$8.1) billion in 1993.[4] Though regionalization efforts have mainly been led by the larger firms, many small and medium enterprises have expanded regionally as well. In most cases, these firms appear to have expanded to neighboring countries, in particular Malaysia. China has seen a significant increase in investment from Singapore in recent years. Though still a net recipient of investment flows, Singapore has become a major source of investments in many regional countries.

Global strategies have generally been important, if only indirectly so, for most Singapore firms. Many firms that have not operated globally or even exported directly have participated in the global marketplace by being component suppliers or service providers to MNCs based in Singapore or elsewhere. Consequently, most Singapore firms appear to have a strong inclination, if not the ability, to participate in the global marketplace. This inclination and the experience of supplying foreign firms have become significant competitive advantages for Singapore firms in their recent drive for regional and global success.

## Singapore's Success in Two Industries

Singapore's success in building up two important local industries—telecommunications and airlines—illustrates very well the strengths of the economy.

### Local Telecommunications Industry

Though the primary purpose of the telecommunications industry is to facilitate communication within and across borders, it does not necessarily follow that telecommunications industries are global. Indeed, government regulation and restriction of telecommunications have been ubiquitous, and the globalization of the industry—in contrast to the globalization of communications—is a relatively recent phenomenon.

Singapore's telecommunications industry, which has been dominated by one major player—Singapore Telecom (ST), the government-linked telecommunications service provider—was an essentially domestic industry until the mid-1970s. This was true, despite the fact that approximately half of ST's revenues were derived from communications with locations outside Singapore. Following the widespread trends of deregulation, privatization, and globalization, Singapore's telecommunications industry began globalizing during the mid-1980s. This took the form of greater foreign participation in the local telecommunications industry, and greater participation in the global industry by ST and other Singapore firms.

A key feature of the ongoing telecommunications revolution is convergence across traditional industry, market, and customer boundaries, with customers in most developed and developing countries wanting similar levels of service from their service providers and technological sophistication in their products. Market drivers, particularly convergence in consumer tastes, are therefore a major force behind the globalization of this industry. With per capita income second only to Japan's in Asia, and with a penchant for electronic goods, Singapore's consumers have been particularly quick to adopt telecommunications devices such as mobile phones and pagers. Penetration levels for both of these products are among the highest in the world.

Competitive pressures are transmitted with relative ease in the telecommunications industry, so that even with government regulation, ST has recently faced significant competitive pressures. Its IDD rates have been reduced significantly since 1994, as a result of pressure from low-cost "call back" services offered by foreign firms. In addition, the desire of regulators to have Singapore's telecommunications services priced at among the lowest in the world has forced ST to achieve world levels of competitiveness in the absence of competition. These efforts are one aspect of the role that government drivers have played in globalizing Singapore's telecommunications industry.

The sophistication of the market, high levels of telecommunications consumption, and market liberalization have attracted a number of telecommunications firms to Singapore. Foreign firms, for example, are participants in all four consortia awarded paging and mobile phone licenses in 1995. Though Singapore's market is small, MNCs find it useful to compete here because of its highly sophisticated telecommunications infrastructure, which has been rated as among the best in the world.[5] Competing in this market is a source of strategic leverage, providing firms with market, cost, and technological experience that converts to competitive advantage when transferred to other countries. The diversity in the country of origin of the telecommunications equipment purchased by ST (with major purchases from several Japanese, European, and North American suppliers) has also attracted multinational telecommunications operators to Singapore. These firms utilize Singapore as their manufacturing base or operational headquarters for the region or the world. In consequence, more than forty-one firms located in Singapore manufactured telecommunications equipment valued at about $1.4 billion in 1991. More than 75% of this output was exported, indicating the importance of the global market for this segment of the telecommunications industry.

ST has itself increasingly ventured out of Singapore and had, by 1994, established more than twenty-five ventures in more than twelve countries, primarily in East Asia and Northern Europe. ST's efforts at globalization have been propelled by four main drivers. First, the small and increasingly mature domestic telecommunications market is unlikely to offer adequate opportunities for ST to maintain its historically high growth rates, particularly with the emergence of competition. The second factor driving ST's globalization is the search for new growth markets. ST's expansion into Asian countries, in particular, has largely been driven by the search for new markets to sustain future growth. ST has focused on new and emerging economies in this regard, as its demonstrated ability in sourcing, implementing, and managing telecommunications services match the needs of these markets. Technological factors are the third set of drivers behind ST's globalization. While it has achieved significant market success, ST has not been able to develop leading edge technological competencies. Many of its ventures in European countries are technology oriented and are probably aimed at enhancing ST's technological competencies. In addition, Singapore's small market hinders the efficient adoption of some large-scale capital intensive technologies. Participation in foreign consortia also allows ST to spread its costs among larger markets and to facilitate ST's access to these technologies. Finally, as a government-linked corporation, ST has been quick to adopt the government's policy of expanding into regional markets to sustain Singapore's future growth. In sum, ST's efforts at globalization have been driven by market, cost, government, and competitive drivers, all of which have played some part in globalizing ST's operations.

## Local Airline Industry

In many respects, market, cost, government and competitive drivers similar to those in the telecommunications industry have driven many other Singapore corporations to globalize their operations. In the airline industry, the high cost of airplanes, ground and maintenance facilities, and information and other systems require that efficient airlines operate on a regional or global basis to achieve significant scale economies. Equally, travel patterns demand that airlines operate across national and continental boundaries to serve as many high-traffic routes as possible. In reaction to these forces, airlines have increasingly globalized their operations, either by introducing flights outside their traditional markets or by establishing alliances with other airlines possessing complementary route networks.

Singapore Airlines (SIA) is widely acknowledged as Singapore's most successful corporation, having established itself as among the highest-rated and most profitable airlines in the world. The total absence of a domestic route network has forced SIA to operate on an essentially global basis from the very commencement of operations. This is strikingly demonstrated by its objective, established in its second year of operation, to position SIA as a top quality intercontinental airline of Southeast Asian origin, offering the best in-flight service in the world. This goal forced SIA to challenge world-leading airlines at an early stage and drove it to match and exceed industry benchmarks of service, efficiency, and effectiveness. This performance has made SIA an attractive partner and has allowed it to establish alliances with Swissair of Switzerland and Delta Airlines of the United States, and more recently with Air New Zealand to establish a global route network. As part of its drive to lower costs, SIA moved some of its operations overseas, shifting some accounting operations to China and software operations to India. The cost-driven globalization of operations reflects the impact that increasingly high operating costs and labor shortages have in driving Singapore firms overseas. The government's provision of a high-quality infrastructure in support of SIA's operations—including prominently an airport consistently rated as among the two best in the world—is representative of the importance of government globalization drivers in this industry. At the same time, government restrictions that SIA and other airlines have faced in attempting to provide services to some countries have constrained the globalization of operations.

# Overall Industry Globalization Drivers

Most of Singapore's globalization drivers are highly favorable for MNCs. Also, as a former British colony in Asia, Singapore has characteristics that are common to both the West and other Asia-Pacific countries.

## Market Globalization Drivers

Market globalization drivers favor integration of Singapore into the global and regional strategies of MNCs. As a modern and relatively Westernized Asian country with strong business, cultural, and language links with North American and European countries, Singapore's retail and industrial consumers have needs common to those of consumers in developed countries. Consequently, Singapore's MNCs have been required to keep up with and, in some cases, lead trends in developed countries. The growing similarity of consumer needs in the region has allowed Singapore firms to transfer their marketing skills and knowledge to neighboring countries. This has facilitated expansion into regional countries, which have often lagged behind Singapore by some years.

Despite its modern outlook, Singapore is an Asian country with cultural, language, and ethnic links to several countries in its region. These links have enabled Singapore firms to establish personal and business contacts and networks in the region, and have been particularly useful in the Southeast Asian region and in China. As Chinese, Singaporeans have had access, at least potentially, to the many Chinese businesses that dominate the economies of Malaysia, Indonesia, Thailand, Taiwan, and Hong Kong. To a much lesser degree, Singapore's Indian and Malay communities have facilitated the country's entry into the Indian and Malaysian markets. These linkages have essentially provided leverage that has facilitated Singaporean firms' movement into the global marketplace, via the intermediate step of regionalization.

## Cost Globalization Drivers

The nature of cost globalization drivers for Singapore has changed in recent years because of Singapore's increasingly high-cost structure. Rather than being a low-cost site, Singapore has become a cost-efficient site, with the benefits of being able to respond quickly to technological change, and greater sourcing and logistical efficiencies, compensating for high land and labor costs. But many MNC managers now rate Singapore poorly in overall availability and other aspects of the labor force (Table 1.7 in Chapter 1).

Singapore's strategy of serving as a regional hub reflects the growing advantages of neighboring countries in different value-chain activities. Recognizing the challenge posed by Taiwan and South Korea, the growing threat of Malaysia, Thailand, and China, and the potential emergence of Indonesia, Vietnam, and India, Singapore has tried to move its manufacturing activities up the value-added chain to avoid intensifying competition. At the same time, it has tried to exploit the more efficient or cost-effective operations possible in these countries by relocating appropriate operations to these locations.

## Government Globalization Drivers

Of all the countries discussed in this book, the Singapore government is the most active in encouraging foreign investment. Singapore has benefited from foreign investment in the past and will continue to do so in the future. To this end, the government places a high priority on creating and maintaining an environment that is conducive to business through a variety of incentive policies.

To reinforce the low-cost attractiveness of Singapore, the government has utilized financial incentives through a range of schemes that provide tax benefits, training assistance, or investment grants. Most of these have been targeted at attracting particular high-technology or high-value-added activities to Singapore. The government and people of Singapore have demonstrated few, if any, sensitivities of the sort that have hindered MNC investments in some emerging countries. Consequently, very few investment, ownership, or repatriation constraints have been imposed on individual or corporate investments in Singapore. The ease and flexibility of carrying out business activities in Singapore has been an important factor in attracting businesses.

Singapore advocates and practices free trade. In addition, there are no tariffs or quota restrictions on imports. Certain goods are, however, controlled or dutiable for health, safety, and security reasons. Furthermore, Singapore is a member of ASEAN which, under the ASEAN Preferential Trading Agreement, allows goods originating or consigned from Singapore a preferential rate of duty in other ASEAN countries.

At 27% for businesses, tax rates in Singapore are lower than in industrialized countries. Furthermore, the government offers a number of fiscal incentives to encourage multinational participation such as the operational HQ incentive and tax concessions of income from offshore activities. Singapore has a highly reliable and predictable legal system, based on English common law. On the other hand, the government has some tendencies to limit freedom of expression, although very mildly so by the standards of some other Asian nations. It may appear that such inhibitions may hurt the development of media-related and information-based industries. However, strong financial and other incentives offered by the government have attracted several media firms to broadcast from, or print in, Singapore for the region.

A main factor driving the emergence of Singapore MNCs is the strong encouragement provided by the government to regionalization.[6] This drive has been adopted as a national effort, has drawn the active support of government-linked corporations, and has galvanized many local businesses to expand their operations regionally. It is likely that for many firms that had not previously operated outside Singapore, the government driver has been the most significant motive for globalization. The support provided by the government has in turn been a significant

advantage, particularly for small- and medium-sized firms that lack the resources to discover, enter, and compete in markets on their own. In general, the impact of such government globalization drivers may have been
the most important factor.

### Competitive Globalization Drivers

By virtue of its small market, Singapore has played a relatively small role
in respect to competitive moves in the global market in most industries.
Nevertheless, in several industries, it has been essential to participate or
manufacture in Singapore in order to maintain competitive parity.

Few firms, whether local or foreign, invest in Singapore with the aim of
capturing the local market. Despite the relatively high per capita income
and wealth of the people, the small population base and land area make
the domestic market in almost all industries tiny relative to markets in
neighboring countries. Thus, most firms that operate in Singapore do so
with the aim of participating in regional and global markets.

## Overall Global Strategies

Singapore has, from the early 1960s, positioned itself as an efficient, low-
cost base for firms seeking to manufacture products for other countries,
particularly the developed Western countries. While continuing to tout
its strengths in this role, Singapore has in recent years emphasized its role
as a gateway to the region. This strategy positions Singapore as a hub that
allows firms operating there to enter or compete in the region more effectively than they could through direct investments. The country's location amid three of the four most populous countries in the world, in the
center of the rapidly growing Southeast Asian region, and its excellent
communications and physical infrastructure have importantly determined Singapore's success in this role.

### Market Participation Strategies

Like Hong Kong, Singapore provides a small but highly affluent market that can afford the best that MNCs can offer. Its per capita GNP of
U.S.$26,730 in 1995, is greater even than Hong Kong's and close behind
that of the United States and Germany; and prices are low enough relative to income that Singaporeans' purchasing power ranks very high also
(Table 1.1 in Chapter 1). Despite its small population, Singapore's GNP
of U.S.$80 billion in 1995, is equal to that of Malaysia or the Philippines.
So this island state can be quite an attractive market in its own right. Furthermore, like Hong Kong, consumption patterns and brand choices in
Singapore have significant influence on its larger, less affluent neighbors.

### Products and Service Strategies

Another consequence of the small size of the Singapore market is that
it is often uneconomic to significantly localize products and services, or
to solely develop them for this market. As a result, many of the products

and services produced or offered for sale here have been those that are popular in other large markets or in the producers' home countries. This process, plus the general outward orientation of Singaporeans, has resulted in most consumers in the country accepting or preferring products and services primarily developed for other markets. Singapore's highly developed infrastructure has also supported the introduction of products developed for more-advanced countries. This trend has generally been beneficial for Singapore-based firms since the process of meeting local demand also provides goods and services that are, potentially, similar to those marketed in other markets, facilitating regional expansion.

## Activity Location Strategies

MNCs have located many activities in Singapore, initially in low-value-added manufacturing, but now increasingly in higher-value-added activities. Most notably, in many electronics-related industries, Singapore undertakes high-value-added activities such as the manufacture of key components or final assembly and testing, while importing components or subassemblies from low-cost manufacturing sites in the region. A similar strategy has seen the country focus on selected services or support activities, such as operational HQs or R&D centers for MNCs, or financial services. Government incentives are often available to encourage firms in these processes and activities.

## Marketing Strategies

Products and services are often marketed in Singapore in the same manner as in other countries, reflecting forces discussed above and the relatively Westernized nature of Singaporean society. Firms operating in Singapore have enjoyed significant advantages in being able to utilize, with relatively little adjustment, marketing techniques and procedures from other markets. A further advantage is that Singapore has been able to play a test or lead market role for other countries. For many products, Singapore has served as a test bed for products and services prior to their introduction in more developed markets. For others, marketing campaigns and techniques adopted from the West for Singapore have subsequently been used in regional countries. The relatively small size of the market allows test marketing to be performed with relatively low cost and minimizes the risk associated with such testing.

## Competitive Move Strategies

Like Hong Kong, Singapore's small size limits the competitive role it can play in MNC strategies. But in some industries, MNCs have to participate in Singapore to coordinate moves with the rest of the world. A particularly significant example of this is the hard disk drive industry, for which Singapore is the largest producing site in the world. Almost every significant producer has manufactured hard disk drives in Singapore, in part to ensure similar access to technology, manufacturing, and cost factors as their competitors.

## Conclusion

It is clear that a major determinant of and the major constraint on Singapore's global competitiveness is its small size and related lack of natural resources. The process of overcoming these constraints has driven Singapore to adopt globalization strategies that make it among the most competitive locations for many firms. These advantages are discussed in greater depth in the following discussions of local and multinational corporations in Singapore. However, for most firms and industries these strategies can be summarized as follows:

*Locate here to access the region.* Firms should exploit Singapore's location and infrastructure advantages by using it as a hub to access the region. For many industries, Singapore is an effective site to manufacture for the world.

*Focus on global products and services.* Many products and services can be manufactured or commercialized here without significant localization. The primary advantage here is that of a test market for more-developed markets and as a lead market for less-developed markets.

*Engage in high-value-added activities.* The limited natural resources available, and its high-cost structure restrict Singapore operations to high-value-added activities that can exploit its relatively highly trained workforce and management, excellent infrastructure, and government support.

*Utilize the high-quality infrastructure.* The excellent all-around infrastructure that Singapore offers can provide an important advantage for industries and firms that are particularly dependent on reliable, efficient, and cost-effective transportation, communications, and operations.

*Exploit government incentives.* The government offers a broad portfolio of incentives for businesses moving high-value-added operations to Singapore or upgrading those already present there. Significant financial and general support for other valued activities indicate that government incentives are an important potential source of advantage.

## Overall Organization and Management Approaches for Singapore

The discussion so far has suggested that Singapore offers many advantages for firms seeking global competitive advantage. One factor that significantly multiplies these advantages is that there are few constraints on organization and management approaches that firms can adopt. An important attraction for MNCs that has contributed significantly to Singapore's success in becoming a global manufacturing and service center is that relatively little adaptation is needed to operate there. Therefore, none of the four organizational factors that influence the formulation and implementation of global strategies represent significant constraints in Singapore.

There are no significant government or other constraints that will hinder firms' choices of organization structures. Government incentives, however, may influence certain structural decisions, such as the location of regional or operational HQs and certain functions in Singapore to take advantage of tax benefits.

Whereas operations in some countries require MNCs to significantly localize procedures, policies, equipment, and other resources, research suggests that MNCs undertake relatively little localization in Singapore. A study of seventy-eight MNCs found that subsidiaries of European, American, and Japanese MNCs operate in Singapore without significantly localizing most aspects of their operations.[7] This study also found that MNC subsidiaries enjoy relatively high levels of autonomy in many aspects of their operations, despite or possibly because of the limited localization necessary.

The shortage of manpower of all types represents a potential difficulty for foreign MNCs. The government's willingness to allow foreigners, particularly technical and managerial personnel, to work in Singapore has alleviated this problem somewhat. On the other hand, the manpower is among the best educated and hardest working in the world. MNCs should beware of one developing weakness. Observers have commented that the highly structured and test-oriented lives of students, the paternalistic government system, and the good life have had a negative influence—leading many Singaporeans to prefer waiting for instructions, to not be entrepreneurial, not be creative, and most of all, to be afraid to risk anything for fear of losing. Singaporeans recognize this weakness and jocularly refer to it as the *kiah su* or *geng sue* ("afraid to lose") syndrome—a phrase even emblazoned on T-shirts.

Singapore's heavy reliance on MNCs has been reflected in a strongly pro-business environment, which imposes relatively few constraints in business matters. Firms have therefore been able to introduce home country routines and procedures with relatively limited adjustment, and have been able to operate effectively. Singapore's relative Westernization, use of English as its language of business and government, and relatively transparent processes of regulation and government have contributed to the limited need for adaptation. Excellent transport and communications facilities also ease the difficulties of coordination with parent HQs. The ability to operate in Singapore as in the home country simplifies managerial and organizational systems, and enhances the competitiveness of this city state.

## Activities by MNCs

Despite the rapid development of Southeast Asian countries and the emergence of Malaysia, Indonesia, and Thailand as direct competitors for MNC operations in the region, Singapore continues to draw heavy MNC greenfield, or expansion, investments. Investment commitments in recent years have increased from already high levels to reach record levels. We have selected the hard disk drive industry, the electronic components industry, and the consumer electronics industry to illustrate MNC activities in Singapore.

# The Hard Disk Drive Industry

An important characteristic of MNC investments in Singapore is the bandwagon effect, which has seen firms from the same industry and, to a lesser degree, from the same country, investing in Singapore. Part of this trend reflects the inherent advantage that Singapore possesses in the production of a particular class of products or in the provision of a particular class of services, as a result of cost, market, or globalization drivers. This trend can also be traced to competitive globalization drivers, particularly the interaction among firms in an industry that pressures them to match the strategies of competitors.

The most prominent example of the bandwagon effect may be the hard disk drive (HDD) industry, which for many years, saw almost every significant independent manufacturer operating in Singapore. HDD manufacturers in Singapore currently include Seagate, Western Digital, Matsushita-Kotobuki Electronics, IBM, and Hyundai. Conner, Maxtor, Micropolis, Imprimis, and others manufactured in Singapore before being taken over by other firms. As a consequence, the country accounted for approximately 70% of world production of HDDs in the late 1980s, earning Singapore the title of "Winchester City" (after Winchester hard drives). Though the industry's leading independent producers of HDDs continue to manufacture here, Singapore's share has declined to approximately 43% of the world output, worth approximately U.S.$8 billion in 1996. HDDs remain among Singapore's largest exports, and in 1994, accounted for 61% of computers and peripheral exports and 20% of all electronics manufacturing.

It is probable that the entry of the first firms was based on the early detection of drivers that made Singapore an attractive global manufacturing site for HDDs. The presence and success of major U.S. electronics component manufacturers, such as Texas Instruments, may have signaled the existence and strength of these drivers, motivating the subsequent entry of HDD manufacturers. The presence of the first firm acted as an important competitive driver and strategic lever in influencing firms to globalize their operations. Significant government incentives to attract electronics industry firms and more specifically, HDD manufacturers, were also important drivers for the relocation of the industry's manufacturing operations from the United States to Singapore. The HDD industry brought in its wake manufacturers of component and complementary products. The emergence of a supplier industry reinforced Singapore's attractiveness for HDD manufacturing and entrenched its position as the most efficient HDD manufacturing center in the world.

HDDs are, arguably, among the most global of products. The product is highly standardized and demand is largely driven by technical and operating characteristics. HDDs are manufactured and utilized almost identically globally, and are easily transportable, allowing manufacturing to be located distantly from consumers without bearing excessive costs. End users have little concern for or knowledge of the country of manufacture. Consequently, firms have flexibly shifted manufacturing in response to changes in globalization drivers. This shift has been from the United States to Singapore in the first instance, and more recently from Singapore to other Southeast Asian countries. This trend is common in, but not unique to the HDD industry. One survey of MNC investment patterns found that of one hundred twenty-eight MNCs that had invested in Singapore, Malaysia, and Thailand, 71% started in Singapore before moving to these other countries.[8] These firms indicated that Singapore serves as a useful hub for their regional operations, allowing easy entry into the region and serving as a base to support these operations.

The negative effects of cost drivers in Singapore and the pull of government incentives in neighboring countries have caused some migration of HDD manufacturing to Thailand, the Philippines, and Malaysia. A particularly popular destination has been the Malaysian island-state of Penang, which bears many similarities to Singapore. For example, by 1995, Singapore no longer enjoyed the 40% material and tooling costs advantages that it had over the United States a decade earlier.[9] Singapore has been engaged in severe competition with Penang to attract new investments and to retain existing investments, with mixed success. Some firms have chosen to locate plants in both of these countries and to phase production across plants. Newer models are often first manufactured in Singapore, being shifted to Malaysia or Thailand after the manufacturing process has been routinized and when the model faces significant market pricing pressures. Other manufacturers, prominently DEC and HP, decided to skip Singapore entirely, to invest directly in Penang.

Even as some HDD manufacturing has moved out of Singapore, investments have been undertaken by new entrants to Singapore and by incumbents in greenfield plants, or to expand existing operations. Matsushita-Kotobuki Electronics (MKE), one of ten Matsushita Group subsidiaries now in Singapore, established its first manufacturing operations outside Japan in Singapore in 1994, the first non-U.S. HDD manufacturer to do so. Generally, Singapore's role in HDD production has declined while its managerial and technological role, particularly in advanced product development has increased. Despite this broad trend, production volumes continue to increase in Singapore, with the 1996 production of forty-five million drives being the largest output ever. The HDD component industry has also continued to grow in Singapore, with many disk media companies commencing operations there. Most manufacturers continue to source components from Singapore. HP, for example, sourced more than half of its HDD components in Singapore, despite not having manufactured there.

Three main drivers explain Singapore's success in the HDD industry. First, government globalization drivers have been particularly important as significant investment incentives. Tax concessions, assistance in facilities construction, and support for human resource training were provided to attract investments. More recently, significant efforts comprising financial and other incentives have been targeted at retaining these investments in Singapore and to encourage new investments. The government has also focused on supporting selected industry clusters, ensuring the presence of producers, supporting and complementary industries, and adequate human and other resources. Second, the existence of a relatively skilled and low-cost work force, and the possibility of Singapore becoming the global low-cost producer of HDDs, represented an important cost driver for the movement of the industry to Singapore. Particularly important in this regard was the emergence of a support industry supplying components for HDDs. Third, competitive globalization drivers are an important explanatory factor. Though a negligible market in terms of revenue and profits for HDD firms, and possibly no longer the lowest-cost production site, Singapore has been and remains the most important manufacturing site in the world for this industry. Investing in Singapore offers significant cost and manufacturing advantages. The failure to establish manufacturing operations there would have prevented a firm from having a manufacturing cost structure similar to those of its competitors and would have prevented early access to product and manufacturing innovations. In addition, the mere presence of the bulk of the industry imposed significant competitive pressures on other firms to locate in Singapore.

## Seagate

Seagate was founded in the United States in 1979, and established its first plant in Singapore in 1982. By the mid-1980s, it had become the largest industrial employer in the country. Seagate has four out of its twenty worldwide plants in Singapore, which also serves as the HQ of its Asia-Pacific operations. Asia-Pacific operations currently account for about 80% of Seagate's total output. It is currently the world's largest independent disk drive manufacturer, with 1994 world sales of U.S.$3.5 billion and market share of 19%.

The factors that attracted Seagate to Singapore were a low-cost but relatively skilled workforce, ten-year reduced-tax incentives, a Generalized System of Preferences (GSP) exemption from U.S. duties, and efficient international transportation facilities. Though Singapore goods no longer enjoy GSP exemption, Seagate has continued to expand its operations there, with total cumulative investments in 1995, of S$1 billion, approximately half of its investments in Asia.

Seagate's operations in Singapore mirror the changes in the advantages that Singapore has offered producers of HDDs. Though initial operations concentrated on the assembly of HDDs from components manufactured in U.S. and other plants, most component manufacturing was quickly shifted to Singapore, with complete production and assembly commencing in 1983. However, the rising costs of production drove Seagate to increasingly shift component production offshore, so that Singapore operations are now concentrated on the manufacture of selected high-value-added components (such as HDD mother boards) and on the final assembly of HDDs.

Though Seagate continues to assemble the majority of its worldwide output in Singapore, it has increasingly moved its manufacturing facilities to Malaysia and Thailand to exploit the lower costs of manufacturing components in these sites. Much of the manufacturing and equipment in these plants has been relocated out of Singapore and is undertaken in support of Singapore-based operations. For example, Seagate's fourteenth Asian plant opened in China in 1995, in a Singapore-operated industrial park, to undertake component manufacture and final assembly of HDDs. Seagate Singapore established and manages this plant, trained its staff, and is a major consumer of its output. Seagate also invested in a wholly owned manufacturing plant in Japan, possibly to ensure access to technological developments in Japan's disk drive industry, which until 1994, had no presence in Singapore.

The dispersion of operations across the region demonstrates the trend of locating in the world's lowest-cost production site for each component of the manufacturing chain. As cost and other drivers differ across countries for different components, even complex products that require a high degree of integration, such as HDDs, end up being manufactured in many different plants in several countries. Under this manufacturing model, efficient logistics management and telecommunications are essential for coordination of the value chain. These remain among Singapore's main advantages, and explain why Seagate has continued to undertake its final assembly of HDDs and its manufacturing of higher-value-added processes in Singapore. Though cost drivers have worked in favor of the relocation of manufacturing outside Singapore, competitive drivers, particularly the need to get new products to market ahead of competitors, have also worked against such movement. Seagate continues to assemble drives in Singapore despite the labor intensity of this process and the shortage and high cost of suitable workers. This can be attributed to the managerial and coordination skills established over many years of sourcing and integrating components for the assembly of HDDs. The labor cost disadvantages have been more than offset by the more efficient engineering, logistics, and general management of operations in Singapore. Singapore's infrastructure, particularly its excellent communications, has allowed more rapid ramping-up of production, thus allowing high-end production to be undertaken in Singapore. In an industry with very short product life cycles, this advantage offsets high manufacturing costs.

## Matsushita-Kotobuki Electronics (MKE)

MKE is a joint venture between Matsushita and Kotobuki Electronics Industries, whose primary business since 1984, has been the manufacture of disk drives under contract to Quantum Corporation, a leading U.S. disk drive firm. MKE became the only non-U.S. manufacturer of disk drives in Singapore in 1994, when it opened its first plant outside Japan there. The rising costs of manufacturing in Japan and the rising value of the Yen were the primary factors that pushed MKE to move its manufacturing operations out of Japan.

Despite the established trend of manufacturing migrating out of Singapore, and the fact that several other Japanese HDD manufacturers have migrated their operations to the Philippines, MKE chose to move its operations there. This choice can be attributed to the availability of skilled manpower, an excellent infrastructure, the presence of established supporting and complementary industries, and the strong presence of parent Matsushita in Singapore. Perhaps the most important attraction was the large presence of Quantum in Singapore. In recent years, MKE has been the major supplier of HDDs to Quantum, which undertakes R&D and design but no manufacturing. Quantum purchases all of MKE's output of HDDs in Singapore, and most of the output of its European and Japanese plants. The desire for proximity was carried to the limit, with MKE establishing its facilities in the same building on the floor above Quantum's operations. A final important driver behind MKE's relocation was the role of the government. MKE was approached directly by top officials, and was offered significant tax incentives and other assistance to relocate to Singapore.

MKE quickly ramped up its production in Singapore, to become the second largest HDD manufacturer on the island. This was possible because of the ease of establishing manufacturing operations in Singapore and because the production facilities were essentially identical to those previously operated in Japan. Quality and reliability of the Singapore operations have also been almost identical to those in Japan, though costs have been lower by approximately 20% because of lower material and labor costs. By 1995, the operations had been highly localized, with only eleven Japanese, albeit in senior technical and managerial positions, among the more than two thousand seven hundred staff. The availability of an extensive network of suppliers has allowed MKE to source almost 100% of its components from Singapore suppliers, though some components are manufactured in-house.

MKE's redeployment to Singapore contrasts with that of other Japanese HDD manufacturers, with NEC, Hitachi, Toshiba, and Fujitsu all moving operations to the Philippines. This suggests a significant deterioration of Singapore's advantage relative to neighboring countries in the manufacture of HDDs. However, the migration of part of the HDD industry into the region confirms that globalization drivers have caused Southeast Asian countries as a whole to achieve significant advantage in the manufacture of disk drives. This is due to development of the electronics industries' human capital skills, the emergence of regional supplier networks, effective infrastructure, and government incentives.

## Electronic Components Industry

The electronic components industry provides another example of heavy MNC participation, although less so than in hard disk drives. We focus on Motorola and Siemens.

### Motorola

Motorola commenced its Singapore operations in 1973, with a minor purchasing office. These operations have grown rapidly in recent years, expanding from about one hundred employees in 1983, to more than four thousand four hundred in 1995. Total investments exceeded S$500 million. Singapore operations accounted for S$2.4 billion in sales, almost half of the group's regional turnover. Motorola explains its presence in Singapore as follows:

> "Motorola decided to expand the Singapore operations because of the Republic's excellent infrastructure, global airport, highly skilled work-force, advanced education institutions, proximity to important customer base and Motorola's excellent results and success during the past nine years."[10] Singapore's strategic location and world-class infrastructure provide a "base to start other manufacturing facilities in the region."[11]

Singapore is now one of Motorola's largest pager facilities and also manufactures mobile data products and communications-related products and components. Singapore is also home to Motorola's Asia-Pacific Operational Headquarters, which houses one of Singapore's largest electronics R&D teams. Dedicated R&D staff of about one hundred fifty and R&D expenditures in 1994, of S$21 million were also relatively high by Singapore standards.

Motorola has several Centers in Singapore, among which are its Excellence Centre, which houses the pager manufacturing facilities. The Innovation Centre conducts product and technology research, as well as design and marketing for the Paging Products Group in the region and beyond. The Design Centre has been responsible for several innovations conceived and produced in Singapore, including the first credit card-sized pager. In addition, Singapore operations serve as the regional R&D center for paging products. This center has successfully introduced a number of products designed for the region, but which have subsequently been adopted globally. Singapore is also one of the six campuses of Motorola University, which provides technical training.

Given Singapore's cost and other advantages in the electronics industry, it is likely the manufacture of paging products in Singapore provided Motorola with significant cost savings. These savings may have played a part in Motorola's success in getting its Flex paging technology adopted by Singapore, Indonesia, and Thailand. The adoption of this technology by these countries is likely, in turn, to provide Motorola with significant manufacturing and competitive advantages. Therefore, while Singapore's small size makes it a relatively unattractive market for paging products (despite the high penetration rate of pagers) the gateway that it offers to the region and beyond is an important aspect of its attractiveness to Motorola and other MNCs. Motorola has also introduced new products in Singapore first, because the consumers' penchant for high-technology products there makes its an ideal test market. By combining manufacturing, product design, and regional management in Singapore, Motorola has been able to react quickly to regional customer needs by customizing products to local tastes and trends. In addition, it has been able to provide high levels of service and responsiveness. Also, Singapore has increasingly served as the springboard for the launch of Motorola's operations in

China and India. Motorola employed technology developed in Singapore for the plants it opened in Tianjin, China, and Bangalore, India. Some managers were also transferred from Singapore to assist in the running of these operations.

A significant component of Motorola's recent activities in Singapore has been geared toward the supply of semiconductors to the disk drive industry, indicating that the presence of this industry has acted as an important strategic lever in getting Motorola to establish or expand operations there. The size and proximity of the HDD industry have allowed Motorola to undertake chip design in Singapore.

## Siemens Components

Siemens Components, a subsidiary of Siemens AG, commenced its Singapore operations in 1970, with a small plant, laboratory, and regional sales office. Siemens Components has since invested more than S$300 million and expects to invest an equal amount in the next few years. Siemens Components employed one thousand six hundred workers in seven wholly owned operations in 1995, and had three other joint ventures there. Sales in 1995 were S$694 million. Singapore is also Siemens Components' HQ for sales, marketing, and distribution in the Asia-Pacific region. In addition, Siemens AG has several other Singapore operations. Collectively, these make Siemens AG the largest German MNC in Singapore. Siemens explains the benefits of operating in Singapore as follows:

> Cost is not the only reason for being here. Singapore is strategically located in the heart of booming markets. Also, the increasing number of qualified engineers and specialists, the excellent infrastructure in Singapore and the strong government support are important for our businesses.[12]

Siemens operations in Singapore are focused on a wide range of electronic components manufacturing for internal and non-Siemens customers. Singapore also serves as Siemen's Asia-Pacific sales and marketing HQ. Customers from the region account for approximately half of Siemen Singapore's sales. Being in the center of the high-growth region of Southeast Asia, particularly Malaysia, Thailand, and Indonesia, and to the emerging economy of Vietnam explains Singapore's attractiveness as a regional HQ.

Among Siemens Components' operations in Singapore is a custom chip design center, which designs application-specific integrated circuits. This center was moved to Singapore in 1994, as part of efforts to decentralize R&D operations outside Europe. The design center is reputed to be as good as any that Siemens operates, while the products manufactured in Singapore have been able to meet in-house and buyer quality standards. The relocation of the center was supported by a grant from the National Science and Technology Board, which aims to encourage R&D activities in Singapore, again demonstrating the impact of the government in Singapore's economic success. Siemens has found that by relocating its R&D facilities to Singapore it has been better able to meet the needs of regional customers by reducing its chip design cycle and its overall time to market. In addition, the time difference between its Singapore and European design centers allows collaborative chip design activities to be conducted almost continuously, with the Singapore center performing its duties during the nonworking hours of the European center, and vice versa.

Despite the success of its local operations, Siemens administered a great shock to the Singapore authorities in 1994, when it announced that it would not be undertaking major new investments in Singapore. Instead, China and India, with their rapidly increasing sales, would be the major recipients of new Siemens investments. This announcement was widely viewed as signaling an emerging economic threat, as competitive and government drivers in Singapore's favor could not offset the combination of low-cost and large-market advantages of other newly emerging Asian economies. This concern was reinforced by the failure of the Singapore authorities to successfully attract several large and high-technology projects in 1994, particularly in the wafer fabrication industry. For this industry, Singapore had few favorable globalization drivers, relative to the United States and Europe, where the plants were located instead. Though efforts to attract the wafer fabrication industry continue, significant government intervention is required, suggesting that in this industry, government globalization drivers are a major source of advantage.

## Consumer Electronics Industry

The consumer electronics industry is one in which MNCs have a very wide choice of where to produce. Many have chosen Singapore. We focus here on Philips and Hitachi.

### Philips

Philips' Singapore operations are among the largest of any MNC on the island, exceeding S$2.5 billion in annual sales in 1995, which comprised close to 2% of GNP. Total investments since its entry in 1951 have exceeded S$500 million, making Singapore among Philips' most important worldwide manufacturing sites. Philips' Singapore operations enjoyed the highest sales growth rates among all its operations worldwide in 1994. Philips has four international production centers (for audio, CTV, tuner, and domestic appliances) in Singapore, and operates six plants employing more than six thousand people. In addition, it has one plant on the Indonesian island of Batam, which is approximately twenty miles from Singapore. Philips also has its operational headquarters for the region here.

As with almost all MNCs operating in Singapore, most of Philips' local production is exported, with the domestic market accounting for a negligible portion of sales—for example, the nine million steam irons and two million hair dryers produced each year greatly dwarf the needs of Singapore's three million people. The plant that produces these irons and hair dryers is Philips' sole "center of competence" for these products, and the world's largest iron manufacturing plant. These "centers of competence" bear responsibility for developing specific product lines for worldwide markets. Four centers are located in Singapore. The fact that design is undertaken in Singapore for the world market suggests that significant similarities exist in customer needs. The cost and design efficiencies of producing in Singapore more than offset shipping and other costs that must be borne to move products to consumers around the world. In addition, Singapore is the world HQ for Philips' Audio Business Group. In this role, Singapore manages eleven audio plants worldwide and accesses R&D on related products from five international sites.

Singapore is also the headquarters for all of Philips' operations in the region and is the site of a regional basic research center. The selection of Singapore for this research center was motivated in part by government funding assistance. The National Science and Technology Board provided a S$5 million grant under its Research Incentive Scheme to finance the establishment of Philip's R&D center. Though not large in itself, this grant demonstrates the ongoing commitment by the Singapore authorities to ensure that Singapore human and infrastructure advantages are matched by its cost attractiveness. Singapore's advantages as an HQ derive from its strength as a communications hub, its strong business infrastructure, efficient logistics, and acceptable cost structure. These advantages result from strong government globalization drivers and, until recently, cost globalization drivers.

The Singapore operations also extend beyond manufacturing to include the design and development of products for the global market. Philips Singapore has the right to introduce locally conceived and developed products globally. In addition, the production of highly complex products, such as robotic modules, has been moved from the Netherlands to Singapore to take advantage of lower production costs and to better meet the needs of Pacific Rim customers. The ability to perform such complex and higher-value-added activities in Singapore has encouraged Philips to increase the amount of R&D undertaken there. An R&D center to focus on manufacturing technology was established there in 1994, moving operations beyond the product-level R&D then being undertaken. This center, one of only three worldwide, differs from other business R&D centers in Singapore in that it undertakes basic research, in contrast to the development and design-oriented focus of most R&D operations in Singapore. This demonstrates that, for Philips at least, Singapore's advantage has moved up the value chain to more technologically and knowledge-intensive activities. This move has been driven by a broad range of forces, including cost drivers (as high-grade engineers can be employed more cheaply), government drivers (financial and other incentives offered by government agencies), market drivers (common needs allow the transfer of activities), and competitive drivers (the need to match competitors' activities in the region).

Singapore is increasingly being used as a springboard to launch operations in the region, especially in China and Vietnam. The greater sociocultural similarity and geographical proximity of Singapore to these countries provides several advantages over Western Europe and North America as an HQ and base for expansion into the newly emerging Asian markets. Reflecting these advantages, several of Philips' ventures in China are managed from its Singapore subsidiary.

## Hitachi Electronic Devices Singapore

Hitachi commenced its Singapore manufacturing operations in 1972, by opening a series of factories to manufacture a wide range of electrical and electronic equipment. These investments were the result of a decision to make Singapore a major manufacturing base for Hitachi's products. By 1994, it had established thirty-two different companies in Singapore and had net sales exceeding S$12 billion. Collectively the Hitachi companies employed more than seven thousand employees and made investments between 1990 and 1994, of about S$750 million.

Hitachi Electronic Devices Singapore (HEDS) was established in 1978, for the production of color picture tubes for television receivers, the first such manufacturer in Southeast Asia. Singapore's attractions for HEDS included the presence of many Hitachi companies, the availability of qualified and relatively low-cost technical workers, a ten-year tax holiday offered by the government, and the difficulty of competing against low-cost Taiwanese and Korean products with high-cost products manufactured in Japan. Another important consideration was the establishment in Singapore of a manufacturing facility by Asahi Glass, HEDS' major supplier of glass tubes. HEDS chose to locate its plant less than a kilometer from Asahi's facility.

Production began in 1979, and has since grown to account for approximately 40% of Hitachi's worldwide production, second only to its Japanese sites. The Singapore operations utilize essentially the same production techniques and technology as the Japanese operations, and match Japanese benchmarks of process reliability and output quality. Nevertheless, some concessions have been made to accommodate local practices. The Just-In-Time (JIT) system has not been introduced at the HEDS plant, because not all local suppliers have been able to meet the delivery conditions. Further, some components are imported into Singapore, which makes a JIT system difficult to implement.

Operations have been heavily localized and the plant is staffed with a largely local workforce, there being only sixteen Japanese staff members in the entire plant. But as is common with most Japanese operations in Singapore, the chief executive and the top few technical staff are Japanese. Components are largely sourced from the region, with approximately 60% of the actual product being made in Singapore by related companies and suppliers.

The Singapore operations have also expanded to include some R&D operations. In particular, R&D for fifteen-inch computer display products will soon be performed only in Singapore, so that HEDS will have world-wide design and manufacturing responsibility for this range of products. The movement of R&D operations was motivated in part by government incentives for conducting R&D in Singapore. However, HEDS has few sales and other responsibilities, so that it remains largely a manufacturing operation. This appears to be true for many, if not the majority of MNCs in Singapore, which are often largely production bases. Despite Singapore's strengths as a potential HQ, many firms retain HQ operations in their home countries.

The availability of many related companies and of alternate suppliers of components is viewed as an important advantage to manufacturing in Singapore. HEDS perceives Singapore to be midway between Japan and the countries of Southeast Asia in terms of its attractiveness and capabilities as a manufacturing site for television and computer display products. The better and more efficient infrastructure continues to offset the more costly human resources in Singapore, so that HEDS is unlikely, in the foreseeable future, to migrate its operations to neighboring countries. Nevertheless, more labor- and natural resource-intensive activities are beginning to be transferred to Indonesia and the Philippines, where they can be performed more cheaply.

## Conclusion

Our analysis suggests that Singapore epitomizes the importance and success of global strategies—that much of the economy's strength can be attributed to its focus, deliberate or otherwise, on the global market. In a sense Singapore is a microcosm of Asia, reflecting and building on the advantages of other Asian economies. At the same time, Singapore's global strategies reflect careful analysis of the few factor advantages that the country possesses and the skillful exploitation of these advantages. Singapore remains possibly the best example of the benefits of globalization and an important example of how globalization drivers can affect the pattern of MNC investment and competitive advantage. The small population base and limited natural resources were partially offset by government and cost drivers, which allowed Singapore to become an efficient and low-cost global manufacturing site, as well as a regional telecommunications and distribution center.

The nature of cost globalization drivers in Singapore has changed in recent years because of Singapore's increasingly high-cost structure. Rather than being a low-cost site, Singapore has become a cost-efficient site, with the benefits of being able to respond quickly to technological change, and greater sourcing and logistical efficiencies compensating for high land and labor costs. In general, and particularly in labor-intensive industries, Singapore's role (and advantage) has gradually moved from manufacturing to engineering, from assembly to coordination, and from operations to HQ functions.

It is clear that Singapore's advantages have not yet extended to the high end of the value chain, as there are relatively few advantages to performing extensive R&D there. In addition, few leading-edge technology operations are performed in Singapore, as cost and competitive drivers are not yet in favor of doing so. When such operations have been undertaken in Singapore, they have often been the result of government drivers, in the form of government-provided incentives, offsetting other unfavorable drivers.

Singapore's strength in terms of market globalization drivers (through access to global customers and channels, transferable marketing, and its status as a lead country whose consumers have needs in common with those in major markets) and competitive globalization drivers (the presence of many global industry clusters with complementary and supporting subindustries, and very high levels of exports) also offset the cost disadvantages of operating in Singapore to serve the global market. For many industries, Singapore's major attraction as a site for businesses seeking global advantage is significantly attributable to government drivers. Highly favorable business, legal, social, financial, and investment policies provide many benefits to businesses that can exploit Singapore's strengths and that fit the country's economic vision.

## NOTES

1. *World Competitiveness Report 1994,* jointly published by the Institute for Management Development and the World Economic Forum, Switzerland. The WEF's *Competitiveness Report 1997* ranked Singapore as number one (see Table 1.10 in Chapter 1).

2. Ministry of Trade and Industry, *Economic Survey of Singapore 1994* (Singapore, 1995). (At end 1995, U.S.$ = S$1.40).

3. Werner Vennewald, "Technocrats in the State Enterprise System of Singapore," working paper no. 32 (Murdoch University: Asia Research Center, 1994).

4. *Economic Survey of Singapore 1994.*

5. Ibid.

6. See, for example, *Singapore Unlimited* (Singapore: Economic Development Board).

7. Joseph Putti, Kulwant Singh, and William A. Stoever, "Autonomy and Localization of American, European and Japanese Subsidiaries in Singapore," in Carl L. Swanson, Abbass Alkhafaji, and Michael H. Ryans, eds., *International Research in the Business Disciplines,* 1 (Greenwich, Connecticut: JAI Press, 1993): 107–23.

8. Natarajan and Tan. *The Impact of MNC Investments in Malaysia, Singapore and Thailand.* (Singapore: ISEAS, 1992).

9. Claire Leow, "Asia's Hard Drive for an Even Bigger Role," *Business Times,* March 18, 1944.

10. Bob Becknall, Vice President and Director of Far East Operations, Motorola Electronics, cited in *Singapore: Your Global Business Architect,* (Singapore: Economic Development Board, 1992) 8.

11. Christopher Galvin, President and CEO of Motorola Inc., cited in "Motorola to Invest $150m Over Next 5 Years in Core Competencies," *Business Times,* September 21, 1994.

12. Harmut Lueck, Managing Editor, Siemens Components, in *National Science and Technology Board, Annual Report 1994–1995* (Singapore: NTSB, 1995).

# CHAPTER 8

# Malaysia—Vision 2020

### Siti Maimon Kamso Wan-Rafaei and George S. Yip

NOW A NATION of twenty million people, Malaysia came into being in 1963, when the former British territories of Malaya, Singapore, Sabah, and Sarawak joined together upon independence. The almost immediate departure of Singapore from this union raised some concerns about the economic and social prospects of the country. But since the 1970s, Malaysia has mostly enjoyed social and political stability and dramatic economic growth. This success spurred Prime Minister Dr. Mahathir Mohamed to set the inspirational goal of making Malaysia a fully developed nation by the year 2020.[1] This "Vision 2020" has become a national theme to create "a society that has a shared destiny, robust and liberated psychologically, culturally tolerant, technologically progressive, caring, economically just, competitive and ethical."[2] In striving toward 2020 Malaysians are imbued with a well-recited slogan *Malaysia Boleh* ("Malaysia can do it"). In this chapter we discuss the reality of this vision and the implications for multinational companies.

## Background

### Economic Performance

In 1996, Malaysia registered its ninth year of high economic growth in the 8% a year range.[3] In 1996, exports of manufactured products equaled 74% of GNP, making Malaysia one of the world's leading countries having a large manufacturing component in its exports. Its 1996 per capita GNP of U.S.$4,447, while well below that of Japan and the "four tigers," placed it ahead of all other Asian nations apart from the oil-rich ministate of Brunei, and at multiples of the per capita GNPs of Indonesia, the Philippines, China, and India.[4] Foreign MNCs have played a major role in this success.

Malaysia's economic transformation can be divided into three stages of growth. The first stage, from 1957 to 1969, was basically led by the export of primary commodities. Since 1957, Malaysia has been, and continues to be, the world's largest producer and exporter of rubber, palm oil, tin, and tropical hard wood. The second stage of growth occurred from 1970 to roughly 1990. During this period, industrialization began and manufactured goods began to overtake commodities as Malaysia's major exports. Malaysia's labor cost advantage, combined with government policies such as financial incentives and the liberalization and deregulation measures adopted in 1985, brought in a substantial inflow of foreign direct investment. As a result, manufactured products began to account for a larger share of Malaysia's total exports. The development of petroleum extraction also played a key role in this stage, and continues to do so— petroleum production in 1996, accounting for 5.9% of GNP. (Malaysia holds about 1% of the world's proven oil reserves.) The third stage of growth stretches from 1990 to the present. Although the government expects the manufacturing sector to lead this stage of growth, greater emphasis will be accorded to the services sector, value-added manufacturing and high-technology industries targeting at global markets. The government plans for the economy to grow at 7% a year for the next twenty-five years based on the spectacular average of 6.7% over the last twenty years and over 8% for the five years from 1990–95.

The Malaysian economy was affected in 1997 when Thailand's currency crisis triggered a corresponding one in Malaysia. The Malaysian ringgit fell between 25% and 30% in value, and stock market values halved. Most observers in the West attribute these declines to recognition of the problems inherent in Malaysia's current account deficit. But many other observers also consider that the financial markets have overreacted. The impending economic slow down will be lessened somewhat as the government has announced the delay of three large projects, viz, Bakun Hydro Project in Sarawak, Malaysia–Indonesia Bridge, and the Kedah–Perak Airport.

Malaysia's industrialization policy has developed two main types of export-oriented industries: resource-based industries, which involve the processing of primary commodities for export, and manufactured goods industries. Domestic companies have traditionally commanded the former while multinationals have dominated the latter. The importance of MNC participation in the economy is reflected in the fact that Malaysia is among the world's top locations for offshore manufacturing operations, and is currently home to more than three thousand international companies from over fifty countries. Total proposed foreign direct investment amounted to RM 9.4 billion by 1996, with Japan (RM2.10 billion) as the largest investor, followed by the United States (RM1.44 billion), and Taiwan (RM 1.44 billion).[5]

## Foreign Participation in Economy

MNC investments have been broad-based, although the light manufacturing, petroleum, electronics and electrical, and chemical and chemical products industries have attracted the most foreign investment. MNCs have contributed significantly in employment creation, income generation, export, and trade. Indeed, the largest foreign companies in manufacturing are usually in export-oriented industries, with the majority of ownership often coming from Singapore, Japan, Hong Kong, the United States, and Britain (Table 8.1).

The heavy MNC investments, Malaysia's rapid development, and labor scarcity have, in recent years, reduced the country's cost advantages. Despite its labor shortage problems, Malaysia still attracts foreign investments. Consequently, MNCs continue to play a major role in the Malaysian economy.

## Domestic Companies

Moving the economy away from the two pillars of the early economy, tin and rubber, toward value-added manufacturing was a deliberate policy by the government. Malaysia's manufacturing sector, however, is still primarily for assembly and not yet for high-technology, skill-based industries. In order to stimulate domestic companies, the government is moving to establish more cohesive linkages in the industrial sector and focusing on the much neglected small- and medium-sized companies.

Currently, domestic companies—indigenous small businesses and large Malaysian corporations—account for 60% of the economy. One element of the Malaysian industrial vision is the creation of a thriving and extensive industrial sector based on locally produced industrial inputs. In the past, Malaysia was only a supplier of raw materials. For the future, Malaysia intends to take the more risky path of upgrading its industrial technological level through linkages among industries to a level consistent with other advanced countries. Malaysia is currently in the process of fulfilling this goal by developing local producers to supply components to multinational manufacturers and also by encouraging MNCs to integrate operating procedures so that all levels of manufacturing can be done— from manufacturing, assembly, design, tooling, engineering, R&D, marketing, and sales, as well as customer service.

In some sectors, local companies are using their roles as suppliers to MNCs to upgrade their activities, particularly from subcontracted assembly to the manufacture of complete products. This has happened particularly in electronics and automobiles under the "vendor scheme."

The government also seeks to create more competitive firms through privatization. Since 1983, the government has privatized eighty-five entities, mostly in road construction, infrastructure, and utilities. In the second half of the 1990s, the government plans to privatize at least 21% of its entities in the manufacturing sector, 14% in the services sector, and 13% in the agricultural sector.[6] Although the government actively encourages foreign investment in Malaysia, it also seeks to hone the competitiveness of Malaysian firms.

The largest Malaysian companies operate in a wide variety of industries, ranging from government-owned concerns in energy, telecommunications, and transportation to private companies in automobiles, steel, heavy industries, chemicals, textiles, petrochemicals, cement, and food

**Table 8.1**
**Largest Foreign Multinational Companies in Malaysian Manufacturing[a]**

| Rank | Company | Nationality | Main Business | Fixed Assets U.S.\$ millions |
|------|---------|-------------|---------------|------------------------------|
| 1 | Shell | U.K./ Netherlands | petroleum | 967 |
| 2 | Matsushita | Japan | consumer electronics/ semiconductors | 478 |
| 3 | Hitachi | Japan | consumer electronics/ durables | 199 |
| 4 | Sony | Japan | consumer electronics | 188 |
| 5 | Esso (Exxon) | U.S. | petroleum | 154 |
| 6 | National Semiconductor | U.S. | semiconductors | 138 |
| 7 | Siemens | Germany | semiconductors | 114 |
| 8 | Intel | U.S. | microprocessors | 110 |
| 9 | Motorola | U.S. | electronics/telecom equipment | 100 |
| 10 | Sharp | Japan | consumer electronics/ components | 77 |
| 11 | Guinness | U.K. | beer | 76 |
| 12 | Fujitsu | Japan | computers | 69 |
| 13 | Hewlett-Packard | U.S. | computers | 68 |
| 14 | Toshiba Electric | Japan | household electricals | 65 |
| 15 | Henkel Ria | Germany | chemicals | 63 |
| 16 | Carlsberg | Denmark | beer | 58 |
| 17 | Dunlop Malaysian Industry Bhd. (DMIB) | U.K. | tires | 54 |
| 18 | Scott Paper | U.S. | paper goods | 53 |
| 19 | Goodyear | U.S. | tires | 51 |
| 20 | BP | U.K. | petroleum | 50 |

*Source:* Malaysian Industrial Development Authority (MIDA); compiled by the authors.
[a]Based on fixed assets in January 1997.

(Table 8.2). Many top nonstate companies have small portions of their equity held by foreign investors. Malaysia's industrial drive is evidenced by the fact that twelve Malaysian companies made *Asiaweek* magazine's list of one thousand leading Asian business concerns for the year 1995, up from ten the previous year. Indeed, Proton, the national automobile company, has become arguably the most successful automobile manufacturer in the developing world, and recently moved from domestic sales only to exporting as well. Proton began with very significant government support and depended heavily on technology and design transfer from Japan's Mitsubishi. In 1996, Proton went global by buying Britain's prestigious Lotus car company.

Currently, Malaysia's manufacturing strategy has been regional rather than global. Domestic entrepreneurs are being encouraged to seek trade

*Table 8.2*
**Largest Malaysian Companies**[a]

| Rank | Company | Main Business | 1995 Revenues U.S.$ millions |
|------|---------|---------------|------------------------------|
| 1 | Petrolium Nasional[b] | oil, gas refining | 6,528 |
| 2 | Sime Darby | trading, commodities | 3,580 |
| 3 | Tenaga Nasional[b] | power generation | 2,145 |
| 4 | Perlis Plantations | sugar, flour, property | 1,831 |
| 5 | Malaysia Airline System[b] | air transport | 1,822 |
| 6 | Telekom Malaysia[b] | telecommunications | 1,712 |
| 7 | Eon | car dealership | 1,692 |
| 8 | Proton | auto manufacturing | 1,143 |
| 9 | Malaysia LNG Sdn Bhd[b] | gas | 1,302 |
| 10 | Federal Flour Mills | flour, animal feed | 1,257 |
| 11 | Berjaya Group | diversified | 1,256 |
| 12 | Petronas Dagangan[b] | oil marketing | 1,232 |
| 13 | Amalgamated Steel Mills | steel, retailing | 1,058 |
| 14 | Multi-Purpose Holdings | investment, property | 990 |
| 15 | Malaysian International Shipping | shipping | 784 |
| 16 | Berjaya Industrial | diversified | 692 |
| 17 | Genting | gaming, investment | 779 |
| 18 | Dunlop Estates | property, investment | 875 |
| 19 | Magnum | property, gaming | 873 |
| 20 | UMW Holdings | vehicle assembly | 705 |

*Source: Asiaweek*
[a]Based on revenues.
[b]Government-owned enterprise.

and investment opportunities overseas, and in pioneer areas for Asian investment such as Africa, Latin America, and Indochina. At the same time, many companies want to maintain their focus on the region. Given the fact that Southeast Asia is growing rapidly and there is interest from multinationals wanting to access the region, many Malaysian companies want to preserve and strengthen their holdings in anticipation of increased competition. Becoming a large player in a significant region, combined with the experience of supplying foreign firms, will be the sources of competitive advantage for Malaysian firms in their drive for global success in the future.

## Overall Globalization Drivers for Malaysia

There are numerous motivators for foreign MNCs to participate in Malaysia, the most attractive being fiscal incentives, infrastructure, trainable labor, and the stable political and legal systems.

### Market Globalization Drivers

Malaysia has mostly favorable market globalization drivers. Its population of twenty million places it at the upper end of the group of small

Asia-Pacific countries, just behind Taiwan's twenty-two million and ahead of Australia's eighteen million. This population has the important characteristic of being about 60% Bumiputra (sons of the soil—i.e. Malay), 30% Chinese, and 8% Indian. The country's British history has made English a common unofficial language that is widely used in business and taught in schools. In addition, many of the elite have received secondary or college education overseas. In consequence, the country is very receptive to Western products and marketing. At the same time, the Islamic faith is a strongly supported and widely practiced state religion that affects many aspects of behavior and consumption. The government also frequently criticizes aspects of Western lifestyles and culture. Japanese influence on popular culture continues to grow with the participation of Japanese companies and products in Malaysia's economy. Into this mélange is added significant influence from the Arab world through increasing business ties fostered by a common religion. For example, it is notable that one of the leading banks in the country is named Arab-Malaysian Bank.

Like the Philippines and Indonesia, Malaysia faces transportation and communication challenges from being spread across 1,300 miles of the South China Sea. East Malaysia, occupying the east and northeast coast of the island of Borneo (Sabah and Sarawah), comprises 60% of Malaysia's land area but only 18% of the population, and is much less developed economically. So in many ways, Malaysia comprises two geographically separate markets. In addition, the 47% of the population living in urban areas differs in many ways from the rural part of the population.[7]

The media and new products and services are rapidly changing consumer needs and tastes. Affluence has brought electricity and good roads and water even to distant villages, or *kampongs*. Ownership of a television, refrigerator, gas-operated cooking stove, and a motorized vehicle is becoming standard in the rural areas throughout West Malaysia. Most household equipment carries MNC brand names, even if made locally. Kentucky Fried Chicken has penetrated into the small towns of Malaysia. Companies selling consumer durables are extending their service networks. For example, UMW, Toyota Motor's local assembler and distributor, is upgrading its customer service through improved facilities and expanded networks. UMW opened a high-tech body and paint service center in Sungai Rasah to serve Toyota owners in the Klang Valley on the periphery of Kuala Lumpur.

As in most developing countries, Malaysians are not only willing to buy foreign products but actively prefer well-known imported foreign brands. Similarly, most types of Western-style marketing are transferable to Malaysia, although with most consumers being both Asian and Muslims, sexual connotations in advertisements need to be reduced or avoided.

Malaysia's importance in the production of electronic products (discussed below) has created the presence of many global customers who need to buy from other global vendors. For example, the presence of Seagate, the computer disc drive producer, has encouraged many of its suppliers to also come to Malaysia. Some negative market globalization drivers are that the proximity of Singapore, with its very highly developed distribution capabilities, has reduced Malaysia's ability to develop as a regional distribution center. Nor has Malaysia yet created companies that are global or regional leaders in their industries.[8] So the country has not achieved lead market status in any sector.

## Cost Globalization Drivers

Malaysia's cost globalization drivers have been very favorable for MNCs but are now deteriorating. The country is a global source for some key commodities—formerly tin, rubber, and palm oil, and more recently petroleum and gas. Despite its relatively small population, the country has done a great deal to create highly favorable cost conditions for foreign companies to locate activities there. In particular, its easily trained, reliable, English-speaking work force has become a primary attraction for MNCs seeking lower-cost production sites in countries that are also easy to do business in. With an increasing portion of the labor force now working directly or indirectly for MNC operations, the country's success has raised labor costs above that of more newly industrializing countries in the region. The hourly labor rate for the Malaysian manufacturing sector in 1995 was RM5.21 (U.S.$2.08) by one estimate,[9] and U.S.$1.59 by another,[10] and is now significantly higher than in Indonesia, the Philippines, and Thailand, Malaysia's most comparable rivals for the location of MNC production. Furthermore, many industries in Malaysia now suffer a shortage of labor.

Concentration of producers from certain industries, particularly semiconductors, telecommunications equipment, consumer electronics, and durables like air conditioners (for which Malaysia is now the world leader in production), has also increased the local availability of input materials and components, thereby reducing the need for more costly imports. For example, the Malaysia-American Electronics Industry Association works to help its member companies, such as Motorola, reduce raw materials imports whenever feasible, as required by the Malaysian government.

Compared with its neighbors in the region, Malaysia has excellent infrastructure in highways, ports, industrial estates, airports, energy, and electricity. Malaysia has been said to have one of the highest quality and most well-developed road systems in Southeast Asia. This system has greatly helped the government policy of dispersing industries to the rural areas of the country and attracting foreign direct investment. For example, sensitive electronic equipment produced by MNCs can be reliably transported on highways of very good quality. On the other hand, booming economic growth is straining the country's infrastructure, with port congestion being the biggest bottleneck.

Lastly, although Malaysia is not yet a creator of technology, the nation is an extensive user and adapter of foreign technology. The country has rapidly studied and converted information technology for modern and future usage within an Asian context, making Malaysia a favorite among suppliers and producers of up-to-date technologies. Once restarted, the setting up of the Multimedia Super Corridor (MSC) of fifty kilometers by

twenty kilometers in Selangor will serve MNCs with fiber links throughout the world.

## Government Globalization Drivers

Government globalization drivers continue to be very favorable. Malaysia, along with Singapore and Japan, has, since the 1960s, enjoyed the
most stable political conditions in Asia. Both Malaysia and Singapore
have government policies that are far more hospitable to foreign companies than are Japan's. In addition, the legacy of the British legal system
and relatively low levels of government corruption all contribute to making Malaysia a very easy place for MNCs to operate. The Malaysian government has fostered many incentives for foreign investment and activity
including free trade zones, double-taxation agreements with major trading partners such as the United States and Japan, and various fiscal incentives such as the Pioneer Status incentive provided for priority and
export-oriented products in the electrical and electronic industries.

Since the 1968 Investment Incentive Act, Malaysia has very actively
sought to attract foreign direct investment, especially in manufacturing
activities. Under the sixth Malaysia Plan (1991–95), the government targeted a total investment of RM 80 (U.S.$32) billion in the manufacturing
sector. Of this sum, domestic-source investment was to account for 60%
while foreign-source investment was to account for 40%. Malaysia has
continued to publicize the country's attractive investment climate, primarily through its industrial statutory body, the Malaysian Industrial Development Authority (MIDA). While all Asia-Pacific economies have similar organizations, Malaysia's seems to be particularly active. MIDA
conducts investment briefings in Kuala Lumpur, organizes investment
promotions and missions overseas, networks through international industrial cooperation, and places advertisements in local and international journals, magazines, and newspapers. It also participates in international industrial exhibitions.

MIDA also orchestrates industrial cooperation programs with other
countries, such as with the German agency for Investment and Development (DEG), the Canadian International Development Agency (CIDA),
the French Association for the Promotion and Development of Industrial
Cooperation (APPROD), and the Ministry of Foreign Affairs for Italy. Malaysia has also begun to promote foreign investment through MIDA centers. The government promotes Labuan (a small island northeast of Borneo) as an international offshore financial center. The program has met
with some degree of success as over forty international banks are now located on the island. Some sources believe that over a hundred international banks should be located there before Labuan can be considered a
fully fledged international financial center.

Malaysia is an enthusiastic participant in ASEAN and its AFTA activi-
ties, as well as in growth areas such as the Singapore-Johore-Riau Growth
Triangle (SIJORI), the Indonesia-Malaysia-Thailand Growth Triangle
(IMT-GT), and the Brunei-Indonesia-Malaysia-Philippines East ASEAN

Growth Area (BIMP-EAGA) (discussed in Chapter 16). So companies seeking benefits from such trade pacts should certainly place Malaysia high on their priority list for locating activities.

Malaysia actively seeks technology transfer, but more as an added bonus than as an exclusionary bargaining tactic, as is practiced by some other countries in the region. Contractual agreements to acquire foreign technology have been on the rise for Malaysia, particularly in the form of transfer agreements. In 1993, of a total of 185 foreign agreements, 153 were technology transfer agreements.[11] These were mainly undertaken for the electronic products industry, followed by the transport equipment industry, and the chemical products industry. Japan took the lead in terms of the total number of agreements signed. In 1993, 91 of 185 agreements were signed with Japan, followed by the United States (34), Korea (8), United Kingdom (8), and Australia (8).[12] About a third (34.6% in 1993) of companies signing agreements for foreign technologies were foreign-owned companies. Another third (30.3% in 1993) were majority Malaysian-owned companies, followed by 23.2% majority foreign-owned companies, and 11.9% wholly Malaysian-owned companies.

Malaysia also takes international technical standards seriously, having set up the Standards Industrial Research Institute of Malaysia (SIRIM) in 1975. SIRIM has gradually made itself into an authoritative body in approving standards for products and systems. It has adopted numerous international standards and nomenclatures for Malaysia.

The country scores relatively high in its commitment to protecting intellectual property rights. Numerous campaigns and confiscations have been undertaken to combat infringements. Perhaps the most distinctive Malaysian government policy is the official program to improve the wealth and condition of the Bumiputras. In 1970, thirteen years after independence (in 1957), Malays held only 2.4% of the country's wealth, while other Malaysians, mainly Chinese, held 46.2%. To achieve social peace after the May 13, 1969, bloody riot, the Malay-majority government instituted a series of policies to provide more favorable economic and educational treatment for Malays, including the creation of financial infrastructure to help redress the disparity. All businesses above a certain revenue level (RM2.5 million or U.S.$1 million in 1996), and all involving foreign investment, require 30% equity ownership by Bumiputras. So by 1990, Bumiputra individuals had increased their ownership share of the country's wealth to 20.3%, although still below the government target of 30% by 1990. Nevertheless, ethnic Chinese continue to dominate most nonstate-owned sectors of business in Malaysia. The economic rise of China has also strengthened the importance of access to the Chinese network.

### Competitive Globalization Drivers

Competitive globalization drivers are mixed. On the plus side, Malaysia is second only to Hong Kong and Singapore in Asia-Pacific in its involvement in trade. Combined merchandise exports and imports average well over 100% of GNP (Table 1.9 in Chapter 1), and over 140% of GDP in 1994, according to the Ministry of Finance. So the economy is exposed to the winds of foreign competition. The country has made itself a vital part of many MNCs' global value chains, thus playing a key role in global competitive battles. Furthermore, such involvement has pulled many local companies into international competition, upgrading their competitive capabilities. On the other hand, the relatively small population and GNP prevents the country from achieving strategic status for reasons of market scale. Nor is Malaysia a lead country in terms of customers, competitors, or innovation. Perhaps the most strategic potential comes from Malaysia as a platform to transfer products and practices to less-developed countries in the region (especially Indonesia with its ethnically similar population, closely related language, and shared religion), as part of the Overseas Chinese/Greater China network, as a lower-cost alternative to Singapore as a regional hub, and as an Islamic link to the wealth of the Middle East.

## Development of High-Technology Industries

Malaysia has become the world's third largest producer and exporter of electronic products and component parts, behind only the United States and Japan. The industry is now Malaysia's largest in terms of sales (RM27.5 billion in 1993). Even the petroleum industry was a distant second (RM13.1 billion). MNCs have played a very major role in building this industry. Foreign investment represented 76% of total investment in the electronics industry for the year 1994, with the United States holding the largest share, 20.3%, followed by Japan with 18.9%. To illustrate this phenomenon, we examine three sectors of the electronics industry in Malaysia—semiconductors, consumer electronics, and personal computers.

Malaysia's cost structure enabled the country to compete with Singapore as a low-cost manufacturing center. By 1996, manufacturing costs in Singapore were nearly three times more than in Malaysia.[13] Although Thailand, Indonesia, and Vietnam boast cost structures that are already luring labor-intensive manufacturing away from Malaysia, the government embraces this shift from low-cost, low-value work. Government incentives have and will continue to play an important role in building the PC industry in Malaysia. The country's aggressively pro-high-tech bureaucrats are well aware that the local industry must leverage all it can from twenty-five years of infrastructure building or face losing its advantage to its fast-rising neighbors. Major investors can expect to achieve pioneer status, paying taxes on only 30% of profits for five years. Companies with significant R&D operations may even qualify for full tax exemption for five years. Manufacturing incentives, however, are not limited to tax breaks. Local governments are upgrading their manufacturing facilities to make them more attractive to foreign investors. The state of Perak, for example, built hostels for workers to make it easier for multinationals to convince workers to come to the region.

## Semiconductor Industry

By offering foreign firms low-cost labor to assemble components, the country became, in the 1980s, one of the world's largest producers and exporters of semiconductors. For example, on Penang, an island off the West Malaysia peninsula, nearly one hundred international companies assemble semiconductors. But a decade later, a scarcity of labor, and rising wages in the economically booming nation have compelled its electronics industry to transform itself into a high-technology, low-labor operation. The semiconductor industry is a key component in the government's plans to encourage the development of high-technology industries. There are neither barriers nor customs duties on the import of supplies for semiconductor production in Malaysia. This results from the original Malaysian decision to foster the growth of an exclusively export-oriented industry.

At the present time, the government aims to develop linkages between the semiconductor industry and the growing downstream commercial and industrial electronics industries in Malaysia. After two decades of serving as an assembly location, Malaysia took a tentative step into the league of high-tech nations in 1996, when it began making its own microchips. The factory built by the Malaysian Institute of Microelectronics Systems (MIMOS) will initially focus on R&D and offer design services on a per-order basis. Its design services and products will be aimed at local users, but for the long term, MIMOS hopes to develop ASIC prototypes for the global market.

To alleviate cost pressures and spur high-value operations, the government has placed greater emphasis toward encouraging MNCs to upgrade their assembly operations to more automated production equipment, requiring higher levels of technical competence from a smaller labor force in such activities as wafer fabrication. Additional tax incentives are given to those firms who source their materials locally and develop ties with other local industries. Malaysia is also developing its infrastructure to provide sufficient supplies of electricity, water, chemicals, and other necessities that many neighboring countries cannot offer. This will allow production of chips from start to finish, from circuit-etching to assembly.

In addition, logistical considerations such as the presence of key component suppliers in Malaysia, and the proximity of suppliers in Singapore may overcome the negative impact of high wages. Malaysia's proximity to Singapore, the largest producing site of hard disk drives in the world, has made the country a convenient site for electronic component assembly. Competitive drivers, specifically the interdependence of manufacturers in Malaysia and Singapore, have offset some cost disadvantages.

## Consumer Electronics Industry

In contrast to the semiconductor industry, the consumer electronics industry is one in which some local manufacturers have emerged to compete with MNCs. The local *ASCON* brand is crowding out Japanese products in a number of fields, particularly air conditioners and refrigerators.

The appreciation of the yen and the ensuing Japanese rush to establish manufacturing bases in Malaysia resulted in a transfer of equipment and technologies Malaysia needed to develop local products. Malaysian firms, taking advantage of easier access to Japanese parts, have utilized their acquired knowledge to put out better and less-expensive products. ASCON has begun to compete regionally with many Japanese, Korean, and Taiwanese consumer electronics companies. But MNCs still dominate the production of consumer electronics in Malaysia. For example, a large Matsushita plant near the airport of Kuala Lumpur produces about one million color TV sets a year for the Japanese market.

The size and affluence of the market has drawn multinationals to produce in and for Malaysia. The nation's nearly twenty million people have seen purchasing power soar in recent years. Malaysia also sits at the center of one of the world's largest emerging markets—ASEAN. With a population of four hundred ten million, ASEAN is larger than either the United States or the European Union.

## Personal Computer Industry

The Malaysian government's plan to turn the country into a center of PC manufacturing that will attract multinational PC makers, as well as developing local suppliers and support industries, is showing signs of success. In 1995, two major U.S. makers, Dell Computer and Gateway, launched manufacturing operations in Malaysia. Gateway's 220,000 square foot personal computer plant in Malacca, (its second-largest worldwide) is conveniently situated next door to another PC maker, Likom Corp. Part of the Malaysian conglomerate Lion Group, Likom supplies PCs on an OEM basis for both U.S. and European vendors. In addition to its inviting economic policy, Malaysia's political stability has made Malaysia increasingly attractive for foreign manufacturers. By contrast, a hostile China flexing its military might in the Taiwan Strait has Taiwan PC makers and others seeking a regional base to the south. Similarly, the takeover of Micropolis Corp.'s disk drive business by Singapore Technologies, a government-owned entity, has Seagate Technology, the largest foreign employer in Singapore, concerned over the issue of business confidentiality.

PC production is a natural progression from semiconductor assembly for Malaysia. In addition, production of disk drives, printed-circuit boards, and a variety of other components made the emergence of the PC industry in Malaysia inevitable. Domestic demand for PCs also helps. Malaysia's strong and sustained economic growth for the last several years has allowed more business sectors to upgrade their present computer systems. The extent and degree of PC penetration in local businesses, industry, and research is at an early stage. There are still many Malaysian companies in various economic sectors that have the potential to implement computerization programs. The market segment for home and small office users has also experienced massive growth in recent years, creating vast opportunities for computer vendors.

For more than twenty years, Malaysia has become increasingly important for multinational electronics companies for locating assembly plants. Now, the region is becoming even more of a focal point for these OEMs, thanks to the exploding demand for PC mother boards and PC laptops. Malaysia's attraction and success as a hub for electronics investments is reinforced by the expansion plans of players already there. The new investments are not just for mature products being transferred out of Singapore and other countries, but for high-value-added products, fresh from U.S. laboratories.

Direct foreign investment combined with the successes of major OEM manufacturers in Malaysia and neighboring Singapore, helped jumpstart several PC-related businesses. Malaysia aspires to be a regional hub for information technology, especially in the fields of manufacturing, R&D, distribution, maintenance, and training. Although Singapore is the current computer center leader (IT) in the region, market, government, and competitive drivers are helping Malaysia narrow the gap.

## Overall Global Strategies for Malaysia

An older generation of MNCs came to Malaysia seeking raw material inputs. A newer generation of MNCs has come to seek both markets and production capabilities, the latter spurred by fiscal incentives, infrastructure, and trainable, educated, but inexpensive labor. In this section we examine the role that Malaysia plays in the global strategies of the six MNCs on which this book focuses—Motorola, Matsushita, Toyota, Philips, Procter and Gamble, and Unilever—and on some other MNCs also, thus drawing broader implications for all MNCs.

### Market Participation Strategies

With few government restrictions, growing affluence, and openness to foreign products, Malaysia constitutes a fairly easy market for MNCs to enter. So despite its moderate size, the country becomes an obvious one for MNCs to add to their roster of markets. In addition, the attractions of Malaysia for production has allowed many MNCs to easily combine local production and selling with both importing and exporting.

All six MNCs view Malaysia as a significant, if small, market. Unilever has been present since 1947, longer than almost any MNC. It began with import substitution activities in the production and sale of foodstuffs, detergents, and household cleaners, basically the same products as those it sells elsewhere. Procter and Gamble began later in similar fashion. It now sells both imported and locally produced products, and also exports processed raw materials.

Philips set up operations in Malaysia in the 1960s in line with the government's import substitution policy in electrical products, particularly lamps for indoor use. Today the company markets a wide range of products in the country, including color and black-and-white television sets, camera systems, central control equipment, business communication systems, alarm systems, access control systems, and voice logging systems, backed by nationwide service networks. Recently, Philips entered the export market in video systems and hi-fi through a joint venture with Japan's JVC. The company is gradually producing more sophisticated products in Malaysia, for example, compact discs for the worldwide market.

Toyota, too, set up in Malaysia in response to the import substitution drive of the 1970s. The company now holds over 20% of the Malaysian automobile market and, in 1994, included Malaysia in the worldwide launch of its global flagship product, the next generation of its *Camry* model (a near-luxury medium-sized vehicle).

Motorola, together with other world electronic products producers, has been a significant contributor to the rapid growth of the electronics industry in Malaysia. In Malaysia the company produces semiconductors, computer components (memory and microprocessors), and communications devices, mostly for export.

Matsushita set up its first subsidiaries in 1965, and produces and markets many products from its worldwide lines—televisions, refrigerators, washing machines, dry cell batteries, fans, irons, rice cookers, vacuum cleaners, and gas cookers. Matsushita located itself in Malaysia during the second (1971–75) and third (1976–80) Five-Year Malaysia Plans, when labor-intensive industries were welcomed. As of 1996, the company had fourteen manufacturing sites, one R&D facility, and two sales companies in the country.

Access to global customers has also become a motivation for participating in Malaysia. The flood of electronic multinationals into Malaysia has allowed semiconductor manufacturers to come into closer contact with their customers, component manufacturers. Many electronic component producers have operations in Malaysia, ranging from microprocessors made by Intel to disk drives made by the three largest drive manufacturers (the U.S. trio—Conner, Quantum, and Seagate), as well as CD-ROMs, and monitors. More important is the recent move into the region by Intel, arguably the most influential force in the PC industry. The chip maker opened a huge PC motherboard production plant in Malaysia, a move that should certainly alter the procurement side of the computer business. Seagate's Senoko and Batam facilities currently produce more than seventy-two thousand printed circuit boards and utilize nearly nineteen million parts daily. But that satisfies only 80% of Seagate's growing internal demand for printed circuit boards that have resulted from the merger with Conner Peripherals.[14] The use of just-in-time manufacturing techniques has made chip availability and expedient delivery major concerns for buyers. So suppliers to Seagate and similar companies have had to locate in Malaysia.

### Product and Service Strategies

The Malaysian market of only twenty million people does not, on its own, justify significant investment in product adaptation. Like most developing countries, its consumer markets can be divided into three major segments. First, the small, but growing, upper-income segment can afford many modern products and services and, through education, travel, and interaction with foreigners, has acquired the taste for such items. MNCs need make few adaptations for this segment and may even lose out by overlocalizing so that products lose their foreign cachet. For example, Malaysian consumers demand a computer system that is rich with features, offers high performance, quality, and is impeccably serviced. Issues relating to marketing, distribution, and service are now as important to consumers as issues of technology, technical features, and performance. So, for example, PC vendors in Malaysia find that they now have to service customers as they would in any developed country. This has also happened with Mercedes-Benz owners.

Second, the large mass market segment would happily buy many foreign goods and services, but can afford only basic or stripped-down versions. For this segment, the appropriate MNC strategy would be to offer low-end items from their product lines. Here also, regionally adapted products can pay their way, spreading the cost of adaptation across several countries with similar economic levels. Toyota's development of an "Asian" economy automobile, the *Soluna*, constitutes a major attempt at such a regional product strategy. Companies marketing ordinary conventional ovens, as opposed to the latest sophisticated ovens, provide another example of regional products.

Third, the teenage market segment has preferences and demands for the same limited set of global products and services that at any time appeal to teenagers all over the world. This segment also demands global standardization—in sneakers, music, consumer electronics, fast food, motorcycles and the like.[15] As many of these global products are produced in Asia, they can be sold at lower local prices, and hence are affordable to local teenagers—for example, denim clothing, sports equipment, and shoes. Similarly, global services, such as McDonalds, depend on local teenagers working at local pay scales for their labor forces, again bringing their prices within reach of this segment. With its per capita income level behind Japan and the "four (developed) tigers," but ahead of all other developing Asian countries, Malaysia most typifies the above three-part segmentation.

For industrial products, the very active role of many MNCs as local customers means that, in most cases, vendors need to supply goods that meet global standards and specifications. For example, Motorola, a very major producer in Malaysia, applies in Malaysia (and all countries) its same "Six Sigma" global quality standards. For professional services, such as accounting and consulting, Malaysian business customers now recognize the need to use world-class providers, but have significant problems with world-class prices.

## Activity Location Strategies

MNCs first set up production activities in Malaysia to benefit from the low-cost, trainable, and reliable labor force, particularly manually-dexterous female workers for electronics producers. These initial activities (still the dominant mode) comprised assembly and packaging rather than complete-product production, especially for high-value items for re-export. For example, Toyota performs final assembly for both the local and export markets, as do Motorola, Philips, and Matsushita. Motorola has in Malaysia its biggest semiconductor plant outside the United States. The company's four plants, in Petaling Jaya, Penang, Seremban, and the Ulu Kelang Free Trade Zone together employ fourteen thousand persons, 10% of Motorola's worldwide work force.

Numerous government incentives also lured MNC operations. Malaysia has benefited from the General System of Preferences (GSP) quota system, which gives priority to developing countries in the form of a reduction or exemption of tariff duties. The Malaysian GSP quota for various types of products was used by Japanese producers, such as Matsushita, to penetrate U.S. markets.

Over the years, several Japanese, Korean, and Taiwanese consumer electronics giants such as Matsushita, JVC, and Hitachi shifted the focus of their overseas production to Malaysia because of its lower production costs. Matsushita now has a total of fourteen plants throughout Malaysia making electronic components and consumer products. Matsushita's production operations in Malaysia constitute that company's largest scale for any of its overseas operations. Faced with falling margins and shorter product life cycles, many personal computer producers shifted some operations into Malaysia in a flight from the soaring costs of manufacturing in their home countries. These cost refugees include U.S. companies such as Apple, Compaq, Dell, IBM, and Texas Instruments; Japanese PC makers, such as NEC, and Taiwanese manufacturers, such as Acer.

Consumer packaged goods companies, such as Unilever and Procter and Gamble, with their high-bulk, low-value products, tend to produce complete products, but use some imported raw materials. In other cases, local raw materials continue to be the basis of MNC activity. Procter and Gamble set up a manufacturing plant in Kuantan, in 1994, to produce for export fatty alcohol, the main ingredient in detergents and cosmetics. The main ingredient for fatty alcohol is palm oil, which is abundantly available in Malaysia. Proximity of the factory to Kuantan Port, on the east coast of the West Malaysia peninsula, also reduces transportation costs significantly in reaching ASEAN and Far East markets.

There are several key developments in the nature of activities being conducted in Malaysia by MNCs. First, as discussed earlier, rising affluence and wage rates are pushing MNCs to move low-value-adding activities to other countries, while moving in higher-value-adding ones. For example, MNCs have mostly moved the production of athletic shoes to Indonesia and elsewhere, but now make tennis rackets, a higher-margin product, in Malaysia. Similarly, other MNCs have shifted some production of personal computers to Malaysia from Singapore, Korea, and Taiwan. As the next to be developed Asian economy, Malaysia stands very much in the middle of the game of "musical factories," in which MNCs move production before costs catch up with the prices they can charge.

Second, improving worker skill and education levels, and technology transfer over the last twenty years are enabling MNCs to shift to the production of technically more-sophisticated products. For example, electronics companies are now able to manufacture more-sophisticated components. Dell, a leading U.S. personal computer company, was one of the first MNC pioneers to help Penang State realize the latter's goal of having all levels of manufacturing done there—from manufacturing, assembly, design, tooling, engineering, R&D, marketing, and sales, to customer service. Intel has made a similar move by adding R&D and sales to its integrated manufacturing process. These MNC changes are very much supported by government policies, as discussed earlier. Motorola has long invested in improving its workers' skills to run sophisticated equipment. The company's machinery operators have been made to be as responsible as engineers for their own quality.

Third, MNCs are trying to reduce dependence on expensive imported parts by enhancing their local ability to develop and produce components and other inputs. High imports of intermediate inputs for reexport yielded low local linkages or value adding. The Philips-JVC (Dutch-Japanese) video joint venture added the assembly of video drums, a difficult core technology in VCR production, in an effort to use more local parts. As a result, Philips-JVC has successfully developed a fully integrated vertical production system, which has enabled the company to significantly increase its production of VCRs. This import-substitution strategy on the part of MNCs is being helped by the widespread improvement in the quality of locally produced components. Most of the parts used in Sony's factories in Malaysia are now bought from Japanese companies based in Malaysia. Sony still needs to import some parts from Japan, mainly because of the lack of a local supporting industry that can meet the standards required by Sony. In the near future, Sony plans to transfer technology to Malaysian-owned small- and medium-sized companies to lift the quality of production in these companies. The consequent increase in local content will reduce for Sony the cost as well as time incurred in importing these products from Japan.

Fourth, many MNCs are upgrading their operations and facilities, spurred by the improving capabilities of workers, labor shortages, and high wages. Matsushita Air Conditioning Group is upgrading its facilities to shorten production lead times through the enhancement of manufacturing processes, better quality control, automation, and cooperation with local suppliers.

Fifth, some MNCs are now adding much-needed R&D activities in the electronics industry. Matsushita has set up an air-conditioning R&D center to design the products it makes in Malaysia. In 1995, Sharp-Roxy, a venture between this leading Japanese electronics company and a Malaysian partner, introduced its first generation of locally produced audio products entirely developed and designed by Malaysian engineers. Sharp-Roxy based this decision on the Malaysian operation's track record for the past twenty years and also because of the availability of local expertise. Motorola is also expanding its R&D facilities to develop technology at lower costs in Malaysia. Its Penang plant now has more than 150 R&D employees, and has developed two-way mobile walkie-talkie radios for low-band VHF and UHF use, and has supported Motorola's *CT-2* product enhancement program for subscriber handsets and public base stations.

## Marketing Strategies

As described earlier, many factors make Western and Japanese marketing strategies easily transferable to Malaysia. In consumer marketing, MNCs are able to use international approaches, adapting mainly for the stage of development of the market and the level of experience that local consumers have with the particular product or service category. For example, U.S.-based Amway sells its households products via kampong peddlers on motorbikes or even bicycles. Or MNCs may need to create a local campaign when their home country one is not exportable. For example, Eveready Battery cannot use internationally its satirical U.S. advertising campaign of the "Energizer bunny that keeps going and going and going," both because of prior international trademarking by its rival, Duracell, and because of international differences in appreciation of humor. So in Malaysia the company developed a TV commercial around the visual device of a continuously stretching arm.

Nevertheless, many MNCs use global campaigns that are little adapted. In the 1994 launch of its new *Camry* model in Malaysia, Toyota used its global advertising campaign that stressed the high-technology content of the car. Both Unilever and Procter and Gamble use many brand names that are international ones: *Lux, Walls, Lipton, Ponds, Persil, Sunlight, Breeze, Comfort, Jif, Vaseline, Pepsodent, Signal, OXO, OMO, Flora, Sunsilk, Brut,* and *Birds Eye* for Unilever; and *Rejoice, Pantene, Vidal Sassoon, Pampers, Whisper,* and *Oil of Olay* for Procter and Gamble. At the same time each company markets some local brands—*Ekonomi Handalan* (a detergent) for Unilever, and *Gheeblend* (a dairy product) for Procter and Gamble. Philips uses a local slogan of "Let's Make Life Brighter."

Marketing by MNCs in Malaysia follows much the same approach as elsewhere. Malaysian buyers are influenced by the media, especially television and radio. Motorola heavily promotes through advertising, emphasizing the quality of its products. Many Unilever brands have become synonymous with their category—*Vaseline* for hair cream, *Lux* for bathing soap, and *JIF* for mild abrasive scouring cleaners.

Advanced retail modes are also reaching Malaysia. For example, personal computers now also sell through retail outlets and superstores, due to the increasing growth of the market segment for home and small office users. Similarly, Dell and Gateway, U.S. pioneers of selling direct to customers, have chosen Malaysia as a site for assembly and regional customer support for the Asia-Pacific region.

## Competitive Move Strategies

So many MNCs now participate in Malaysia and so many depend on the country as part of their global value-adding chains that competitive moves there often have regional or worldwide implications. The presence of rival MNCs also makes Malaysia a good testing ground for products and ideas. On the other hand, the relatively small size of local markets for most products and services, with the exception of high-volume supplies for locally based global factories, reduces the stakes. So MNCs can afford some mistakes in Malaysia, although not too many.

## Overall Organization and Management Approaches for Malaysia

Malaysia's lengthy experience with British administration, a largely Western-educated elite, and long-time involvement with foreign MNCs mean that Western management methods are familiar and accepted. Because of language and cultural differences, Japanese MNCs have more difficulty applying their management approaches.

### Organization Structure

The major issue affecting an MNC's organization structure regards the selection of a local partner. As discussed earlier, ethnic Chinese continue to dominate most sectors of nonstate-owned business, but are also subject to extensive restrictions through the Bumiputra preference system. A foreign MNC should select an ethnic Chinese partner if particular types of expertise are needed, or particular connections, especially to the expatriate Chinese network or to China itself. An ethnic Malay partner would be particularly helpful for long-term security and access to the government. Partners from the smaller ethnic Indian community can also be useful for their particular skills and contacts, especially now that the Indian economy is opening up.

There is less need for government as a majority partner since government participation in business has been significantly reduced through the Privatization Programme. Government partnership is now largely confined to large and sophisticated operations in strategic sectors such as telecommunications (e.g., satellite programs). At the same time, as in most Asian countries, partnerships with relatives of government officials can be a plus. Also, capable local partners from the private sector have become more available in various industries in recent years. Lastly, unlike in some other Asian countries, the military plays no direct role in business. However, retired military personnel do involve themselves.

Like most other countries in the region, the government would like to attract more regionally headquartered operations. Singapore is, of course, the dominant choice in Southeast Asia. In a 1996 survey of regional executives,[16] Kuala Lumpur ranked third (albeit distantly) behind Singapore and Hong Kong. For example, Dell Computer runs all of its Asian operations from Penang. To switch to Malaysia, MNCs would need to balance Malaysia's lower cost of HQ operations (e.g., rent, salaries, and utilities) against Singapore's better communications and transportation infrastructure.

## Management Processes[17]

Ever since the colonial era, Western influences on management in Malaysia have been significant. In general, medium- and large-size organizations that are not family-owned adopt Western-style management practices. Once the customary handshakes and courtesies are completed, business is more straightforward in Malaysia than in Indonesia or Thailand. At the same time, small companies and the few medium and large family-owned businesses may incorporate management approaches that have been brought by migrant groups from China and India. Consequently, there is no distinct Malaysian style of management. This absence of a distinct Malaysian management style and the willingness to adapt to foreign business practices has enabled MNCs to use global management processes in Malaysia. Different MNCs have varied management processes depending on their origin and their perceptions of and responsiveness to local requirements. For example, Motorola uses in Malaysia the same participative management programs that it has elsewhere. One program solicits suggestions from employees. For Motorola Seremban alone the total number of suggestions amounted to five hundred per month in 1995.

The rise of Islamic banking in Malaysia is becoming well-received. The system essentially substitutes equity participation for interest in banking transactions. Malaysia has become the pioneer, ahead even of Middle Eastern countries, of Islamic banking methods and can boast of its "Father of Islamic Banking," Nor Yakcop Mohamed.[18] Islamic banks now hold perhaps 30% of the Malaysian market.

### People

The government has strongly encouraged "Malaysianisation" of MNC work forces and management. The relatively high standard of middle-class education has allowed MNCs to replace most of their expatriates with locals. Training local managers has been supported by the government's Malaysianisation Programme since the mid-1970s. Both Procter and Gamble and Unilever have very Malaysianized management teams. Philips recently made its management team more Malaysian. In high-technology industries, most American MNCs are highly Malaysianized, with locals as CEOs. In contrast, most Japanese MNCs have, as in most other countries, retained senior positions for Japanese nationals, citing language and culture as justifications. Some MNCs also transfer Malaysian managers to other countries. Motorola has more than thirty senior executives from Malaysia running operations all over the world. Singapore Airlines increasingly hires pilots and flight attendants from Malaysia (and a few other countries) paying them the same as native Singaporeans.

Skilled managers, however, continue to be in short supply. The government has to some extent eased the problem by allowing MNCs to recruit foreign personnel in areas where there is a shortage of trained

Malaysians. But foreign companies still face difficulties and delays in getting work permits for expatriate staff.[19]

## Culture

Malaysia's mix of three ethnic groups, a state religion of Islam, and numerous expatriates in business, creates a complex business and management culture. As in most countries, each group has strong beliefs about the capabilities of, and distinct roles that should be played by, each of the other groups. National cultural practices reinforce these views. For example, the ethnic groups take turns in running organizations during festive seasons involving the three respective races. Most MNCs try to avoid allocating jobs by race, and probably do best by promoting a global corporate culture that is also sensitive to the various local cultures.

## Conclusions

Perhaps more than any other Asia-Pacific economy, Malaysia poses the most issues of transition and change for MNCs. Over the past three decades, Malaysia has joined the ranks of the fastest-expanding markets in the Pacific Rim. The economic transformation from a producer of primary commodities such as natural rubber and tin to a world exporter in manufactured goods has been remarkable. The rapidly growing economy has led to a growing middle class, higher living standards, full employment, a strong MNC-dominated corporate sector, an expanding local supplier base, and increased integration into global trading systems. However, as Malaysia heads toward developed country status (as articulated in *Vision 2020*), it is encountering several challenges to its continued expansion, including rising costs, shortages of skilled labor, and infrastructure bottlenecks, and its current financial crisis.

Malaysia exemplifies the success of a global strategy for both itself and for MNCs. There is no doubt that Malaysia has enjoyed high growth due to foreign investments in plants and equipment in their respective manufacturing sectors. In return, Malaysia has given MNCs reliable conditions (location, market size, resource base, stable political system), stable macroeconomic management, clear and consistent policies toward investors, a favorable attitude to private enterprise, good infrastructure, and various deregulation and liberalization measures that allow MNCs to operate in internationally competitive conditions.

The role of Malaysia in global strategies has changed over the decades. At first foreign companies invested in Malaysia because of cheap labor and government incentives. Yet as wages rise amid labor shortages, Malaysia may no longer have a cost advantage in assembling labor-intensive products. In its place, market and competitive drivers now encourage MNCs to shift to higher-value-added fields and pursue greater productivity. MNCs need to be vigilant in adjusting their strategies for Malaysia as that country's situation continues to develop and as that of competing countries also changes.

For MNCs, Malaysia constitutes an attractive market in its own right. In many ways, its small, middle-income population provides a relatively easy market for Western MNCs, particularly for those seeking an easier, early experience in Asia. On the one hand, standards are sufficiently below most Western ones that MNCs will find it relatively easy in many cases to have a competitive advantage over local producers. On the other hand, standards are not so far below those of affluent nations that MNCs need make drastic adjustments. Also, as an economy in transition from developing to developed, experience in this market can be leveraged up or down the scale of other Asia-Pacific economies.

Malaysia's stable political system, which strongly supports foreign investment, also makes it an easy country for MNCs. At the same time, MNCs do need to find ways to build connections into the government, either directly or through partners, perhaps from the Overseas Chinese network. MNCs can also develop partnerships with the growing number of large and capable local companies that are themselves internationalizing (see the list in Table 8.2 earlier).

MNCs should find Malaysia attractive for many activities in the value chain. While purely low-skill, low-cost assembly activities are no longer economic, many semiskilled production activities should be viable in Malaysia through the year 2000. But perhaps more than in any other country in the region, MNCs will have to plan for the gradual upgrading of in-country activities, as wages and costs continue to rise. Today MNCs can consider locating in Malaysia every value-chain activity from research to customer service, or even a regional headquarters. Lastly, managing in Malaysia will pose the usual challenges of any foreign environment, but not excessively so. MNCs can push to apply global methods and standards of management.

## NOTES

1. "The ultimate objective that we should aim for is a Malaysia that is a fully developed country by the year 2020. . . . We should be a developed country in our own mould." Prime Minister Mahathir Mohamed, 1991.

2. Mahathir Mohamed, *The Way Forward* (Kuala Lumpur: Government Printers, 1991).

3. Minister of Finance, Malaysia, *Economic Report 1996* (Kuala Lumpur: Government Printers, 1996).

4. Not counting the Middle Eastern states as Asian.

5. Malaysian Industrial Development Authority (MIDA), *Annual Report 1995* (Kuala Lumpur, 1996).

6. Rodney Smith, William Sullivan, Lynn Wallace, "Malaysia: Moving From Public to Private," *Asian Century Business Report* 4, no. 1 (February 1995).

7. *Asiaweek*, October 1996, 51.

8. One exception is Royal Selangor Pewter in pewter products.

9. Department of Statistics, *Manufacturing Industries Survey* (Kuala Lumpur: Government Printers, 1995).

10. See Table 1.2 in Chapter 1.

11. MIDA, 1994.

12. MDIA, 1994.

13. LaPedus, Mark, "Asia-Pacific Gets More Important in PC Assembly," *Electronic Buyers' News,* January 29, 1996, 28.

14. "Seagate Technology Expands PCBA Operations Into Malaysia," *Business Wire,* June 3, 1996.

15. Theodore Levitt, "The Globalization of Markets," *Harvard Business Review* (May–June 1983), 92–102.

16. Survey of over 6,000 executives around Asia, conducted by Survey Research Singapore in 1996.

17. This section on management processes is partly based on Gregory Thong Tin Sin, "Managing Process in *Bumiputra* Society—Malaysia," in Joseph M. Putti, *Management: Asian Context* (Singapore: McGraw-Hill Book Co., 1991).

18. See also Dr. Yahia Abdul Rahman, *Lariba Bank: Islamic Banking* (Hiawatha, Iowa: Cedar Graphics, 1994).

19. Murray Hiebert, "Playing the Hi-Tech Card," *Far Eastern Economic Review,* April 27, 1995, 40–42.

# CHAPTER 9

# Thailand—Tiger by the Tail?

*Kanoknart Visudtibhan and George S. Yip*

THAILAND IS IN THE third wave of Asian countries after Japan and the "four tigers" to embark on rapid and widespread industrialization. Once known as the Kingdom of Siam, Thailand is the only country in the Southeast Asian region never to have been colonized by the West. Rooted in Buddhist heritage and a democratic system within a constitutional monarchy, the country has enjoyed a relatively stable political and social climate compared to other countries at a similar stage of economic development. The country's relatively large population, rapid economic growth, and position next to the emerging economies of Indochina, combine to make it highly attractive as both a market and a location for production and distribution. Thailand has had one of the fastest growth rates of the Asian tigers. Its financial and economic crisis beginning in 1997 suggests that Thailand's rulers now have this tiger by the tail! Can Thailand recover its growth, or are its halcyon days over? While the crisis hurts the Thais, opportunities can still abound for foreign investors and economic participants.

## Background

Thailand's economic development policies have been relatively conservative with an emphasis on a competitive free-market philosophy. The industrialization process was largely characterized by an import substitution policy in the 1960s, an export promotion policy in the 1970s, a foreign direct investment promotion policy in the 1980s, and a trade liberalization policy in the 1990s. Differential tariff rates on imports have been most frequently used by various Thai governments to influence the pace of industrialization. Other measures include import quotas, credit assistance for exports and imports, local content requirements, and tax rebates for export goods production.

Thailand's economic policy formulation has been guided by a series of five-year National Economic and Social Development Plans, first implemented in 1961. The goal of the Seventh Plan (1992–96) was for the country to achieve improvements in economic liberalization, investment

in basic and social infrastructure, industrial development at the provincial level, and in environmental protection and energy conservation
programs.

## Economic Performance

The Thai economy has experienced exceptional rates of GDP annual
growth in recent decades with growth peaking at over 10% from 1988–90.
Since 1991, the average annual rate of GDP growth has been about 8%.
Before the financial crisis of 1997, the International Monetary Fund
(IMF) predicted that the economy will continue to grow with an average
annual rate of 7.6% from 1995–2002, making Thailand the eighth fastest-
growing economy in the world. Thailand's National Economic and Social
Development Board (NESDB) has projected that by the year 2000, the
GDP will be U.S.$289 billion, making Thailand the largest economy in
Southeast Asia.[1] In July 1997, Thailand's economic prospects were
thrown into doubt by the sudden collapse of its currency. The Thai baht
plunged by about 20% in just a few days, forcing the government to drop
its fixed rate for a floating one, but still retaining exchange controls. This
crisis was precipitated by a large deficit in the balance-of-payments and by
the recognition that many Thai banks held debts of questionable quality.
In response, the International Monetary Fund put together a support
package with strict terms. By November 1997, the Thai baht was down
33% in value relative to the U.S. dollar from a year previously, and stock
market values were down by nearly 50%.

Accompanying the economic growth has been a structural shift from
agriculture to manufacturing. A milestone occurred in 1985, when manufacturing achieved a larger share of the GDP for the first time. Industry
share of GDP at the end of 1992 stood at 39%, of which 28% was from the
manufacturing sector. Similar phenomena can be observed in international trade activities. The manufacturing share of total exports increased
from 30% in 1980, to 80% in 1993. Most of this increase took place in
light and labor-intensive industries. Textile products, computers and
components, and electrical appliances have been the three leading manufacturing exports. Export of integrated circuits, however, is becoming
increasingly important.

In 1994, Thailand's exports totaled over U.S.$40 billion. Thailand's
major trading partners are industrialized countries, including the United
States, Japan, and Germany. However, Thailand increasingly takes part in
intraregional trade, largely through Singapore and Hong Kong, with
total direct investment from Asian NICs recently outweighing that of
Japan. Leading imported products are machinery (nonelectric and electric), other consumer goods, and chemicals.

## Foreign Investment in Thailand

MNCs, such as Shell, British-American Tobacco, Singer, and Unilever,
were present in Thailand even before World War II. A significant increase

in foreign investment in the country, however, began in 1957, with the industrialization of the country during the Field Marshall Sarit Thanarat regime. In order to promote and render assistance to private investors, the government established the Board of Investment (BOI) in 1958. It also formed the National Economic and Social Development Board to regularly produce five-year development plans to guide investment.[2]

Because of the country's import substitution policy during the 1960s and 1970s, direct foreign investment concentrated on production for the protected domestic market. A shift in government emphasis from import substitution toward an export orientation and changes in the BOI's promotional criteria in 1983, to complement the new government policy, has led to a higher inflow of export-oriented foreign investment. The surge of investment can also be attributable to the Plaza Accord agreement in 1985, which resulted in a favorable realignment of exchange rates for Thailand. Between 1980 and 1988, direct foreign investment more than tripled.

The net inflows of foreign direct investment in Thailand at the end of 1994 were U.S.$1 billion. Since 1985, the inflows have shifted more to the production of labor-intensive products for export to Northeast Asia, the United States, and Europe. Leading sectors of foreign investment, in terms of value, have occurred in industries such as food, textiles, metals, electrical appliances, and construction.

Japanese automobile companies dominate the top twenty list of foreign MNCs (Table 9.1). But companies in consumer products, electronics and computers also play significant roles.

## Local Companies

The private sector in Thailand possesses three distinct characteristics. First, it is dominated by a well-integrated local Chinese-Thai business class, unusually free from ethnic and religious divisions. Second, the private sector plays a large and active role in policy making. Third, it has not been eclipsed by the recent surge of MNC foreign direct investment. To the contrary, Thai capital accounts for a significant share of assets in the key industrial sectors, for example, 45% in the automobile and textile industries.[3]

Some Thai companies are aggressively expanding internationally. The first wave of Thai multinationals began in the agricultural sector. Today, however, Thai firms are doing everything from building dams and highways in Indochina to operating manufacturing plants in the United States. Table 9.2 lists the twenty largest domestic Thai companies.

Most of these top companies are very active in the international arena. For example, Chareon Pokphand Feedmill, the sixth largest public local company, is part of the C. P. Group conglomerate that is the largest foreign investor in China. This privately held concern typifies many Thai family-based concerns and conducts many different activities, including agribusiness, aquaculture, international trading, marketing and distribution, real estate and land development, petrochemicals, automotive and

*Table 9.1*
**Largest Foreign Multinational Companies in Thailand**

| Rank | Company | Nationality | Industry | 1995 Revenues U.S. $millions |
|---|---|---|---|---|
| 1 | Toyota Motor Thailand | Japan | automobile | 1,372 |
| 2 | Shell Company of Thailand | U.K. | oil | 1,148 |
| 3. | ESSO Standard | U.S. | oil | 1,068 |
| 4 | Tri Petch Isuzu | Japan | automobile | 990 |
| 5 | Seagate Technology (Thailand) | U.S. | computer | 850 |
| 6 | MMC Sittipol | Japan | automobile | 840 |
| 7 | Thai Honda Manufacturing | Japan | automobile | 576 |
| 8 | Siam Nissan Automobile | Japan | automobile | 539 |
| 9 | Caltex Oil (Thailand) | U.S. | oil | 528 |
| 10 | Honda Car Manufacturing | Japan | automobile | 367 |
| 11 | Thai-Hino Motor Sales | Japan | automobile | 319 |
| 12 | Lever Brothers (Thailand) | U.K. | consumer products | 287 |
| 13 | Thai Suzuki Motor | Japan | motorcycles | 246 |
| 14 | Fujitsu (Thailand) | Japan | computer | 241 |
| 15 | Siam National | Japan | consumer electronics | 201 |
| 16 | Mitsui & Co. (Thailand) | Japan | electronics | 198 |
| 17 | Minebea Electronics (Thailand) | Japan | electronics | 196 |
| 18 | Cal-Comp Electronics (Thailand) | Taiwan | computer peripherals | 190 |
| 19 | Volvo Thailand | Sweden | automobile | 185 |
| 20 | Singba Thailand | U.S. | appliances | 176 |

Source: Financial Day 2000, (First edition), Bangkok: Manager Information Services Co. Ltd., 1996 and Thailand Company Information, 1996–1997.
Note: Exchange rate = US$ 0.02621 to 1 Baht

industrial products, telecommunications, and the production of petroleum. The ninth largest public company, Italian-Thai Development, a property concern, is investing $40 million in central Laos. The eighth largest public company, Saha-Union group, operates a modern textile plant in the United States. C. P. Group and Shinawatra were recently ranked in an *Asiaweek* survey as the first and eighth Asian companies with the greatest potential for growth.[4]

Thai investment overseas at the end of 1994 was $323 million, the largest recipients being China, the Philippines, and the United States. The leading three sectors of Thai investment overseas were industry, services, and real estate.

## Overall Globalization Drivers for Thailand

Most of Thailand's globalization drivers favor the participation of foreign MNCs. In addition, Thailand has become increasingly attractive as a gateway and hub for the emerging economies of the Indochina region.

**Table 9.2**
**Largest Companies Listed on the Bangkok Stock Exchange**

| Rank | Company | Main Business | 1995 Revenues in U.S.$millions |
|---|---|---|---|
| 1 | Siam Cement | building | 4,173 |
| 2 | Thai Airways International | transportation | 3,069 |
| 3 | Bangchak Petroleum | energy | 1,240 |
| 4 | Siam Makro | commerce | 1,231 |
| 5 | Petrochemical Industry | petrochemical | 997 |
| 6 | Charoen Pokphand Feedmill | agribusiness | 954 |
| 7 | Shinawatra | communication | 784 |
| 8 | Bangkok Produce Merchandise | agribusiness | 758 |
| 9 | Italian-Thai Development | property | 731 |
| 10 | United Communications | communication | 626 |
| 11 | Robinson Department Store | commerce | 588 |
| 12 | Saha Union | textiles | 545 |
| 13 | Siam City Cement | building | 542 |
| 14 | Advanced Information Service | communication | 495 |
| 15 | TPI Polene | chemicals | 491 |
| 16 | Siam Suk | foods | 479 |
| 17 | Alphatec Electronics | electronics | 476 |
| 18 | Thai Central Chemical | chemical | 408 |
| 19 | International Cosmetics | commerce | 386 |
| 20 | Land & House | property | 378 |

*Source:* Stock Exchange of Thailand
Note: Excludes banks and financial companies. Exchange rate = US$ 0.02621 to 1 Baht

## Market Globalization Drivers

Thailand's rapid industrialization and GDP growth have made it a target both for global corporations seeking new customers, as well as for those MNCs seeking to take advantage of Thailand's still cheap prices for raw material and labor inputs. The local market is relatively large, with a population of over sixty million, and has a growing GDP per capita of over $2,000.

The high rate of economic growth has led to the emergence of a new burgeoning middle-class category of Thai consumers, known as the "have somes."[5] Thai consumption patterns are increasingly similar to those of industrialized Western nations. A communications and media revolution coupled with the rising middle class has fueled a proliferation of televisions (reaching 100 per 1,000 population by 1994).[6] Young Thai consumers are now buying fresh food and vegetables at a fixed price in air-conditioned supermarkets instead of going to open-air fresh markets. Other indications of converging consumer needs include the rapid expansion of fast food chains, such as Kentucky Fried Chicken, which increased its outlets from 71 in 1994, to 111 in 1995; the wine market, which is growing at 30% annually, with consumption around 2.7 million liters a year and a market value of about U.S.$40 million; and the construction of large shopping malls, one of which is a megamall that ranks among the world's four largest. Kellogg, the U.S. cereal company, believing that Thai consumers would forego *Kaw Tom* (rice porridge) for a healthy, more convenient breakfast, is investing 300 million baht (U.S.$1.2 million) in a cereal-producing plant in Thailand to serve both the domestic and other Asian markets.

Although some marketing adaptation is always required due to language and cultural differences, Thailand offers MNCs a relatively high degree of marketing transferability, especially with brand names. Western television and increasing tourism have helped increase consumers' awareness of the latest Western trends and products. Foreign brand names are well recognized and often preferred by Thai consumers. Advertisers use Western sports figures and movie stars, from Carl Lewis to Sylvester Stallone, to endorse their products.

MNCs have increasingly included Thailand in their regional distribution systems because of its strategic location as a gateway to the newly emerging neighboring economies of Vietnam, Laos, Myanmar, and Cambodia. In retailing, companies such as Costco and J. C. Penney of the United States, and David Holdings of Australia, are forming joint ventures with local partners to operate and coinvest in distribution centers. On the other hand, relatively few MNCs maintain regional offices in Thailand, compared with Hong Kong or Singapore.

## Cost Globalization Drivers

Thailand is a global source for customers seeking cheap labor or material inputs. The country is rich in natural resources—tin, rubber, natural gas, tungsten, and timber being a few examples. The country is a major source for agricultural products.

Thailand also has an abundant supply of low-skilled labor with high participation rates in the work force—86% for males and 67% for females in 1995.[7] At the same time, the country is the most developed in Southeast Asia, making for a relatively reliable work environment. In consequence, foreign companies use Thailand as a production base in labor-intensive and light industries such as textiles, consumer electronics, and auto parts to serve their regional networks.

Thailand's comparative advantage of labor cost is, however, slowly eroding. The threats have come from the opening of China's and Vietnam's markets with their even cheaper labor sources. The minimum wage rate of Thai labor in 1996 was 135 baht (U.S.$5.40) per day, compared to $1.25 per day for MNCs in Vietnam and about $3.50 per day in China. The eroding comparative advantage in labor cost is aggravated by increasing electricity, water, and office operating costs (Table 9.3). The severe devaluation of the currency in 1997 should improve Thailand's cost position.

Strategically, Thailand has a comparative advantage in size and location with its four international airports and two major seaports. In prac-

*Table 9.3*
**Cost Comparison—Japan, Thailand, China**[a]

|  | Japan | Thailand | China |
|---|---|---|---|
| Wages | 100 | 6 | 4 |
| Short-term interest rates | 100 | 1,188 | 1,513 |
| Plant-site land | 100 | 1 | 10 |
| Construction cost | 100 | 45 | — |
| Overland transport | 100 | 25 | — |
| Customs expense | 100 | 33 | 130 |
| Warehouse leasing | 100 | 20 | 20 |
| Power | 100 | 45 | 28 |
| Tap water | 100 | 100 | 1 |
| Office operating cost | 100 | 70 | 20 |
| Corporation tax | 100 | 80 | 88 |

*Source: The Economist,* March 16, 1996.
[a]Japan = 100

tice, however, the rapid economic growth has created bottlenecks in an overwhelmed infrastructure. At the end of 1992, there were only 1,000 kilowatt hours of electrical power per person, 31 telephone lines per 1,000 persons, 841 kilometers of paved road per million persons, 50% of which was in good condition. Comparable figures for Korea were 2,996 kilowatt hours, 357 telephone lines, 1,090 kilometers of paved road, 70% of which was in good condition; and for Hong Kong, 6,051 kilowatt hours, 485 telephone lines, and 268 kilometers of paved road.[8] In addition, about 95% of Thailand's international trade depends on ships, 90% of which are foreign-owned. Dependence on foreign-owned transportation, in turn, limits the country's ability to be cost competitive.

One hope for Thailand is to increase its technological capabilities. The country suffers from a shortage of skilled managers, scientists, and engineers, with only 0.2 scientists and technicians per 1,000 people during 1988–92, compared with Korea (2.3) and Japan (7.0).[9] In parallel, foreign MNCs seldom transfer much technology to the country. When MNCs engage in a production strategy, they normally limit it to one using low levels of technological sophistication. Recognizing these problems, the government has embarked on various programs such as expanding research and development, improving education, luring expatriate scientists and engineers home, and attracting foreign direct investment in technological projects. It has also designated human resource development as a key factor in national development for the Eighth National Economic and Social Development Plan (1997–2001). The potential role of Thailand as a lead country will be contingent on the success of this plan. Local companies are beginning to play a part. For example, Siew Company, the local joint venture partner of Matsushita, has embarked on a joint investment, PKS Development, with the Crown Properties Bureau and the NEP to make Thailand a transfer base of technology from Japan.[10]

## Government Globalization Drivers

The Thai government is relatively stable and business friendly as newly industrializing countries go, although it does maintain careful watch on and regulates the activities of foreign MNCs in Thailand. Most foreign MNCs consider the Thai economy to be highly attractive with its relatively peaceful political atmosphere and the highly liberal foreign trade and investment policies pursued by various governments.[11] For example, in the insurance industry foreign companies are now allowed 25% ownership, with a target of 49% allowable by 2000, and foreign branch establishment by 2005. In banking and finance, the Thai government aims, somewhat ambitiously, to compete directly with Singapore to become "the Asian financial center." The government has initiated the country's Financial Master Plan to ensure the stable progress of the capital and money markets. The Finance Ministry has adopted a scheme to increase the country's savings, minimize exposure to currency fluctuations, and to undertake swaps to hedge against foreign-exchange loss. In addition, the Ministry has introduced electronic data interchange to speed up custom and exchange procedures.

To attract investment in the provincial areas and tighten control around Bangkok, the Board of Investment (BOI) adjusted its criteria in 1993, offering greater incentives for businesses to relocate to underdeveloped rural provinces. Maximum foreign equity allowances in promoted projects stood at 49% in 1997 for primary production, mining and service sectors, and manufacturing due mainly for domestic distribution. Majority share holding is allowed in manufacturing projects whose production is at least 50% export. If 80% of the products are exported, 100% ownership is allowed. In newly privatized industries such as public utilities, environmental projects, and infrastructure, ownership is considered on a case-by-case basis by the ministry concerned. Thailand has been aggressive in pursuing economic cooperation with its neighbors. In the south, an economic triangle has been formed between northern Sumatra in Indonesia, the five southern provinces of Thailand, and the four northern states of Malaysia. In the north, the Indochinese Economic Quadrangle has been formed between Thailand, Laos, Myanmar, and the south Chinese province of Yunnan. Additional economic cooperation with Vietnam and Laos is under study. The success of this cooperation will certainly enhance regional investment, trade, and tourism.

Thailand is a member of ASEAN, APEC, and the World Trade Organization. As part of the Asian Free Trade Association (AFTA) agreement, free movement of goods among ASEAN countries is promised by December 2008. Of the fifteen products that will undergo fast-track tariff rate harmonization, Thailand will implement the scheme for many additional products. However, for pharmaceuticals, chemicals, plastics, and vegetable oil, Thailand will accept and implement the scheme only if satisfactory reciprocation is received from other member countries. On the negative side, Thailand has historically been notorious in its near total disregard for the protection of trademarks and intellectual property rights. In recent years, though, Thailand has dramatically increased its enforcement of these laws, with highly publicized burnings of bogus Gucci bags and pirated cassette tapes. Still, Thailand remains a leader in the production and distribution of knock-off products, ignoring international copyright protection.

In technical areas, Thailand is slowly moving toward international standards. The country subscribes to ISO 9000, and has had the Thai Industrial Standards Institute manage compliance since 1991. However, the number of certificates granted to date is quite low. Compared to the Philippines, and India, which established technical offices at about the same time, three certificates had been granted in Thailand by 1995, as against twenty-three in the Philippines and over one hundred in India.[12] Thailand also has governing bodies issuing regulations pertaining to the control of food and drugs, prices, monopolies, advertising, and labeling. For example, importers and producers of pharmaceutical products are required to register the drugs' ingredients with the Ministry of Health before obtaining import or production licenses. The National Environmental Protection and Promotion Act, B.E. 2535 (1992) has brought Thailand closer to the international standard by setting up and ensuring Environmental Quality Standards (EQS).

Lastly, MNCs need to be aware that in some industries, especially those that were recently privatized such as telecommunications, energy, and airlines, they will have the government as a competitor as well as a regulator.

## Government Liberalization in the Automotive Industry

The automotive industry provides a primary example of the Thai government's efforts at trade liberalization. While Thailand remains a well-protected car market, the government continues to pursue liberalization efforts first initiated in 1988. In October of that year Thailand signed the ASEAN BBC (Brand-to-Brand Complementation) agreement (described in Chapter 16). Since 1991, Thailand has undertaken unilateral measures to liberalize the automotive industry in an attempt to make itself the regional center for automotive assembly and components. The government significantly reduced high import duties on fully assembled cars in 1991. It also announced, in 1994, a tariff rebate of more than 90% on imported CKD (completely knocked down) car kits that would be reexported as assembled vehicles. The Board of Investment has expanded its promotional incentives for assembly plants to be located in provincial regions. These incentives include a seven-year tax exemption on income earned from exports, reduced duties on imported machinery, and government subsidies for construction, transport, and power. As a result of these liberalizing measures, Thailand is relatively less protected than its neighbors. Auto manufacturers can also expect further relaxation in the local content requirements as the Thai government implements WTO agreements.

AFTA is another example of the government's liberalization policy. Thailand is taking part in three schemes: Brand-to-Brand Complementation (BBC), the ASEAN Industrial Joint Venture Programs (AIJVs), and the Common Effective Preferential Tariff (CEPT) scheme (described in Chapter 16). Through BBC, assemblers in participating countries are able to import components from other members and obtain local content points and a 50% reduction in the normal import duty. In Thailand, Toyota, Honda, Mitsubishi, Nissan, and Volvo are trading parts under this scheme.

## Competitive Globalization Drivers

Thailand is increasingly becoming both a battleground, as MNCs fight over its domestic market, and a staging area, as MNCs use its location, its cheap labor, and resources as a springboard to regional and global markets. Thailand is becoming an important market for both local and foreign businesses. Thai businesses are major players in the garment, textile, agricultural, gem, and jewelry industries. In the hotel business, MNCs such as Quality Inn and Best Western have made their presence known. Thai hoteliers have also been aggressive in acquiring foreign properties, for example the Dusit Group with its purchase of Germany's Kempinski group in 1995 and with its expansion in Texas. In information technology, the National Electronic and Computer Technology Center (NECTEC) is studying how to reposition Thailand as a center for software R&D for global leaders in the industry.[13]

Thailand is also becoming an important part of globally interdependent business systems, and hence, global competitive battles. Foreign MNCs, Japanese in particular, have used Thailand as a production and export platform to compete internationally and to bypass some trade protection measures of its trading partners. For example, in the consumer electronics industry, Japanese manufacturers exported to the United States through their Thai subsidiaries to bypass the Voluntary Export Restraint Quotas affecting U.S./Japan trade.

## Overall Global Strategies for Thailand

MNCs from Europe, Japan, and the United States have all pursued different strategies in the Thai market. Yet their common view of the country as an important market results in a major emphasis on marketing strategy. The companies also view Thailand as important for their regional strategies, driving an export focus for production. In all industries, competition is increasingly intense and the strategies pursued by these companies partially reflect the growing global pattern of competition.

We focus on the strategies of six MNCs that are successful in Thailand—Nestlé, Unilever, Toyota, Matsushita, IBM, and Procter and Gamble. Except for IBM, which now ranks third in the personal computer market, all are leaders in their core products. Nestlé is the largest branded foods company in Thailand. It enjoys a 30% market share for milk products and an 80% market share in the instant coffee market. Unilever is dominant in seven of the twelve markets in which it competes, including laundry detergents, ice cream, and hair care products.[14] Procter and Gamble dominates disposable diapers, and holds near-leadership positions in feminine hygiene, skin care, and hair care products. Toyota and Matsushita, respectively, lead in automobile and consumer electronic products (notably televisions and radios).

## Market Participation Strategies

Thailand is large enough to be an attractive market in its own right and now has the added attraction of being a conduit to Indochina. All six companies entered the country with export strategies and subsequently engaged in direct investment strategies by setting up wholly owned subsidiaries or forming joint ventures with local partners. The direct investments of Unilever and P&G occurred through wholly owned subsidiaries, while those of Nestlé, Toyota, and Matsushita took the form of joint ventures with local companies. However, Nestlé subsequently acquired shares from its partners in the joint venture and currently wholly owns Nestlé Thailand.

Of the six companies, Unilever is the oldest and P&G the youngest in Thailand. Unilever first established its wholly owned subsidiary, Siam Industries, Ltd. (subsequently changed to Lever Brothers Thailand, Ltd.), in 1932, to produce and market soaps. P&G Thailand was established in 1987, when the parent company acquired Richardson-Vicks worldwide in 1985, and took over that company's operation in Thailand. IBM, Matsushita, Toyota and Nestlé's initial investments were made respectively in 1952, 1961, 1962, and 1967. Matsushita created a joint venture with a local company to assemble imported parts and components to supply domestic market demand.

The success of Toyota and other Japanese MNCs in the auto industry can be attributed to their early entrance to set up production facilities in Thailand. Their distribution and service networks are well established, affording them a high degree of consumer loyalty. Pushed by the increasing value of the yen, and pulled by growth in local demand as well as by the Thai government's liberalized policies and incentives, Japanese producers have increasingly relocated auto parts factories to Thailand, and have embarked on expansion plans to increase production capacity there.

Auto companies often pursue an alliance strategy when entering Thailand. For example, the Auto Alliance Co., Thailand of Ford, Mazda, and local partners produces pick-up trucks. Fiat and Italsiam combined to make the *Fiat 178* world car, while Isuzu, Nissan, and Toyota partnered to produce and exchange parts in order to meet the current 54% local content requirement for cars assembled in Thailand.

Partnering with local companies or the government is particularly important in regulated industries such as telecommunications. For example, AT&T of the United States has partnered with Shinawatra, OTC International of Australia with Samart Group, and Cable and Wireless of the United Kingdom with Sophonpanich Group.

## Product and Service Strategies

Most products and services need only minimal to moderate adaptation for Thailand. MNCs, on the whole, try to leverage their strong global products in the Thai market with some tailoring to meet local needs. Nestlé's products in Thailand include both global brands and those developed domestically. Nestlé's product strategy in Thailand reflects its policy for "brands to be local, people regional, only the technology goes global,"[15] and mirrors its corporate philosophy of broadening the market and pursuing market share with a limited number of brands. In contrast, Unilever pursues market share by blanketing the market with a wider range of brands in four main divisions, with subcategories within each brand. It has also demonstrated its corporate citizenship by being one of the first firms to incorporate an environmental conservation strategy in their product strategy. P&G Thailand follows the "megabrand" approach, with eight major brands within six categories. For consumer products, additional modification varies by product type and by regulations of the Thai Food and Drug Administration. For example, the automobile's steering wheel is on the right, electrical voltage is 220, and because of the climate, ultraviolet sun ray protection and moisturizing aspects are important for beauty products.

IBM's product strategy is regionally integrated through Singapore. It uses Thailand as a destination for a limited number of advanced technologies and design configurations. Matsushita, through its global product development network, considers Thailand to be one of its key markets for receiving new products. Like IBM, Matsushita focuses on advanced technology products backed by its well-established brand names and quality. Toyota markets its globally standardized world cars in Thailand, but also produced in Thailand and launched in late 1996, an "Asian car" for the Southeast Asia market.

## Activity Location Strategies

The low cost of local production has encouraged many MNCs to produce in Thailand either for the local market, for export, or both. All of these six MNCs use Thailand as a production base to supply the local market and to export. All are conducting factory expansion projects to increase their production capabilities. Toyota has the highest degree of regional integration for value-added activities. A relatively developed backward linkage in the Thai auto industry has allowed Toyota to successfully pursue the strategy of vertical integration. Toyota makes extensive use of the BBC scheme set up in ASEAN. As illustrated in Figure 9.1, Toyota produces diesel engines, stamped parts, and electrical equipment in Thailand and ships these around the region in partial exchange for other components and parts.

The Thai production base is part of Toyota's regional strategy. Jigs and dies were exported to Japan, Taiwan, Malaysia, and Indonesia even before it implemented the BBC scheme. In 1992, the first completely built-up (CBU) unit was exported to Laos. While the current activities are con-

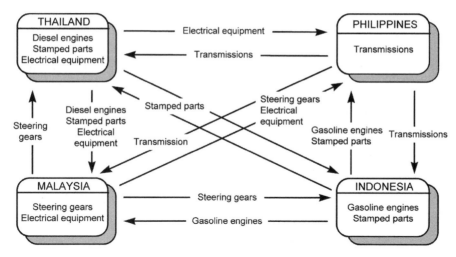

**Figure 9.1** Toyota's Logistics Under the BBC Scheme. *Source: Asian Business,* April 1990.

centrated on sourcing and manufacturing, Toyota plans to use Thailand for the design and development of new car models.

Nestlé pursues a policy of creating products from local ingredients and has invested significantly in developing the indigenous industry to assure the quantity and quality of its product ingredients. For example, the company, teaming up with the Livestock Cooperative of Sakol Nakorn province, has set up an experimental station for the crossbreeding of Thai Zebu cattle with Simmental cows through artificial insemination. It also invested in the Arabica Coffee experimental farm, a frozen vegetable project, and also built a production plant for green coffee. In an example of regionalization in Thailand via the ASEAN Industrial Joint Venture (AJIV) project, Nestlé Thailand has been designated the company's supplier of its "Coffee Mate" product to the entire ASEAN market.

P&G views Thailand as the future production hub for its key product brands such as *Pampers* disposable diapers, *Whisper* sanitary napkins, hair care products such as *Rejoice, Ivory, Head & Shoulders,* and *Pantene;* and *Oil of Olay* facial skin care products. In 1996, the company opened a second, U.S.$60 million plant. This has helped not only to reduce Thailand's reliance on imports of its brand name products, but has made the country an important distribution center for P&G products for Australia, the Philippines, Singapore, Malaysia, Indonesia, and Taiwan. Citing overall investor-friendly economic policies as one reason for its future expansion, P&G announced plans to increase its investment in Thai production facilities to U.S.$140 by the year 2000. In an example of localization, P&G distributes its products through nine Sales District Offices (SDO) that are jointly managed with a local, Thai owner. Each SDO is technically independent and operates within a clearly defined radius, but because they have a common interest in promoting their products, information and ideas are often shared.[16]

P&G has planned to participate in the AIJV. It has proposed to invest five billion baht over a five-year period in four countries—for the production of detergent and soap in the Philippines; sanitary napkins, skin care moisturizers, shampoo, hair conditioners, and diapers in Thailand; soaps and fatty acids in Malaysia; and cosmetics in Singapore. So far, Singapore and the Philippines have given approval to P&G to proceed. In contrast, the Thai government has decided not to participate for fear that P&G's expansion would crowd out local consumer goods manufacturers.[17]

For both Matsushita and IBM, manufacturing activities are for labor-intensive products or components with relatively low levels of technological sophistication, such as low-capacity disk drives. As discussed earlier, Thailand will have to upgrade its technical capabilities before attracting higher-value-added activities.

## Marketing Strategies

With the increasing convergence of customer needs and tastes in Thailand to those of Western nations, MNCs are eagerly jumping at opportunities to build their share of this market. All companies are able to use their global brand names in the Thai market. On the other hand, they share a need for local adaptation—translating information on product packages and enclosed documents (including production description and usage) into the Thai language. Advertising strategy plays a critical role for all of the companies mentioned. As in their home countries, these companies emphasize television as the primary advertising outlet, followed by radio and newspapers. In addition to advertising, Nestlé positions some of its products differently than in other markets. For example, coffee is promoted as a beverage that provides relaxation from urban stress rather than as a stimulating drink. Nestlé emphasizes and introduces new products around its core local brand, *Bear*. The brand is used for sweetened condensed milk, evaporated milk, sterilized milk, and powdered milks, which are further differentiated by Bear brand *(BB) Full Cream, BB Honey Milk, BB Plus*, and *BB Honey UHT*.

Because their products have prices that are high relative to local incomes, IBM and Toyota use creative financing schemes, such as leasing. IBM also employs direct marketing techniques, such as by cooperating with American Express through the "IBM ThinkPad offer for American Express Members." Special incentives for this project include lower product prices, product upgrades, preloaded software, free delivery, and payment flexibility. To support its direct marketing campaigns, IBM has a telesales staff to answer customer questions, an increasing number of service centers, including "Remote service" and "Remote service vans" for customers outside of Bangkok, and otherwise pools service resources among its five dealers.

Matsushita and IBM do not prioritize competitive pricing as a strategy. Price is justified by high product quality and service. However, others, such as Toyota, employ a preemptive price cutting strategy in Thailand.

## Competitive Move Strategies

Competition has been and will continue to be increasingly intense for all these companies. MNCs face a mixture of foreign and local competition, depending on the industry. Some, like Toyota, might enjoy a more comfortable lead than others. In general, the higher the level of technology, the less likely there are to be significant local competitors. So Nestlé faces local competitors in milk products like Nong Pho Dairy Cooperative and Thai Dairy Industries Ltd. Co., and Unilever competes with the local Saha Pathanapibul Group, as well as with Western and Japanese MNCs. But Toyota and Matsushita compete primarily with other Japanese MNCs. IBM's local rivals are mostly its American compatriots—Compaq, Hewlett-Packard, Packard Bell, AST, and Digital. Lastly, the added attraction of access to Indochina's markets has raised the stakes for competitive success in Thailand itself, and added an increasing need to coordinate regional competitive moves.

# Overall Organization and Management Approaches for Thailand

MNCs view Thailand less and less as a separate market. To the contrary, a regional view prevails and, therefore, operations in Thailand are becoming increasingly linked with those in other countries. In addition, MNCs are making significant efforts to upgrade management processes and skills. Unilever, for example, attempts to exploit regional benefits while protecting individual subsidiaries' local advantages by coordinating various product decisions through "Product Champion Groups." Such groups consist of managers representing various functions from each country in the region, and are led by a senior manager from one of those countries. To assure global strategic consistency, the Product Champion Groups are integrated in corporate networks.

Nestlé, IBM, and Toyota have engaged in some reorganization to better coordinate their regional activities. In its marketing division, Nestlé established Business Groups and Business Units to enhance responsiveness and flexibility in sales and marketing. For example, the Milk Department was formed by combining the Milk 1 and Milk 2 groups in the previous structure. The department now has eight marketing managers handling twelve milk products under four brands. The company also established an Indochina & Myanmar Business Unit in its Thai subsidiary, indicating its increasing regional market orientation. It has already obtained authorization to build a fully owned factory for Milo and Nescafé in Vietnam.

IBM went through an extensive restructuring in 1994, the same year as Nestlé's, involving the shift of authority for many of IBM Thailand's business units to regional offices outside Thailand. Seven business segments now report directly to worldwide and regional business headquarters. These segments include finance, insurance, manufacturing, banking, petroleum, transport, and travel. The country managing director retained responsibility for general business, which includes government, health, utilities, communication, education, crossindustries, and construction.[18]

In the PC business, IBM centralized all the inventory and warehousing for individual countries into a few centers, namely Hong Kong, Singapore, and Korea. All PC shipments to countries in ASEAN are carried out through Singapore. IBM also set up a headquarters in Singapore to supervise the Southeast Asia PC business.

Both local and foreign companies realize that human resource problems act as growth inhibiting factors and are, therefore, slowly incorporating human resource aspects into their strategies. Toyota's reorganization included development of training programs to provide its local employees with opportunities to advance to higher positions in the administrative hierarchy.[19] These MNCs have made significant efforts to globalize, or at least regionalize, their top management teams. Judging from the career path of top management teams in the six companies, one can conclude that global or "geocentric"[20] human resource practices and culture are emphasized. For example, Nestlé circulates managers constantly between developed and developing countries where they can pick up new ideas or new products. In Asia, managers are shuffled around the region at four- or five-year intervals.

Although Unilever is the only one of the six MNCs that had a Thai Managing Director as of 1995, many positions on the top management teams of all companies are occupied by local nationals. All these MNCs recognize and emphasize the human resource problems of Thailand, in particular the fact that the type of education provided is sometimes ill-suited to labor market requirements. They are committed to help improve the situation. Nestlé implemented its attempt at improving human relations by encouraging involvement in the "Five S's Program" (*Kaizen*) originated by its subsidiary in Japan. It incorporates five steps: identify waste, organize, clean the plant, clean one's self, and maintain self-discipline. P&G enhanced teamwork to improve production efficiency through a "vertical start-up team," whereby a product core team is assembled to identify areas that need support or improvement. The team then develops an execution plan to ensure efficiency of production systems, the operating capability of personnel, and overall system standards. Matsushita will relocate its training courses for Thai employees from the regional office in Singapore and house them in their new $28 million head office.

Lastly, all MNCs must recognize that some adaptation to local culture is required to operate successfully in Thailand. For example, building a factory will always involve a ground breaking ceremony to ward off evil spirits, and the opening of any new factory will always involve a blessing ceremony.

## Conclusions

The economic imperative that first attracted foreign MNCs to Thailand was their search for a low-cost production base. The political imperative that continued to pull these companies to the country was the Thai government's protectionist economic policy. Over time, as the prevailing political imperatives evolved, the companies' strategies have also changed. Although they still observe the role of Thailand as a production base, additional strategic dimensions for Thailand are becoming evident. Thailand is now a gateway to Indochina and, in some industries, has become a platform to exploit regional and global strategies. Participation in regional trade pacts and growth triangles is also playing an increasingly important role, with significant implications for the strategies of MNCs.

Thailand remains a prime source for efficient and cheap labor and materials, but its reputation is slowly eroding as its infrastructure gets overwhelmed by development, and as its less developed neighbors begin to offer their even cheaper labor and material resources. There are severe, probably short- to medium-term clouds over its economic prospects. The terms imposed by the U.S.$ 17 billion financial bailout arranged by the International Monetary Fund in late 1997 should help Thailand to restructure.

The ability of Thailand to sustain its economic growth and to play a more vital role in the globalization process of MNCs depends very much on how Thailand develops its human resources and increases its ability to absorb high-value-added technology. The government has already committed to pursue this objective, at least in the next five years of the NESD plan. Some Thai companies have tried to catch up through the shortcut strategy of strategic alliances. Foreign MNCs already present in the country should try to incorporate technology transfer and human resource development strategies into their overall corporate and regional strategies.

## NOTES

1. "Thailand: Still Plenty to Smile About," *Asia Business,* February 1995.
2. A. Suehiro, *Capital Accumulation and Industrial Development in Thailand* (Bangkok: Chulalongkorn University Social Research Institute, 1985).
3. For a detailed discussion, see Anek Laothamatas, "From Clientelism to Partnership: Business-Government Relations in Thailand," in *Business and Government in Industrializing Asia* (Ithaca, N.Y.: Cornell University Press, 1994).
4. "Asia's Most Admired Companies," *Asian Business,* May 1995.
5. "Economic Review Year-end 1994," *Bangkok Post,* December 30, 1994.
6. Thailand: Statistics, *Asian Business,* February, 1995.
7. The World Bank, *World Development Report 1995* (Oxford University Press, 1995).
8. Ibid.
9. United Nations, *Human Development Report 1994* (New York: New York University Press, 1995). For a specific analysis on Thailand, see Chatri Sripaipan, "Technology Upgrading in Thailand: A Strategic Perspective," in Denis F. Simon, ed., *The Emerging Technology Trajectory of the Pacific Rim* (M. E. Sharpe, Inc., 1994).
10. *Bangkok Post,* February 8, 1995.
11. The World Economic Forum in its *1994 World Competitive Report* ranked Thailand twenty-third.

12. Pussadee Polsaram, *ISO 9000 in the EC: Are Thai Exporters Sufficiently Prepared,* unpublished manuscript (Chulalongkorn University, 1995).

13. "Year-end Review," *Bangkok Post,* December 29, 1995.

14. "'Asian Delight' Tempts Thai Palates—How Lever Brothers Has Benefited from the Growth of Ice Cream Consumption," *Financial Times,* May 12, 1994.

15. "Nestlé's Brand Building Machine," *Fortune,* September 19, 1994.

16. Company source: SDO Fact file.

17. *Bangkok Post,* April 7, 1995.

18. "IBM Thailand Head to leave for New Company," *Bangkok Post,* December 30, 1994.

19. Company publications, 1994.

20. Howard V. Perlmutter, "The Tortuous Evolution of Multinational Corporations," *Columbia Journal of World Business* (January–February 1969).

# CHAPTER 10

# Indonesia—Finding Ways to Takeoff

*Albert Widjaja and George S. Yip*

WITH ITS TWO HUNDRED million people, Indonesia constitutes the world's fourth most populous country, after China, India, and the United States. Its currently low per capita income of about U.S.$1,100 (in 1996) stems from a legacy of the nation's long struggle for independence, followed by misdirection of the economy until the mid-1960s, with a resultant low-growth performance below 2% per annum during the period 1945–65. Its future prospects come from the high economic growth rate of 7% per annum from 1969 to the present. So Indonesia has now joined the group of dynamic East Asian economies, albeit as a latecomer. In the next twenty-five years the Indonesian government aims to quadruple per capita income to reach $4,000. Multinational companies are rapidly discovering Indonesia as both an enormous potential market and as a major source of production.

On the other hand, Indonesia has also suffered from the 1997 regional turmoil, with both its currency and its stock market falling a third from 1996 levels. The nation has accepted an International Monetary Fund rescue package worth perhaps U.S.$40 billion. In exchange, the government has had to agree to shut down banks, break up government monopolies, and dilute the business interests of relatives of government officials.[1] Furthermore, the economy suffered in 1997 from the extensive uncontrolled forest fires in Sumatra and elsewhere.

## Background

Prior to 1986, the economy could be characterized as resource-based (using oil and other natural commodities as the engine of growth) with import substitution manufacturing and a pervasive role for the public sector. The result was a high-cost economy with excessive protection and monopolies, oligopolies, or cartels in many industries, discouraging broad investments by both domestic and foreign entrepreneurs. Meanwhile, the oil sector began to decline from 22.3% of GDP in 1983, to 2.4% in 1996.

From 1986, Indonesia embarked on a new economic strategy—developing nonoil sectors, especially manufacturing, relying much more on the private sector, launching an export drive as the engine of growth—supported by a series of deregulation and liberalization moves. This new policy orientation succeeded in generating economic growth of 7.9% per annum between 1990 and 1996, with inflation in one digit.[2] As of mid-1995, the government was still targeting the level of economic growth at a rate of 7.0% per annum for the next five years.

Indonesia's economic structure has been transformed toward a more balanced one in the last ten years, joining the global economy with fast growth both in exports and imports. The manufacturing sector has gained impressively, from only 8.4% of GDP in the early 1970s to 24.6% in 1996, gearing up to sophisticated technology (such as engineering products, chemicals, and aircraft), with extensive foreign direct investment. In contrast, the role of the agricultural sector (including fishery and forestry) has shrunk from 50% of GDP in the early 1970s to only 15.2% in 1996. Nevertheless, the agricultural sector still employs around 50% of the total working population. The mining sector (including oil and natural gas) accounted for 9.2% of GDP in 1996. The capital intensity and high expertise required in this sector has led the government to encourage the participation of foreign investors.

The fast growing construction sector accounted for 7.9% of GDP in 1996. The trade, hotel, and restaurant sector (including wholesale and retail trade) expanded to 16.7% of GDP in 1996. Only recently has the wholesale sector opened for foreign investment, along with the retail sector through franchising. Japanese retailers, such as SOGO, Yaohan, and Seibu, have been quick to respond to the opportunity, followed by the Netherlands' Makro, and the United States' Wal-Mart and Toys 'Я Us.

Trade constitutes a moderate share of Indonesia's economy (exports being 26.8% of GDP in 1996). But the country has a healthy trade surplus, and the structure of exports has also changed dramatically, shifting away from overdependence on oil, gas, and other primary commodities. In 1981, oil and gas accounted for 82% of total exports, but fell to 23.5% by 1996. Manufacturing exports have surged to become 64.5% of total exports, contributed by textiles, wood products, electrical goods, footwear, rubber products, machines and automobiles, coconut and palm oil, pulp and paper, basic chemicals, gold and silver, and new products generated by new domestic and foreign investments in such fields as synthetics and electronic goods. In fact, Indonesia has established a name as a major world supplier of textiles, footwear, and plywood.[3]

While Indonesia still maintains a surplus in merchandise trade, recently imports have grown faster than exports, especially of final consumer goods. Imports of raw materials and intermediate products for production have risen consistently since 1990 to U.S.$23.1 billion in 1994, and U.S.$29.6 billion in 1996, indicating strong demand from the manufacturing sector.

The direction of exports and imports has also shifted from a strong trading share with European countries to a greater share with Asian economies and the United States. In 1996, Japan led both exports and imports, with the United States second in both categories.

## Largest Domestic Companies

Leading local private companies emerged mostly in the past thirty years. Many of them grew from their business ingenuity, taking advantage of the facilities and protection provided by the government. These companies are concentrated in three hundred conglomerates whose assets equaled 69% of GDP and whose sales accounted for 44% of GDP in 1993.[4] Initially involved in the service sector (trade and finance), these companies broadened their base by seizing opportunities opened by the maturing of industries in developed countries, such as textile manufacturing. The business scope of these companies grew rapidly through mergers and acquisitions, both domestically and internationally, so that many are now diversified conglomerates (Table 10.1). Many of these companies are now

**Table 10.1**
**Largest Indonesian Public Companies**

| Rank | Name of Company | Major Business | 1996 Revenues U.S.$ millions | 1996 Net Profit U.S.$ millions |
|------|-----------------|----------------|------------------------------|--------------------------------|
| 1 | PT Astra International | automotive | 5,245 | 200 |
| 2 | PT Gudang Garam | cigarettes | 2,800 | 280 |
| 3 | Indocement Tunggal Prakarsa | cement | 1,824 | 236 |
| 4 | PT Idofood Sukses Makmur | food and beverage | 1,207 | 150 |
| 5 | PT H. M. Sampurna | cigarettes | 1,010 | 169 |
| 6 | PT Indah Kiat Pulp & Paper | pulp, paper | 774 | 113 |
| 7 | PT Bakrie & Brothers | telecom, infracture | 671 | 80 |
| 8 | PT Polysindo Eka Perkasa | textile, garment | 600 | 73 |
| 9 | PT Pabrik Kertas Tjiwi Kimia | pulp,paper | 594 | 62 |
| 10 | PT Gajah Tunggal | automotive, component | 422 | 57 |
| 11 | PT Barito Pacific | wood industry | 406 | 37 |
| 12 | PT Bimantara Citra | telecom, automotive | 380 | 67 |
| 13 | PT Astra Graphia | photocopy, electronics | 380 | 6 |
| 14 | PT Smart Corporation | food, beverages | 361 | 16 |
| 15 | PT Semen Cibinong | cement | 328 | 45 |
| 16 | PT Prasidha Aneka Niaga | food, beverages | 317 | 13 |
| 17 | PT Tri Polita Indonesia | chemical | 308 | 11 |
| 18 | PT Indo-Rama Synthetics | textile, garment | 290 | 52 |
| 19 | PT Modern Photo Film Company | camera, photo materials | 284 | 27 |
| 20 | PT Bakrie Sumaatera Plantation | agriculture | 258 | 18 |

*Source:* PT Indonesia Business Data Centre: *Informasi,* Jakarta: PDBI, June 28, 1997.
*Average exchange rate:* Rp. 2,342 to U.S.$ 1 (1996).
Note: The list above does not include banking and construction, which are only a few of the largest ones.

shifting their attention to global growth industries that are also capital intensive, such as chemicals, electronics, and telecommunications.

State-owned companies are also significant players in the economy, as required in the nation's constitution. A total of 180 state enterprises contributed approximately 25% of GDP in 1993,[5] engaging in a broad range of products and services (Table 10.2). The after-tax profitability of state enterprises averaged 4% from 1993–96, and is much lower than that for private enterprises, except for those engaged in modern businesses such as telecommunications. Most of the largest state enterprises operate in resource-based industries, telecommunications, transportation, and aircraft assembly. The government has started some privatization through domestic and international capital markets. The size of the state-owned sector is shrinking rapidly.

After the mid-1980s a growing number of Indonesian companies also began to undertake foreign investment in many countries. These companies internationalized in several ways: (1) small- and medium-sized companies exporting solicited or unsolicited orders, as in the garment, shoe, and toy industries; (2) through export promotion of products into the global market by establishing trading subsidiaries in strategic countries, with a purpose of gaining international experience, such as Bimantara Group's Mindo Commodities, in Hong Kong;[6] (3) through portfolio direct placements that also provided experience in managing a multinational company, such as Bakrie Brothers' purchase of a majority share in Link Telecommunications of Australia; (4) through a "U-Turn strategy," by which cash-rich, diversified companies with limited international experience acquired foreign companies to gain access to technology, management, and global distribution that would lead to new flows of international trade and investment from Indonesia (such as Salim Group's acquisition of Hagemeyer [Netherlands] with all of its operations in different countries); (5) through a management expansion strategy, by which internal resource advantages in cost efficiency, quality management, and marketing skills are utilized in offshore operations, such as LIPPO Group in the finance business in Hong Kong; and (6) through resource-based vertical integration and greenfield investment in other countries to gain access to markets, as when pulp and paper company, PT Inti Indorayon Utama, formed a global company, Asia-Pacific Resources International, Ltd. (APRIL), to enter manufacturing in China and other countries with funds raised through the New York Stock Exchange, and with subsequent dramatic enhancement of APRIL's international competitiveness by learning from global competition.

## Largest Foreign Companies

The twenty largest multinational companies (MNCs) operate primarily in various resource-based industries, and in the automotive and electronics industries (Table 10.3). Japan accounts for half of these companies, while

**Table 10.2**
**Largest Indonesian State Companies**

| Rank | Company | Main Business | 1995 Revenues U.S.$ millions |
|------|---------|---------------|------------------------------|
| 1 | PT Pertamina | oil | 12,856 |
| 2 | PT BADAK NGL | natural gas liquefaction | 4,029 |
| 3 | PT Arun NGL | natural gas liquefaction | 3,913 |
| 4 | PT PLN | electrical energy | 2,627 |
| 5 | PT Garuda Indonesia | airline | 2,377 |
| 6 | PT Telekommunikasi Indonesia | telecommunications | 2,211 |
| 7 | PT Krakatau Steel | steel | 972 |
| 8 | PT Pupuk Sriwidjaja | fertilizer | 932 |
| 9 | PT INDOSAT | telecommunications | 453 |
| 10 | PT Industri Pesawat Terbang Nusantara | aircraft | 412 |
| 11 | PT Semen Gresik | cement | 354 |
| 12 | PT Tambang Batubara Bukit Asam | coal | 323 |
| 13 | PT Petrokimia Gresik | petrochemicals | 314 |
| 14 | PT Merpati Nusantara Airlines | airline | 307 |
| 15 | PT Adhi Karya | construction | 247 |
| 16 | PT Perumka | railroad | 243 |
| 17 | PT Waskita Karya | construction | 227 |
| 18 | PT Jasa Marga | tollroad | 225 |
| 19 | PT Pupuk Kalimantan Timur | fertilizer | 221 |
| 20 | PT Tambang Timah | tin mining | 218 |

*Source:* PT CISI Raya Utama, *600 Largest Companies 1995.* Jakarta: CIC, 1996.
*Average exchange rate:* U.S.$1 = Rp. 2,308

the United States accounts for only one-seventh. In 1993, these MNCs' profit levels averaged 9.2%, quite below their local counterparts' average of 11.9%, due to higher overhead costs such as expatriate staff, costs of indirect distribution, or high import contents based on transfer pricing.

Foreign investment in Indonesia has grown rapidly from a low base— 0.2% of GDP in 1980, to 2.64% in 1995. For realized cumulative direct foreign investment from 1967 to January 1995, Japan had the highest value at U.S.$9.6 billion, followed by Hong Kong, the United States, and Singapore. After 1986, most of the investment inflows to Indonesia came from the newly industrialized economies of the East-Asian region, because of high costs of land and labor, and foreign exchange appreciation in the investor countries.[7] European investment, specifically from the Netherlands and the United Kingdom, also increased in recent years, while investment from the United States has declined.

MNCs have succeeded in many different ways. Unilever's dominance of the consumer packaged goods sector comes partly from its in-depth knowledge of the market needs of Indonesia's diverse population and of ways to reach these customers. The company makes significant use of the

*Table 10.3*

**Largest Foreign Multinational Companies in Indonesia**

| Rank | Company | Nationality | Main Business | 1995 Revenues U.S.$ millions |
|---|---|---|---|---|
| 1 | PT Caltex Indonesia Company | U.S. | oil | 932 |
| 2 | PT Toyota Astra Motor | Japan | automotive | 856 |
| 3 | PT Freeport Indonesia Company | U.S. | mining | 741 |
| 4 | PT Indomobil Suzuki International | Japan | automotive | 742 |
| 5 | PT Unilever Indonesia | U.K./ Netherlands | personal care | 581 |
| 6 | PT National Gobel | Japan | electronics | 533 |
| 7 | PT Kaltim Prima Coal | U.K. | mining | 433 |
| 8 | PT Charoen Pokphand Indonesia | Thailand | animal feed | 424 |
| 9 | PT Socfin Indonesia | Belgium | plantation | 419 |
| 10 | PT Japfa Comfeed Indonesia | Netherlands | animal feed | 351 |
| 11 | PT Yamaha Motor Kencana | Japan | motorcycle | 342 |
| 12 | PT Sony Electronics Indonesia | Japan | electronics | 336 |
| 13 | PT Yamaha Indonesia Motor Manufacturing | Japan | motorcycle | 312 |
| 14 | PT International Nickel Indonesia | U.S. | mining | 293 |
| 15 | PT Astra Daihatsu Motor | Japan | automotive | 271 |
| 16 | PT Petrokimia Nusantara Interindo | U.K., Japan | polyethylene | 221 |
| 17 | PT Adaro Indonesia | Australia | coal mining | 220 |
| 18 | PT National Panasonic Gobel | Japan | electronics | 210 |
| 19 | PT Star Motor Indonesia | Germany | automotive | 208 |
| 20 | PT Asahimas Subentra Chemical | Japan | chemical | 199 |

*Source:* PT CISI Raya Utama, *600 Largest Companies 1995.* Jakarta, 1996.
*Average exchange rate:* = RP. 2,308 to U.S.$1 (1996).

indigenous distribution channel of street stalls. Selling through thousands of these tiny stalls throughout the country helps Unilever penetrate deep into the national market. For example, Unilever offers low-priced shampoo in sachets and toothpaste in minitubes to be hung in the fronts of stalls across the country.

Sunkyong Group, a Korean *chaebol,* has developed a close relationship with its local partner, Batik Keris, as its basis for future growth in polyester resin manufacturing. Success has come from predicting the input demand structure in the textile industry, leading to focus in polyester filament yarn, providing low-cost products through productivity improvement supported by intensive training of the local staff in Korea. In just three years of operation, Sunkyong was able to gain 40% of the market.[8]

Charoen Pokphand Group, a leading MNC from Thailand, recognized the underdevelopment of supporting businesses in many industries in Indonesia, especially agribusiness. So it established value-chain activities through vertical integration, achieving fast growth by involving small-scale farmers in its production process. Charoen produces baby chickens, animal feed, shrimp feed, poultry equipment, and polyethylene woven bags. It also provides credit, in order to support farmers raising chicken and shrimps. The company offers up-front contracts to farmers to produce chickens that Charoen then sells locally and overseas. The farmers do not need experience to enter the business, except for some training by Charoen, and have low risks because Charoen guarantees supplies and sales. Charoen has developed small factories across the country to support this chicken industry.

Increasing privatization of state enterprises has become a major entry mode for many MNCs, through either bilateral direct capital placement, multilateral international capital markets, joint venture, or through various alliances such as build-operate-transfer (BOT) in the telecommunications industry, build-operate-own (BOO) in the construction industry, and power purchase agreements (PPA) in the public electric company. AT&T has a BOT alliance with PT Indosat for submarine fiber optics. Siemens set up a 51% joint venture with PT INTI to manufacture automatic digital telephone equipment, while Korea's Lucky-Goldstar has a joint venture with PT INTI as well as with private PT Pioneer Trading in manufacturing electrical equipment.

## Overall Globalization Drivers for Indonesia

The huge size and diversity of Indonesia's population and geography dominate how globalization drivers for the country affect MNCs. Its two hundred million people speak two hundred fifty regional dialects and languages, and are scattered over some thirteen thousand seven hundred islands that stretch for over three thousand miles (more than the continental United States). It has the world's largest Muslim population, over one hundred seventy million, and one of its most densely inhabited places, the island of Java, while other parts are almost unpopulated.[9]

### *Market Globalization Drivers*

As a market, Indonesia exhibits the typical characteristics of a rapidly growing middle class that eagerly seeks modern goods and services and a very large mass class that desires but can afford only the most basic foreign offerings. Families in urban centers are rapidly converging on the Western/Japanese model of small units with a growing number of two earners per family. Such consumers are responsive to new product offerings, and their purchasing decisions are increasingly made by women.[10] Both this fast-growing middle class and new potential customers among the rural populations are exposed to domestic and international television networks. The large population, rising income, different educational levels, and divergent ethnic communities also provide opportunities for selling to many different market niches.

At the same time, consumers still exhibit traditional forms of behavior that can trip up even the most experienced MNCs. Unilever failed, for example, in its introduction of a concentrated detergent, *Rinso Ultra*. Users needed only one spoon of powder to wash one kilogram of dirty clothing. But middle-class Indonesian households still have servants to wash their clothing. These servants used the same large quantity of *Rinso Ultra* as they had done with regular detergents. So customers switched back to the cheaper regular powder rather than pay the high prices for concentrated detergent. Unilever has also had difficulty switching consumers to its *Bon Vivant Croissant* for breakfast, from their usual rice, noodles, porridge, or fresh bread from bakeries.

Indonesia probably requires MNCs to make more efforts at marketing adaptation. Special aspects of advertising rules are that advertising should not insult or humiliate the dignity of religion, good manners, culture, or ethnic groups. On the other hand, its Dutch colonial past has also helped familiarize the country with Western practices and culture. The great differences between the lifestyles of urban and rural populations (typical of newly developing countries) also poses obstacles to national, let alone global, marketing standardization. Also, Indonesia is not yet a lead market for any significant product or service categories.

## Cost Globalization Drivers

With one of the lowest labor costs in the region, averaging U.S.$0.30/ hour in 1995, a huge work force, and improving infrastructure, Indonesia has highly attractive cost globalization drivers. Many MNCs, especially those seeking low-skilled labor have recognized this and relocated production there. Higher technology MNCs, such as Motorola, Siemens, and Lucky-Goldstar are also discovering the country. Increased education of the work force (brought by compulsory education to the ninth grade) has enhanced skills and productivity, and increases in wages are still behind the inflation rate. Excessive costs caused by bureaucracy, red tape, and corruption are declining as the government is committed to attract foreign investments. On the other hand, the country has also attracted negative publicity from harsh treatment of labor organizers and human rights advocates. Politically sensitive or socially responsible MNCs also need to take extra care to ensure decent treatment of their work forces, or more difficult, for those of their subcontractors and suppliers.

The costs of local supplies are also falling. Government protection of many local companies in upstream industries has created high costs of production in the downstream industries populated by MNCs. But such protection and resultant high costs will soon be phased out as the World Trade Organization enforces its nondiscriminatory national treatment principle. Nevertheless, the economy still overheats periodically, resulting in high interest rates and continuing depreciation of the Rupiah currency, thereby raising the costs of imported raw materials and supplies.

For selected products the huge home market can contribute significantly to achieving regional and global economies of scale, especially when MNCs use Indonesia as a production base. This has become the case, among others, for automobiles (Toyota), consumer electronics (Matsushita and Sony), and telecommunications equipment (Motorola). On the other hand, the country has difficult logistics and an uneven spread of infrastructure.

## Government Globalization Drivers

Indonesia's government is heavily involved in regulating business both officially and unofficially. Furthermore, individual members of the government and the military are themselves extensively involved in business, particularly the children and relatives of the highest officials. Indonesia is also noted for its high levels of corruption, ranking forty-third out of the forty-eight countries surveyed in the *World Competitiveness Report* (Table 1.10). Nevertheless, the government has made great strides in recent years to liberalize the economy. The major reason for the export upsurge came specifically from government policies—the foreign exchange policy was directed to give incentives for nonoil exports by gradual depreciation of the real exchange rate at an average of 2.6% per annum since 1987;[11] foreign exchange has been completely free since 1967; excessive bureaucracy dealing with exports and imports has been gradually reduced; and protection of domestic "infant" industries is being gradually phased out.

In addition, MNCs will find problematic the relationship between the government and the tight-knit business community. Indonesia exhibits substantial practice of monopoly, oligopoly, and cartels through the mechanisms of coalitions (between government and private players), regulation of entry and exit, and price and distribution controls. Examples of government/business coalitions include: government funds being placed in large private companies that have been chosen as the preferential winners of tenders for large government projects; special licenses to specific private companies to produce, buy, import, and sell specific products such as cloves and wheat; and many other transactions lacking transparency between the government and private companies, such as in acquisitions of state enterprises by the private sector.

Trade policies are improving. Tariffs have been steadily reduced from an overall average of 22% in 1990, to 7% in 1996.[12] In the June 1996 Package, all items with a tariff rate of 20% or less will be gradually reduced to 5% or less by the year 2000; items with tariff rates of more than 20% will be gradually reduced to 10% or less by the year 2003; with the immediate target of a maximum 20% in the year 1998. Items with high tariffs, now exempt from the across-the-board cuts, such as automobiles, will be reduced according to a set timetable. Tariffs on chemical and metal products will be reduced via a separate timetable to a maximum tariff of 10% by 2000. Furthermore, tariffs on 249 items have been eliminated altogether, such as paper, cooking oil, wood products, tiles, ceramics, and glassware. Within ASEAN, Indonesia will reduce tariffs under the Common Effective Preferential Tariff scheme (CEPT) from an average of 11.6% in 1996, to 4.3% by the year 2003.

The government is also liberalizing foreign direct investment. Between 1967 and the mid-1980s, foreign investment policies underwent pendulum swings between liberalization and restriction, depending on the abundance or shortage of capital (particularly from oil revenues) for development financing, the rise or fall of nationalistic sentiments, and the relative competitiveness of other developing economies in Asia in attracting foreign investment.[13] But since 1986, consistent liberalization has been launched to promote export-oriented investments, to relax requirements for equity participation by Indonesians, to extend operating licenses to a thirty-year period, to shorten the list of business sectors closed to foreign investment, to encourage foreign participation in the domestic capital market, and to provide incentives for investment in East Indonesia.

In May 1994, the government issued Regulation No. 20, which offered the most substantial liberalization on foreign investment to date. The May Package allowed straight 100% foreign ownership either by individuals or enterprises (except in infrastructure and agribusiness), allowing the continuation of foreign majority control, permitting joint ventures (with majority shares by a local partner) in "nine vital sectors" related to infrastructure investment—seaports, airports, shipping, roads, railroads, power, telecommunications, nuclear power generation, and public drinking water—and eliminating the minimum requirement on the amount of capital investment. Investment in mass media is expected to be gradually liberalized. In September 1997, the government liberalized further to allow MNCs to hold majority control of domestic companies.

Indonesia's government is sensitive to foreign dominance of some key industries. Foreign participation in the nine vital sectors listed above, as well as banking, can occur only through joint venture with Indonesian citizens or legal entities. Some sectors are entirely closed to foreign investments—defense, retail (except wholesale for MNCs' own products or via franchising), forestry concessions, mining (except by production sharing or through government work contracts), real estate (except as a contractor), and agribusiness (except with the government). Final approval for all foreign investment projects must come from the President of the Republic of Indonesia.

Extensive privatization has become a major drive to make state enterprises more efficient and competitive, and less dependent on government financing. Hence many previously government-owned competitors to MNCs have become private competitors, or in many cases have become, through alliances, potential partners and customers, as is strongly shown in the telecommunications industry.

Participation in ASEAN and AFTA is helping to liberalize trade. But the Indonesian government also sometimes goes against free trade. In early 1996, the Indonesian government granted PT Timor Putra Nasional (a joint venture of Korea's Kia Motors and a local company) the status of "national car" for its local brand, *Timor,* (based on Kia's *Sephia* model). This national car was exempted from import tariffs and luxury taxes (gaining a 40% price advantage), provided that it incorporates 60% local content within three years. This government decision has raised significant controversy as a violation of World Trade Organization rules. Specifically, foreign car makers who invested in plants in Indonesia now face duty-free competition from a Korean import. Japan, the United States, and the European Union have brought this issue to the WTO to redress discrimination and to reconfirm the principle of national treatment. Furthermore, this designation violates the spirit of the Bogor Declaration of 1994 (discussed in Chapter 16).[14]

Unlike China, Indonesia has a reasonably reliable legal system, based on Dutch law, and, hence, similar to most continental European systems. Nonetheless, protection of trademarks and intellectual property is a major weakness, but improving. Indonesia is a party to the International Community for the Protection of Industrial Property. However, piracy is active in many industries, such as book publishing, video recording, and fashion apparel. Indonesia used to grant to any first party the right to register a trademark locally, even for global brands. So Sony had to pay U.S.$50,000 to a local producer to cease using the Sony name on his underwear products. New legislation in 1993, however, recognizes international registration. A court ruling in 1995, for example, supported Levi Strauss's ownership of its brand name over a local party who had previously registered Levi's as a trademark for jeans production. But patent protection is still limited. For example, Patent Law No. 6/1989 allows the Indonesian pharmaceutical industry to import and freely copy fifty types of pharmaceutical products, such as atenolol and sulprostone, even while the product is under patent protection internationally. However, Indonesia is currently revising the law to meet the ruling of the Trade Related Intellectual Property Rights (TRIPs) of the WTO.

## Beginning to Emphasize Technology

Indonesia's industrial policy has emphasized labor-intensive industries, and is still maintained that way. The government is beginning to recognize the need to shift toward higher-technology activities. The country is known for its abundant supply of low-cost labor. Policy makers and business leaders are aware, however, that long-term dependence on low-cost labor will not enhance economic growth, exports, or a higher standard of living. Debate has surfaced on how much the country should advance into high-technology industries versus labor-intensive (or employment-generating industries), and their respective implications for Indonesia's competitiveness in the world market. Some critics argue that progressing into high-technology industries (such as aircraft assembling) is currently beyond Indonesia's capacity, both in financing and human resources. However, there is a consensus that high-technology industries based on real market demand will lift Indonesia's competitiveness and increase its share of value-adding activities. Investment in labor-intensive industries has leveled, as has that for resource-intensive ones, while investment in capital-intensive industries is increasing. Government policy now also encourages capital-intensive industries to attract high-technology business, such as the electronics industry (including semiconductors) and the manufacturing of telecommunications equipment.

Some examples of the shift toward higher technology occur in the textile, electronics, telecommunications, and semiconductor industries. The textile industry has entered into advanced technology mode by producing high-quality synthetic materials. The electronics industry has been successful in exporting with an average rate of growth of 50% per annum in the first half of the 1990s. Telecommunications has emerged as the fastest-growing industry, attracting into the country state-of-the-art technology such as the latest Global System for Mobile Communications (GSM) and large-scale mobile satellite communications. Investment in semiconductors, the foundation of high-technology industries, began to flourish from around 1990.

## Competitive Globalization Drivers

Indonesia's competitive importance is growing. In addition to its size, its central location in the Asia-Pacific region—equidistant between Japan and Australia—makes it an increasingly important site for MNC marketing and production activities. Growing integration of the region's markets means that MNCs can ill afford the gap of such a large country and economy in their regional strategies. As in China, competitive imitation is also becoming a driver for MNC activity in Indonesia.

The country increasingly provides an attractive base for export and hence regional and global competitive advantage. Local firms are also becoming more competitive and increasingly invest overseas, either through acquisitions, mergers, or portfolio participation, and so are enhancing their capabilities. This internationalization also helps local firms to better serve domestic demand and to better compete with the entry of foreign MNCs.

## Overall Global Strategies for Indonesia

Large MNCs have already penetrated well into Indonesia, as into most other ASEAN member countries. Several companies have been there since the 1970s. As an Anglo-Dutch company, Unilever has been present in Indonesia since the pre-World War II colonial period. Motorola has been in Indonesia since 1991, while Motorola products have been sold there since the late 1940s. Primarily, the original interest of MNCs likely lay in Indonesia's large population and high projected economic growth rate. However, in terms of global strategy, MNCs are finding that Indonesia presents a good location for low-cost production and for gaining a foothold in the Southeast Asian region. Consequently, Indonesia is becoming a major source of production for many MNCs. Economies of scale can be reached with the help of the local markets, and increased tourism stemming from liberalization (open skies) helps gain market exposure. In addition, a production strategy involving several Southeast Asian countries (including Indonesia) can help to optimize the tax and tariff preferences throughout the region. The Jakarta and Surabaya stock exchanges also present capital-raising opportunities in the country; the capitalization of the Taharta Stock Exchange was U.S.$92 billion at the end of 1996.

## Market Participation Strategies

Like China, Indonesia is too large a potential market to ignore. The six featured MNCs illustrate the different types of market participation strategies that MNCs have undertaken in Indonesia. All have significant local ownership, except Motorola, which started with 100% ownership after the new deregulation allowed it to do so.

Unilever has long been the dominant consumer products player in Indonesia, and is currently ranked as the largest consumer goods manufacturer in the country, as well as a market leader in food and personal care products. Unilever's long involvement in Indonesia, with a high degree of autonomy, has given the company a strategic edge in expanding and penetrating local markets. As a result, the company's sales in the country have increased steadily from U.S.$300 million in 1990, to just over U.S.$600 million in 1995, or an average annual rate of 19.8%, compared with a much lower rate of growth (about 7%) for Unilever's global sales during the same period. The company also provides 15% public ownership of its Indonesian subsidiary.

Procter and Gamble entered Indonesia through its 1986 acquisition of Richardson-Vicks, hence its local subsidiary, which had gone public on the Jakarta Stock Exchange in 1980, selling 27.8% of its shares. In recent years, PT P&G Indonesia has moved from loss to profit by adding to the original Richardson-Vicks business the company's global products, such as hair care and cosmetics.

Motorola has a long-standing and steadily increasing presence in Indonesia, initially selling radio equipment. The company then established trade representatives to supply communication systems and switching equipment/components to state enterprises and private companies. Some of the switching equipment is presently supplied from manufacturing operations elsewhere in Asia. In 1994, Motorola applied as a foreign investment company (with 100% ownership) to strengthen its support for sales and marketing, allowing it to directly serve end customers and to provide related consulting and professional services. In addition, Motorola will consider investing to produce semiconductors, which is Motorola's global core competence in its high-technology business, and to assemble two-way radio communications in the land mobile sector.

As a Dutch company, Philips was another early entrant, setting up a wholly owned subsidiary in 1941 that, in 1969, became a joint venture company with 14% owned by an Indonesian partner. Its products and services include lighting, consumer electronics (e.g., interactive CD- and HD-TV), domestic appliances (e.g., irons, air and water cleaners, autosensor hairdryers), professional systems (e.g, rural telephone systems, public radio telecommunications, industrial electronic systems), and medical systems. For Philips, Asia is a major part of its future, with Indonesia play-ing a major role. The multiplier effect of the development in physical infrastructure and communications systems in Indonesia creates a strong market for Philips' products and services. However, Indonesia's impor-tance for its total global strategy stems primarily from its being a source of low-cost production and a contributor to global economies of scale.

Matsushita was an early MNC mover in manufacturing in Indonesia. Beginning in 1970, the company established its position in the consumer electronics industry through many joint ventures between its subsidiaries and the National Gobel Group, a diversified local conglomerate with over thirty subsidiaries and affiliates. (Among Gobel's businesses are consumer electronics, chemical manufacturing, trading, watch assembly, construc-tion, agricultural equipment, and cargo services.)

Toyota relies on Indonesia as a key part of its total Asian strategy. Toy-ota divides its manufacturing of automotive components, engines, and transmissions among different countries in Southeast Asia through spe-cialization to enhance cost efficiency, quality, and expertise. As discussed in the chapter on Thailand, this allows Toyota to gain preferential treat-ment within ASEAN from the Brand-to-Brand Complementary Scheme at half of the regular tariff rates. In Indonesia, Toyota operates through a joint venture owned 49% by itself and 51% by PT Astra International, the country's largest private company.

## Product and Service Strategies

So long as they are allowed into the market, MNCs generally find their products and services easy to sell in Indonesia. Driven by common cus-tomer needs, many markets are growing rapidly, especially in the area of basic consumer products. The country's development of its infrastructure also presents opportunities for large systems and technologically ad-vanced products and services. In addition, the country has a large enough population that a product strategy can be wide and also deep. For example, in consumer electronics, companies have entered with audio, video, and other products as well. With respect to personal care and home appliances, full-line product offerings are achieving success by the dominant MNCs. Generally, MNCs mostly introduce standardized products with minimal adaptation and globally recognized brands first. Later, some MNCs encroach upon established local company products (such as tea) with significant success.

Unilever has achieved strong acceptance of selected global brands, such as *Lipton Tea,* benefitting from its early entry. The company is now concentrating on more locally tailored new products such as *Teh Siap Pakai* (Ready-to-Drink Tea). This product entered the lucrative tea drink market controlled by a local company, Sosro Teh. Unilever has also launched *Sari Wangi Teh* with several locally appealing varieties such as or-ange and mango tea. One major problem that Unilever now faces in In-donesia is the alarming rate at which its products are being duplicated by local competitors.

P&G takes a similar approach to Unilever's, also making some adaptations to achieve greater local appeal. For example, *Vicks Throat Drops* are presented in six different flavors, with modified packaging and advertising.

Toyota adapts to the Indonesian market, not by changing its products, but by focusing on lower-power, lower-priced cars. In 1995, Toyota dominated the market for cars with 1,100–1,300 cc engines with its *Starlet* and *Corolla* models holding a 46% share of that category, and an overall 25% share for all categories of vehicles. Key to Toyota's success is its extensive network of sales and service outlets, supported by a global brand name and world-class quality. But Toyota is now being challenged by new comers from Korea, such as Kia Motor, with its recent creation of the *Timor* national car, and local models like Suzuki's *Baleno* and Hyundai's *Bimantaya Cakya*, trying to seize the huge low-end market by offering small standardized cars with prices half those of Toyota in the same engine size. The *Timor* is being sold at about U.S.$15,000, about half of the price of Toyota and other major brands with the same engine size (1,500 cc). In addition, Mitsubishi, Toyota, Suzuki, Isuzu, and Daihatsu all sell in Indonesia (as well as in Thailand and Malaysia) a car that is really a utility vehicle or "fan," the latter category making up 90% of all passenger cars. These cars are commercial vehicles but appeal because their low price, fuel economy, and large carrying capacity suit very well the large, low-income population.

In Indonesia Matsushita relies very much on its globally standardized products. The company has achieved strong customer preference, especially in audio and video equipment in brands such as *National, Technic,* and *Panasonic*. In 1993, the company achieved a market share of 22% in sales of consumer electronics. Matsushita continues to make new investments allowing it to manufacture more products in Indonesia. Among its major products being manufactured currently are audio (e.g., radio-related products, stereo-related products, speaker systems, hi-fi components), video (e.g., television, HD-TV, video tape recorders), home appliances (e.g., refrigerators, air conditioning, electric irons, washing machines, water pumps), and full manufacturing of components (e.g., speakers, tuners, transformers, and coils).

Philips offers full product lines and special services in several businesses. Philips' product strategy for Indonesia is to apply global technical standards using its strong R&D center in Europe. However, slight modifications are often required to enhance customer satisfaction due to climate, physical conditions, and the usage behavior of local customers. Government requirements on technical standards are still being developed as well, for example, in the case of advanced communications systems that require compatibility with other global systems.

Motorola focuses on the supply of general systems and associated services, all from its global line of products and services. The largest businesses of Motorola in Indonesia currently are in the supply of cellular telephone systems. Another large sector is mobile products, including analog and digital two-way radios and systems for conventional, shared, and private applications. Motorola's third largest sector is the messaging, information, and media sector. This sector represents a significant business for the company, though it is not a major business with respect to global sales. It includes pagers and paging systems, wireless and wire-line data communications products, infrastructure equipment, systems, and related services.

## Activity Location Strategies

The huge local market can contribute significantly to achieving regional and global economies of scale when MNCs use Indonesia as a production base. Although certain upstream activities are not completely sufficient in Indonesia (e.g., packaging materials suppliers), many MNCs have established complete value chains for various products from R&D centers, to manufacturing, to distribution for local markets. This is particularly true for the personal care and other consumer product markets. MNCs such as P&G, Unilever, and Matsushita have long been manufacturing in Indonesia, and are increasing their activities located there. Additionally, Indonesia is becoming a testing ground for products and marketing concepts for other Asian countries. In cases where full production of products from start to finish is not taking place, such as in automobiles, the principals maintain complementary production of different parts in different countries to keep intact their control of the value chain.

Unilever has located a full range of activity in Indonesia. Practically all of Unilever's products offered in Indonesia are manufactured in the country, except some intermediate goods, with continuous new investment as product offerings are widened. On the other hand, the company needs to import large portions of raw materials, such as flavors for food, fragrances, and silicates for cleaning and personal care products, and even raw materials for packaging, such as aluminum foil and fine paper. But Unilever is also increasing Indonesia's technical role. In the early 1990s, Indonesia was assigned as the regional center for innovation on mouth care products. P&G engages in full manufacturing and distribution of products in Indonesia. The company has had manufacturing plants located in Jakarta since 1975, for pharmaceutical products, personal care products, and candy products (*Vicks Throat Drops*). These plants have been expanded several times to increase manufacturing capacity for current products, and to add other products such as sanitary napkins.

Toyota uses Indonesia as an important part of its global cost reduction strategy. Greater relocation of component production into Indonesia has become an important factor in lowering costs and adapting to local requirements. Toyota will transfer more component and engine manufacturing to Indonesia and other ASEAN countries. Eventually, each country will be a regional and global supplier for major parts.

Philips' activity location strategy revolves around logistics and experience curve effects. Philips' long involvement in Indonesia with strong sales has resulted in steep experience curve effects for the company in basic products such as lighting manufacturing. This has resulted in greater quality and variety of products, better R&D, and higher labor productivity. With more advanced products, Philips attempts to create regional economies of scale from manufacturing centers in the region. Logistics is a critical aspect for Philips in moving and storing raw materials in regional or national manufacturing centers, as well as moving products to final customers. This requires efficiency, timeliness, and safety—all significant challenges given the country's still developing infrastructure. For basic products, such as lighting and home appliances, logistics constitute 10% to 15% of the total cost of production. To improve the lead time for transportation and efficiency on the costs of inventory, some of these products are produced regionally, and manufacturing for basic products in Indonesia continues to expand. Additionally, Philips is using the Indonesian market to experiment with a new marketing technique for the region by creating a "Lighting Application Center" in the country.

Motorola has an increasing commitment to locating activities in Indonesia. In its present role as a supplier of cellular phones, pagers, and computer hardware to local distributors, Motorola uses its U.S.-based and Asia-based (Malaysia, Singapore, and others) manufacturing, information systems, and technical support for serving the local market. However, Motorola has now committed itself to establish a long-term presence in Indonesia.

Matsushita's establishment in Indonesia increasingly serves as an export center for the company to destinations around the world. The company has set up manufacturing of electronics, electrical home appliances, components, and batteries in Indonesia and operates through the National Gobel Group. The substantial manufacturing capacity established in the country allows the company to compete effectively against other manufacturers as well as importers. National Gobel has also globalized its operation in Indonesia with the production of VCRs for export to North America.

In conclusion, Indonesia can provide an excellent location for manufacturing activity. Primarily because of the large market, in many cases MNCs can locate manufacturing in Indonesia with the assurance that production economies will be reached. This is clearly evidenced by Unilever and P&G's vast manufacturing activities in products for personal use and consumption. Once manufacturing has been established, Indonesia presents a viable location for exporting activities to other parts of Asia and the rest of the world. Alternatively, as with Toyota, Indonesia can play a participatory role for the manufacturing of parts.

## Marketing Strategies

MNCs are finding that successful marketing strategies in Indonesia are not too dissimilar from those used in other, more developed countries. The critical issue, however, is how to penetrate this market with its diverse population, uneven geographic spread and transportation system, and wide variations in ethnic culture. Of course, government regulations restrict some activities, such as owning retail distribution and mass media, including wholly foreign-owned advertising agencies. Overall, brand-driven marketing is common, as is the use of globally standardized marketing and packaging, including logos and advertising concepts. Many MNCs, such as Toyota, Motorola, Philips, and Unilever rely heavily on strong relationships with local distribution networks, from tricycles to computer-based networking. Marketing strategies can also be somewhat sophisticated as in more developed countries. For example, P&G focuses largely on applying global brands to a wide variety of needs along several dimensions, and Unilever attempts to identify specific future needs through detailed market research. In many cases, local customs and preferences can be incorporated relatively easily with existing standardized approaches by MNCs.

Toyota has developed a rather consistent global marketing mix, including product design, positioning, brand name, advertising, and extensive repair services. For example, the company recently changed its worldwide logo to consist of three ellipses with different sizes crossing each other. This global logo is widely publicized in Indonesia to create enthusiasm among consumers. Toyota's local advertising depicts a car driving up a mountain or hard desert road, much as can be seen in other countries. Pricing, however, depends largely on government tariffs and other taxes. In Indonesia, the industry has already moved from a seller's market to a buyer's market. Hence, dealer and service networks and marketing promotion are crucial to the business.

Motorola also uses global marketing approaches, but in Indonesia places extra stress on personal selling to establish close cooperation with state enterprises and local private distributors. In another local adaptation, Motorola uses the advertising message, "your true partner." "Partnership" is central in the Indonesian business culture, as the constitution emphasizes familial relationships to be the norm in business relationships. This relationship marketing approach is both globally transferable, and at the same time, consistent with the local culture.

Philips and Matsushita both illustrate the importance of building local distribution in this geographically complex country. In the consumer electronics industry, consistent with government regulations, producers do not involve themselves with distribution. Producers establish an affiliate as the single national distributor, who then selects an external agent to distribute products in each province as the main provincial distributor. These distributors in turn distribute the products to electronic retailers in the particular province. For imported home appliances, the importer serves simultaneously as a sole agent as well as a national distributor who can distribute the products directly or indirectly to retailers. Companies offering products related to telecommunications infrastructure, such as Philips, need to develop close relationships with state-owned customers, who control most of the business. Such customers include PT Telkom for design, development, and manufacture of telecommunications equipment, and the national electricity authority (PLN), for services regarding energy conservation. In June 1996, however, a new deregulation allows MNCs to be wholesalers for their local products, and to import complementary products to be sold in a package with their own local products.

## Competitive Move Strategies

For Indonesia, competitive moves are typically orchestrated with the entire region in mind. Specifically, certain incentives have been established by the ASEAN Industrial Joint Venture program encouraging intra-ASEAN trade as well as trade outside of ASEAN. Competitive advantages can be created by establishing manufacturing facilities in the various economies, including Indonesia. This provides MNCs with an opportunity to formulate strategic competitive plans for the larger market in the region. In addition, the local manufacturing capacity helps MNCs cope with increasing import competition from newly industrialized countries. Most of the MNCs we studied have already, or are planning to, take advantage of this type of philosophy in Indonesia. Additionally, MNCs are establishing close ties with government entities and educational institutions in the country to solidly fix themselves as part of the developing infrastructure. These strategies too create competitive advantage.

Toyota's competitive moves in Indonesia are typically orchestrated with moves in other Southeast Asian countries as the integration of the market increases. Such moves include introducing more multipurpose vehicles at affordable prices, building extensive sales and service outlets, and making other local adaptations without sacrificing standardization for economies of scale. Philips Indonesia has been assigned as a regional center to serve the public telecommunications systems business in the ASEAN region. Philips' success in building the state of the art in digital microwave radio systems for Indonesian communications will be leveraged to serve the entire region.

For competitive advantage, MNCs increasingly need to include Indonesia as part of an overall strategy for Southeast Asia. Certain ASEAN trade incentives have been established that should be taken advantage of in any integrated manufacturing plan. In addition, many MNCs are putting substantial amounts of capital toward operations in Indonesia, thereby making it a regional center for certain efforts, and a significant manufacturing base for others.

# Overall Organization and
# Management Approaches for Indonesia

In Indonesia, MNCs have selected various organizational structures that meet the needs of their markets. Some companies have taken a more centralized approach, while others have acted in a more decentralized fashion for local empowerment. For some MNCs, it has been important to join forces with one major Indonesian partner, whereas others have built distribution systems using many local partners throughout the country. While important in nearly all Asian countries, local partners can be particularly helpful here. For example, Matsushita relies heavily on its joint venture relationships with The National Gobel Group. This strong relationship has allowed Matsushita to enter a variety of businesses with the benefits and insight of a major local partner, giving Matsushita a significant competitive advantage. Compared with the situation at the beginning of the 1980s, it is now not difficult to find qualified local partners. In fact, many local companies are eager to form partnerships with foreign investors. Such local alliances can help MNCs break into the tight-knit Indonesian business community, the latter being characterized by extensive alliances (such as interlocking directorships, direct equity placements, special credit facilities, joint marketing, buyer and seller relationships, mergers, and acquisitions). Examples of MNC alliances with Indonesian partners include Nihon Cement with Indocement, Frito-Lay and Nissin Biscuit with IndoFood (Salim Group), and Mitsubishi Bank and Nikko Bank with Indovest Bank.

Management processes in Indonesia have been undergoing tremendous change from the conventional management style based on hierarchy (vertical control), authority (top decision making), exemplary role of the leader (an emphasis in the national culture), preferential relationships (with relatives or close friends), short-term profitability, intuition, simplicity (avoidance of complexity), and stability (resistance to change—business as usual) into an approach emphasizing adaptive management and business growth. This approach is based on rational professionalism, delegation of authority, shared leadership (or partnership), socialization (building up common corporate culture), transparency (within and outside organization), the importance of a business concept (not purely based on intuition) to ensure long-term growth, social responsibility (seeking social acceptance through promoting economic distribution and environmental concern), flexibility (reduction of organizational bureaucracy), strategic planning based management, technical procedures, problem-solving oriented, and continuous learning through training and seminars. The change has been brought by Western-oriented management education of top managers, multicultural management brought by MNCs (with a high percentage of MNCs' local employees changing jobs to higher positions in local companies), and pressure to globalize business operations at least to deal with new foreign competitors. The national ideology of *Pancasila* (five principles of belief in God, humanity, national unity, democracy, and justice) is also gradually affecting business practices, as shown in some corporate stakeholders' philosophy of caring for employees, social responsibility and economic equality, either voluntarily launched by the companies or increasingly demanded by Indonesian society. Decision making, business cooperation, or long-term transactions are taken through consensus building, based on strong personal relationships.

The importance of human resources development is certainly recognized by MNCs, and this is particularly true in Indonesia where technology and infrastructure are still in the developing stages. Many MNCs and local firms have special local training centers, besides regional or global centers. The government provides significant tax incentives for training expenses. Indonesia can also present a good location for training facilities, and a source of local and global managers. Unilever maintains a modern training facility in Mega Mendung Puncak (south of Jakarta) that is used not only by the Indonesian employees, but also by employees from other countries. But training may also draw from other countries. P&G's major training programs for Indonesia are supplied from the company's Singapore regional center. For some companies, education goes beyond specific skills training, and more toward ethical management, continuous improvement, and crosscultural communication.

Unilever "internationalizes" some of its Indonesian managers as part of a global program. The company carries out swap programs on personnel, exchanging junior managers between countries in the Asia-Pacific region for six months at a time. On the managerial level for future leaders work internships in other countries for two to three years are conducted in regional and worldwide placements. In 1995, eight Indonesian managers were serving in other countries as part of a "tour of duty." These employees may return later at higher levels of responsibility.

MNC compensation systems in Indonesia often accommodate local needs. Toyota's salary system, for example, is decided on locally. The compensation system employed by The Gobel Group provides housing to all employees, following Matsushita's system. However, many MNCs face challenges from international labor organizations or human rights groups for the low compensation to local employees, even though consistent with the local minimum wage policy.

Increased waves of strikes by workers throughout industrial locations in Indonesia (from 19 strikes in 1989, to 296 strikes in 1994) provide evidence of worker discontent, but at the same time counter the idea that the Indonesian work force is complacent, underemployed, or unemployed, desperately hanging on to a job and willing to receive any pay. Employment grew 6% per year from 1986 to 1994. For many years wages increased more slowly than inflation. Since 1990, minimum wages increased at an average rate of 10% to become U.S.$0.30 per hour, while women's earnings grew 50% faster than men's as MNCs found female workers to be more teachable and productive. However, productivity growth has kept pace with the increase in the minimum wage except that, since 1993, the minimum wage has increased substantially.[15] Much of the social unrest is caused by the failure of employers to meet the minimum wage required by law. Most Western MNCs, however, prefer to pay more than the minimum wage, to sustain loyalty and motivation.

In adapting their corporate global cultures to Indonesia, MNCs need to incorporate the emphasis on personal relationships, group spirit, and consensus building. Matsushita provides a good example of this adaptation. Its corporate motto for employee motivation says "dare to be creative, dare to challenge." These injunctions counter the Indonesian culture of loyalty to the leader. To adapt to the local culture, Matsushita has recast its motto in terms of the banana tree as an example or model of sacrifice for the benefit of society. The banana blossom opens up to give

birth to its new generation before it dies. This is related to the importance of the preparation for succession of leadership in the company
(which is a major problem in Matsushita's home base and in Indonesia).
Banana trees grow throughout the archipelago of Indonesia, always together with other trees and with their own offspring, indicating the need
for the employees to be well informed about the changing market. The
sacrifice and benefit shown by the banana tree is expected to inspire Matsushita's employees to work in happiness together, and to work in teams
in order to "accelerate the transformation of new technologies into products and businesses of tomorrow."

## Conclusions

Indonesia is one of the three giant emerging markets in the Asia-Pacific
region, behind only China and India in population, but ahead of both in
economic development and probably easier for Western MNCs to operate in. The nation has effectively redirected the economy to achieve sustained high economic growth, double digit growth in many industries
(such as consumer goods manufacturing, communications, transportation, construction), rates of imports growing faster than exports, an increase in the number of affluent customers, an easily trainable labor force,
a switching of investment demand to capital goods and high technology,
greater receptivity to foreign investment, a growing number of expatriates
working for local companies, and aggressive business practices by a new
generation of Indonesians eager to expand both domestically and internationally. Overall, the Indonesian economy is finding ways to take off and
the large government role is reducing. Short-term political uncertainty
from the presidential succession and the subsequent uncertainty of the
regulatory infrastructure provide a major cloud, as does the financial crisis
that broke in 1997. Nevertheless, the country presents very attractive
prospects for MNCs, both as a market and for production activities.

### NOTES

1. "Rescuing Asia," *Business Week,* November 17, 1997, 116–24.
2. Central Bureau of Statistics, press release, May 1997.
3. Citibank, *Indonesia: An Investment Guide,* APEC ed. (Jakarta: Citibank, 1994) 10.
4. Indonesian Central Business Data, *Information: Monthly Newsletter* no. 1, 1996, 3.
5. Heru Sotojo, "A Report of Survey on Privitization: Indonesian Case," Faculty
of Economics, University of Indonesia, 1995.
6. Donald J. Lecraw, "Outward Direct Investment by Indonesia Firms: Motivation and Effects," *Journal of International Business Studies* (Third quarter 1993):
589–600.
7. Thee Kian Wie, *Industrialisasi di Indonesia: Beberapa Kajian* (Jakarta: Pustaka
LP3ES Indonesia, 1994).
8. Citibank, *Indonesia.*
9. M. S. Dobbs-Higginson, *Asia Pacific: Its Role in the New World Disorder* (London: Mandarin Paperbacks, Reed Consumer Group, 1995) 305.

10. Yanti B. Sugarda, "Tinjuan Perilaku Konsumen di Indonesia." A paper presented for national discussion on "Power marketing 1995–96," organized by the faculty of Economics, Management Institute, University of Indonesia, June 1, 1995.

11. World Bank, *Indonesia: Improving Efficiency and Equity Changes in the Public Sector Role* (Washington: World Bank, 1995).

12. Coordinating Ministry of Industry and Trade, press release, "Deregulation of June 4, 1996," Jakarta.

13. Mary Pangestu, "Deregulation of Foreign Investment Policy." Paper presented at the seminar of World Bank and ISEI (Association of Indonesian Economists) on "Building on Success: Maximizing the Gains from Deregulation," Jakarta, April 26–28, 1995.

14. "In the Driver's Seat: Indonesia's National Car," *Far Eastern Economic Review,* June 20, 1996, 5.

15. World Bank, *Indonesia: Dimensions of Growth,* Country Report (Washington: World Bank, 1996).

# CHAPTER 11

# The Philippines—
# Overcoming the Past

*Emanuel V. Soriano and George S. Yip*

IN HIS BOOK, *Asia Pacific*, M. S. Dobbs-Higginson,[1] former chairman of Merrill Lynch Asia-Pacific, wrote that the Philippines is a country still in search of an identity. In James C. Abegglen's book, Sea Change,[2] the Philippines is referred to as "the sick man of East Asia." However one looks at the situation, it is clear that, for the Philippines, future prosperity will require overcoming historical, social, and political handicaps. In short, the Philippines has a lot of catching up to do, not only with respect to Asia, but with respect to its ASEAN partners as well.

To understand the obstacles that the Philippines must overcome, it is useful to briefly review its rocky history. Filipinos struggled for independence during more than three centuries as a Spanish colony, fifty years as a colony of the United States, and four years of Japanese occupation. As a popular saying goes, "The Philippines has spent three centuries in a Roman Catholic monastery, followed by fifty years in Hollywood."[3] Filipinos won their independence twice: on June 12, 1898, from Spain, the first Asian country to win freedom, and on July 4, 1946, from the United States, following the destruction of World War II. For the four hundred years prior to the 1946 independence, the Philippines was primarily an agricultural economy; only in the last fifty years has some industrialization developed.

In 1946, the Republic of the Philippines had the highest per capita income in Asia outside Japan. Today, its per capita income of about $1,130 (1996) is barely ahead of Indonesia's, is less than half of Thailand's, and only a third of Malaysia's. But although most of the other ASEAN countries have had a head start in industrialization, the Philippines is poised, over the long term, to do well in the region because of its relatively highly educated and largely English-speaking population of seventy million. That is, of course, if the country can overcome its past.

## Background

The difficulty of the Philippines becoming a business economic center lies largely in its social and political landscape. At least, this is the perception.

Even as many past obstacles are showing signs of retreat, this remaining negative perception looms like a shadow over the country. Understanding the social and political trends are key to understanding the Philippines and any business strategy there.

## Social and Political Trends

The majority of Filipino citizens, like Indonesians and Malaysians, are of the Malay race. Over the last four centuries, those with Chinese, Spanish, American, and Japanese ancestry have become a significant part of the population. Overseas Chinese are taking an increasing role in the business landscape.

Significantly, the Philippines is the only predominantly Christian country in Asia. The vast majority of Filipinos are Roman Catholic, with Protestants constituting a small minority. This is important to understand because it explains the historical lack of either a Protestant or Confucian "work ethic" in the country. In 1992, Fidel V. Ramos, with the endorsement of former President Corazon C. Aquino, was elected President of the Philippines—notably, the first Protestant to be so elected. Although Filipinos are hardworking in general, it is only in recent decades that they have come closer to the economic discipline characteristic of those with Chinese ancestry. This trend is expected to continue.

A striking fact in the Philippines is the enormous discrepancy between rich and poor. This gap remains a major social problem. In the early 1990s, 45% of the families were below the poverty line and the unemployment rate was 10%.[4] With this said, there are presently two types of elite: the Spanish mestizo, who descended from colonizers, and those of Chinese ancestry. Members of these two groups control many of the largest Philippine business organizations. Unlike the Spanish mestizos, some of whom have become political leaders, the ethnic Chinese have kept a low profile, preferring to make money with which they can buy political insurance. These two types of elite are expected to remain very significant, and this contributes to skepticism about the country's high levels of business and political corruption (see Table 1.8).

Conflict in Philippine society, although existing, has not been as severe as in other societies. Some conflict exists among the following: labor and management, peasants and landowners, the urban poor and some local governments, isolated communist rebel groups and those opposed to their ideology, some military rebels and their superiors, and Muslim secessionist groups among themselves. Peace talks are ongoing and the conflicts that exist are being resolved. Labor-management relations are improving (certainly better than what it was in the United States at the height of labor activism); agrarian reform still awaits more effective implementation but progressive legislation is in place; local communist rebels, with no support from the defunct USSR or China, have been marginalized and peace negotiations are going on; peace talks are also taking

place with Muslim rebels with the help of Indonesia. Thus, in the matter
of resolving social conflict, the prospects are good.

Amidst the several concerns regarding business in the Philippines, the
country has some very positive features. Most importantly, the Philippines
has one of the most extensive higher education systems in Asia. At the secondary level, in the early 1990s, about 73% of the age group was enrolled
in schooling; at the primary level it was 99%.[5] The literacy rate was about
96% in 1995, and is expected to reach 98% toward the end of the century.[6] In addition, depending on how measured, the Philippines has either the third or fourth largest English-speaking population in the world.

## Political Trends

For its region, the Philippines' political trends are as notable and distinct as its social trends. From 1972 to 1986, the Philippines was governed
as a virtual dictatorship by President Ferdinand E. Marcos. In 1986, Corazon Aquino, wife of the murdered Ninoy Aquino, became president following a "people power" revolution and Marcos went into exile. Aquino
was succeeded peacefully in 1992, by Ramos. In 1997, a major focus of political attention was on a possible amendment to the constitution to per-
mit Fidel Ramos to remain in office beyond his single term, scheduled to
end in 1998. Eventually, Ramos had to abandon this attempt in the face
of much popular opposition. Economic reform may be less sure under
the next president.

## Economic Performance

In the 1950s, the Philippines was one of the strongest economies in
Asia. A subsequent combination of economic, political, and natural disasters brought the country near to collapse. In the 1960s, the economy suffered a major setback when import substitution was given priority over export promotion. This has since been rectified, but much catching up is
needed. Following this mistake, the flow of capital and aid from the
United States dried up in the late 1970s after the Vietnam war, and for all
practical considerations ended when the two U.S. military bases (Subic
and Clark) were phased out in 1991. Today, the Philippines is in search of
new economic benefactors, the current primary prospects being Japan,
South Korea, and Taiwan.

Economic recovery began in 1986, when Aquino became president.
Under Ramos this recovery is continuing. A few months after becoming
president in 1992, Ramos deregulated foreign exchange transactions.
This was welcomed by the business community and was followed by legislation to encourage foreign banks to enter the banking systems. As of late
1995, ten foreign banks had been granted licenses to open full-service
branches in the Philippines, joining the four that have long been there.[7]
These foreign entries have brought severe competition and have put
pressure on Philippine banks to improve. Many are rising to the challenge. Since 1992, ten new Filipino commercial banks have opened,
some being the rebirth of banks closed a decade previously. Also, al-

though a few families continue to control the economy, the government has started serious efforts to spawn new entrepreneurs in an effort to reduce this problem.

The economy's growth rate in the 1990s has allowed the Philippines to join the ranks of other high-growth Asian countries. From 1987–91, GNP grew at a rate of 4.5% yearly, at a rate of 5.5% yearly from 1994–97, and is expected to continue this rate though the end of the 1990s.[8] A continuing economic problem in the Philippines is the relatively lower savings rate as compared to its ASEAN partners. The Philippines savings rate declined from 21% of income in 1965, to 15% in 1992, mirroring the experience in the United States, whereas the savings rate in Thailand grew from 19% to 34%; in Malaysia from 24% to 30%; and in Indonesia from 8% to 36% over the same period.[9] In addition, the Philippines has had a history of a negative balance of trade that is expected to persist until the end of the 1990s.

But the Philippines has also suffered from the regional economic crisis of 1997, with its currency declining nearly 30% relative to the U.S. dollar and its stock market falling 50% from 1996 levels. On the other hand, not having expanded as fast in the 1990s as its ASEAN neighbors, the country does not have the same overhang of excessive foreign investment and potentially bad business loans.

The country continues to be technology importing. R&D expenditure is only about 0.2% of GNP—way below the 1% prescribed by the United Nations. Export-processing zones have been established, including former U.S. military bases Subic and Clark, which are being developed quite successfully as special economic zones. Although there is much to overcome, the prospects for a positive future in the Philippines include the eradication of utter poverty, a higher level of industrialization, and a more entrepreneurial class of citizens.

## Role of Domestic Companies

Significant international activities of local companies emerged only during the last two decades. Foreign exchange policy, giving priority to import substitution projects starting in the early 1960s, is the main reason for this. Despite the unfavorable export policy, some companies, like the country's largest, San Miguel Corporation, had the good sense to perceive exporting as in their, and the country's, best interest. Thus, they pursued exporting as part of their corporate strategy. Some, like the mining companies, had no other way to survive but to export. Other companies are essentially subsidiaries of multinational corporations (MNCs) using the Philippines as a manufacturing base. Table 11.1 lists the twenty largest exporting domestic companies. It is notable that most are in primary extraction, agriculture, food, or other basic industries.

Notably, San Miguel Corporation accounts for about 4% of the Philippine's GNP and pays 6% of its taxes. According to the company, its vision is to become Asia's best beverage, food, and packaging company. San

*Table 11.1*

**Largest Exporting Domestic Companies in the Philippines**

| Rank | Company | Main Business | 1994 Revenues U.S.$ millions |
|---|---|---|---|
| 1 | Petron | naphta | 1,880 |
| 2 | San Miguel | beverages | 1,560 |
| 3 | Purefoods | shrimp | 260 |
| 4 | General Milling | leaf pellets | 260 |
| 5 | RFM | sauces, fruit | 240 |
| 6 | La Tondena Distillers | alcoholic beverages | 190 |
| 7 | Rustan Commercial | handicrafts | 180 |
| 8 | Jollibee Foods | food preparations | 140 |
| 9 | PICOP Resources | plywood | 130 |
| 10 | Victorias Milling | tuna | 130 |
| 11 | Legaspi Oil | coconut oil | 130 |
| 12 | Benguet | copper concentrate, gold, chromite | 130 |
| 13 | Granexport Manufacturing | coconut oil | 110 |
| 14 | Philex Mining | copper ore | 90 |
| 15 | Concepcion Industries | aluminum plates | 80 |
| 16 | Philippines Appliance | refrigerators | 80 |
| 17 | Marcopper | copper concentrate | 70 |
| 18 | United Coconut Chemicals | coco chemicals | 70 |
| 19 | FILSYN | fiber, yarns | 70 |
| 20 | WDO & LYM | coconut oil | 70 |

*Source: Business World.*

Miguel is on its way, having opened thirty factories since 1988, and invested forty billion pesos (U.S.$1.5 billion) during the period 1995–97. Since it formed its first joint venture in China in 1991, the company has operated two breweries in China, and San Miguel's beer has become the largest selling foreign brand in Guangdong province.[10]

## Role of Foreign Companies

The history of MNCs involvement in the Philippines has been like the wind, blowing hot and cold. When the business and government environment was good, foreign direct investment, primarily from the United States and Japan, came in; when the business and government environment became hostile, investment either dried up or left the country. In recent years, there has been a more conscious effort by the government to establish a stable and attractive business policy environment. From 1986–91, Japan represented 29% of foreign direct investment in the Philippines, whereas the United States represented only 14%; the newly industrialized economies of Korea, Taiwan, Hong Kong, and Singapore represented 25%, and the rest of the world represented the remaining 32%.[11] MNCs have primarily come for two reasons: (1) to capture part of the local market (e.g., Shell), and (2) to establish a manufacturing base (e.g., Motorola, Matsushita, Philips). Table 11.2 shows the twenty largest

*Table 11.2*

**Largest Foreign Multinational Companies in the Philippines**

| Rank | Company | Nationality | Main Business | 1994 Revenues U.S.$ millions |
|---|---|---|---|---|
| 1 | Shell Petroleum | U.K./ Netherlands | petroleum | 1,320 |
| 2 | Caltex | U.S. | petroleum | 1,150 |
| 3 | Nestlé | Switzerland | food, beverages | 760 |
| 4 | Texas Instruments | U.S. | consumer electronics | 700 |
| 5 | Coca Cola | U.S. | beverages | 670 |
| 6 | Toyota Motors | Japan | automotive | 450 |
| 7 | Philippines Automotive (Mitsubishi) | Japan | automotive | 440 |
| 8 | Procter and Gamble | U.S. | household, personal care | 440 |
| 9 | Shell Gas Eastern | U.K./ Netherlands | gas | 310 |
| 10 | Unilever | U.K./ Netherlands | household, personal care | 240 |
| 11 | Matsushita Electric | Japan | electrical | 210 |
| 12 | Uniden | Japan | telecom equipment | 200 |
| 13 | Matsushita Industrial Communication | Japan | telecom equipment | 200 |
| 14 | Citibank | U.S. | banking | 200 |
| 15 | Dole Philippines | U.S. | food | 190 |
| 16 | Nissan Motors | Japan | automotive | 170 |
| 17 | Colgate-Palmolive | U.S. | household, personal care | 160 |
| 18 | Pepsi Cola | U.S. | beverages | 160 |
| 19 | Del Monte | U.S. | food | 150 |
| 20 | Wyeth Philippines | U.S. | manufacturer | 140 |

*Source: Business World.*

MNCs and their local revenues—they span a wide range of industries and come from the world's elite companies.

Interestingly, in 1995, San Miguel Corporation purchased the *Dari Creme* and *Star* margarine brands from Procter and Gamble Philippine Manufacturing Corp., for 1.35 billion pesos (U.S.$52 million). These are among the best-known brands in the Philippines and had been owned by the P&G unit for sixty years. P&G explained the sale by saying that the brands were not a good fit for its long-term interests.[12]

There are increasing opportunities for foreign companies to participate in the Philippines by way of joint venture. In addition, the trend toward privatization continues in the country and a more liberalized policy and regulatory environment is progressing. For example, foreign partners have been signed for airport development at Manila and Clark, and the government is now planning to sell 14% of the equity in the Philippine National Bank, which will drop the government's stake to below 50%.[13]

## Overall Industry Globalization Drivers in the Philippines

The perception of the Philippines is that business and political corruption exist alongside political uncertainty. Although this is perhaps true in a relative sense, improvement is ongoing. As a result, there are many positive globalization drivers that should not be overlooked when considering global strategy. In addition, the government is making major efforts to liberalize and catch up to its neighbors as an attractive business location.

### Market Globalization Drivers

The historical Spanish, American, and Japanese involvement in the Philippines, and its Western (Catholic) religion, make its population and companies more amenable to foreign products and services than any Asian country other than highly Westernized Hong Kong and Singapore. Only low purchasing power prevents greater acceptance of global goods. Except for vital commodities, like rice and fish, which must be available at affordable prices to low-income families, the needs of Filipino consumers, even in remote rural areas, are similar to those of most consumers the world over. The "blue seal" mentality (i.e., foreign brands are better) prevails all over the country. Thus, foreign brands are able to easily penetrate the Philippine market. Only a few local products, like refrigerators, processed meat, and beer, are at a standard to compete with foreign products.

A mass market exists for low-cost consumer products. However, high-priced items, like motor vehicles, personal computers, and other electronic products, are affordable only for middle- and high-income families and business organizations. So the Philippines is not a lead market for product innovation.

Global and regional customers operate in the country in a few industry sectors, particularly resource-based industries like mining and coconut. This is also true for industries where for some MNCs, like Toyota and Motorola, the country is now playing a global and regional role.

Like Indonesia, but smaller, the Philippines occupies an archipelago of seven thousand one hundred islands sprawled over one thousand miles of sea, with resulting physical segmentation of its markets. At the same time, the country's position midway between Northeast and Southeast Asia gives it great, although mostly as yet unrealized, potential as a regional distribution hub. Further improvements in infrastructure and government policies will be needed to realize such a role.

MNC marketing approaches are readily transferable to the country. The population's facility with English makes English-language television, print, or radio advertisements easily understood in all cities and provinces.

Typically, the only marketing modifications made by MNCs with consumer products is the use of endorsements from local sports and movie personalities, of which there are many.

## Cost Globalization Drivers

The Philippines' cost globalization drivers are mostly favorable for MNCs. The market is large enough to support local production at the minimum efficient scale and above, as Unilever, P&G, Matsushita, Philips, and others have found. Or in industries where the Philippines market is insufficient, some MNCs, such as Toyota, use the country as a base to exploit economies of scale available in the ASEAN market.

Logistics is still a problem but solutions are underway. On the one hand, seaports and airports barely meet world standards. On the other hand, Subic (the former U.S. naval base) is world class. For products that are economical to transport by air, some processing zones (e.g., Mactan, Subic, Clark, and Cavite) are ideal. Domestic water transport is inadequate but the whole country is covered by air cargo service. International container cargo facilities are available in major ports but the level of technology is behind that of Singapore or Hong Kong. Infrastructure is also a problem, particularly in electric power, communications, and transportation. But progressive legislation is in place and foreign investments should ensure dramatic improvements in a few years.

Other country costs are competitive. Average wages of about U.S.$0.70/hour in 1995, cost of land, energy, and various services compare favorably with much of Asia. So attractive margins are possible with the present level of costs in the Philippines. Geothermal energy is about to become available in larger capacities. A very large gas field is now being developed by Shell and the Philippine National Oil Company. The country also easily adopts the latest in manufacturing technology. Finally, land is readily available. Many industrial estates, government and private, are accessible to local investors and to MNCs.

Technical skills are abundant. The excess is such that the "brain drain" has been a long-time phenomenon. The Philippines, for many decades, has been a technology resource in agribusiness for many Asian countries. Most Thai agribusiness technologists were trained in the Philippines. The world center for rice research is in the country. R&D workers in plant genetics are world class. In the area of computer software development and IT services, the country has a competitive edge because of the availability of professionals and skilled workers. But, overall, the Philippines, except in agribusiness, is a technology-importing country.

Owing to a long history of technology importation, the technology standards are those used by MNCs the world over. Exporters of Philippine products use world standards as a basis for determining the specifications of their products. Total Quality Management is gaining ground among leading companies in the private sector.

A negative cost factor is that annual natural disasters should be expected, the most frequent being the tropical typhoon. This natural phenomenon affects agriculture the most, presenting both a problem and an opportunity. Companies that can offer low-cost logistics for agricultural products (rice, fish, vegetables, etc.) will find the Philippines a good market. Over the last two hundred years, only three typhoons passed the large island of Mindanao in the South. So, Del Monte pineapple is there and Dole Pineapple transferred its plantations in Hawaii to Southern Mindanao. Earthquake and volcanic operations are frequent occurrences. However, the locations of danger areas are well known and can be avoided.

Another negative cost factor is that the Philippines is a relatively litigious society, this aspect being inherited from the fifty years of American rule. An example illustrates this problem. In 1995, the government secured ITT Sheraton and Renong (a Malaysian Group) as strategic partners to invest in the Manila Hotel. Together these foreign companies offered the highest price for a 51% stake. The losing bidder, a Filipino company, obtained a temporary restraining order from the Supreme Court on the grounds that the constitution stipulated that a Filipino company should have priority in the acquisition of state assets. The losing bidder had submitted a bid 5% lower than the ITT/Renong bid, but later matched the winning bid.[14] Still, litigious as the country is, good legal counsel is helpful in arriving at win-win compromise agreements.

Crime against executives, particularly kidnapping, is also a problem for MNCs. To date, most such crime has been targeted at prominent local businessmen and their families, particularly ethnic Chinese. But such crimes are also reaching foreign executives.

## Government Globalization Drivers

Government involvement in the economy and consequent corruption has been a major disincentive for MNCs. But conditions are improving rapidly with the opening up of the economy. For decades the country had a policy of protecting "infant industries." But that era is now over. Globalization is in the consciousness of Filipino business. Only the retail sector remains closed to foreign companies. In the four decades prior to the early 1990s, the government had a dominant presence in commerce and industry. But from the mid-1980s, privatization was successfully pursued. Only in the generation of electric energy is the Philippine government dominant. Even in this sector, privatization plans are in place. By 1997, the oil industry was to be fully deregulated and to operate based on international market forces. Foreign investment is also welcome in the energy sector. Except for industries related to national defense, an area of sensitivity, the government encourages the private sector (local and foreign) to be the engine for development.

Political instability has also been a deterrent to MNCs. For example, until the several coup attempts during the term of President Corazon Aquino, the Philippines was a training center for Philips executives in the Asia-Pacific region. It has been temporarily transferred to Singapore and may be returned to the Philippines. But the stability under President

Ramos has calmed MNC fears. A peaceful transfer of power in the next presidential election in 1998 should cement this calm.

Privatization of business is now an established policy. Government has successfully phased out of direct involvement in business. It does remain a significant customer for many products and services that have to do with national defense, peace and order, health, education, and public works.

Trade is opening up—imports now account for over 30% of GNP. The Philippines is a recent signatory of GATT. Before that the country signed the ASEAN Free Trade Agreement discussed in Chapter 16. But tariffs are still mostly higher than in the rest of ASEAN. Rules on foreign direct investment have become more hospitable and this trend will continue. The whole Philippine economy is now open to foreign direct investment. The only limits are in the ownership of land and in the development of natural resources (open up to 40% of equity). But these two constraints do not pose serious problems. The Philippines is an active participant in trade blocs and the economic future of the country is tied up with ASEAN. Within and beyond ASEAN, the Philippines seeks greater involvement in growth triangles (e.g., the East-Asia Growth Area: Southern Philippines, Eastern Indonesia, East Malaysia, and Brunei).

In the early 1990s, the banking system was opened to foreign banks. Immediately, ten foreign banks entered the Philippine banking system. This was welcomed with open arms by the business community. At about the same time, the telecommunications industry was opened up, a development that was felt as long overdue. By 1995, seven local groups and their foreign partners had franchises to develop the telecommunications capability of the country.

Tax policies are comparable to other Southeast Asian countries, so the Philippines offers no significant tax advantages. In 1996, General Motors was deciding, supposedly based on tax incentives, between the Philippines and Thailand in its effort to establish a major Asian presence. GM ultimately chose Thailand, but it is doubtful that the company's decision turned mainly on tax considerations. The overall policy environment was probably more crucial.

While copyright infringement and theft of intellectual property occur, as in the rest of Asia, the Philippines does not stand out in this regard. The Philippines is a signatory to international conventions on intellectual property and technology transfer. The government makes serious efforts to respect patents and intellectual property rights.

Unlike China or Malaysia, the Philippine government is not aggressive in seeking technology transfer from MNCs. For example, the Department of Science and Technology has, for many years, proposed a Science and Technology Incentives Law. But, the legislature does not seem to be listening. The importance of R&D is recognized in official government planning, but R&D expenditure is well below the levels of South Korea, Singapore, and Taiwan; and state-of-the-art R&D is nonexistent. However, some MNCs, like Toyota and Motorola, have benefited from new ideas in manufacturing processes, which are now being adopted in other plants around the world. So it is really up to the MNCs to decide what technology to transfer, as the country does not have a strong bargaining position in this regard. In contrast, government policy toward MNCs is more concerned with job creation. The brain drain and worker emigration have been long-standing phenomena. There are now about two million Filipinos, mostly workers, in the United States. There is also a very large number of overseas contract workers (OCWs), many in the Middle East, which has a positive and negative impact on family life. Thus, job creation has been a top priority of all administrations.

Economic zones, including former U.S. military bases, play an increasingly important role. Subic Bay is attracting investments from several MNCs. A handful of American companies account for a third of the pledges for Subic as of 1995. Federal Express plans to spend $100 million and locate at the airport; Enron, a major U.S. energy company, has built a $150 million plant in the zone; and AT&T has a joint venture with a local company to upgrade Subic's telecommunications facilities at a cost of $20 million.[15] The country is also bidding, like its neighbors, to become a location for the regional head offices of MNCs, offering numerous incentives. The Philippines is particularly targeting Hong Kong-based MNCs, who may be fearful of that territory's return to China, citing that Manila is only two hours flying time away.

The legal system is very similar to that of the United States and some European countries. Decades of trading with Asian and Western countries have integrated the Philippine legal system with those in the rest of the world. Legal, tax, and financial consultants are readily available. One drawback is the slow process in arriving at decisions by the courts. Thus, out-of-court settlements are often resorted to.

Western, and most Asian, MNCs will find the Philippines an area for creative marketing. Rules and regulations are minimal. Self-restraint among marketing organizations is the prevailing mode of behavior.

### Competitive Globalization Drivers

The Philippines' competitive globalization drivers are not compelling for MNCs. The country is in catch-up mode in making itself globally or regionally strategic. A few industries provide exceptions. An obvious example is a whole range of personal and home care products. Unilever, P&G, and Kao of Japan are the major MNCs in this industry. Beyond the prospect of revenues and profits, and the presence of global competitors, the country is a major source for raw materials such as coconut oil. Another example is the automobile industry where major Japanese manufacturers are using the country as a manufacturing base for ASEAN. Computer software is another industry where high-skilled lower-cost professionals and workers are available who can speak and write in English. Software companies there now service major customers in the United States.

Internationalized domestic competitors are nonexistent except for the airline industry. Although the country has no global companies, there are strong domestic competitors in certain industries like food, garments, and pharmaceuticals. Local companies with significant export activity are usually linked up with MNCs or foreign partners. In every key industry, foreign competitors are operating in the country. Except for the motor vehicle industry, where U.S. and European manufacturers are absent, MNCs from Asia, the United States, and Europe compete in just about every key industry in the country.

## Overall Global Strategies for the Philippines

The appropriate strategies for the Philippines depend on the industry and the company, but several generalizations can be made. In addition, all six of this book's featured MNCs operate in the Philippines.

### Market Participation Strategies

Participation in the Philippines is profitable in many industries, the country being larger than many in Asia and Europe. With a large and growing population and rising incomes, the Philippines is becoming increasingly attractive for many types of MNCs. Some MNCs have participated in the Philippines for a long time, including our six focus MNCs. Most, but not all, MNCs begin in joint ventures with local partners. Often, local production is established with agreements on technology transfer and the use of foreign, global brand names.

P&G has operated in the Philippines since 1908, and this subsidiary is the company's oldest in Asia. P&G has consistently been among the top thirty corporations in the country. It offers a wide range of products and is the market leader in many categories. P&G's rival, Unilever, acquired the Philippine Refining Company in 1929, since renamed Unilever Philippines (PRC) Inc. In 1995, this company had one thousand five hundred employees and was the largest private employer in Manila, with ten warehouses in various locations. Like P&G, Unilever markets in the Philippines a very wide range of its global products.

Philips established its presence by marketing lighting products and short-wave radios in the Philippines in the 1920s. It was in the 1950s, however, that Philips laid the firm foundation for what was to become a diversified Philippine operation. By 1995, the Philips Group of Companies was composed of the following: Philips Electronic and Lighting, Inc., Philips Industrial Development, Inc., Philips Semiconductors, Inc., and Philippine Glass Bulbs, Inc. Together, these companies employ more than three thousand Filipinos. Philips has an extensive and diversified participation in the Philippines. Its head office is in Makati (the main business district of Metro Manila); the plant site and industrial complex is in Pamplona, Las Pinas (a town bordering Metro Manila); there is a showroom and information center in Cebu City (about four hundred nautical miles from Metro Manila) in the Visayas in central Philippines, and another showroom and information center in Davao City (about seven hundred nautical miles from Metro Manila) in Mindanao which is in the southern Philippines.

As one leaves the Ninoy Aquino International Airport toward Manila, the first neon sign an arriving passenger sees is that of *National* and *Panasonic*—global brand names of Matsushita. This sign is symbolic of the company's presence in the Philippines. Matsushita is composed of two companies in the Philippines, Matsushita Electric Philippines Corporation (MEPC) and Matsushita Communication Industrial Corporation of the Philippines (MCP). MEPC began as a joint venture (51% owned by Matsushita and 49% by local partners) in 1967. Less than two years later, MEPC was registered with the Board of Investments as a local manufacturer of electronics products. By the early 1990s, MEPC had about two thousand employees. MCP originally was a department of MECP. In 1988, MCP became a separate corporate entity and had about 1,500 employees.

Motorola Philippines, Inc. (MPI), is part of the Semiconductor Products Sector of Motorola Inc. MPI was established in 1979 to assemble integrated circuits (ICs). MPI produces varied kinds of ICs and plastic chips for export to other Motorola plants around the world. Some of Motorola's global customers, such as IBM and AT&T, are supplied from the Philippines. In brief, today MPI is an international production center for Motorola. It does market Motorola products in the Philippines (cellular telephone, pagers, etc.), but the bulk of its business is exporting components made in the Philippines to overseas users. Local sales should, however, grow rapidly once the country's telecommunications infrastructure is completed in the late 1990s.

Toyota Motor Philippines Corporation is a relatively new joint venture founded in 1988, during the presidency of Corazon Aquino. The corporation's predecessor closed down for many reasons including mismanagement and its previous stockholders being linked to the disgraced and exiled President Ferdinand Marcos. By 1989, a Toyota model, the *Corolla* sedan, was the best selling passenger car in the country. By 1990, Toyota was the overall market leader with over 50% of the passenger car market and 34% of all vehicles.

## Product and Service Strategies

The strong driver of globally common customer needs, discussed earlier, means that most MNC products and services can be offered in the Philippines with relatively little adaptation, particularly if MNCs select lower-priced items from their product ranges.

For P&G, global products such as *Tide, Ivory, Pantene, Pampers, Whisper, Vicks Vaporub, Always,* and *Camay* have wide acceptance in the country. Many of these products have been marketed for decades now. The company also offers some locally developed brands. Unilever has a similar product strategy, marketing global products and brands in detergents, personal care, and food products, such as *Lux, Surf, Sunsilk, Pepsodent, Rexona, Vaseline,* and *Lipton,* mostly with very little adaptation.

Philips offers a broad range of products and services that have found wide acceptance in the Philippines. This range includes consumer electronics (digital compact cassettes, high definition TVs, compact discs);

domestic appliances (food processors, vacuum cleaners, flat irons, hair dryers, electric shavers); lighting products; mobile and handheld cellular telephones; medical, telecommunications, and industrial electronics; and electroacoustic products. Some of these products are very advanced, such as magnetic resonance systems, linear accelerators that destroy cancerous cells, and digital vascular and cardiac imaging systems that help prevent heart disease. Similar to Philips, Motorola offers a wide range of global products and services, its cellular telephone and the radio pager being the most popular in the country. Matsushita, too, markets in the Philippines most of its global range of products.

Toyota's global products are popular in the Philippine market. Some localization is part of the production process, but the overall basic designs remain the same. Toyota's market research showed that there is a significant demand for a vehicle suitable for Philippine and ASEAN conditions, especially in rural areas. Hence, Toyota introduced, in 1991, the *Tamaraw FX*, a jeep-plus-van vehicle ("jipny") suitable for the rural areas and named after a rare animal (a small buffalo) indigenous to the Philippines.

## Activity Location Strategies

Because of its large and young labor force, low wages, and widespread English-language capability, the Philippines has become increasingly attractive for MNCs to locate activities there, despite continuing problems with productivity, infrastructure, transportation, and bureaucratic inefficiencies. But, as discussed earlier, these drawbacks are decreasing. Some MNCs, such as Toyota, Federal Express, P&G, and Matsushita, use the country for regional and global roles in their value chains.

Unilever locates here all production and downstream value-chain activities for the domestic and export markets. In addition, the company is locally active in conducting R&D in the use of chemicals derived from coconut and its by-products, in detergents, foods, and personal care. The company also uses coconut by-products as an alternative energy source in its cogeneration plant. Unilever also sources coconut raw material from the Philippines for its operations elsewhere. P&G takes a similar approach. In addition, as the most mature of all P&G Asian subsidiaries, the Philippines unit has served as a resource group to newer units.

Philips locates raw material processing, intermediate production/subassembly, final production/assembly, marketing, selling, distribution, and customer service (but not R&D) in the Philippines. Philips in the Philippines has evolved from just an importer/distributor in the 1920s to that of a manufacturer and global supplier of parts and components. For example, an ISO 9002 certification for manufacturing operations enables Philips to provide customers with world-class products in domestic and foreign markets. Philips' semiconductor operation is one of the major Dutch investments in the country, and counts a number of major electronics companies in the world as customers. Recently, Philips inaugurated an expanded production facility, indicating a larger role for the country in the company's global network.

Motorola's main activity in the Philippines is as an international production center for ICs and plastic chips for export to other Motorola plants in the world, and to service the requirements of some customers like IBM and AT&T. In 1993, the Philippine capacity was expanded to serve a bigger role in the global semiconductor products sector of Motorola.

Matsushita is using the Philippines as a key international production center for the export market which includes Japan, the United States, and many other countries around the world. The Philippines is also a base for R&D in product quality improvement. Thus, all activities in the value chain exist in the Philippines for its various products.

When it started in the Philippines, Toyota had only assembly operations for semiknocked-down units. This evolved into assembly of completely knocked-down units. Engine assembly previously done in Japan is now done in the Philippines. Within four years of its founding, Toyota established a subsidiary to manufacture auto parts. Then, Toyota began to produce the *Tamaraw* for the entire ASEAN market. All these activities involve R&D, procurement, raw material sourcing, final production and assembly, marketing, distribution, and customer service. So the Philippines is very significant in the overall value chain of Toyota, and the company plans to double local assembly capacity by 1997.

## Marketing Strategies

Most MNCs use global marketing approaches in the Philippines. The main modifications are in the use of Taglish (a combination of English and the Filipino language, Tagalog) and of local personalities for advertising campaigns.

Most of Unilever's marketing techniques are applicable in the Philippines. Through its market research on the Philippine market, some local habits have been considered in product development. For example, the introduction of a nonsoap detergent bar was designed to address the local habit of washing clothes by hand. Otherwise, all other marketing approaches used in the United States and Europe are applicable. P&G practices its worldwide marketing approaches in the Philippines. However, to penetrate lower-income groups, local brands, such as *Perla,* a laundry soap, have been successfully developed and sold. In their advertising both Unilever and P&G make extensive use of the Filipino language and of local movie and other personalities.

Given the presence of competitors in the Philippines like Matsushita, Philips has an aggressive marketing approach in the country. In terms of positioning, brand name, labeling, advertising, promotion, personal selling, and service, Philips has an extensive presence in the Philippines. Matsushita, too, markets heavily in the Philippine market. Motorola's domestic marketing is handled through dealers who are served by a relatively small Motorola office in Makati. Motorola has an aggressive and continuing advertising campaign, especially in Metro Manila, which delivers its global advertising message that Motorola is the "world leader in mobile communications." Toyota's marketing practices used all over the world are also effective in the Philippine market.

### Competitive Move Strategies

Given its lag as an Asian economic power, the Philippines does not yet feature as very strategic when MNCs make regional or global competitive moves. But in the cases where MNCs, such as Toyota, Matsushita, Motorola, and Philips, have made the Philippines part of their global supply and value chains, competitive moves are made with the country in mind. This can also apply in the sourcing of raw materials. The Philippines is potentially strategic in industries such as software that need English skills.

Toyota's moves in the Philippines are coordinated with moves in other parts of the world, especially in auto parts and in the introduction of the *Tamaraw FX*. Toyota of Japan became involved in the ASEAN brand-to-brand complementation (BBC) programs partly with the objective of developing and producing an affordable and efficient ASEAN car through the manufacture of common car parts by participating subsidiaries in the ASEAN region. Thus Toyota Autoparts Philippines, Inc. (TAP), became the company's first transmissions factory outside Japan, with the mission to produce top-quality transmissions for export to ASEAN and Japan.

Lastly, MNCs need worry little about competition from purely local companies. Most such companies are in joint ventures with MNCs. But this also means that local competitive battles can spill over into broader ones as MNCs make multicountry and multimarket moves.

## Overall Organization and Management Approaches for the Philippines

In the Philippines, MNCs mostly have classic subsidiary organization structures, but often with local partners. In addition, perhaps because of the country's history of turbulence, MNCs tend to maintain tight control of their local operations. Sometimes this has not been enough. For example, Pepsico suffered a very embarrassing financial scandal in the early 1980s when the top management of its Philippines subsidiary was found to have rigged performance numbers in order to win corporate bonuses.[16]

Philips entered the country in partnership with Filipinos, and historically, has operated as an autonomous subsidiary. In recent years, with the parent company's focus on global integration, it has operated as a tightly controlled extension of the head office in the Netherlands. Motorola, Matsushita, and Toyota have always tightly controlled their Philippines operations.

Western and Japanese management processes and practices have been readily accepted because these approaches are not alien to Philippine culture. So P&G Philippines has adopted, almost totally, the practices of the parent company in advertising, finance and accounting, management systems, market research, personnel, maintenance, logistics, purchasing, product development, and sales. The Philips operation follows management practices prescribed by the world head office. Japanese companies make extensive use of the *kaizen* quality circles, suggestion schemes, and other typical worker participation processes.

Management talent is abundant in the country. In fact, many Filipinos occupy key managerial positions in other ASEAN countries such as Indonesia. World-class management training programs are available and the Philippines serves as a regional training center for management with graduate students coming from throughout Asia. But despite this availability of local managers, some MNCs still have expatriates occupying positions. In others, however, Filipino managers have replaced expatriate managers. In 1995, after decades of doing business in the Philippines, P&G finally appointed the first Filipino to head its Philippine subsidiary. Today, the managerial corps of P&G Philippines is Filipino. In fact, P&G has been a regular source of effective managers for other Asia-Pacific subsidiaries, Europe, and the United States. Unilever appointed Filipinos to top positions much earlier than did P&G. The company also supports strong family ties in personnel and human resource policies, giving preference to children of retirees for employment, other factors being equal. In Shell, alternating expatriates and local managers has been a long-standing practice so that merit, regardless of country of origin, is viewed as the main consideration. Shell has also transferred Filipinos to other countries.

Culture, including organizational culture, is not a major issue in Philippine business organizations. If at all, the issue is whether a better culture is needed. Thus, as a society, the Philippines is generally open to the best that is available. For example, Motorola Philippines' organizational culture follows that of the parent company, emphasizing human resources, the Six Sigma quality program, continuous process improvement, and participative management. Motorola does, however, address local concerns such as basic needs and benefits for local employees, including free meals, a sack of rice every month, scholarships, housing loans, and a Christmas package.

## Conclusion

In conclusion, the Philippines is rapidly making up for lost time. Political, social, and infrastructure improvements are all making it increasingly attractive for MNCs. With a large, growing, increasingly affluent, English-speaking population, and a highly pro-Western government, the Philippines has to be seriously considered by any MNC as both a market and as a location for most value-adding activities. The country's active participation in ASEAN adds a significant bonus. Wage rates are still low enough that the country can compete for labor-intensive activities with the lowest-cost countries such as China, India, and Indonesia. But added inducements for MNCs include the English-language capability, the democratic government, and educated and adaptable Filipino managers. The Philippines has a memory of economic prominence. Foreign investment can help quickly restore that past to current reality while allowing MNCs to profit from a near ground-floor opportunity. Lastly, the Filipino currency and economy were hurt by the Asian crises of 1997. But having expanded less rapidly than its ASEAN neighbors, the Filipino economy has attracted less speculative investment, and should weather the crises more easily.

## NOTES

1. M. S. Dobbs-Higginson, *Asia-Pacific: Its Role in the New World Disorder* (Hong Kong: Longman Group [Far East], 1994): (London: Mandarin Paperbacks, Reed Consumer Books, 1995).

2. James C. Abegglen, *Sea Change: Pacific Asia as the New World Industrial Center* (New York: Free Press, 1994).

3. Reported by Dobbs-Higginson, 1995.

4. National Economic Development Authority.

5. National Economic Development Authority.

6. World Bank.

7. National Economic Development Authority.

8. *Country Report: Philippines* first quarter (London: *The Economist Intelligence Unit,* 1996).

9. Abegglen, *Sea Change,* tables 1–4, 9.

10. "San Miguel's Big Push," *International Herald Tribune,* April 20, 1995.

11. Abegglen, op. cit., tables 2–3, 74.

12. "San Miguel Buys Two Food Brands from Manila Unit of P&G," *Bloomberg News Service,* April 19, 1995.

13. The Economist Intelligence Unit (1996).

14. The Economist Intelligence Unit (1996).

15. "Back in Business," *Far Eastern Economic Review,* December 14, 1995, 62–64.

16. But such misdeeds are not necessarily country or culture specific. The Hong Kong subsidiary of Bausch and Lomb featured in a similar scandal in 1995.

# CHAPTER 12

# India—Giving Multinationals a Chance

*K. Ramachandran and George S. Yip*

BY 2050, INDIA'S POPULATION is expected to exceed China's, thereby making it the world's largest market. Characterized by a largely English-speaking, skilled work force and a solid middle class of two hundred million Indians, India represents a potential bonanza for many MNCs. However, while these attributes point to a relatively transparent market situation and the promise of a big pay-off, restrictions intended to put Indian companies on a level, or favorable, playing field confound even those multinational corporations (MNCs) with the best intentions.

## Background

After forty-four years (1947–91) of outright hostility to free markets and foreign companies, India is finally giving markets and MNCs a chance.

### India's Patchy Liberalization

Despite independence in 1947, following two hundred years of colonial rule, India continued to fight domination from outside sources. India adopted a self-reliance policy as a reaction to exploitation by the British, and restricted any significant level of foreign investment in India until 1991. In July 1991, the national government started the process of economic liberalization by removing several controls on industrial investment.

Economic reform, designed to cut the fat from the socialist government and bring India into a more competitive position, opened key industries—such as automobiles, telecommunications, consumer electronics, and power—to both Indian and overseas private investors, and it removed stringent licensing requirements. But from 1995, the liberalization process slowed down significantly—domestic companies applied pressure to even the level of competition before completely opening the flood gates to foreign investment. Local companies complain that MNCs indulge in dumping and benefit from better factor advantages (such as a lower cost of capital). Even though the flow of investment from abroad has not posed a major threat to India's local industry, the government is carefully considering various factors before allowing any additional investment. Currently, overseas investors have to obtain clearance from the Foreign Investment Promotion Board to enter the Indian market. The Annual Budget for 1997–98 and subsequent discussions indicate that the reforms are back on track with the government adopting an aggressive investment-friendly strategy without sacrificing support for the poor.

## The Appeal of the Indian Market

India's population of over nine hundred million, and its growing consumption of goods and services, attract both domestic and overseas companies. The increase in the number of nuclear families and working couples has fueled increased levels of consumption among the middle class. Moreover, rising literacy rates and incomes should expand demand for high-quality global products. As employment and education is made more available to women, there will be a surge in demand for household gadgets that help reduce routine work and increase leisure time. India now has a population, 40% of which, has an income criterion above Rs 12,500 (U.S.$350) per annum. Fourteen percent of the population has income over Rs 25,000 (U.S.$700). While these numbers seem low, their parity purchasing power equivalents are about four times greater. However, the promise of expanding consumer markets needs to be tempered against the current reality that India remains largely a poor country. Over three hundred fifty million Indians live in poverty and the nation's average per capita income barely exceeds U.S.$300 a year. Furthermore, the nation has huge regional, ethnic, religious, and language differences, all affecting consumer behavior.

Nevertheless, India promises continued growth and, therefore, Indian as well as overseas investors are keen on developing a production base in India. Additionally, the availability of low-cost, qualified, skilled labor, a Western accounting and legal system, and the fact that many Indians speak English provide added attractions. For these reasons, many overseas investors seem to prefer India to other countries such as China.

## Economic Performance

The economic changes that make India more attractive to outside investment are predicted to continue. All political parties are committed to the economic reforms and there does not appear to be a threat of reversal of the liberalization process. India's economy has started to show signs of structural changes and faster growth. Exports rose from U.S.$8.5 billion in 1980–81 to U.S.$ 35 billion in 1996–97. About 78% of the exports came from manufactured goods and 16% from agricultural products, while capital goods and petroleum products comprise 25% each of imports. Considering the growth in the volume of trade, India's trade gap has decreased significantly. This situation is likely to continue with the increased import of capital goods and sustained efforts to push exports.

When economic planning started in 1950, the government decided to open only some industries to private investment, either Indian or foreign. This policy restricted free and fast expansion of private investment. Economic policy focused strictly on import substitution. For the next thirty years, the government controlled industrialization through the imposition of a socialistic approach. Private industry could invest only where the government allowed and, even then, needed several licenses to operate. In the 1980s, many companies, lured by India's vast, untapped market, doggedly attempted to defy government controls and, as a result, India saw moderate growth in industrial investment. However, India's turning point did not occur until the 1990s when liberalized investments and accelerated exports led to economic development. Although India has benefited from economic reform—exports growing at 22–29% during 1992–96[1], corporate profits growing at 10% annually, the economy growing at 6–8%, up from 1.5% in 1991—India's economy is still only the size of Belgium's. It is against this backdrop that one must examine the opportunities for overseas and domestic companies.

## Domestic Companies

Due to the government's import substitution approach, domestic companies in public and private sectors have been more active than foreign companies in India. In addition, the key role played by the government in industrialization is reflected in the fact that only four of the twenty companies listed below are in the private sector. Some of the details of the twenty largest local companies are given in Table 12.1. The export performance of these domestic companies is not very impressive. An exception is Titan watches, India's first consumer brand to go global successfully. Titan combines low production costs and foreign technology to produce a relatively inexpensive, high-quality product that challenges Swiss and Japanese watchmakers. But Titan's advertising downplays its Indian origin, stressing, instead, an international heritage. Titan also benefits from being part of the U.S.$10 billion Tata Group, one of India's largest.[2]

India's private sector is dominated by a number of very large family-based corporate groups, such as Tata, Bajaj, and Mahindra. Their complex ownership structures hide their overall strength. Historically, these groups have provided the best joint venture partners for foreign companies. Today, the groups also pose domestic competition for foreign MNCs entering India on their own, and potentially can become global competitors in the future.

## Foreign Participation in Economy

The first large overseas company to operate in India, The British East India Company, initiated a history of British activity in India that lasted nearly a century. Many English firms followed suit and opened offices in India to serve production and trade functions. The Netherlands' Philips

**Table 12.1**
**Largest Indian Companies**

| Rank | Company | Main Business | 1995 Revenues U.S.$ millions | Ownership |
|---|---|---|---|---|
| 1 | Indian Oil | petroleum | 11,920 | State |
| 2 | Steel Authority of India | steel | 3,861 | State |
| 3 | Oil & Natural Gas | petroleum | 3,475 | State |
| 4 | Hindustan Petroleum | petroleum | 2,964 | State |
| 5 | Bharat Petroleum | petroleum | 2,249 | State |
| 6 | Tata Engineering & Locomotive | automobile | 1,926 | Private |
| 7 | Reliance Industries | textiles, petroleum | 1,739 | Private |
| 8 | Tata Iron & Steel | steel | 1,462 | Private |
| 9 | Bharat Heavy Electricals | power transmission | 1,242 | State |
| 10 | VSNL | communication | 1,232 | State |
| 11 | Larsen & Toubro | engineering | 1,108 | Private |
| 12 | Mahanagar Telephone Nigam | communication | 978 | State |
| 13 | Cochin Refineries | petroleum | 940 | State |
| 14 | IPCL | petrochemicals | 846 | State |
| 15 | Grasim Industries | VSF, cement | 762 | Private |
| 16 | Mahindra and Mahindra | automobiles | 658 | Private |
| 17 | Bajaj Auto | scooters | 634 | Private |
| 18 | Madras Refineries | petroleum | 599 | State |
| 19 | Shipping Corporation | shipping | 587 | State |
| 20 | ACC | cement | 562 | Private |

*Source:* "BS 1000: India's Corporate Giants," *Business Standard,* November 1996.

opened shop in 1930. The Unilever group has operated in India since 1932. Only after India's independence in 1947 did investments from other countries increase by any considerable amount. Government restrictions on investment and repatriation of profit, especially under the Foreign Exchange Regulations Act, restrict the flow of multinational investments into India. However, since the liberalization era started in 1991, restrictions on foreign exchange movements have been eased greatly. Some key data about the major MNCs in India are given in the Table 12.2. A British firm, ITC ( formerly Imperial Tobacco Company), with interests in cigarette, hotel, edible oil, and software currently achieves the highest level of sales in India. Unilever, Procter and Gamble, Philips, Motorola, Suzuki, and Matsushita, as well as Johnson and Johnson, Nestlé, ICI, ITC, Siemens, Bata, Cadbury, and Boots have manufacturing and marketing operations in India through their subsidiaries. Most of their products are adapted versions from abroad. Maruti Udyog is an Indian government joint venture with Suzuki of Japan. The third and fourth ranked Hindustan Lever and Brooke Bond Lipton India are part of the Unilever group.

*Table 12.2*
**Largest Foreign Multinational Companies in India**

| Rank | Company | Nationality | Main Business | 1995 Revenues U.S.$ millions |
|------|---------|-------------|---------------|------------------------------|
| 1 | Maruti Udyog | Japan | automobiles | 1,797 |
| 2 | ITC | U.K. | cigarettes | 1,423 |
| 3 | Hindustan Lever | U.K. | soaps and detergents | 1,051 |
| 4 | Brooke Bond Lipton India | U.K. | beverages | 587 |
| 5 | Ashok Leyland | U.K. | automobile | 571 |
| 6 | Philips India | Netherlands | electricals, electronics | 441 |
| 7 | Nippon Denro Ispat | Japan | steel | 381 |
| 8 | Indian Aluminum | Canada | aluminum | 328 |
| 9 | Siemens | Germany | machinery | 327 |
| 10 | Nestlé India | Switzerland | food | 277 |
| 11 | Shaw Wallace | U.K. | fertilizers | 274 |
| 12 | Motor Industries | U.S. | auto components | 260 |
| 13 | Glaxo India | U.K. | food, pharmaceuticals | 256 |
| 14 | Asea Brown Boveri | Switz./Sweden | electricals, electronics | 249 |
| 15 | Coats Viyella India | U.K. | yarn, thread | 245 |
| 16 | Colgate-Palmolive (I) | U.S. | toothpaste | 236 |
| 17 | Dunlop India | U.K. | tires | 227 |
| 18 | Castrol India | U.K. | petroleum | 203 |
| 19 | ICI India | U.K. | chemicals | 174 |
| 20 | VST Industries | U.K. | cigarettes | 169 |

*Source:* CIMM Data Base, Center for Monitoring Indian Economy.

While companies such as Unilever, Philips, Nestlé and Siemens came to India on their own in search of markets, others such as Coats, Shaw Wallace, Indian Aluminum, and Nippon Denro came through the partnership route. The partnership model typically involved an Indian partner inviting those companies with technology and capital to make use of locally available resources to produce for the local market. Since 1991, MNCs have also started scouting actively for local partners.

## Overall Industry Globalization Drivers in India

India's globalization drivers play a dual role. For example, while many market globalization drivers encourage MNCs to participate in India's huge consumer market, India's government drivers often limit the ability to execute a global strategy in India.

### Market Globalization Drivers

India boasts the world's fifth-largest economy based on purchasing power parity. Couple that alluring draw with India's expanding middle class, estimated at two hundred million, and strong market globalization drivers emerge.

The legacy of Gandhi combined with the tenets of self-restraint extolled by India's major religion, Hinduism, have historically worked to weaken the acceptance of Western-style consumerism. Recent economic growth, however, is propelling India to become more outwardly focused through the encouragement of foreign investment. As Indian consumer needs become increasingly Westernized, modern amenities are closer to becoming requirements rather than unattainable luxury items. *Kentucky Fried Chicken, McDonald's* (with vegetarian and lamb burgers, instead of beef burgers, because of the Hindu reverence for cows), *Coke*, and *Pepsi* are all courting Indian consumers and Indian consumers are accepting their advances. Indian ownership of consumer durables is also growing rapidly.

The explosive transformation of television in the early 1990s, with the arrival of StarTV and ZeeTV from Hong Kong, swiftly brought Western attitudes and consumption behavior to millions of Indians. ZeeTV challenged the monopolistic reign of government-run Doordarshan TV and spread Western culture in the form of modern soap operas such as the "Bold and the Beautiful" and "Baywatch."[3] About forty-two to forty-seven million television households view ZeeTV. By scattering the seeds of Western consumer behavior among millions of Indians, Western-influenced programming has increased market demand for global products by making consumers more brand conscious. As a direct result of new television channels, many Indian consumers—previously unaware of brand names and used to buying a week's portion of bulk commodity product—now demand the branded products they see in television commercials.

India's location in Asia, although outside the Pacific Rim, makes it an attractive location for MNCs to base production and distribution. In addition, many MNCs are beginning to depend more heavily on India for global sourcing. Rhone-Poulenc Rorer has made India a regional sourcing center for pharmaceuticals, McDonnell Douglas plans to source components for two new aircraft models in India, and Airbus Industrie currently sources airplane parts.[4] India's potential to become a global supply base is most evident in the garment industry. India already competes with Hong Kong in supplying mass-produced garments that are later branded by clothing companies in other countries. With a greater number of global customers, Indian garment manufacturers will be driven to improve quality, standardize products, and fill international orders in a timely fashion: all factors which are shaping the global garment industry. The established distribution channels are via retailers, but exclusive outlets and direct marketing are imminent.

## Cost Globalization Drivers

Removal of import restrictions and targeted gradual reduction of import taxes to the level of ASEAN countries by the year 2000 will make India an attractive production site.[5] Local production can contribute to external markets. For example, exports fuel India's growing software industry. Global scale economies may be on the rise, however, as the base of personal computers in India continues to grow—from two million PCs to ten million by the year 2000.

While India's labor force of over three hundred million is one of the largest in the world, with the second-largest scientific manpower, the compensation package is relatively low. In 1994, an engineer earned U.S.$8,000 in Bombay, while his counterpart in Frankfurt was paid U.S.$52,000, U.S.$21,000 in Seoul, and U.S.$11,000 in Jakarta.[6] Similarly a skilled worker earned U.S.$6,000 in Bombay compared to U.S.$30,000 in Frankfurt, U.S.$13,000 in Seoul, and U.S.$9,000 in Jakarta. One analysis comparing the cost/productivity ratio for an Indian versus a Taiwanese worker demonstrates India's cost advantage: an Indian worker costs only 5% that of a Taiwanese worker, and is 85% as productive.[7] While the limited supply of educated business managers makes Indian professionals increasingly expensive to hire, the overabundant manual labor supply will continue to keep overall labor costs low.

It is estimated that India requires U.S.$100 billion in new investment to adequately develop its infrastructure by the year 2000.[8] Current infrastructure problems such as frequent power shortages, poor roads, and a weak phone system prevent the maximization of global cost drivers. The infrastructure sector is almost entirely state-controlled, although liberalization has already shown its effects on air, road, sea, mail, and telephones, and there are indications that this trend will continue. The national government has already indicated that it will encourage foreign investment, especially in infrastructure and technology-intensive industries. In addition, India benefits from a well-structured banking system, an English legal system, and over twenty-three stock markets with 7,000 listings.[9]

India is a base for developing technology. In the late-1980s Texas Instruments set up a software design subsidiary in Bangalore, India, in order to access the low-cost, but highly-skilled, technical workers available there. This subsidiary communicates with Texas Instruments' R&D center in the United States via satellite each day, thus operating very much as part of a global network. Bangalore has become the base of India's software industry and one of the world's largest software exporting centers. However, the supply of automotive grade steel, glass, plastic, and electronics of the required quality is still a problem in India. The R&D capabilities of the industry have to go a long way before becoming globally competitive. At the moment, the industry spends only about 3% of its turnover on R&D.

## Government Globalization Drivers

The government proves to be the most formidable limitation to India's inclusion in MNC strategies. The 1995 cancellation of the Enron power plant project in the state of Maharashtra and subsequent renegotiation on somewhat more favorable terms for the state provides evidence of the government's heavy-handed control over foreign direct investment. U.S.-based Enron eventually lowered costs and electricity rates partly to salvage the project, as it needs the Indian plant as a buyer for fuel from another gas processing plant in the Middle East.[10] Enron has, however, evinced keen interest in investing in a few new projects. During the 1970s, IBM, Coca-Cola, and Mobil suffered as India put limits on ownership by foreign companies. MNCs in low-technology fields continue to face hostility from some quarters such as India's Bharatiya Janata Party (BJP; favoring Hindu nationalism) and leftist parties. Threat of competition to government monopolies comes in the way of its permitting foreign investments. But the 1997–98 budget indicates further welcome changes for MNC investments.

The government cleared 390 overseas investment proposals in 1995–96 as against only 107 in 1992. There were a total of 524 joint ventures and 300 wholly owned subsidiaries of Indian companies operating abroad at the end of 1994.[11] Most of these operations are either extensions of domestic operations or largely independent entities in terms of managerial processes and control. In 1997, the government lowered corporate tax rates to an effective rate of 35%. Income tax rates have also been lowered significantly for the first time.

The maximum tariff rate has been lowered from 400% to 40%, with restrictions minimized on the import of most consumer goods.[12] But the government still guards many key industry sectors from outside competition. Although competition now exists in previous public sector monopolies such as airlines and power generation, government bureaucracy and red tape present formidable stumbling blocks, especially in the steel, petroleum, and coal industries. Other industries that continue to be controlled by the government are defense products, atomic energy, and railways.

The government fears that MNCs will source key competencies outside of India, and use India for less-significant links of the value chain. Therefore, the government favors industries that contribute to technology transfer in India such as electronics and computer software. The opposition party, the BJP, popularized the slogan "microchips, not potato chips" to express their preference for technology industries rather than consumer goods. Due to government partiality, technology-related investments will move forward more rapidly than other FDI projects. The government intends to improve over the next few years India's share in international trade, from a level of 0.72% in 1992.

Indian law severely restricts a company's freedom to shut down plants. Barriers to exit prevent unprofitable firms from closing operations and forces companies to stay in markets that cannot support existing volume. Furthermore, the law makes firing workers extremely difficult and expensive.

India does not now participate in the most important regional economic groupings, AFTA and APEC, that can help MNCs conduct crossborder activities. But the country is beginning to develop some cooperative arrangements. It already belongs to SAARC (South Asian Association for Regional Cooperation), which has seven members (India, Pakistan, Bangladesh, Nepal, Bhutan, Sri Lanka, and the Maldives) and is emerging as a trade block, although not a very strong one. India has also joined with South Africa, Australia, and Singapore to found the new Indian Ocean Rim Association.

Television as well as other forms of media are highly regulated. In particular, advertising directed toward children, students, and women, as well as advertising that makes any health claims is restricted.[13] The government has not made adequate provisions for protection of trademarks. The ambiguity surrounding trademark protection stalls arrival of MNCs in industries where trademarks are core to business such as entertainment, publishing, and media. For example, Disney Consumer Products waited to enter India until they felt copyright laws were adequately enforced by the Indian government.[14] Although India does not have patent legislation covering software, a patent is given if it is combined with hardware. It is, however, likely that new legislation in tune with the GATT agreement will be introduced in India in the near future.

MNCs also need to understand the consequences of India's federal system of government and consequent high degree of state autonomy, similar to the situation in the United States. Federalism results in large differences in policies and regulations among different Indian States. These governmental differences combine with ethnic, linguistic, cultural, educational, and economic differences, to greatly complicate life for foreign companies seeking to implement national strategies.

## Competitive Globalization Drivers

As long as the government continues to limit competition, MNCs' participation in India will be limited. Conversely, those industries that have the most domestic competitors tend to be the most competitive in global markets. Thus, the limitation of domestic competition impairs both Indian companies and MNCs. MNCs' entry will help accelerate the integration of India into the world economy.

To varying degrees, India's strategic importance can be supported by all of the following drivers:

- large source of revenues and profits
- significant market of global competitors
- source of industry innovation
- home market of global customers
- home market of global competitors.

The presence of MNCs in India provides evidence of India's global strategic importance. For example, close to three hundred foreign companies now compete in India's financial industry, which was closed to foreign activity prior to 1992.

## Overall Global Strategies for India

The MNCs that are present in India have been able to apply much of their global strategies, while also making some significant adaptations.

### *Market Participation Strategies*

The country is undergoing a consumer metamorphosis and there is growing demand for almost all products. The industries that are likely to achieve exceptional growth are computers and software, automobiles, electronics, food processing, and infrastructure. Participation in India is a high priority because it is viewed as a strategic market for MNCs' sales growth. A notable change in the structure of India's overall export market is that India now sells more to Europe, Japan, and the United States, as opposed to Russia, Eastern Europe, and Africa a few years ago. This is a reflection of the improving competitiveness of Indian manufacturers and their capability to compete in advanced countries.

The recent opening of the Indian economy is spurring interest on the part of many MNCs such as Coca-Cola, which has invested U.S.$70 million since reforms began in 1991. In addition, a few MNCs, such as Unilever, have long participated in India. Unilever's Indian subsidiary, Hindustan Lever Limited (HLL) is the largest MNC operating in India. Although currently HLL accounts for only 4.5% of Unilever's U.S.$40 billion global turnover, it is expected that this number will rise to 10% by 2000. This optimism is based on the company's current annual global growth rate of 4% compared to a 20% growth in India. With the rapid expansion of the middle-income segment and growing rural market, India is going to be an important market for Unilever.

Many global players, who initially employed a gradual approach to India, have realized that to adequately match competitors' commitment, they would need to bring in all of their brands. For example, P&G entered the Indian market with the acquisition of the Richardson-Vicks company worldwide in 1986, but soon realized that they would have to expand beyond the *Vicks* umbrella brand to compete with heavily entrenched consumer products competitors such as Unilever. Therefore, to achieve growth, P&G reversed its initial market participation strategy and introduced all of its major product lines in India. The company's heavy investment in market development confirms its new commitment to reach the vast Indian market.

Timing of entry into India's markets is a key success factor: the earlier the entry, the better. One segment of India's market, consumer durables, is currently growing at 15–20%, and those companies willing to endure the risks involved with early entry are in the most favorable position to earn a big pay-off. For example, Matsushita earned a uniquely advantageous position to grow in India by building brand equity through six joint ventures spread over several years since 1972, when they began manufacturing batteries in India. By the year 2000, the company intends to have operations expanded by 1300%, and Matsushita hopes to have a market share of 15–20% in each of the product categories it enters. The company's policy is to introduce into the Indian market almost every product available in the Matsushita basket worldwide.

Philips' market participation strategy is supported by a policy of launching a new product every month for over eighteen months from 1993–95. By pursuing the continual launch policy and offering more products and a wider range in most categories, Philips intends to achieve a bigger presence in the market. Evidence of the success of Philips' market participation strategy lies in increased market share in highly competitive segments such as the color TV market. Philips now has 13% of the market compared with 1% in 1991. In short, the message is that big players need to be present in all segments of the market to maintain position.

The vastness of India's market makes possible many new product introductions, despite the immaturity of the market. For example, because the pager and cellular phone industries show promise of big growth— there will likely be eight million pager users in India by the end of 1998— Motorola had, by 1996, already launched several models of pagers and cellular phones in India. While this strategy may appear risky, Motorola plans to gain advantage in the long term by establishing itself early in the growth stage of this market. Motorola has now expanded operations to cover various products that demonstrate growth potential such as mobile radios and semiconductors. For now, their India operations are insignificant, but it is expected that in five years they will contribute about 3–5% of the global revenues of Motorola.

The government's economic policy has restricted commercial business up until the past five years. Under the 'license raj,' foreign industry could invest only where the government dictated. Therefore, government alliances proved imperative for entry into key industries, such as the automobile market. Now, the artificially suppressed latent demand for automobiles has been released and there is a flood of interest in the latest models. One such example is Maruti Udyog, established in 1982, by a joint alliance between the government and Suzuki of Japan. Suzuki's Maruti venture now holds over a 70% market share in the domestic car market and Maruti Udyog is the largest car plant of Suzuki outside Japan, bigger than the Suzuki-GM project in Canada. Suzuki uses Maruti Udyog as a model production unit for its other Suzuki family members. Other foreign producers are also establishing joint venture production operations.[15]

## Product and Service Strategies

The fact that some products are highly successful globally does not mean that they are always successful in India. Because price sensitivity is high and quality consciousness is increasingly important, new products are most successful if a preexisting need develops among consumers. For example, General Foods' failure with the powdered drink mix *Tang* attests to the importance of proper positioning in the market. Because a cheap substitute, *Rasna*, already existed in the market and breakfast habits were different, consumers did not respond to *Tang*'s positioning as a powder-based natural soft drink. Kellogg also finds the going tough and hopes to change the breakfast habits of Indians gradually over several years. Automobile companies, however, generally do not have this experience. Indian consumers are reasonably familiar with several global auto brands and have interest in vehicles that are superior to what, historically, can be found in the local market.

It is imperative to employ the same rigorous evaluation of the marketing mix for entry into India's market as in the home countries where MNCs operate. Simply exporting global brands will not sufficiently motivate buyers if attention to local details is overlooked. P&G's experience with the introduction of globally accepted products in the Indian market indicates that not all products will pass the Indian consumer acceptance test. For example, while their *Whisper* sanitary pads gave Johnson and Johnson stiff competition, P&G's decision to take the premium market segment route (like most other products from advanced countries) to introduce *Ariel* detergent proved costly as they accumulated a loss of Rs 221 million (about U.S.$7 million) in 1992–93. P&G did not realize that most Indians use a laundry soap or detergent bar along with a detergent powder for washing clothes. Subsequently, they introduced an *Ariel* bar and cheaper variations of the powder. At the same time as the *Ariel* launch, P&G successfully introduced *Camay* soap in India. Because *Camay* is familiar to many Indians, especially in urban areas, thanks to gifts from visitors abroad, P&G did not have problems selling this product.

Because India follows British electrical standards and Indian houses and apartments are comparable to those in Europe in terms of size, many consumer electronics companies encounter few problems when introducing low-cost global products in India. Nonetheless, it is important to note that the quality of power supply, roads, air, and water available in India is inferior to those in advanced Western countries, making it necessary to examine the need for adaptation. Some washing machine manufacturers paid a heavy price before realizing this. Similarly, although automobiles are generally standardized across the globe, modifications are needed in India to accommodate the quality of roads, local competition, and regulations on permissible emission limits. General Motors is currently designing a car appropriate for Indian conditions.

Often the mix of global products offered in India requires regionalization. Differences in product selection arise for two reasons: lack of competition and a low level of infrastructure development. For example, although most Motorola products tend to be global and do not require major adaptation, major differences exist in the range of models available at any given time. Furthermore, since the Indian market is in its nascent stage, Motorola has not as yet resorted to detailed market segmentation and differentiation. Additionally, Motorola limits the number of product features on many products. Motorola also made adjustments in products to match India's supply communication infrastructure. For example, line voltage is different in India so voltage fluctuation is high and, hence, products must be able to bear this fluctuation. Because of behavioral differences (Indians tend to talk longer per call) and the resulting heavy load on telephones, there is a need for adaptation of the product to India's requirements. Additionally, products such as pagers are localized to contain messages in local languages.

## Activity Location Strategies

Most MNCs' initial attraction to India arises from observing India's huge growing market and considering stagnating demand at home and in most advanced markets. Other MNCs, many in historically international Indian industries such as leather, computer software, and automobile components consider India to have a unique combination of sourcing advantages. Suzuki exports *Maruti* and *Zen* cars from its joint venture with the Government of India. As already described, Texas Instruments sources software from India. MNC sourcing strategies cover essentially all value-chain activities from raw material sourcing to R&D centers. India is emerging also as a major R&D sourcing center. Companies such as Abbott Laboratories, Acer Computer, Akzo, Du Pont, Eli Lilly, FMC, General Electric, Haldar Topsoe, Hewlett Packard, Hughes, Lummus, Motorola, Nova Nordisk, Smith Kline Beecham, Telstra, and Unilever have R&D alliances with government-run laboratories under the Council for Scientific and Industrial Research or with private companies. Companies with local R&D can implement product adaptations more quickly than those companies exporting from other markets. With the opening of the South Asia regional office in New Delhi, India is gearing up to play a key role in the activities of Matsushita.

Motorola set up a corporate research center in Bangalore to develop software for all Motorola companies worldwide. Where Motorola finds sufficient market demand it commits complete manufacturing operations. For example, while semiconductors continue to be imported, pagers for the Indian market are manufactured locally. Furthermore, Motorola created an R&D center for pagers in Bangalore that will develop pagers capable of transmitting Hindi and Gujarati messages.

Manufacturing in India presents a lucrative alternative to the high, tariff-imposed, cost of importing. In extremely price-sensitive industries, cost control is a decisive lever to gain consumer acceptance. Local manufacture provides the additional benefit of enabling quick market response. Because Philips in India is being integrated with its parent company at a fast pace, the Dutch parent plans to source manufacturing of many globally distributed products in India such as precision tools, computer software, and lights.

## Marketing Strategies

India is home to eleven major languages, not including the national language, Hindi. The fact that many Indians speak English can create the false illusion that a single English-language marketing approach can be applied to a culture that is radically different from other English-speaking countries. The complexity of the demographics of the Indian market can be a limiting factor and need to be kept in mind.

Price must be adapted to the Indian market because the majority of customers in the middle-income group are generally price sensitive. Several MNCs, including Reebok, incurred huge losses before realizing this fact. Therefore, MNCs will have to be careful about their overhead expenses including those for marketing. In the case of Unilever, the company follows a strict policy of low overhead to maintain low prices in the Indian market. Additionally, Unilever follows a policy of offering products for various segments at affordable prices. Price is especially crucial if the brand name is unknown in the Indian market. Because brand name and distribution are critical for the successful marketing of products in India, P&G's alliance with the local brand of Godrej Soaps, though short lived, proved wise for two reasons. First, Godrej is a strong brand name well known to Indians. Second, Godrej owns a large retail chain from its takeover of another local Indian company, Transelektra.

India's infrastructure falls below many MNCs' expectations and is a difficult obstacle to the execution of a global marketing plan. The nation's transformation into a modern market economy occurred suddenly and the infrastructure may not be ready to support total access for consumers to all sophisticated products. In order to ensure functional distribution channels, Philips created several exclusive showrooms, especially to sell its expensive products. Philips based the showroom model on the success of similar approaches used by local companies such as Titan Watches and BPL consumer products.

Matsushita transcended India's infrastructure difficulties by investing heavily to build a viable distribution network. Also, in 1994, Matsushita established a national sales company, National Panasonic India Pvt. Ltd. The company assigned geographic areas to a network of sales and service dealers. Then, huge warehousing facilities were located on strategic nodes in the network to ensure a reliable inventory supply. Part of the strategy rests on treating dealers like entrepreneurs. To promote entrepreneurial behavior, Matsushita provides exceptional benefits to develop individual dealers including retail training, inventory management, and customer service programs. Indian dealers have responded very positively to the entrepreneurial management policy and Matsushita expects all their dealers to become exclusive *Panasonic* sellers that offer a wide range of products by the year 2000.

Many MNCs modify global advertising plans to meet local Indian tastes. For example, Motorola adapted advertisement themes by featuring traditionally dressed commodity traders using pagers to do business. Unilever modifies advertising content to respect the beliefs and sociocultural feelings of Indian customers. Advertising is further tailored by choosing media based on the best return on investment. For instance, the cost of a television and print advertisement are highly disproportionate in

India compared to advanced countries. Therefore companies have to carefully choose the medium to assess its impact. People generally believe that products advertised on television are likely to be good.

Widespread and fast communication, heightened levels of travel, and developing media make Indians increasingly aware of all products available in the world's markets. For this reason, MNCs must be sensitive to offer the best quality to the Indian market. Motorola is world renowned for its in-house, Six Sigma quality standard, and its Indian operations follow suit. Even though the company could probably survive in the Indian market with lower-quality norms, it does not want to compromise on the quality front at any cost.

## Competitive Move Strategies

Many competitors consider India an integral part of their global competitive strategy. For example, Microsoft introduced Windows 95 in India simultaneously with its launch elsewhere, and Bill Gates wants to see India a major center for its software development. Those competitors who want to exploit the huge market potential of the country will have to bring their latest technologies and products into India.

Global competitors in India prefer to associate themselves with local companies to build business, in some cases, through brand acquisition or facility buy out. Local acquisitions allow companies to reduce the number of competing brands and to compete against other heavy hitters in the fight for market share. An aggressive acquisition strategy, as shown by Unilever's history in India leads to energetic growth. India's liberalization policy enabled Unilever to execute an assertive growth strategy by acquiring a series of medium to large firms in the recent past. The list includes the takeover of Tata Oil Mills (TOMCO) for soaps and detergents, Kissan for processed foods, Kothari General Foods for coffee, and Dollaps, Quality, and Milkfood for ice cream. Unilever's activities follow a clear strategy of the acquisition of established brands in all these cases. On a global scale, Unilever has formed joint alliances to fight head-on with other MNCs, namely P&G. HLL's exclusive alliance with U.S.-based Kimberly-Clark in India raises the stakes in competition. Established brand equity and presence in many product categories makes it easier for MNCs with a historical presence in India to erect barriers to entry.

## Overall Organization and Management Approaches for India

Partnership is the most common and favorable model for organizational structure in India, from both a business and regulatory outlook. By partnering, many MNCs overcome restrictions placed on foreign companies that limit ownership. Those MNCs that formed joint alliances with the best Indian companies now enjoy considerable advantage over those that waited. GE partnered with Godrej in appliances and kept its partner's name for refrigerators, rather than using GE's name, due to consumer familiarity with the existing brand name. The Godrej name has 40% of the market. Only in the last few years have MNCs entered the Indian market as wholly owned subsidiaries, unassisted by local partnerships.

The government's active role in key sectors, though significant, is gradually shrinking. Still, MNCs usually do not prefer government partnerships, as these may lead to conflicts of interest. The Maruti-Suzuki alliance, 50% owned by Suzuki and about 48% owned by the Government, clearly demonstrates this reality. The alliance jointly holds 70% of India's domestic car market. The government alliance poses some degree of conflict in terms of capacity expansion and globalization goals. For example, the government's globalization strategy may want Maruti to export its different models, including to countries where Suzuki may have its own operation, or at least to neighboring countries. A cash-strapped government partner may not wish to approve expansion plans that reduce its equity stake.

Indians overseas total ten million and their aggregate annual income approximately equals the GDP of all of India, around U.S.$300 billion. Overseas Indians (often referred to as NRIs, or Nonresident Indians) provide a powerful source of contacts, business acumen, and insight. Aligning with Indians living abroad often facilitates MNCs' investment in India as the government encourages foreign investment from Indians.

Indian management can trace its roots to an early guild system that laid down strict rules and regulations for conducting business in ancient India. Dharma,[16] or moral norms and societal values, was key to the management process. To this day, Indian management stresses the importance of leadership, noble conduct, and practical wisdom extolled by religious texts such as the *Bhagavat Gita*. With British influence, management in India emerged as a more defined set of formal processes and scientific approaches. Today, Indian management is characterized by loyalty to the chief executive, a centralization of power, and decentralization of activities. Hierarchy is key to management coordination.

Western-style management is gaining in popularity as demonstrated by the huge excitement over management consultants and gurus coming to India on the lecture circuit and demand for hiring management consultants. As of 1997, McKinsey had fifty consultants in India, while Andersen Consulting, Coopers and Lybrand, and A. T. Kearney all actively pursue Indian clients.[17] Many firms adopt a hybrid approach that combines both traditional Indian management style with an increasingly popular Western approach. For example, while Motorola applies the same type of performance appraisal systems across their global operations, remuneration follows local standards. Similarly, Motorola localizes titles for some positions in India, while internally, the company has a separate set of titles comparable across countries.

The sudden growth in operations of existing firms and the entry of new ones has created a shortage in the supply of professional managers in the country. Salary levels have shot up, though they are still far lower in international terms. Job hopping is becoming common. Regardless of staffing policy, most MNCs in India emphasize the importance of communication throughout their worldwide networks of subsidiaries. For example, P&G installed an information system accessible to all its executives throughout the world and Unilever set up a computer e-mail network to allow managers to access information from colleagues anywhere in the world. Unilever is also linking its thirty-two production units across India through satellite links and a network of 131 dish antennae. This will enable Unilever to track every item as it leaves each factory and passes through the forty-four clearing and forwarding agents to its 350 wholesalers and 600,000 retailers.

Many MNCs staff their offices with Indian managers. Unilever India is managed almost entirely by Indians. As much as possible, Motorola follows a local hire policy. To ensure crossfertilization and exposure of local managers to technological development, senior managers are often transferred to India from developing countries and back. The goal is to inculcate the Indian subsidiary with the Motorola culture.

Indian civilization first emerged around 3,000 B.C. and many modern social characteristics can be traced back to ancient traditions. The caste system, which binds individuals to a clearly defined social group, regional identity expressed through language and territory, and solidarity of family and kinship groups, continues to exert major influence on Indian culture. Indians are accustomed to lifelong employment and the permanence of membership in caste, family, and corporate groups. This sense of fatalism often works to decrease productivity and stagnate change. Teamwork proves to be very effective as collective wisdom is highly valued in Indian culture. Education in India holds great importance; literacy in certain cities and states is as high as 100% and India has the second-largest population of newspaper readers in the world. Inequality in education, however, lowers India's overall literacy rate to 48% and sends a clear message of the side effects of a rigid caste system that continues to label about 25% of the population as untouchable.[18] The election, in 1997, of India's first "untouchable" as the nation's President, symbolizes the effort to change.

## Conclusions

Transcending a previously highly controlled regime, the Indian economy has registered high growth rates in recent years. Opportunities and prospects for MNCs depend largely on the degree of government intervention affecting each industry. Controls are being gradually removed and tariff rates are expected to be on a par with ASEAN countries by the year 2000. This is especially so in technologically intensive areas. Untapped huge market potential and favorable costs of operation such as abundant supply of cheap skilled labour and scale economies are the key attractions for MNCs. Besides, commonalities with the West in terms of legal system and technical standards make the country attractive for investment.

MNC success in India largely depends on the ability to manufacture and market products and services at affordable prices. MNCs should try to understand the pulse of the market before formulating their strategies. They should be prepared to adapt various components of their strategy to local conditions. It is useful to remember that India is not a uniform market for all products. While automobiles and consumer durables may work with the same product-market strategies for the country, the same may not hold for nondurables such as breakfast cereals. In any case, product features, including technical specifications, may have to be adapted for the climatic and infrastructure conditions of the country.

MNCs that are new to the country tend to take the joint venture route when entering India primarily to reduce risks of operating on an unknown terrain. After the breakup of several recent partnerships, many potential partners are now skeptical, however, about MNCs' genuine interest in joint ventures. There is an impression that MNCs want to use them to gain entry and throw them out later. Yet another route is to employ Indian managers, now common in plenty of key positions in MNC subsidiaries.

The acceptance of the concept and process of liberalization by opposition parties and trade unions indicate that India will not go back on economic liberalization. The process may be slow but it is steady. Although the Indian government has historically restricted investment in order to protect industries vital to India's well being, the lure of technology should cause it to lower previously erected barriers. This is happening in a variety of industries, including those in core sectors. Computerization of operations (as in banks) and the spurt in growth of the information technology industry are interrelated. Efficiency, core competence, competition, and total quality are in common parlance. In this environment, MNCs may enter India to take advantage of the growing market and low cost advantages. Although foreign investment is welcome, permission is not automatic as the government wants to ensure that resources are properly utilized. One bleak area is infrastructure, which is already overstretched. It will be a while before new infrastructure investment yields results. In short, India offers attractions to MNCs that are ready to understand the environment before formulating their strategies. They should not, however, be carried away by their experiences in other countries and be overconfident about their capabilities. It would be advisable for MNCs to make an entry now and reap the benefits as they go along.

## NOTES

1. Centre for Monitoring Indian Economy, various volumes, 1996.
2. "Foreign Foray," *Far Eastern Economic Review,* July 10, 1997, 64–67.
3. "A Survey of India," *The Economist,* 1996, 4.
4. Economist Intelligence Unit Country Report, Fourth Quarter 1995.
5. "A Survey of India," *The Economist,* February 12, 1997.
6. *India Today,* November 15, 1995, quoting various World Bank Reports.
7. *The Economist,* January 21, 1995, 39.
8. *International Business,* January 1995.
9. *The McKinsey Quarterly* no. 2, 1995.

10. *Business Week,* January 22, 1996.

11. *Business World,* May 3–16, 1995.

12. *The Economic Times,* March 1, 1997.

13. Leo Burnett Advertising.

14. Informal discussion with manager of international marketing at Disney Consumer Products.

15. "A Survey of India," *The Economist,* February 12, 1997.

16. S.K. Chakraborty. *Management Values: Towards Cultural Congruence.* (New Delhi: Oxford University Press, 1991).

17. "A Survey of India," 8.

18. Ibid., 23.

# CHAPTER 13

# Vietnam—Capitalism Now

*George S. Yip[1]*

AFTER SUFFERING THE twin ravages of war and communist business planning, the economy of Vietnam is finally showing signs of development and hope. The stifling blanket of state control has been lifted enough to allow the growth of new opportunities in every sector of the nation. The nation has received the endorsement of membership in ASEAN. Foreign investor sentiment has been riding high, and the government is active in promoting international business projects. However, this blanket has been removed only to be replaced by the entangling red tape of an omnipresent bureaucracy. Initial investor enthusiasm in Vietnam has been replaced by guarded optimism. Much like its neighbor to the north, China, Vietnam offers both great frustrations and great rewards for those attempting to do business during this time of transition. MNCs have only just begun to enter or return to Vietnam. So, unlike the more extensive analysis provided for the other countries in this book, we can give in this chapter only a brief analysis of possible strategies for multinational company (MNCs).[2]

## Background

In 1986, ten years after the end of the Vietnam War, and after ten years of communist business planning and an American embargo, the nation was weathering a severe economic crisis. People were going hungry and Vietnam had to import 1.5 million tons of rice just to survive. Partially out of desperation, and partially out of the changing nature of world communism, Vietnam embarked that year on a path of economic reforms known as *doi moi* (renovation). After a decade of *doi moi,* Vietnam has become the third largest rice exporter in the world, and by 1995, had the greatest GDP growth rate of all ASEAN nations at 9.5%. Nevertheless, Vietnam's nominal GNP of U.S.$19 billion in 1996 is only a third that of New Zealand's, and the per capita GNP for its eighty million people is only U.S.$250 a year, or two-thirds that of India.

Liberalization of foreign investment laws in 1987 brought in swarms of Taiwanese, Japanese, Korean, and French investors. In late 1992, the U.S.

government allowed American firms to set up representative offices in Vietnam. The United States lifted its trade embargo on Vietnam in February, 1994, and normalized relations with Vietnam in July 1995, sparking general business euphoria for the investment prospects in this relatively untapped country. From 1987–95, over nine hundred foreign investment projects with a value in excess of US $17 billion were granted operating licenses in Vietnam, with 50% of that total coming in 1994–95.[3] The optimistic growth figures for Vietnam are counterbalanced by several points. The nation still lacks a modern infrastructure (to put it kindly), and the logistics of doing business can become a nightmare. The legal framework is a nebulous developing creature that can take a bite out of operations when least expected. Accounting and tax systems are similarly evolving, and any financial statistics must be taken with a grain or two of salt. Also, the state economic planning bureaucracy is by no means a thing of the past. Delays, corruption, confusion, and contradictions characterize much of the MNCs' dealings with the government. And while the government is taking steps to improve the honesty, consistency, and transparency of state business activities, it is by no means relinquishing control of the economic policies of the nation. As a representative of the Ministry of Planning and Investment put it: "We are becoming a market system, yes, but a market system under state control."

GDP Growth from 1991–94 averaged nearly 8% yearly, and about 9.5% for 1996. The Vietnamese government had a plan to double GDP from 1990–2000, but has revised the goal to say they now hope to increase GDP 2.5 times by 2000.[4] Yearly inflation, which had averaged 57% from 1989–91, dropped to 5.2% by 1993, but had risen to 12.2% by October 1995, and was predicted to be as high as 19% for 1996.

Vietnam's largest domestic companies are still mostly divisions of state monopolies, the largest of which is Petro Vietnam. An exception is the Hachiba conglomerate, which is a power in textiles, and has diversified to execute an exclusive bottling agreement with Coca-Cola and a joint venture with Carlsberg.

Foreign companies have begun to return to Vietnam. As of 1997, the largest international firms in Vietnam include the Daewoo conglomerate from Korea; Antara Koh Development company from Singapore; Mitsui, Honda, Marubeni, and Suzuki from Japan; and British Petroleum, Occidental Chemical, GEC/Alsthom from Europe. U.S. firms with planned or established presence include the big three automakers (General Motors, Ford, and Chrysler), Coca-Cola, which has two large bottling plants in operation; United Technologies with an aggressive expansion program, Citibank with two offices and participation in a variety of projects, and the Big Six accounting firms, all of which are consulting with the Vietnamese government on financial services. Added to these are a variety of oil exploration firms, freight forwarders, and infrastructure companies (construction, electric, and telecommunications). Over U.S.$10 billion in foreign direct investment was made from 1987 to 1995, with Asian countries dominating (Table 13.1).

**Table 13.1**
**Foreign Direct Investment in Vietnam by Country**[a]

| Country | # of Projects | Total Capital U.S.$ billions |
|---------|---------------|------------------------------|
| Taiwan | 231 | 3.29 |
| Hong Kong | 181 | 2.13 |
| Japan | 175 | 1.92 |
| Singapore | 113 | 1.60 |
| South Korea | 130 | 1.44 |
| United States | 48 | 1.03 |

*Source:* State Committee for Cooperation and Investment, reported in *Vietnam Economic Times*, December 1995.
[a]Since 1987 and as of November 1995. List is for projects that are actually operating.

# Overall Industry Globalization Drivers for Vietnam

Most of Vietnam's current globalization drivers, other than labor costs, are unfavorable. But most should steadily improve with further liberalization and economic development.

## Market Globalization Drivers

Vietnam's market globalization drivers are low but improving. At least in Hanoi and Ho Chi Minh City, a newly affluent urban worker has a choice between whole streets full of shops offering the latest stereo, TV, and VCR equipment. The official statistic of average annual income belies the ability of the urban worker to afford similar consumer goods as those offered anywhere in the world. Thanks to the high volume of smuggled goods entering the country, American brands have been quite popular for years before the lifting of the embargo. While Ho Chi Minh City (formerly Saigon) in the south is characterized as more flamboyant and more Western in its consumer purchasing habits, trends that begin in Ho Chi Minh City usually filter north to the more staid Hanoi in a period of months.

Global and regional customers are emerging. Vietnam's accession in 1995 to membership in ASEAN gives it a more active role in participating in this regional market of 420 million people. Vietnam is quickly becoming an active member of the ASEAN development sphere. Vietnam also benefits not only from its close investment ties to Asian business communities, particularly overseas Chinese, but from remittances by overseas Vietnamese workers and emigrated family members. This web of investments and flow of goods is expected to integrate Vietnam more closely with its neighbors, at least in a business sense.

Vietnam is becoming an Asian source for many raw materials and commodity goods, but an archaic infrastructure makes it unreliable. Vietnam's coffee production, for example, boasts the world's highest yields, and a very popular taste among worldwide customers. Unfortunately, Vietnamese coffee producers have such a bad reputation for late delivery, uneven quality, and payment problems, that the industry's output remains stagnant.[5]

Global marketing is not easily transferred to Vietnam. Like China, Vietnam has a tonal language that poses problems in marketing communications for firms. Studying English is becoming popular though, as are American movies and music. Satellite TV has been making inroads into hotels, bars, and wealthy homes, giving MNCs a beachhead in their marketing efforts. According to Bakerville Communications, TV penetration in Vietnam's fourteen million households has increased to 50%, and, in addition, 89% of urban homes own TVs, and 43% own VCRs.[6] Billboards for foreign products cover open spaces in the cities, and MNC sponsorship of sporting and other events keeps their marketing messages prominent. The Vietnamese government, however, has recently made ominous rumblings regarding regulation of advertising, and in January 1996, closed down a popular and advertisement-filled foreign-published magazine and confiscated all copies for vague reasons. Many other advertising restrictions have been applied. Furthermore, foreign companies cannot get advance approvals of advertising before incurring production expenses, and may meet rejection from both the authorities and the media. Lastly, Vietnam does not set trends in marketing and consumption but follows them, especially from its ASEAN neighbors.

## Cost Globalization Drivers

Vietnam's most favorable cost globalization driver is its large, low-cost labor force. Other drivers are much less favorable. Vietnam offers only limited potential for global and regional scale economies—high barriers and tariffs for imports make doing so difficult. At the present time, the purpose of local MNC production is to gain local market share. The size of scheduled auto plants, however, shows that given even optimistic market growth projections, they will have massive excess capacity, presumably fueling exports. Korean companies, in particular, hope to use manufacturing bases in northern Vietnam to eventually produce goods for the wealthy southern provinces of China, reaching a total market of three hundred million people. But not until this market becomes reachable both politically and logistically will MNCs be able to take advantage of regional scale economies.

The country also offers limited scope for sourcing efficiencies. Vietnam has high royalty rates for the export of raw materials, and a weak local infrastructure with which to transport sourced goods. Omnipresent government involvement requires any sourcing project to produce tangible benefits for Vietnam, thereby limiting the scope of its efficiency.

The country has decent outbound logistics but very poor logistics internally. The long, narrow shape of the country, with its two major cities at opposite ends (and almost one thousand miles apart by road), make travel distances disproportionately long and expensive. The fastest train takes over two days to get from Ho Chi Minh City to Hanoi. The Vietnamese government has stated that 45% of its national highway network is in "poor to very poor" condition, with about 65% of other networks in "poor to bad" condition. Also, 87% of the road system is dirt, including one-third of the top-grade national roadways. And despite the long coastline of the nation, because of inadequate port facilities, shipping moves only 2% of internal freight traffic.[7] Despite the failings of the national transport infrastructure, usage is increasing dramatically. Trucks are banned from the cities during business hours due to overwhelming congestion. The number of four-wheeled vehicles increased 500% from 1989–94, and traffic congestion has increased proportionately. The number of traffic accidents has also increased at a rate of 22% per year,[8] possibly as a result of the common feeling that traffic laws are merely suggestions and not hard rules. Even with its inefficiencies, transport costs are rising dramatically. The cost of transporting a container from the main port in Saigon to nearby factories increased 300% between 1994–95. In Haiphong Port, the closest deep-sea access to Hanoi, a bureaucracy-created backlog of several hundred containers has stifled the flow of goods to nascent entrepreneurs.

Vietnam does have very cheap labor, with a $35 minimum monthly wage, and an average rate for industrial workers of $55 per month in state enterprises, and $47 per month in foreign-invested companies. Overall monthly wages are estimated at $60 a month, excluding benefits.[9] This sourcing benefit is outweighed by logistical problems of transporting products within, and outside of the country.

While in many instances MNCs can find favorable terms in negotiating rural land leases, land use fees in Hanoi and Saigon are beginning to make costs more closely resemble those of Manhattan, not a developing country.[10]

Lastly, Vietnam cannot play a technological role for MNCs. Vietnam is trying very hard to get technology transferred on joint venture deals, but is far behind even its ASEAN neighbors in terms of technological resources. It is playing a catch-up game in terms of technology, with woefully out-of-date scientific equipment in its universities, outdated factories, and a technically lacking infrastructure. Vietnam is aggressively pursuing technology transfer deals and World Bank-funded infrastructure projects. While Vietnam could be considered a leader in terms of yields on agricultural crops, this is often from the benefit of overuse of fertilizers, which is beginning to cause significant environmental damage.

## Government Globalization Drivers

Vietnam has the least-favorable government globalization drivers of the countries and economies in this book. Vietnam has a highly regulated import/export trade market, with a variety of constantly changing tariffs, quotas, and outright banned goods. Vietnam has committed, on paper at least, to abide by ASEAN bylaws that state it must reduce (almost) all tariffs to 5% by 2006. In the mean time, the maximum tariff on imported goods has been reduced from 200% to a still extreme 60%.

Vietnam is experimenting with the special Export Processing Zone (EPZ) concept, which would allow foreign firms exemptions on import/export duties, and special tax incentives. But as with most projects in Vietnam, there are still a few bugs in the system, and the EPZ plan still has not come to reach its potential as of yet.

Given the constantly changing nature of the market, it is possible for MNCs who wield enough political clout to either get special exemptions from specific trade policies, or to actually convince the government to change these policies. As of 1996, the government was considering changing its policies on the import and production of small motorcycles at the behest of both local importers (MNCs such as Honda) and end users complaining of price gouging.

Vietnam has very stringent rules on foreign direct investment. But investment was still up by 30% between 1994–95. Per capita foreign investment in Vietnam in 1994 was twice that of China. Vietnam's foreign investment law, for example, requires a two-thirds interest in the paid-up capital of a joint venture company to gain even a nominal majority of the board of directors of the company. And even with such a majority, many decisions require unanimous board consent, somewhat complicating the joint venture concept. Capital contributed is subject to valuation by the minority partner and the Ministry of Planning and Investment, making things even more subject to local whim.[11]

Vietnam's government is sensitive about foreign activity in many sectors, so government political agendas get in the way of many projects. For example, Total, the French oil giant, recently pulled out of a multibillion dollar refining project due to conflict with government planners over siting of the refinery. The Vietnamese government wanted to site the refinery at Dung Quat Bay, located near the impoverished Da Nang central region of the country, which has not recovered from the ravages of the war. Total wanted the refinery in the industrial Vung Tau area, located close to Ho Chi Minh city, as well as to producing oil fields. It found the costs of locating the refinery at Dung Quat to be infeasible, and given that the government was completely unyielding on the location issue, Total pulled out.

But because of Vietnam's current popularity in the world of international investments, replacements for Total should not be hard to find. Two South Korean firms and an Iranian interest, among others, were reported in 1996 to be submitting proposals to design refineries wherever the Vietnamese government wants them.

The Vietnamese government is eager for MNCs to transfer technology. For example, the government is pushing its new Build-Operate-Transfer (BOT) framework for foreign investment. Under this framework, the foreign investor builds an infrastructure property, manufacturing center, or some other major creation, operates it for a given period of time, and finally is obliged to transfer ownership to the Vietnamese party. Obviously, foreign firms are not enthusiastic about giving away their investment in Vietnam, and the government is constantly coming up with new provisions to make this framework either more attractive, or more required.

Vietnam is working hard to institute what it feels is an appropriate system of taxation. It is consulting with most of the leading Western auditing firms concerning system development and accounting standards. All of the U.S. big six accounting firms have been accepted to open operations, and the door has been shut at the present time to any new entrants. As of the end of 1995, there were only eighty-four certified Vietnamese accountants, which is a fitting statistic to show the development of this sector.

In July 1995, Vietnam became the seventh member of ASEAN. The group recognizes Vietnam's slow start in the development race, and has given it an extra ten years to abide by the group's tariff reduction plan. Vietnam is also a member of the Mekong River Commission, a group coordinating the development in and around the Mekong River's route through the member nations of Cambodia, Laos, and Thailand. China and Myanmar have been asked to join the Mekong group, but do not want to abide by some of the cooperative agreements. Vietnam's participation in these groups shows an increased willingness to work with its neighbors in a coordinated business sense.

The Spratly Island issue has become less of a sticking point, as China agreed in 1996 to abide by impending negotiations, and there have been no incidents since the Chinese were discovered at the aptly named Mischief Reef in 1995.

Technical standards are being established rapidly, creating a race between MNCs in attempts to be the first to institute a technical standard in a variety of areas. Noninfrastructure companies find themselves at a disadvantage when trying to set up their operations in this environment. For the telecommunications market for example, the U.S. Foreign Commercial Service noted that although there is "a continuing market for products used in extending the national system to rural areas, a swiftly growing market for end-user telecommunications equipment" and other goods, "there are no signs of allowing competition in providing services, the procurement system is opaque, and U.S. equipment suppliers must be prepared to work within Vietnam's apparently wholesale adoption of ITU standards."[12]

The government recognizes it has a major problem with a lack of laws governing bankruptcy and bad credit as an increasingly large number of newly created firms and joint ventures go bad. The tax system is still under development, with conflicting and evolving rules confusing foreign and local firms alike. The sketchy rules governing foreign investment and operations has created an environment where corruption and bribery are endemic. Vietnam provides very poor protection of trademarks and intellectual property. Visitors to any major Vietnamese city can find cheap pirated book, music, and video items from around the world openly sold in stores and on the streets. Many of the items are Chinese made, and get smuggled into Vietnam by land and sea. Even confidential business plans and proposals have found their way, in photocopied form, to these street vendors. Bugged fax and phone lines create an atmosphere with a serious lack of security and integrity for intellectual property rights. MNCs have found that their greatest competition is often from their own goods smuggled (duty free) across the Chinese or Cambodian borders. The government line is that they recognize the problem and are working on it, but it does not seem to be their greatest priority at the moment.

A confusing legal framework leads to many frustrations for MNCs in Vietnam. Advertising and access to media are issues that are currently under debate, and the decisions here could serve to restrict a variety of marketing channels for the MNCs.

Lastly, foreign MNCs face in Vietnam many government-owned competitors and customers. To say the government is active in business would be an understatement. In 1994, government bureaus and businesses accounted for over 40% of GDP, growing from 33% in 1988. The twenty-two thousand companies registered as sole proprietorships, limited liability, and joint stock companies accounted for only 18% of the assets of registered companies, leaving state companies with 82% of registered assets.[13] This is, of course, discounting the tremendous amount of understated or unreported private activities in Vietnam. High tax rates and government interference, coupled with ineffective checking mechanisms, make for an overly modest private sector when it comes to financial reporting. The unreported smuggling of trade goods over Vietnam's land borders, has been conservatively estimated at over $1.5 billion a year, or one-fifth of all imports.[14] Employment in state firms fell from 4.1 million to 2.9 million between 1986–93, and the sector's share of total employment fell from 14.6% to 8.9% in the same period.[15] This shift in labor represents a hope for more private sector output in the future, but with the state still controlling the vast majority of assets, this transition may be quite slow.

## Competitive Globalization Drivers

Vietnam currently has limited global strategic importance, although it has eventual potential as a low-cost source of labor, and as a concentrated homogenous customer base in the north and the south. But returns will come only in the long term, and must wait for improved infrastructure, laws, and financial frameworks. As a stand-alone market, Vietnam offers potentially attractive returns only on the long-term horizon. It is doubtful whether Vietnam, in and of itself, will be a significant market of any global competitor (aside from Honda motorscooters, which virtually everyone in the country owns), but it does represent a potentially good secondary market and production facility for Southeast Asian expansion.

Global rivals are often present. Vietnam is becoming a prestigious nation as MNCs hustle to be the first in their industry to tackle this latest developing nation challenge. But no MNC has yet been able to use their operations in Vietnam as a springboard for global expansion.

## Summary of Globalization Drivers

Vietnam could eventually become a large source of revenues or profits. Vietnam has a large population (eighty million) for a smaller country. Aside from the north/south disparity, its consumers are largely homogenous, and offer the potential of rapidly increasing disposable income in the future. Present political and logistical problems make import, production, and distribution of goods difficult, but in the long-term, these problems may be solved.

## Overall Global Strategies for Vietnam

Many MNCs seek market participation in Vietnam as a high priority, believing they will gain a first-mover advantage by moving quickly in Vietnam. Any look in the streets will demonstrate Honda's complete dominance of the lucrative motorbike market. Add to this the prestige value of conquering a newly opened country, as well as its proximity to the Chinese market, and MNCs become very bullish about participation in Vietnam. Recently, however, this optimism is beginning to be tempered by reports of the troubles firms face in actually reaping any rewards from their participation. One extreme example had Chrysler representatives going to look at the site for their proposed U.S.$200 million factory and getting accosted by an ax-wielding local farmer who was evidently not happy with the development plans. Three years and five consulting firms later Chrysler received its license to build, but did not expect to break ground before another year of permit wrangling.[16] With such stories becoming more public, and the media's love of hyping any new perceived trend, Vietnam may yet be touted as the model of the hopeless international venture. The reality, of course, is that Vietnam is somewhere between these two extremes of a sure-fire opportunity and hopeless quagmire, and it is up to the management skills of an organization (coupled with a little luck) to achieve hoped-for results.

MNCs can market both global and local products. Foreign products have a definite prestige value in Vietnam, both for industrial and consumer goods. Foreign whisky (to note one example), like elsewhere in Asia, has become the drink of choice for newly rich local businessmen and government officials. Local brands though, especially in foodstuffs, are gaining popularity as they extend their scope of operations across the country. However, the questionably named *Nitrogen Fertilizer* brand of local sparkling wine may need some marketing input before exports are considered.

In terms of value-chain strategies, given present tight laws governing imports and exports, short-term returns will be seen only in the local production and distribution of goods. The EPZ concept will possibly change this, but it is still in the development phase.

In marketing, MNCs need to use a mixture of global and local approaches. Foreign products are featured in most billboard and newspaper ads, but local companies are beginning to learn about marketing. Advertising is a combination of English (targeted at the increasing number of expatriates and tourists) and Vietnamese. Many ads feature only brand trademarks while research is being conducted to determine the most effective niche-targeting methods. The earliest and most visible foreign advertisers have been for spirits, beer, soft drinks, and cigarettes.

## Overall Organization and Management Approaches for Vietnam

To ensure quicker entry, many foreign firms are teaming with local partners to do business in Vietnam. Naturally, this process is creating or aiding potential competitors, particularly in the BOT (build-operate-transfer) framework. As previously mentioned, a changing legal framework makes such agreements very complicated and open for interpretation from a somewhat capricious government. Unquestionably the most important aspect for MNC development in Vietnam is a close tie to bureaucrats in appropriate government ministries. Unfortunately, it is often a mystery, even to the Vietnamese, about which bureau truly holds the power in a particular deal, and which people are pulling the strings behind it. Much has been made about the inability of Western managers to break into this network of government bureaucracies, with one Japanese general manager stating that it is "impossible for Americans to comprehend the complex relations needed to succeed here. It is even hard for the Japanese who are used to such a situation."

The Ministry of Planning and Investment (MPI) now holds official power for the evaluation and granting of investment licenses. This power seems straight forward, but MPI is the recent creation (in October 1995) of a merging of the old State Committee for Cooperation and Investments (SCCI) and the State Planning Commission. How many people will remain from these old ministries, and in what context, is still not known. Even if the key players at MPI were known, the MPI still must gain consensus with the Ministry of Finance and other "appropriate ministries" to see if any proposed foreign investment is in conformity with the government's "master plan" for economic development. That this "master plan" is still under construction adds just one more challenge to navigating the high seas of government relations in Vietnam.

To have a "government partner" means something entirely different for some businesses than it does for others. The 1995–96 revelations in Korea of the *chaebols'* massive and sustained payoffs of their own government officials points to one method of building and sustaining a network of government partners. Some say that it is no coincidence that it is these same *chaebols* who now enjoy the best relations with Vietnamese government officials, and are getting their projects approved at an astonishing rate. While the Vietnamese government makes a lot of noise about curtailing corruption, and local newspapers publish regular stories of crooked officials being punished, the fact remains that corruption is endemic in Vietnam, and MNCs must develop a strategy to cope with it.

Vietnam has a huge overseas Chinese business community which is fueling growth, especially in the south. Chinese families in Vietnam are "digging up the gold from the backyard" to begin investing in local business. The over two million Vietnamese contract workers, along with relatives abroad and the overseas Chinese, are sending remittances to Vietnam at a rate estimated over $500 million a year.[17] A foreign investor would be wise to link with this informal investment network in order to launch or expand operations in Vietnam.

Increasingly, those Vietnamese who fled the country after the war are returning as prosperous businesspeople from abroad. American-born or raised Vietnamese are finding themselves in demand from companies attempting to crack the market. In Vietnam, however, these prosperous overseas Vietnamese sometimes find themselves facing locals resentful of their perceived swaggering Western attitude, not to mention suspicions of links to the old southern regime. But as business ties increase, and as a transparent profit motive becomes more acceptable, people from any background or nation are being welcomed to at least attempt to do some business.

The Asian model of consensus management holds in government bureaucracies, and the Chinese model of the family network is also applicable in business. With former or present military figures running many of the ministries and state corporations, a certain amount of autocratic rule is no surprise. The ongoing transformation to a market economy has put many of the old state and military management processes in total flux. Managers are confronted with the opportunity of pursuing free market objectives while still constrained by state controls. The rampant corruption is a result of this conflict: the line between regulation and opportunity has been blurred in both government and business. Basically, everyone wants a piece of the pie and, with the rules still under construction, many use any means necessary to achieve it.

Vietnam has a serious lack of trained middle managers, as everyone in charge has been following communist business planning for the past thirty years. Prewar managers and newly graduating business students are beginning to grab opportunities with firms, but they have either been out of the loop for too long, or have never been in it to make an immediate impact. MNCs also have difficulties in training their Vietnamese hires abroad due to complicated exit visa procedures. The general population is quite literate (88%), and well educated, but still lacks a background in market economy fundamentals. Schools are undergoing a rapid makeover to teach students business basics, while current communist managers are eagerly employing Western consulting companies to lay the groundwork for the country and themselves to think in terms of a market economy.

Any view of a street in any city of the country will show the rampant entrepreneurial attitude of the nation. Every streetfront house is used as some kind of business, from bicycle repair to sweet shops. People with no more capital than a chair, scissors, and a mirror open for business as barbers on random sidewalk strips. The people have whole-heartedly embraced the transition to a market economy and are ready for capitalism now.

Despite having a thousand-year history of foreign military interference, the Vietnamese seem to hold no grudges when business is concerned—"the past is for history books" is a commonly spoken refrain. Naturally, when businesses progress beyond the entrepreneurial level, the government steps in with its regulations and political agendas. But for the time being, the culture of Vietnam is very business friendly. It is just a matter of using this attitude to circumvent the many logistical and political problems of the nation.

## Conclusions

Vietnam offers both many challenges and many potential rewards for an MNC seeking to expand its global strategy to Southeast Asia. There is no question Vietnam is a developing nation, and will be so for quite some time. Even at its present high GNP growth rate of 9.5%, it will take Vietnam almost twenty years to reach the GDP level of Thailand, whose annual growth in GDP is currently greater than Vietnam's total output. Managers have to plan for long-term investment, and be patient waiting for results both in Vietnam, and also for the contribution these operations will make to their global networks.

The question remains as to whether a company will want to brave the nebulous legal, financial, and political system of the present for the reward of solid status in a more stable future economic environment. Certainly those companies with interests in infrastructure projects or other issues specifically addressing the needs of a developing nation will benefit from the current situation. But for the global consumer product company, the risks remain great.

Companies can benefit from the entrepreneurial, hard-working attitude of the general populace and the current atmosphere of the nation, which favors doing whatever is necessary to earn money. The Vietnamese government has shown a relatively large amount of flexibility (for what amounts to a dictatorship) in terms of modifying the system to favor business development. Vietnam's central location in the ASEAN region, its shared border with the strong southern economic region of China, and its large and literate population all point to good reasons to include Vietnam in any globalization plan. The first movers in such a setting can benefit from influencing developing regulations to favor their own business, from building the long-term relations so necessary for doing business there, and from simply establishing a presence before their competitors can reach the market.

However, the lack of physical, legal, and financial infrastructure makes reaping the benefits of, or even reaching, these objectives very difficult. A corrupt, communist-trained bureaucracy suspicious of foreigners can make even the best-planned ventures into lingering failures. Political re-lations with China and the United States are present stumbling blocks to globalization, and more problems could develop in the future.

The euphoric business optimism that accompanied the opening of Vietnam's markets has now faded to be replaced by well-publicized pit-falls of many of the first entrants. Nevertheless, the fact remains that Viet-nam is a country situated at the crossroads of socialism and capitalism, and those companies that can tailor their operations to the unique re-quirements of Vietnam's developing economy can reap the very large benefits of this capitalism now.

## NOTES

1. I particularly thank Bill Fink, M.B.A., Anderson Graduate School of Man-agement, UCLA, for his help with this chapter.

2. For some practical guides to doing business in Vietnam, see Neil Ashwood, *Vietnam: A Business Handbook* (London: Graham & Trotman, 1995); Joseph P. Quin-lan, *Vietnam: Business Opportunities and Risks* (Berkeley: Pacific View Press, 1995); Cisca Spencer and Gitte Heij, *A Guide to Doing Business in Vietnam* (Perth, Australia: Asia Research Center, Murdoch University, 1995); and *Vietnam Investment Database* (Hanoi: Vietnam Investment Review).

3. Bill Pietrucha, *Journal of Business Strategy* (November 1995): 36.

4. Ibid., 35.

5. *EIU Vietnam Country Report,* Fourth quarter (London: The Economist Intelli-gence Unit, 1995) 24.

6. *Market Asia Pacific* 5, no. 2 (February 1996).

7. Henry Kamm, *Dragon Ascending,* (Boston: Little Brown, 1996) 211.

8. EIU, 13.

9. EIU, 20.

10. Frederick Barke (Baker & McKenzie law firm), interview, *Business News In-dochina,* February 1996, 3.

11. Ibid., 2.

12. Pietrucha, 40.

13. EIU, 17.

14. Kamm, *Dragon Ascending,* 217.

15. Ibid.

16. Mark Mitchell, "Viewpoint," *New York Times,* February 18, 1996.

17. James C. Abegglen, *Sea Change: Pacific Asia as the New World Industrial Center* (New York: Free Press) 1994.

# CHAPTER 14

# Australia—Asian Future

*Peter FitzRoy, Susan Freeman, and George S. Yip*

AUSTRALIA LIES BEYOND Asia proper but is rapidly integrating with its Asian neighbors. For MNCs looking to enter or expand activities in the Asia-Pacific region, Australia can function as a convenient, westernized gateway to Asia while also providing access to a country with high living standards, an advanced educational system, excellent infrastructure, and significant consumer purchasing power.[1]

Although Australia's actual role in the rapid development of the region is as yet unclear, the country's intentions are certain. Australia is moving in the direction of shedding its European affiliation and strengthening its ties with Asia. In 1994, trade between Australia and ASEAN countries reached A$11.1 billion (U.S.$8.0 billion) and has grown at 20% annually in recent years.[2] (About 76% of Australia's merchandise exports were directed to APEC economies in 1995–96, up from 64% in 1975. Exports to ASEAN countries have been growing particularly rapidly. Imports from APEC countries have risen to 67% of total merchandise imports by 1996, up from 52% in 1995.)[3] Immigration from Asia to Australia continues to grow and, today, there is a higher representation of Asian languages in Australia than anywhere else in Asia. Indeed, one in eight inhabitants of Sydney, Australia's largest city, is of Asian origin. In addition, Australia has developed defense ties with various Asian nations through training and military exercises. Prior to 1973, only 24% of Australian companies exported to East Asia. By 1994, over 50% made that region their first export focus and primary destination.

The Asia-Pacific Region as a whole now accounts for about half of global production and about 40% of global trade. More than 60% of Australian merchandise exports are sold to Asian economies, while North Asia and Southest Asia account for over 60% of Australia's total growth in merchandise exports between 1983–93. Of Australia's top twelve markets, eleven are members of APEC.[4]

## Background

Australia is turning from a British past to an Asian future. Permanent European settlement of Australia began in 1788, when the British colonized

Australia. Today, Australia is an English-speaking, highly industrialized, Western-style economy with eighteen million inhabitants. From the 1930s through to 1973, Australia enjoyed preferred trading status with the United Kingdom due to the latter's favorable policies for British Commonwealth countries. When the United Kingdom joined the European Community in 1973, Australia's ability to export agricultural goods into the United Kingdom was severely limited. Australia's loss of its favored trading status, along with the Australian government's continued protectionist polices initiated during the second World War, significantly curtailed its global participation. It was only recently that Australia began to look beyond its own borders.

After the election of a Labor government in the late 1970s, following a Liberal-Conservative government in power for thirty years, the Australian economy underwent considerable change. While the Australian economy can still be described as managed, the Labor government was responsible for introducing, in stages, an open economy in most sectors. For example, the then Labor government introduced a deregulated financial sector and a free-floating exchange rate in the early 1980s. In late 1995, a Liberal-Conservative government returned to power but, like the previous Labor government, favors an open economy and has instituted further privatization programs.

Compared to neighboring Asian countries, the Australian population is more heterogeneous, but also much smaller. Given that the natural increase in population is very low by Asia-Pacific standards, the population is not likely to grow to the national target of twenty-three million without continuing immigration. This issue is highly sensitive to Australians from a political and social standpoint. When considering the economic standpoint, however, further immigration is desirable in order to expand the local market and to take advantage of the rich diversity of benefits resulting from a wide, culturally dispersed population base.

## Economic Performance

In contrast to many of its Asian neighbors, Australia has a slower rate of growth—3%—and has a mature economy. Australia does not come close in comparison with many of Asia's economies, which are experiencing rates of growth more than twice the Australian figure. It also has one of the lowest proportions of exports to GDP ratios among OECD countries. While its economy depends on international trade, Australia accounts for merely 1% of world trade and is ranked seventeenth in per capita income worldwide.[5] The previous Labor government in Australia had experienced a record seventeen successive quarters of growth in GDP. Yet the economy is moving at a slowed rate of growth.[6] Australia still has to exert pressure to attain access to markets for its primary products but the desire to have domestic economic autonomy and maintain tariff protection has diminished remarkably since the mid-1980s.[7] This change has created a need for Australian companies to look further afield. Australia is now intent on promoting foreign investment to help drive its industrial policy through reforms to the taxation system—as mentioned in a recent review initiated by the Australian Federal Government, the *Mortimer Report*, which has recommended a number of incentive schemes to promote and encourage foreign investment levels in and out of Australia.[8]

Investment in Australia by selected countries tended to see greater amounts of Asian investment in Australia than out of Australia. During 1995, total foreign investment in Australia reached A$400,943 million. The biggest foreign investor in Australia for 1995 was the United States, totaling A$88,649 million, followed by the United Kingdom at A$76,034 million, Japan at A$50,913 million and Hong Kong at A$14,047 million. As regards country groups, the OECD countries are the largest in Australia investors at A$271,172 million, followed by the APEC countries at A$177,411 million, the EU at A$112,212 million, ASEAN countries at A$8,436 million, and the OPEC countries at A$1,638 million.

When analyzed by industry, the largest inflows of investment for 1994–95 were into government administration and defence (A$12,537 million), finance and insurance (A$6,039 million), and manufacturing (A$95,644 million). Net withdrawals of investment were recorded for a number of countries, the largest being retail trade (A$1,805 million). In summary, the largest inflows of foreign investment in Australia in 1994–95 came from international capital markets (A$11,533 million), the United States (A$2,148 million), and the United Kingdom (A$2,130 million).

## Domestic Companies

Australia already has some very large domestic companies (Table 14.1), although many of these have foreign origins or ownership. BHP, a major steel and mining company; Coles Myer and Woolworths, both retail chains; and the National Australia Bank, are the four largest. Most Australian firms have a limited international presence. Australia's closest neighbor to the south, New Zealand, continues to be its major export destination despite the increased attention focused north toward Asia. In 1992–93 exports to New Zealand represented 64% of total exports. Yet, in 1995, foreign investment in Australia by New Zealand reached A$7,930 million and Australian investment in New Zealand was A$10,746. While an increase in investment in Asia is a major objective of the Australian government, in reality Australian companies still show a preference for doing business in other English-speaking countries.

For 1995, Australia's investment abroad in terms of its most significant countries were the United States, totaling A$35,683 million, followed by the United Kingdom, at A$27,709 million, New Zealand at A$10,746, and Japan at A$8,718 million. With regard to country groups, the OECD countries were the most significant location for investment during 1995, totaling A$106,317 million, followed by the APEC countries at A$71,399 million, the European Union at A$39,021 million, and the OPEC coun-

**Table 14.1**
**Largest Australian Companies**

| Rank | Company | Main Business | 1996–97 Revenues U.S.$ millions |
|---|---|---|---|
| 1 | BHP | diversified resources | 14,221 |
| 2 | Coles Myer | retail | 13,534 |
| 3 | Woolworths | mass retail | 10,010 |
| 4 | National Australia Bank | banking | 9,822 |
| 5 | News Corporation | media | 9,365 |
| 6 | Australia and New Zealand Bank | banking | 8,327 |
| 7 | Jardine Matheson | automotive distribution and properties | 7,417 |
| 8 | Westpac | banking | 6,588 |
| 9 | Commonwealth | banking | 6,249 |
| 10 | Pacific Dunlop | diversified industrial | 5,628 |
| 11 | AMCOR | packaging | 5,157 |
| 12 | TNT | transport | 4,989 |
| 13 | CSR | sugar, building products | 4,806 |
| 14 | Jardine Strategic | automotive distribution, properties, and food | 4,462 |
| 15 | Dairy Farm International | dairy produce | 4,381 |
| 16 | Pioneer International | building products | 4,325 |
| 17 | Foster's Brewing | beer | 3,898 |
| 18 | Boral | building products | 3,881 |
| 19 | Goodman Fielder | food manufacture | 3,154 |
| 20 | Cadbury Schweppes | food, beverage manufacturing | 3,100 |

*Source: Jobson's Yearbook of Public Companies 1996–97: A Guide to Australian and New Zealand Companies,* Dun & Bradstreet Marketing Pty. Ltd., 1996.

tries at A$8,154 million. Total Australian investment abroad by selected countries and country groups during 1995 was A$141,226 million. The largest withdrawal of investment (net outflow) was recorded for Singapore, at A$919 million. The largest outflows of Australian investments abroad in 1994–95 were to the United Kingdom, at A$1,053 million. The largest withdrawals of investment (inflow) were received from Japan (A$3,479 million) and the United States (A$2,103 million).[9]

Thus Australia's investment abroad, continues to focus on the United States, United Kingdom, New Zealand, Japan, and Europe. Australia has yet to demonstrate a commitment to investment in a meaningful way in the Asia-Pacifc Rim. The gap between what is said and what is done still needs adjustment, but that gap is closing. However, APEC countries as a whole are likely to become the focus.

The importance of Asian markets can be seen on closer inspection of Australia's major exports for 1992–93 and their principal markets:

- coal, A$7,538 million—12% of total exports: Japan (50%), Republic of Korea (12%), Taiwan (6%), and India (5%).
- nonmonetary gold, A$4,315 million—7% of total exports: Singapore (44%), Japan (19%), and Hong Kong (14%).
- beef, A$2,991 million—5% of total exports: Japan (42%), United States (32%), and Canada (8%).
- iron ore, A$2,895 million—5% of total exports: Japan (49%), South Korea (17%), and China (15%).[10]

Australia also continues to increase its trade links with the Asia-Pacific Rim. For example, New South Wales continues to be Australia's major state for exports. New South Wales's top merchandise export markets in order of volume include Japan, New Zealand, South Korea, the United States, Taiwan, Singapore, Indonesia, China, and Thailand. Nine of New South Wales's top ten export destinations are Asia-Pacific countries. These top ten destinations account for almost 70% of all New South Wales exports.[11]

Historically, Australia has been an exporter of primary products and commodities, although recently exporters have encompassed the more value-added end of the spectrum. The most significant increases in value-added exports occurred for road vehicles, petroleum products, and machinery specialized for particular industries. One sector where Australian value-added exports do particularly well is in manufactured goods. Australia has more than seven hundred emerging high-value-added exporters in all manufacturing industries.[12] The fastest growing firms are found in photographic, professional (finance, property, and business services), and scientific industries, with 56% of all firms exceeding annual growth of 15%.

Many Australian companies have undertaken very significant investments in Asia, including Alliance Properties (consultancy) in Indonesia, Malaysia, and Thailand; Amway Asia-Pacific (manufacturing) in Hong Kong, Thailand, Taiwan, Malaysia, and China; Australia and New Zealand Bank (financial services) in Hong Kong, Indonesia, Japan, the Philippines, Singapore, and India; Commonwealth Bank (financial services) in China, Hong Kong, Vietnam, Indonesia, Japan, and South Korea; and Faulding (pharmaceutical) in Hong Kong and Singapore.[13]

Australian MNCs are very active in developing telecommunications networks throughout Asia, and the Australian media are forging a strong link between Australia and Asian markets. Rupert Murdoch, CEO of News Corporation, and Kerry Packer of Consolidated Press have formed partnerships in a number of Asian markets, China being one of the most important and largest. Of growing significance is the Australian Broadcasting Commission's Asian satellite television venture, Australian Television. The recent launch of a new satellite from Cape Kennedy in Florida will allow the broadcaster to reach an area encompassing one-third of the globe. The new satellite will also take in first-time viewers from Beijing in the north to Sydney and New Zealand in the South. According to Australia Television's CEO: "We are going to be a global village . . . and Australia Television is making Australia closer to the peoples of the region."[14] The service is run from Darwin, the Australian city closest to Asia (nearer to Jakarta than to Sydney), and has established a considerable audience in Asia, with programming rebroadcast by more than one hundred regional broadcasters and cable operators.

Many other Australian MNCs also have global ambitions. Pacific Dunlop has many divisions and is a large and very diverse global company. Two large consumer industries, Ansell International (household/surgical gloves and condoms) and Pacific Brands (clothing and footwear) are the major consumer products divisions. It is also one of the two major participants in the Australian tire industry and is the largest Australian operator. In 1996–97 revenue was close to A$7,306 million. In Australia, the tire market is heavily influenced by the level of economic activity. The fall in 1990–91 was reflected in a decline of 11%, to 10.9 million units, and demand since then has focused on cheaper new and second-hand tires, as in Europe and Asia where consumers are becoming increasingly price conscious during a slower period of economic growth.[15]

In the packaging industry, Australia's AMCOR has two major focuses as part of its international expansion. Firstly, it wants to establish a market niche for fiber packaging and secondly to then build paper-making facilities.[16] This downside approach or backward integration will ensure that AMCOR has control over its paper supplies and will thus be insulated to some extent from the worldwide fluctuations in paper prices. AMCOR, to avoid substitution by major competitors, has focused its product mix around a range of market segments. Horizontal integration has proved to be a valuable strategy for AMCOR and has guarded against cycles and changes in consumer preferences. However, vertical integration has been an even more important long-term strategy for AMCOR. It has acquired large holdings in pulp and paper sources and manufacturing to ensure raw material supplies on a regional and global basis.[17]

## Foreign Participation in Economy

The largest foreign-funded companies operate primarily in extraction, including oil resources and mining (Table 14.2). The second largest foreign group of companies are all in the automotive industry. While Australia is eager to attract investment from throughout Asia, the United States, the United Kingdom, Japan, and the rest of the European Union are the current sources of major foreign investment in Australia and it appears that investment by Asian countries (other than Japan) will not grow markedly until the next decade.[18] However, in 1995, Hong Kong was the fourth largest foreign investor in Australia, totaling A$14,472 million, and Singapore was Australia's tenth largest foreign investor at A$6,658 million. However, China was still very low, totaling only A$1,956 million, the fourteenth largest investor.[19] In 1995, the United States was the main source of the net inflow of foreign investment into Australia for the fourth

*Table 14.2*

**Largest Foreign Multinational Companies in Australia**

| Rank | Company | Nationality | Main Business | 1995 Revenues U.S.$ millions |
|------|---------|-------------|---------------|------------------------------|
| 1 | Shell Australia | U.K./ Netherlands | oil and gas | 6,297 |
| 2 | Mitsui | Japan | general trading | 4,537 |
| 3 | Mobil Oil | U.S. | oil and gas | 4,020 |
| 4 | Mitsubishi Motors Australia | Japan | general trading | 4,016 |
| 5 | British Petroleum | U.K. | oil and gas | 3,916 |
| 6 | Ford Motor Company | U.S. | motor vehicle manufacturing | 2,366 |
| 7 | General Motors Holden | U.S. | motor vehicle manufacturing | 2,254 |
| 8 | Marubeni Australia | Japan | export/import | 1,893 |
| 9 | Toyota Motor Sales | Japan | motor vehicle import | 1,711 |
| 10 | Alcoa of Australia | U.S. | aluminum products | 1,643 |
| 11 | Mitsubishi Motors | Japan | motor vehicle manufacturing | 1,615 |
| 12 | Toyota Motor | Japan | motor vehicle manufacturing | 1,595 |
| 13 | Sumitomo | Japan | export/import | 1,585 |
| 14 | Itochu Australia | Japan | export/import | 1,522 |
| 15 | IBM Australia | U.S. | information technology | 1,296 |
| 16 | Esso Australia Resources | U.S. | oil and gas | 1,259 |
| 17 | Philip Morris | U.S. | tobacco products | 1,214 |
| 18 | Nissho Iwai Australia | Japan | export/import | 1,172 |
| 19 | Nestlé Australia | Switzerland | food manufacture | 1,044 |
| 20 | Unilever | U.K./ Netherlands | manufacturing | 916 |

*Source:* "Top 500 Companies," *The Bulletin,* December 5, 1995.

consecutive year, followed by the United Kingdom and Japan. The level of foreign investment was highest in the finance, property, and business services category, followed by manufacturing, mining, and wholesale and retail trade. The largest foreign-owned companies in Australia are Shell, Mitsui, Mobil Oil, Mitsubishi Motors, and British Petroleum (Table 14.2).

## Overall Industry Globalization Drivers in Australia

Australia's globalization drivers present great contrasts. Its developed status and Western heritage make for mostly favorable market globalization drivers. Its relatively small population and high wages cause mixed cost globalization drivers. Its stable political system and open policies provide for mostly favorable government globalization drivers. Its position is at the edge of Asia and its relatively small economy limits competitive globalization drivers.

## Market Globalization Drivers

Australian consumers have customer needs common to highly advanced, Western economies. Consumption patterns of key lead product categories including automobiles, telephones, TV sets, VCRs, and personal computers are indicative of a Western economy in a mature stage of growth. For example, in Australia, in particular, as in many Asian countries, the mobile telephone market has grown dramatically (70% in 1994).[20] By the late 1990s, Motorola Australia sees the country as possibly having the highest penetration of any in the world for cellular phones— driven by Australians' appetite for new knowledge and receptivity to new technologies.[21]

Yet even though Australians have distinctly Western consumption patterns, the country has a relatively small market size by Asian standards. This limits the extent to which corporations behave as regional customers and purchase and source from Australia.

Australia is generally seen by major global and regional companies as a lead country in research, development, and innovation. For example, Motorola Australia is building a large, multifaceted R&D center in Sydney over the next few years. Currently, Motorola Australia is doing software development in Adelaide, employing approximately three thousand five hundred people. Similarly, Toyota sees Australia's role in the next ten years as one that will contribute more significantly to innovation in areas including braking, safety, and design. While R&D is small in comparison to its global activities, Toyota has a sizable engineering team in Melbourne for the development of braking design, and is in the process of setting up its third R&D center, worldwide, in Australia.

## Cost Globalization Drivers

Australia's cost globalization drivers are mixed. The small population and economy limit the potential for both global and regional economies. But this limit is offset by the ability to export from Australia-based operations, particularly of higher-quality items. For example, the Australian market is relatively small for household and surgical gloves but the opportunity for exports is considerable. Extra capacity has been possible through numerous acquisitions as part of Ansell's (Pacific Dunlop) integrated international strategy in overseas markets. Ansell's performance has also been enhanced by the Sri Lankan medical and industrial gloves plant and the condom manufacturing plant in Alabama. Automation is a major focus, especially in the Asian facilities. In fact, before the Perry

(U.S.) acquisition, 90% of Ansell's business revenue was international and is now as high as 95%. The percentage spread of worldwide business revenue for Ansell is diverse. Japan is the biggest percentage source, namely 16%, followed by France at 12%, the Middle East at 11.3%, Australia at 8.3%, and Germany and Ireland at 8.0 and 7.9 respectively.[22]

Australia can offer significant sourcing efficiencies of both its abundant natural resources and its quality production in selected sectors. For example, there is strong demand in Southeast Asia for Australian steel and iron exports, especially to Taiwan, which is Australia's largest country market for iron and steel exports in volume, ahead of the United States. One large Australian company, BHP, is responsible for 80% of total domestic production/output in Australia, making the market a difficult one to enter by foreign companies.

In terms of outbound logistics, Australia is primarily an unfavorable location at the southern end of the Asia-Pacific region, and its major cities, other than Darwin (with a very minor population and business significance), are not on the northern coastline, but the eastern and southern tips of the coast. But Australia has acceptable logistics for high-value-added products such as steel. Offsetting the poor external logistics, Australia has excellent infrastructure. Transportation, communications, and utilities all work extremely well.

Australia's biggest cost disadvantage lies in its relatively high labor costs—$14.40 hourly labor costs in manufacturing in 1995, compared with $1.59 in Malaysia, and $0.30 in Indonesia (see Table 1.6 in Chapter 1). In addition, Australia has the strongest labor unions in the region. Offsetting these disadvantages are the high quality of the labor pool, its availability, and its low turnover rate (see Table 1.7 in Chapter 1).

Lastly, Australia can play a significant technological role for MNCs because of its high educational levels and the presence of many domestic companies that have developed strong technological capabilities, particularly in sectors related to Australia's natural resources—agriculture, mining, and minerals. Australia appears to be making moves to establish stronger technological ties with its Asian neighbors. For example, Australia recently signed a multimedia sister industry development agreement with Japan designed to create collaborative links between software engineers, content developers, and hardware experts in both countries. In general, Australia adheres to worldwide standards for telecommunications, favoring the digital over the analog system for future needs.

## Government Globalization Drivers

The Australian government actively supports Australia's globalization by enacting measures to encourage international investment and assisting Australian companies in penetrating international markets.[23] In order to improve access to the growing markets in the Asia-Pacific region the government has created a positive investment climate in Australia, with a number of recent studies, in particular the *Mortimer Report*, suggesting an increased focus on the need to attract investment from the Asia-Pacific Rim.[24]

In 1988, then-Treasurer Paul Keating announced the government's desire for a more flexible and open economy. Since then, many measures have been implemented to reduce protectionism. By 1996, there were to be no tariffs in excess of 5%, apart from motor vehicles, clothing, textiles, and footwear.[25] A recent announcement by Prime Minister John Howard, in September 1997, set tariffs in the CTF industry to remain at 5% until 2005. The auto industry has also been singled out for existing tariff level protection through 2005. Moreover, trademarks and intellectual property are well-protected from imitation in Australia.[26]

Deregulation opened the aviation industry to private investment in the late 1980s and utilities in the 1990s. The two most recent examples of deregulation are the floating of the national aviation authority, Qantas, in late 1995, and the partial sale of the government-owned telecommunications body, Telstra, in late 1997. The Telstra partial sell-off is likely to net the government approximately A\$2.5 million.[27]

In addition to initiating deregulation of key industries, recent and current Australian governments have encouraged foreign investment by lowering tariffs and showing an ongoing commitment to establishing AFTA (ASEAN Free Trade Area), support for APEC and a free trade area (CER) with New Zealand. In general, the Australian trade policy is one that seeks to promote an open, multilateral, and liberalized international economy.

In order to take full advantage of the recent decline in barriers to trade, foreign investment restrictions must also be relaxed. Australia must attempt to liberalize the foreign investment regimes of its traditional and growing markets so that Australian firms can have complete market access. This is the reason that APEC has included investment in its trade facilitation agenda and why the APEC Bogor declaration states that there will be free and open trade investment by 2000.[28] The recently released *Mortimer Report* in Australia is also recommending a freeing-up of investment restrictions in Australia for foreign companies.

The 1994 APEC summit at Bogor, Indonesia, was seen as a real success with Australia playing an important role. Australia is likely to gain an annual trade dividend of A\$7 billion when the agreement is finally implemented. Australia's real output is expected to rise by 3.8% and real National Income by approximately 1.2%, or A\$6.8 billion per annum. This would more than double the expected real income gains for Australia if the Uruguay discussions prove fruitful.[29]

Australia, like many other nations, recognizes the need to develop comprehensive disciplines for foreign investment policy. The OECD countries, including Australia, have commenced negotiations on a multilateral agreement, with a completion target date of 1997. In 1994, APEC trade ministers signed the APEC nonbinding investment principles (Australian initiative under the then Prime Minister, Paul Keating). It advocates the complete removal of all foreign investment restrictions in

Australia, including the abolition of the foreign investment board. This has been supported by the recent release of the *Mortimer Report,* in 1997. The WTO, in Singapore in 1996, established a new committee to investigate foreign investment.[30]

As a middle power in trade diplomacy, Australia will have to play a stronger role in ensuring that investment rules developed in the multilateral arena in the APEC, OECD, or WTO groups are made consistent with the existing Australian trade policy and orientation. A five-part general framework has been adopted by APEC and the OECD, with five major provisions relating to transparency, national treatment, and most-favored nation status. The fourth refers to a code of government behavior, with the fifth related to dispute resolution. Unfortunately, the transparency provision relating to all Australian laws and regulations, means they will have to be specified clearly. Most developed countries would have little problem, but for Australia this will be a considerable effort and overhaul.[31]

The most difficult provision to address will be that related to the national treatment of foreign investment and investors. Australia has recently sent out conflicting messages here, especially with recent handling of the Campbell-Arnotts, RTZ-CRA, and Dream-World Case. Foreign investment is on the policy agenda in APEC and the OECD and will form part of the WTO agenda. Australia's commitment to an open and equitable trading system will be tested in these forums. So far, Australia has not responded to the challenges of foreign investors, but the recent *Mortimer Report* and changing government attitudes, which recognise the enormous importance of trade and investment for Australia, both from and in the Asia-Pacific Rim will help to hasten this change. Australia remains one of the few developed countries that screen foreign investment proposals in all sectors, but removal of this has been a major recommendation of the *Mortimer Report.* Most of Australia's counterparts require foreign investors to notify the authorities after they have completed the transaction. Foreign investment is on the policy agenda in APEC and the OECD and by 1997 will form part of the WTO agenda. Australia's commitment to an open and equitable trading system will thus be tested within these forums. But the challenge to adapt their foreign investment policy remains a high priority in Australia, with the recent announcement by Prime Minister Howard, that Australia needs to adopt a more Asian-style approach to its industrial policy.[32]

The taxation system is another area that needs serious review with regards to attracting international investors, which again has been addressed as a priority in the *Mortimer Report.* The previous and current governments' recent moves to increase the corporate tax rate to 36% may hurt the push to attract regional headquarters (RHQ's) as it goes against a trend of declining tax rates in the region and may also create uncertainty among investors. Some tax experts argue that the government is wasting its time trying to attract RHQ's unless it neutralizes the Australian tax disadvantage against Asian countries.[33] The Federal Government has recently acknowledged and pledged to address this issue as a result of the *Mortimer Report.*

The taxation system in Australia does not encourage local companies to invest or expand overseas, either. When a company is presented with the opportunity to expand into a foreign country, all of the income, although taxed overseas, would also be subject to Australian tax.[34] The company is also obliged to claim foreign tax credits in Australia, keep detailed travel diaries, and is unable to claim entertainment expenses as a deduction. These tax impediments do hold back Australian businesspeople when they have to compete in Asia. The current changing of the words of the Tax Act, without changing the substance, will do little to ease the compliance burden on small Australian businesspeople. Much of the complexity of the Australian taxation law is systemic and needs to be fundamentally altered.[35]

Professor Vann of Sydney University Law School, who has worked with the IMF and OECD on tax systems, states that much of the complexity that arises is mainly relevant to large companies. For example, the French and Germans are able to keep their legislation short by relying on reported income when taxing listed companies. For this reason, there is a powerful incentive for listed companies not to minimize their reported income as this would cause the market to take an adverse view of them. Professor Vann has also pointed out the almost unlimited potential in Australia for employment deductions, which should be greatly simplified. With the current piecemeal approach to tax reform in Australia, Vann sees the systemic problems remaining. Submissions by industry and professional bodies, including the Minerals Company of Australia, show there are still major flaws and unresolved issues in the legislation presented by the tax law improvement project (TLIP) set up by government to report to federal parliament.[36] A new team is needed if a radical overhaul of existing tax measures in Australia is to be achieved. This seems likely in the light of recommendations from the recent *Mortimer Report.*

Technical standards is another area for concern. The technical standards set by government bodies in Australia and other countries do affect the potential for a globally standardized product. Specific modifications are needed in Australia because there are definite requirements for modifications on technical product attributes in every market.

In many industries declining industry protection has caused increased competition and cost containment measures. For example, auto producers now demand better and cheaper service for automotive components due to declining industry protection. This is causing some rationalization and falling tariff levels in the context of a more competitive environment. However, overall governmental factors in Australia point toward globalization in most lines of business. Recent change in the economic environment is resulting in further deregulation of the financial sector (with no barriers to foreign ownership) and of the telecommunications sector, with a 25% sale of the state-run monopoly (previously the only operator), but now competing with the new privately run consortium, Optus. Optus is currently at logger heads legally with Telstra to obtain the right to compete in the offering of the domestic call facilities segment of the market.

## Competitive Globalization Drivers

Australia's competitive globalization drivers are probably the weakest of the four. The country is strategic in very few industries, and most of these being agricultural or extractive rather than manufacturing or services. So MNCs have not found it vital to make Australia part of their global or regional networks or value chains. Australia's best hope in building its strategic importance lies in R&D. MNCs should be conducting more such activities there. Motorola-Sydney is building a research center for technology development for the next ten years and beyond. Telstra is setting up its third R&D center, globally, in Melbourne. Australia may also retain some strategic importance because of first mover advantage. Many American and British MNCs went there first because of historical ties or linguistic and cultural familiarity. Such MNCs want to at least maintain their position in Australia. So, for example, even though Motorola no longer manufactures in Australia, it still considers it important to remain in Australia, emphasizing the R&D advantages of operating in the long run in Australia. All of its main competitors are there and Motorola wants to maintain its number one or two ranking in each of its markets worldwide. R&D will however, become increasingly important. Motorola-Sydney expects its current building project in Sydney, a Research Center for technological development, to be at the leading edge in telecommunications for the next ten years and beyond.

## Overall Global Strategies for Australia

MNCs can probably develop profitable strategies for Australia, particularly if they are leveraging significant competitive advantages, such as brand names, products, or technology. But, in most cases, MNCs should probably expect such attempts to be self-supporting rather than contributing to a broader regional or global strategy. Hence, Australia is likely to play a different role from most other Asia-Pacific economies in an MNC's portfolio.

### Market Participation Strategies

While the Australian market is fairly limited in size and growth potential, its consumers are generally receptive to foreign brand names, packaging, and advertising. They are also very amenable to marketing strategies and approaches used in other countries. Moreover, the country offers comfortable proximity to some of the world's fastest-growing economies. Those companies that can benefit from locating activities in Australia can also take advantage of the swelling consumer and financial markets just to the north in Southeast Asia. On the other hand, the financial crisis that hit Southeast Asia in 1997 will cause Australia to suffer an immediate decline in export sales to this region.[37]

The extent of global customers who purchase or source from Australia is expected to grow. Australia's packaging industry provides such an example. As countries in Asia lower barriers to foreign brands, the three largest players in consumer brands (cigarettes) are entering those markets: Philip Morris, BAT Rothmans, and R. J. Reynolds. Not surprisingly, they want their suppliers to follow. For example, AMCOR, the largest Australian firm in the industry, through its Rentsch subsidiary, is a major supplier for Philip Morris. AMCOR is providing capacity and capital for Rentsch to continue to follow this global customer into newly emerging markets.[38]

## Product and Service Strategies

Most global products are well accepted in Australia. For example, in the photocopier market, products are standardized globally, apart from slight frequency and technical variations.[39] Very little adaptation is required for the Australian market, although some items experience greater acceptance when slightly tailored. The Toyota *Camry* manufactured in Australia is a globally standardized product except for some minor features. For example, the color preference for the *Camry* in Australia tends to be dark and glossy, while the color preference in Malaysia and Saudi Arabia is for steel gray with little gloss. Thus, autos destined for the Australian domestic market differ from those exported to the Asia-Pacific Rim. Otherwise, only minor differences exist in the made-for-Australia *Camry* such as adaptation of the braking and suspension system to more demanding road conditions.

## Activity Location Strategies

Australia's potential or actual importance for different value-added activities is confined to locally driven activities including marketing, selling, distribution, service, and general management. In contrast, Australia holds little attraction for manufacturing activities largely due to its unfavorable labor costs and external logistics. For example, Panasonic and Motorola Australia found electronic product manufacturing in Australia to be approximately 25–50% more expensive than in the European Union and the United States, although less than in Japan.

Some companies do use Australia as an export base. Toyota has adopted a policy to increase production in Australia and raise the proportion of locally produced vehicles in its total unit sales. This trend is not simply for domestic sale but, more importantly, for export to other markets (e.g., *Camry* models to Malaysia, replacing exports from Toyota's higher-cost Japanese factories). Moreover, by the end of 1996, Toyota had hoped to increase offshore production by about 50% over the 1993 total of 890,000 units. The executive vice president of Toyota Australia has stated that the company is trying to increase local content in its production facilities because the parts from Japan are increasingly expensive.[40] In mid-1997,plans were made to make further investments in manufacturing, to the tune of several million dollars over the next few years, in order to produce exports mainly to Southeast Asia. In return, the Australian Government has fixed tariffs to remain at 5% until 2005, providing continued protection for this industry over the next decade.

Australia lies close enough to Asian markets that transportation is cost effective, at least for high-value products. For example, Toyota hopes to position Toyota Motor Corporation Australia (TMCA) as a finished vehicle manufacturing base for Asia and raise its exports to 20,000 units per year.[41] Investment levels over five years beginning in 1997 should ensure this. Toyota will spend A$1.1 billion (U.S.$867 million) in the 1990s on new plants, tooling, and facilities alone. Meanwhile, Toyota headquarters is focusing on the global production and distribution of finished vehicles; a global procurement system for auto parts and materials; and finally, cooperation with overseas automakers. Australia has become significant to the company in all three of these areas. Furthermore, consistently strong growth in the Asia-Pacific auto market reflects the region's strong economic growth rate and suggests an increasingly important role for Australia.[42]

In the steel industry, a clear shift in the global patterns of steel production and consumption, with increased demand in Asia, heralds enormous potential for Australia. Asian countries are expected to consume close to 47% of the world's steel supply by 2000, compared with 34% in 1990.[43] China, India, and Korea stand out as major markets. For example, Korea is Australia's second-largest export market and fourth largest trading partner with exports in 1995–96 at A$6,608 million. Of particular interest and focus are nonmonetary gold, coal, and iron ore, with rapid growth in recent years in the export of Australian manufacturing, reflecting Australia's increased competitiveness in nontraditional areas and the success of efforts to promote Australia as a source of high-tech and high-value-added products.[44] Steel-producing companies are aware of the need to follow their global customers into emerging markets to provide them with the familiar levels of service they have come to expect.[45] While worldwide steel production slowed to 1% annual growth in 1994, Australian steel production increased by 6.5%. Increased production resulted from higher domestic economic demand and improving exports. This is an industry where shipping costs are a significant factor, thus favoring Australia, relative to Europe and the United States, as a steel manufacturing location for Asia. BHP, Australia's largest steel-producing company is well placed domestically and globally to take advantage of the expected large increases in demand in the growing Asia-Pacific Rim, with a competitive advantage, regionally and globally, based on a strategic location of value-added activities and also vertical integration.

In consumer packaged goods, P&G has located high-quality, high-volume manufacturing plants in a number of Asian locations for particular products to cater to the growing demands of Asia. Unilever also manufactures in the region, including Australia.

Because of the supply of technically trained staff at costs that are low relative to other advanced economies, Australia can be attractive for locating R&D activities. For example, the Melbourne division of Toyota has a research center of Australian engineers who are involved in R&D issues in the areas of braking and road suspension that are used on a worldwide basis. Motorola, too, has set up a R&D center in Sydney. This R&D Center will now expand this activity in Australia recognizing the expertise that Australia offers with regard to its highly trained engineers. Additionally, Australia is also considered to be valuable as a source of financial services.

Many multinational firms favor Australia for training programs, corporate conventions, and shareholder meetings given its proximity to Asia, combined with the convenience of a fully Westernized environment. For example, Toyota has located the training center for its Oceania region in Australia. Some MNCs have found Australia to be an effective and economic location for customer service centers and other back office operations. Swire Pacific, the giant Hong Kong trading company has moved some of its back office operations to Sydney, Australia. These operations are primarily crew and route management. American Express has centralized its Asia-Pacific billing and customer service center in Sydney, primarily due to the high representation of Asian language proficiency in the work force.

Many large corporations have regional headquarters for distribution or other significant operations in Australia, not so much because of its location, which is not central for the region, but more for its highly advanced infrastructure and telecommunications. Campbell Soup, a U.S. company, uses its Australian location for production and has mainly been involved in processing in the last three years. Cadbury Schweppes is a United Kingdom based company involved in production in Australia and is increasing its concerns in Australia. Kraft, a U.S. company, has been in Australia since the 1930s and uses the Australian site for R&D. It is now expanding its R&D operations in Australia. Dun and Bradstreet is a U.S.-based company offering financial services in Australia since around 1990. They are now using the Australian location for their regional HQ for data distribution. Crédit Suisse (Switzerland) uses its Australian site as the regional bullion trader. It has been in Australia for two years. Saab, a Swedish company has located its regional HQ in Australia too, and has been in Australia since early 1997. Oracle, a U.S.-based company involved in software systems now has its regional HQ located in Australia. These companies see Australia as valuable because of the language skills and highly skilled labor force. Overall, there are approximately one hundred regional HQs from MNCs in Melbourne, Victoria, alone, and this is an increasing trend in both Melbourne and Sydney.

## Marketing Strategies

MNCs typically take a globally uniform approach to their marketing mix in Australia—the same brand names, packaging, pricing, advertising, promotion, selling, and distribution. One exception is the importance of avoiding heavily discounted promotions, the Australian market being too small to recoup such expenditures. This market size limitation effects all elements of the marketing mix to some degree.

MNCs also make some marketing adaptations in Australia. For example, Toyota Australia's local marketing director created Toyota's local brand image by featuring a chicken. While this may seem an unusual approach to marketing automotive brands, it has given Toyota an edge and an identity in what is regarded a fairly pedestrian advertising segment.

Many Australian consumers, affected by the ongoing recession of the 1990s, want value and will not buy unless convinced they are getting the best value possible. While many firms use discounting, ultimately discount-driven advertising, whether it be through large national sales or less-prominent promotion, is considered to be "financially suicidal" in a limited market the size of Australia's. Many executives believe that brand equity is very important for the long-term viability of business in Australia.[46] This premise has affected all elements of the marketing mix in Australia, from P&G's hair care products to Toyota's contracts for fleet car sales.

Despite Australian consumers' familiarity with an established brand, some MNCs have been able to change local brand names to fit with global strategies. For example, Matsushita changed its product line in Australia from *National* to *Panasonic* in 1988, in an effort to regroup its subsidiaries and turn its *Panasonic* product ranges into a global brand. The name change was a gamble, as *National* consumer products accounted for nearly 75% of the company's turnover in the late 1980s. However, the *Panasonic* name now covers one thousand six hundred products and models in Australia and worldwide.

Introductions of global hair care products in Australia have had particular problems with their pricing and advertising strategies. The Australian market is littered with the casualties of premium-priced brands that failed. Furthermore, brand promiscuity is high. Consumers regularly hop from one brand to another, driven primarily by the belief that they need to change their shampoo and conditioner brand from time to time to get a better end result, as well as by temporary price reductions and new product entries. Successful products in Australia are those that recognize that customers are more educated about hair care now.[47] P&G Australia's *Pantene Pro-V* brand has been very successful due to advertising that reinforces the product's hair care benefits.

Lastly, Australia is experiencing many of the global trends in distribution and selling. Retail ownership continues to concentrate—more than four million people already shop at Coles Supermarkets and Woolworths every week—so manufacturers are increasingly exploring in-store marketing strategies to influence consumer purchasing. Following the international trend of contracting out company sales and merchandising forces, P&G Australia, Vodaphone, Philip Morris, and Pepsi-Cola have appointed or are testing out field marketing agencies to handle their merchandising and in-store sales functions.

## Competitive Move Strategies

Due to its small size and relative isolation, Australia is often not included as part of a crosscountry subsidization strategy or of a globally coordinated sequence of competitive moves. Most MNCs conduct their strategies and competitive reactions on a local basis. This is particularly true in those few industries where competition is much more limited than in other markets. For example, there are only three groups of motor vehicle manufacturers operating in Australia and all are foreign owned— Ford, Mitsubishi, and United Australian Automotive Industries (UAAI), a joint venture company formed in March 1992 (equally owned by General Motors-Holden's Automotive Ltd. and by Toyota Motor Corporation Australia Ltd.). So, in such industries, the competitive game tends to be simpler and more local in Australia.

In most industries, competitors act locally in Australia. For example, Panasonic Australia makes its own competitive moves independent of global moves. The Australian division is kept informed about competitive moves elsewhere, but acts on its own. With regard to strategies for dealing with competitors in Australia, Panasonic has a policy of "our own boat, own shop." Each business unit in each country is left to carry out its own individual functions while following global policies. The business strategy used in Australia is not very global, although the parent company is regarded as extremely global. Panasonic believes that a local approach in Australia is the optimal position. Philips has adopted the same strategy, allowing for local autonomy. On the other hand, Toyota does not consider Australia an independent market when deciding competitive moves. All decisions concerning the value-added activities of the company are decided in the home country and are directed to the overseas sites. Toyota hands down plans originating in Japan that are then delivered to its overseas facilities, where they are carried out largely at the executive level, staffed primarily by Japanese.[48] They have thus adopted a more strategically integrated approach.

## Overall Organization and Management Approaches for Australia

Given its developed status and Western background, Australia rates very highly for MNCs being able to use global organization and management approaches. First, foreign MNCs can easily operate without local partners. Second, Australian managers are more than qualified to be given a high degree of local autonomy. For example, Matsushita's and Philip's organizational operations in Australia are largely carried out as autonomous subsidiaries. Motorola Australia also acts fairly independently of the head office, although it is directed by guidelines.

In some industries, however, home country management sets major policies. For example, from the outset, Australians have had relatively little say in how their foreign-owned auto industry is managed. Over the last fifty years, the industry's long- and medium-term decisions have been made by management outside Australia. This is not likely to change a great deal despite a directive from the government in the 1984 Button Auto-Plan for a preference for Australian managers. The government desires a greater number of Australian managers in the automobile industry. This seems even less of a possibility as the local industry becomes more internationalized.[49]

Third, Australian subsidiaries of MNCs can easily use and participate in global account management processes—education, language, culture, and experience all facilitating such involvement. Australian business practices are considered very international.[50] Australians benefit from a high educational level, with 46% of the population possessing an educational standard of 12 years of completed formal education or higher.[51]

Fourth, Australia has many highly capable managers, many of whom have taken high-level positions in the Asian and other subsidiaries of MNCs. And MNCs do not seem to have much difficulty in persuading Australians to relocate. For example, Ford has thirty Australians working in overseas operations ranging from the United States and Japan to Taiwan, Britain, Venezuela, Indonesia, Italy, and New Zealand. On the other hand, most Japanese MNCs have not found ways to really use senior Australian (or other non-Japanese) executives. The lack of opportunity for senior personnel in some Japanese companies is seen by some as frustrating, while others are cynical of the way Japanese companies publicly present an Australian management structure, while at the same time relying on a network of Japanese advisers who shadow their Australian counterparts and often report directly to the head office.[52] For technical personnel, Australia's software developers, for example, are considered to be among the best in the world, particularly in medical software and education training and curriculum titles.

Lastly, Australia's culture has many aspects of both British and American culture (British from the shared heritage, and American from the shared frontier experience). Increasing immigration since the 1980s has also made Australians much more open to foreign cultures, as has the long-standing tradition of world travel by young Australians. So MNCs from most countries should find little difficulty in applying to an Australian subsidiary their particular corporate culture.

## Conclusions

Australia is a Western country in the Asia-Pacific region that is now focusing its attention on Asia. It has the advantages of a developed infrastructure, well-educated population, and increasing Asian immigration that brings dynamism, language capabilities, and Asian connections. Moreover, Australia is an educational destination for many affluent Asians, resulting in implications for networking in the short term and long term.

Australia is trying to retain its role as a site for MNC regional HQs. Its distance from the rest of Asia is somewhat offset by its location in the same time zone. Furthermore, Australia is an attractive location for value-added activities, such as marketing, distribution, and services, but not for production. Meanwhile, its labor costs are now competitive with developed parts of Asia, making it increasingly attractive for white-collar activities requiring highly educated employees and managerial capabilities. Australia also offers stability and receptivity to new and highly technologically advanced products. Conversely, Australian companies are attracted to Asia by the vast population, the rapidly growing economies, and geographic proximity. Some Australian companies have gotten into difficulties because of their failure to recognize the different customs and ways of doing business in Asia. As a result, more Australian companies are now forming joint ventures as a preferred entry mode into Asia with local partners who may be either free enterprise or government. Also, many of Australia's larger companies, such as Brambles, Lend Lease, and CSR, have taken a very cautious approach when entering the Asia-Pacific Rim, but other companies—for example, National Australia Bank and Telstra—are proving through their successes that they have the ability to compete very effectively in many industries, ranging from building and construction, such as Leighton Holdings, media (News Corporation), telecommunications (Matrix) and general manufacturings (Pacific BBA).

In recognition of the importance of the Asian markets, the Australian Stock Exchange recently introduced an Asian Company index which is made up of Asian companies that have Asian affiliates based in Asia and are listed on the Australian Stock Exchange. The index consists of twenty-six stocks that have 75% of their profit generated in Asia, or 75% of their revenue generated from Asia, or 75% of their assets located in Asia.[53] These companies are successfully competing in many highly competitive markets in Asia, including a wide range of activities such as food, building, and investments.

Even though Australia is a small market with stagnant consumer demand, which therefore does not offer significant potential for MNC globalization efforts, this fact belies the strategic importance of Australia. GDP growth in the Asia-Pacific region will propel demand forward at an accelerated pace, despite the current financial crisis in this region. Those companies with ties to Australia will be in a strategic position to jump over to Asian markets. Closeness to growing markets, an easily understandable and reliable business and legal system, combined with an easy lifestyle for MNC expatriates, give Australia a potentially healthy future.

## NOTES

1. Department of Foreign Affairs and Trade (DFAT), "Winning Enterprises," Canberra: Australian Government Publishing Service, 1995.

2. Murray Hiebert, and Bandar Seri Bagawan "Wizard of Oz," *Far Eastern Economic Review,* 1995): 26.

3. Australian Bureau of Statistics, Year Book Australia, 1997.

4. Ibid.

5. World Bank, *World Development Report 1994: Infrastructure for Development* (Washington, D.C.: Oxford University Press for the World Bank, 1994).

6. *Australian Chamber of Commerce and Industry Report of Business Expectations,* November, 1995.

7. Speech by Prime Minister, Mr. R. Hawke at the Uruguay Round of GATT, the Center for European Policy Studies, Brussels, February 4, 1995.

8. Released in the second half of 1997.

9. Australian Bureau of Statistics, cat. no. 5363.0, 1994–95: BOP and International Investment Position: Australia—14-4.

10. *The Australian Year Book,* 1995.

11. Australian Bureau of Statistics, *Report on Foreign Trade,* no. 5410.0, 1995 and unpublished data.

12. Emerging exporters can be divided into three main categories: start-up or established firms with foreign sales of less than A$2 million, exporters with foreign sales of A$2–50 million, and large, established firms with foreign sales greater than A$50 million. Source: *Emerging Exporters: Australia's High Value-added Manufacturing Exporters,* McKinsey and Company, Australian Manufacturing Council, June, 1993.

13. *Jobson's Year Book of Public Companies,* 1996–1997 (Dun & Bradstreet Marketing Pty. Ltd., 1996).

14. *The Australian,* February 2, 1996.

15. *Standard and Poor's Industry Profiles—Tyres,* July 15, 1995.

16. *Australian Financial Review,* October 31, 1994.

17. AMCOR—annual company report and interviews with senior company personnel, 1995.

18. *International Investment Position,* Canberra: Australian Bureau of Statistics, no. 5306.0, December 1993.

19. Australian Bureau of Statistics, cat. no. 5363.0, 1994–95.

20. P. Budde, *Telecommunications Strategies, Featuring Superhighway Developments 1995–96.* Paul Budde Communication Pty. Ltd., Bucketty, NSW, 1995.

21. *Motorola Annual Report,* 1995.

22. Pacific Dunlop—senior company personnel interview and annual reports, 1995.

23. *Doing Business in Australia,* Price Waterhouse, 14.

24. Ibid., 18.

25. Economic statements made on May 25, 1988, and the PM Industry Statement in March 1991.

26. Senior company personnel interview, 1988.

27. *Australian Financial Review,* September 16, 1997.

28. "The Trade Winds Blow," *The Australian,* February 2, 1996, 29.

29. *Australian Weekly Economic News Highlight,* U.S. Embassy, Canberra, Australia, November 11–18, 1994.

30. "The Trade Winds Blow," 29.

31. Ibid.

32. Ibid.

33. *The Financial Review,* November 16, 1994.

34. "Tax Project should be axed and the law fixed."

35. Ibid.

36. Ibid.

37. *The Business Age,* September 16, 1997.

38. *Australian Financial Review,* November 16, 1994.

39. Senior company personnel interview, 1995.

40. *Business Review Weekly,* April 25, 1994.

41. *Japan Industrial Journal,* April 18, 1994, 22.

42. Data for Australia is from the Automotive Industry Manufacturing, December 15, 1993.

43. Sheffield Steel Consultancy Reports.

44. Australian Bureau of Statistics, *Year Book Australia,* 1997.

45. George S. Yip, *Total Global Strategy: Managing for Worldwide Competitive Advantage* (Englewood Cliffs, N.J.: Prentice Hall, 1992).

46. *B & T,* February 5, 1993.

47. *Sunday Age (Melbourne),* September 11, 1994.

48. *The Bulletin,* September 14, 1993, 86.

49. Ibid.

50. Senior company personnel interview, 1995.

51. *Morgan Gallup Poll,* 1996.

52. Ibid., 86.

53. The largest company in the index is Aurora Gold Ltd., which has a market capitalization of $314 million and accounts for about 30% of the index.

# CHAPTER 15

# New Zealand—Resource Play

*Wayne Cartwright and George S. Yip*

WITH A POPULATION OF under four million people, New Zealand is a small country and market but has a relatively high level of per capita income for the Asia-Pacific region. Its population is comparatively sophisticated and much of the demand for consumer goods and capital equipment is satisfied by imports. These conditions provide a small but rewarding environment for distribution subsidiaries of multinational companies (MNCs). Other MNCs participate in development of the indigenous resource base for both domestic and export markets.

New Zealand lies on the periphery of Asia in terms of both geography and psychological distance. The country has strong historical links with the United Kingdom and more recent cultural affinity with the United States and Canada. These ties to primarily European cultures have been strengthened by economic, political, and sporting associations with neighbouring Australia. However, as Australia has reached out to Asia and has worked to be recognised as a part of the region, New Zealand has followed in its own way, albeit later. Tangible linkages between New Zealand and Asian countries are numerous. Japan is New Zealand's largest trading partner. Exports to China, Korea, Taiwan, Malaysia, Singapore, and Indonesia are also important, and significant foreign direct investment by New Zealand firms in some of these countries supports local marketing, distribution, and production. Investment from Japan, Malaysia, and Singapore in the New Zealand economy is accelerating. Since the late 1980s there has been substantial immigration of professional and entrepreneurial people from Hong Kong and Taiwan, motivated in part by favourable educational opportunities in New Zealand, a course followed earlier by Malaysian Chinese families. New Zealand is an enthusiastic member of several politicoeconomic institutions in the region, the principal one being APEC.

However, despite this strong move to develop Asian relationships, New Zealand retains crucial trade and investment linkages with North America and Europe, and has emergent ties also with Latin America and Middle Eastern countries. Hence, it appears unlikely that New Zealand will develop a specific regional focus. Rather, it will seek to establish and retain favourable relations with all of these regions.

Since the early 1980s, New Zealand has progressed through profound change in both its economic and its sociocultural perspectives. Prior to this time, the New Zealand economy was relatively closed, through import controls implemented via quota licensing and punitive tariff regimes, and rigid foreign exchange controls with fixed exchange rates. Originating in the 1930s, this economic and social ideology was essentially socialist, favoring full employment and an economy managed by a centralized public service and government regulation. By 1983–84 almost unserviceable levels of public foreign debt and high levels of inflation led to widespread recognition that this form of economy had failed. A change of government and a rapid shift in economic policy followed. Surprisingly, the new government, which supposedly held strong socialist views, actually implemented conservative policies based on neoclassical free trade theory, monetarist (Friedmanite) principles, and substantial reduction in the influence and size of government. Successive governments have supported these initiatives with the result that New Zealand's economy is now one of the most open and unregulated in the world. Apart from a few residual (and declining) tariffs, trade is unrestricted and capital flows are free. Many of the previous commercial government operations have been privatized or sold into state-owned enterprises that are managed as ordinary companies. Previous laws that required collective wage bargaining have been replaced by labour contracting at the enterprise and individual level. These economic reforms have become known as "Rogernomics," in recognition of Roger Douglas who led the process as Minister of Finance.[1]

Despite the spectacular results and macrolevel success of these economic policies, the social cost has been perceived as high by many citizens. Previous principles of egalitarianism and the values embraced in a welfare state are perceived to have been severely challenged and even ignored. The distributions of income and wealth have widened, the effectiveness of the 'trickle-down' effect has been questioned, and unemployment remains around 7%.

## Economic Performance

The indicators of spectacular economic turnaround are compelling. Since 1984, inflation has fallen from around 15% to around 2%. From stagnation, the economy has moved into growth ranging from 2–5% per year. All public foreign debt has been retired and the New Zealand dollar has steadily appreciated against all major trading currencies. Foreign investment is still scrutinized but is almost always approved. Less tangibly, but of great importance, New Zealand firms and people now recognise that they are part of a global economy.

Overlying this process of change is another, with deeper roots and a longer period of resolution. This is the process of adjustment to a multicultural ethos. The main thrust of this comes from the indigenous Maori people (14% of the population), who have succeeded in bringing strong political focus to grievances resulting from claimed expropriation of land, fisheries and other rights in contravention of the Treaty of Waitangi signed by Maori representatives and Britain in 1840.

Claims resulting from this process are returning significant land holdings and fishery quotas to Maori ownership. Such changes of ownership do not, however, seem to prevent commercial utilization of the resources. Further, there is growing public acceptance for recognition of other cultures, especially those of the Pacific Islands (more Pacific Island people live in New Zealand than in their homelands) and of the Chinese immigrants from Malaysia, Hong Kong, and Taiwan.

Two major patterns emerge from study of New Zealand exports and imports. First, New Zealand relies on exports of resource-based industries and on imports of more sophisticated manufactured goods. The principal resource-based exports are those based on pastoral agriculture (dairy products, meat, wool), on renewable or plantation forestry, and on fruit growing (apples and kiwifruit). The chief categories of imports are fuels and oils, electrical and other technical equipment and machinery, vehicles, and industrial raw materials.

The second pattern is that several New Zealand industries have a high level of export market dependency. Thus, for example, more than 90% of dairy products are exported, and over half of forestry and meat products are marketed offshore. New Zealand now has a very strong sense of the need for its industries to compete favourably in regional and global markets. Trade and investment policy follows this principle.[2]

## Foreign MNC Involvement in New Zealand

With its history as a colony and then a dominion of the British Empire and Commonwealth, New Zealand's economy was dominated until the early 1960s by the United Kingdom. This was manifested at government-to-government level (such as 'advice' from London, facilitation of government borrowing, and bulk purchase arrangements for primary commodities), and also through British firms having preferential access to New Zealand markets and resources. Thus, during this period MNC involvement was predominantly British. Examples include Vestey and Borthwick in frozen meat processing and exporting, and Dalgety in primary products trading, BP, Shell, and Castrol in petroleum products, ICI in chemicals, P&O in shipping, and Norwich and Lloyds in insurance and banking. Mobil and Caltex (Texaco) were among the few American MNCs. The United Kingdom's movement toward membership in the European Common Market (now the European Union) in the late 1950s, coincided with the appearance in New Zealand of more American MNCs, such as Dow Chemical (agricultural chemicals), Caterpillar (agricultural and construction equipment), and Knudsen (hydrodam construction).

But these initiatives were modest and levels of investment were subject to strict government regulation. During the same period strong government import substitution policies resulted in establishment by MNCs of manufacturing/assembly operations that had very high costs by international standards. This policy embraced cars (Ford, General Motors, British Leyland and Rootes), foods (Unilever), television and radio equipment (Philips), and early computer developments (IBM, Burroughs, ICL, and Digital).

The rapid deregulation of the economy that began in 1984 resulted in a flood of MNC arrivals, especially relating to telecommunications and information technology, office and home electronics, wood processing, banking and financial services, and advertising. The twenty-five largest foreign MNC operations in New Zealand, in terms of turnover in New Zealand, are listed in Table 15.1. The rankings reflect more the earlier historical pattern than recent entries. Many Asian MNCs and those based on high technology are still relatively small. For example, the New Zealand turnover, in 1995, of Philips was NZ $124 million (U.S.$84 million), that of Unisys NZ$119 million (U.S.$84 million), Sony NZ$96 million (U.S.$65 million), and Motorola NZ$133 million (U.S.$90 million). Examples of Japanese trading houses are Marubeni NZ$156 million (U.S.$106 million) and Mitsui NZ$118 million (U.S.$80 million).

Several key themes emerge when industry groupings are considered. In terms of aggregate MNC turnover, the largest foreign involvement is in forestry, wood processing, and paper. The key MNC players in this industry are International Paper, Rayonier, Sumitomo, and Juken Nissho. This industry is based on a natural environment that favors rapid growth of coniferous plantation forest species, and sustainable-yield forests. The MNC approach here is investment to produce wood fiber that is exported as logs, but also increasingly as processed products such as panel wood, moldings, lumber, paper, and pulp. The long-established oil/petroleum MNCs make the second group, comprising BP, Mobil, Shell, Caltex/Texaco and Castrol. About 40% of New Zealand oil demand is met from home-based resources. The MNCs distribute both imports and locally derived products. Banking and other financial services account for the third-ranked industry for MNCs and include Lloyds Bank, Bank of Scotland, National Mutual Life, Bankers Trust, Norwich Union, CML, Guardian, Sun Alliance, CIGNA, CitiBank, and Hong Kong Bank. New Zealand has a vigorous international financial market, with some apparent advantage as the first time-zone to open for business each day.

The motor vehicle sector ranks fourth, including assembly (declining), importing (increasing), and distribution. Ford (with Mazda), Toyota, Honda, General Motors, and Nissan are the key players. The MNC theme here is the traditional one of establishing a distribution, marketing, and support presence in a small offshore market. Food processing ranks fifth, largely through the involvement of Heinz, Nestlé, and Unilever, but this industry is actually dominated by New Zealand-owned companies that focus on dairy foods and meat processing.

## Table 15.1
### Largest Foreign Multinational Companies in New Zealand

| Rank | Company Name | Main Business | Nationality | 1995 Revenues U.S.$ millions | Rank in NZ Top 200 |
|---|---|---|---|---|---|
| 1 | International Paper (via Carter Holt Harvey) | paper | U.S. | 1,880 | 5 |
| 2 | Lloyds Bank (as National Bank of New Zealand) | banking | U.K. | 912 | 3[a] |
| 3 | BP | petroleum | U.K. | 824 | 12 |
| 4 | Mobil | petroleum | U.S. | 792 | 13 |
| 5 | Shell | petroleum | U.K./Netherlands | 774 | 14 |
| 6 | Newscorp (as Independent Newspapers) | media | Australia | 630 | 15 |
| 7 | Heinz (as Heinz-Wattie) | food | U.S. | 576 | 17 |
| 8 | Caltex (Texaco) | petroleum | U.S. | 438 | 26 |
| 9 | Comalco | aluminum | Australia | 363 | 33 |
| 10 | Ford | automobiles | U.S. | 341 | 36 |
| 11 | Toyota | automobiles | Japan | 307 | 40 |
| 12 | Bank of Scotland (as CountryWide Bank) | banking | U.K. | 297 | 7[a] |
| 13 | Pacific Dunlop | rubber goods | U.K. | 292 | 44 |
| 14 | National Mutual Life | insurance | U.S. | 290 | 11[a] |
| 15 | Norwich Union | insurance | U.K. | 273 | 15[a] |
| 16 | Mitsubishi Motors (as MMC) | automobiles | Japan | 271 | 53 |
| 17 | Unilever | food | U.K./Netherlands | 252 | 57 |
| 18 | BTR | carpets | U.K. | 226 | 51 |
| 19 | ICI | chemicals | U.K. | 208 | 64 |
| 20 | Honda | automobiles | Japan | 195 | 66 |
| 21 | Nissan | automobiles | Japan | 172 | 70 |
| 22 | General Motors (as Holden) | automobiles | U.S. | 163 | 77 |
| 23 | Nestlé | food | Switzerland | 161 | 74 |
| 24 | IBM | computers | U.S. | 158 | 73 |
| 25 | Cadbury | food | U.K. | 124 | 83 |

*Note:* Companies that are primarily located in Australia/New Zealand are excluded. These include three of the four largest banks and the largest insurance company.
[a]Separate rankings of financial institutions

A broad information technology/electronics importer-distributor grouping ranks next, and includes firms such as IBM, Microsoft, Digital, Fujitsu, Motorola, Matsushita, Ericsson, ABB, Canon, Sony, Philips, Fuji-Xerox, Unisys, and Honeywell. Although this MNC sector is comparatively small, a significant theme is that the New Zealand market tends to be regarded as a low-cost and low-risk test site for new products, particularly in the telecommunications, information technology, and office equipment markets.

The final industry to be ranked here is the importation and distribution of chemical products by such MNCs as ICI, Shell, Bayer, Ciba-Geigy, BASF, Dow-Elanco, Du Pont, and 3M. All these companies run essentially importer-distributor operations. Until the late 1980s most MNC pharmaceutical companies had subsidiaries in New Zealand. Less than half remain; the others now manage their New Zealand business from subsidiaries in Australia.

In general terms, then, the MNCs that operate manufacturing or processing operations in New Zealand do so in order to utilize country-specific resources, mostly in forestry and agriculture. Distortions caused by import substitution policies obliged MNCs to establish low-volume high-cost local assembly sites for cars and consumer electronics. Removal of these policies in the early 1990s has resulted in closure of most such operations, and in reliance on importing by MNC subsidiaries. Many MNCs now view Australia and New Zealand as a single market, with some choosing to maintain just one subsidiary for the two countries. A majority of these are sited in Australia, but some—such as Motorola and Heinz—have regional group management in New Zealand. This situation is likely to continue. However, there is a strong emerging theme of the higher-technology MNCs viewing New Zealand as a favored location for test launches of emerging products in a relatively sophisticated but small (and hence low-risk) market.

## Development of New Zealand Companies

New Zealand's largest domestic companies mostly have substantial international involvement, or the potential to do so. These companies operate in four major sectors. Table 15.2 provides information about the twenty largest firms that have effective management control in New Zealand.

The first sector lies in forestry products and is dominated by New Zealand's largest company, Fletcher Challenge. The latter is a mature MNC with forestry, wood processing, pulp, and paper operations in Canada, the United Kingdom, Chile, Brazil, Australia, and New Zealand, and is the second-largest newsprint producer in the world. The company also operates construction businesses in the United States and New Zealand; manufacture, domestic distribution, and exporting of building supplies, and produces energy in New Zealand, Canada, and several other countries.

*Table 15.2*
**Largest New Zealand Companies**

| Rank | Company Name | Main Business | 1995 Revenues U.S.$ millions | Percentage Revenue Derived Offshore | Rank in NZ Top 200 |
|---|---|---|---|---|---|
| 1 | Fletcher Challenge[b] | forestry, pulp and paper, building products | 5,941 | 70[a] | 1 |
| 2 | New Zealand Dairy Board | dairy products, international marketing | 3,560 | 100 | 2 |
| 3 | Air New Zealand | airline | 2,057 | 40[a] | 3 |
| 4 | Telecom New Zealand | telecommunications | 2,008 | 5[a] | 4 |
| 5 | Brierley | investment | 1,838 | 40[a] | 6 |
| 6 | Progressive Enterprises | retailing | 1,534 | 7 | |
| 7 | New Zealand Dairy Group[c] | dairy products | 1,416 | 10[a] | 8 |
| 8 | Lion Nathan | brewing | 1,188 | 10[a] | 9 |
| 9 | ECNZ | electricity generation | 1,076 | 2[a] | 10 |
| 10 | Foodstuffs (AK) | retailing | 1,054 | 0 | 11 |
| 11 | Foodstuffs (WT) | retailing | 603 | 0 | 16 |
| 12 | Skellerup | investment | 582 | 30[a] | 18 |
| 13 | Alliance | meat processing | 555 | 95[a] | 19 |
| 14 | AFFCO | meat processing | 548 | 95[a] | 20 |
| 15 | Fisher & Paykel | appliances, office equipment | 538 | 30[a] | 21 |
| 16 | Primary Producers | food distribution | 505 | 0[a] | 22 |
| 17 | Foodstuffs (SI) | retailing | 495 | 0[a] | 23 |
| 18 | DB | brewing | 493 | 5[a] | 24 |
| 19 | Wrightsons | agricultural supply | 487 | 15[a] | 25 |
| 20 | NZ Post | postal services | 451 | 2[a] | 27 |

[a]Estimated
[b]Fletcher Challenge shares are approximately 55% offshore-owned, but management control remains with NZ.
[c]The New Zealand Dairy Board has statutory rights as the sole exporter of dairy products. NZ Dairy Group and Kiwi Dairies are the largest two of thirteen manufacturing cooperatives that supply the Dairy Board. These manufacturers hold licenses for direct exporting to Australia and other limited offshore markets. They operate independently in the domestic market.

A second sector is a vertically integrated dairy products system, comprising thirteen manufacturing cooperatives in New Zealand, offshore marketing by the New Zealand Dairy Board, and a network of R&D sites. This system is essentially a two-tier cooperative, the Dairy Board having statutory rights as the sole exporter of dairy products, the continuation of these rights being determined by the wishes of milk producers, who also own the cooperatives. The Dairy Board, itself, is an MNC with more than one hundred twenty offshore subsidiaries and joint ventures. Although exports from New Zealand dominate product offerings, manufacturing also takes place in the United States, the United Kingdom, Australia, and Chile. Marketing addresses two broad segments in accessible world markets—branded consumer and food service business, and food ingredient producers whose needs range from highly specialized and differentiated products to requirements for bulk volumes of standard specification products. The board aims to lead or be a close second in its key markets and is succeeding with this objective.

A third sector, meat based, is represented in Table 15.2 by Alliance and AFFCO which produce chilled and frozen lamb, beef, and venison for consumer and food service markets and manufacturers in numerous world markets. This group, which also includes about fifteen significant smaller companies, is trapped in the upstream end of the value system. Poor profitability, low equity ratios, and a traditional emphasis on investing in New Zealand operations have severely limited the financial resources and expertise available for offshore processing, packing, and marketing. The firms in this group are exporters, not true MNCs.

A fourth sector, fruit based, is represented by two other grower-controlled statutory marketing boards, one for apples and the other for kiwifruit. Both compete successfully in often turbulent and rapidly changing business environments. Both have invested in foreign market distribution and marketing. They have also initiated programs to source fruit from other countries, to maintain continuity of supply to retailers, given seasonal production variation. Thus, they are emergent MNCs but currently maintain an exporting focus.

Other industry sectors contain firms that have the potential to become MNCs. Examples are wine, seafood, agritech, and marine leisure products. Each sector has firms that have invested significantly offshore and some are actually small MNCs, but all have limited capabilities for achievement of rapid growth and global significance. Networking and/or mergers and acquisition would be necessary to achieve this.

A dominant theme is that the New Zealand firms that have achieved, or are in reach of, sustainable MNC scale and offshore presence are all a part of resource-based value systems that originate in forestry, production of milk, fruit, and meat, or hydro and gas-based energy. Several other manufacturing and service industries contain firms with the potential to be globally competitive but are either in specialized niche markets (such as, for example, electric fencing, racing yachts, and seismic engineering) or require enhanced capabilities to expand into broader market opportunities.

## Overall Globalization Drivers in New Zealand

New Zealand's globalization drivers vary particularly by the level of export dependency of individual industries. Industries that are focused on serving domestic markets have their potential for globalization limited by the relatively small size of these markets. On the other hand, several industries that are resource-based provide productive capacities much greater than domestic demand. The inherent export dependency of these industries requires regional and global perspectives, and their globalization drivers are not limited by the size of the New Zealand economy.

## Market Globalization Drivers

Even more so than Australia, New Zealand has primarily favorable market globalization drivers that are offset by its very small market. New Zealand consumers have a pattern of needs and expectations broadly consistent with those in other highly advanced Western economies, and marketing strategies applicable in those markets are generally transferable to New Zealand. For example, the country is among world leaders in terms of the rate of adoption of personal computers, cellular phones, and access to the Internet. The propensity for early adoption of new product concepts in consumer electronics, information technology, office equipment, and telecommunications has led to the New Zealand market being chosen by MNCs such as Motorola, Ericsson, Digital, and NEC as an early test site for distribution and marketing of new products.

New Zealand is a lead country through distinctive innovation in several industries. Examples include

1. Specialized dairy-based products, such as a calcium-enriched milk powder for Asian women seeking to avoid osteoporosis, and high-technology milk protein derivative ingredients for health foods.
2. Development of large-scale sustainable-yield conifer forests and downstream wood fiber value systems.
3. Leisure marine products (yachts, launches, and fittings) based on use of leading edge technology and design skills derived from New Zealand's preeminence in yacht racing. This racing reputation has been leveraged into success in world markets for cruising yachts and launches as well as components and fittings.

In summary, New Zealand does not contribute significantly to market globalization in terms of market scale, and is integrated with Australia to achieve further scale economies in marketing many product categories. However, its role as a test site for high-technology electronics, information technology, and software is of substantial interest to MNCs in those fields. Further, New Zealand demonstrates leadership through distinctive innovation in a number of industries.

## Cost Globalization Drivers

Given its small size and relatively high costs, New Zealand's cost globalization drivers are mostly unfavorable except in its resource-based sectors. For example, New Zealand is the world's lowest-cost producer of milk and first-stage processed dairy products. This is due to development of sophisticated farm management systems that make effective use of a temperate climate, and also results from implementation of large-scale processing plants for milk. But New Zealand markets mostly do not assist

MNCs materially with regional or global-scale economies. MNCs that link New Zealand with Australia achieve cost gains, but even when the two country markets are combined the scale is moderate by the standards of the Asia-Pacific region.

One plus is that the economic and social reforms implemented since 1984 have provided an excellent infrastructure for MNC operations, especially relating to freedom of capital movement and investment, communications, energy, roads, and a labor union movement with much reduced power.[3] Some internal country costs are relatively favorable, resulting from cheap hydroelectric sources of energy and open competition in markets for resources, products, and services. Against this, New Zealand is disadvantaged in transportation costs to its key export markets in North Asia, North America, and Europe.

## Government Globalization Drivers

New Zealand has among the most favorable government globalization drivers in the region and, indeed, the world. New Zealand is extraordinarily free of government control of enterprises, being ranked fifth out of fifty-three in the World Economic Forum's *Global Competitiveness Report 1997*, and second only to Hong Kong among Asia-Pacific countries. There are no restrictions on capital flows. While scrutinized, investment by foreign firms is approved on a very liberal basis. Tariffs still exist to protect some domestic industries (especially footwear and clothing) but these regimes are being phased out rapidly.

A peculiarity of government intervention does, however, characterize the three most successful resource-based export industries: dairy products, apples, and kiwifruit. All three international marketing operations—including investment in offshore locations and activities—are owned by producer boards that are essentially cooperatives of farmers and orchardists. Each organization has statutory authority to be the sole exporter of the defined product category. There is no other government involvement, so that the organizations operate on a fully commercial basis in offshore markets. The key rationale for these structures is to ensure that producers receive the benefits accruing from offshore processing, distribution, and marketing activities. Investment in these industries by MNCs (or any other firms) in exporting activities—and, in the case of the dairy industry, processing as well—is effectively precluded. However, the New Zealand Dairy Board has some one hundred twenty offshore enterprises, about half of which are joint ventures with foreign firms. Some forms of alliances with MNCs in downstream marketing activities are entirely feasible.

## Competitive Globalization Drivers

New Zealand's competitive globalization drivers are among the weakest in the region, probably ahead of only Vietnam's. This position derives from its small population, geographic isolation, and costs that are higher relative to most Asia-Pacific neighbors. Furthermore, many MNCs increasingly combine New Zealand with Australia for management purposes. Only in the limited number of industries, primarily resource-based, in which New Zealand is a world leader, do competitive globalization drivers encourage MNC participation.

In such industries, the major strategic position held by New Zealand is as a secure southern hemisphere source of food products derived from an environment that is apparently free of major pollutants and derived through sustainable systems of production. The value of such a source, particularly to northern hemisphere customers, lies in the counterseasonality of products, and in the reliability of supply of product that is free from major environmental contamination. This strategic positioning applies particularly to dairy products, venison, lamb, apples, and kiwifruit. The sustainable yield characteristics of New Zealand's pine forests is also an emergent source of competitive advantage in markets for furniture parts, house framing, and panel board, due to customer preferences for product origins that meet certain environmental standards.

## Overall Global Strategies for New Zealand

Recommended global strategies for New Zealand vary greatly by both the type of strategy and the industry, more so than for any other Asia-Pacific economy in this book. This variation arises from the small and specialized nature of the New Zealand economy.

### Market Participation Strategies

Because the population is small, MNCs can consider market participation strategies on a primarily opportunistic basis. On the other hand, the openness of the economy makes participation easier than in almost any other country in the region. New Zealand's high degree of similarity with Western nations in terms of both income levels and tastes also makes entry easy. Additionally, New Zealand's increasing integration with Australia makes it easy for MNCs to treat the two countries as a common market and achieve the economies of combined operations.

Each of this book's nine "focus" MNCs participates in the New Zealand market. Both Procter and Gamble and Unilever treat Australia and New Zealand as a single market, and import many products from Australia to New Zealand. Motorola is a leading importer and distributor of cellular phones in New Zealand and also operates as a reseller of airtime. The country accounts for very small volumes for Philips but is seen by that company as an important site of marketing innovation. Matsushita considers the New Zealand market to be small but to have sophisticated requirements. The company's *Panasonic* brand is a leader in several categories. Toyota participates in New Zealand by locally assembling passenger cars from imported CKD ("completely knocked down") parts and by importing assembled trucks.

## Product and Service Strategies

New Zealand's Western heritage and high standard of living mean that most global products and services are readily accepted and need little adaptation. Furthermore, the market is too small to justify adaptation. So the recommended product/service strategy for MNCs is to select from the many products and services that need little or no adaptation for New Zealand, and to forget about the few items that require external change. Both P&G and Unilever take such an approach, marketing global brands and product specifications, with sometimes minor changes in packaging. Motorola has found that global product standards are fully accepted and expected in cellular telephones. Indeed, New Zealand was an early adopter of the new digital technology. Philips and Matsushita both bring in standard products from offshore. Toyota provides an instance of some product adaptation. New Zealand's hilly, rural roads provide some special conditions. Toyota makes a ritual of the necessary adaptation, using an internationally renowned New Zealand racing driver (Chris Amon) to "suspension-tune" its vehicles. Toyota has transferred this technical adaptation to other markets with similar roads.

## Activity Location Strategies

New Zealand's high costs and remote location make it unattractive for MNCs to conduct activities there to serve foreign markets. So New Zealand can seldom play a significant role in the global value chains of MNCs. Even for serving the New Zealand market, most MNCs locate value activities elsewhere, except those requiring immediate proximity—perhaps a procurement function for raw material sourcing or selling or service activities. So P&G, Unilever, Philips, and Motorola manufacture elsewhere, but maintain local distribution, selling, and customer support functions. Matsushita relies on a third-party agent to perform the latter activities. As mentioned earlier, Toyota also conducts final assembly from imported kits for the New Zealand market, and R&D on suspension and tuning for both the local and other markets with similar needs.

## Marketing Strategies

New Zealand's cultural closeness to Western nations and its use of English make global marketing readily accepted. So most MNCs need make little adaptation of their marketing. In particular, many marketing elements, such as advertising, are often directly transferred from the United States or Australia—a common practice for P&G. Unilever also uses mostly global marketing, including for brands, although it does market some local brands. Motorola makes little adaptation in its marketing. Philips, however, produces its advertising locally and places significant stress on building local customer relationships. Matsushita uses *Panasonic* brand brochures and manuals that are standard for its English-speaking markets. Toyota also creates local advertising and ties to position itself as a "New Zealand company" through such activities as sponsoring New Zealand teams in the America's Cup Challenge in sailing.

## Competitive Move Strategies

Lastly, New Zealand's small size minimizes its role in the global competitive moves of MNCs. So in most MNCs, local New Zealand managers make only local competitive decisions and have little involvement in global competitive moves. Exceptions include New Zealand's role for Toyota in developing design-based competitive advantage in specific product aspects. Also, Motorola uses New Zealand as an early adopter site. Hence, new product introductions are made there early in the international roll-out schedule, providing information about customer and competitor response. In some instances, as in Motorola for cellular phones, the New Zealand organization is given management responsibility for the Asia-Pacific region.

## Overall Organization and Management Approaches for New Zealand

Similar to Australia, New Zealand lends itself easily to MNCs to use global organization and management approaches. In addition, many companies manage Australia and New Zealand together as a single entity, frequently with regional control in Australia. Unilever does this and has category managers in New Zealand reporting to Australia. An exception to this is brewing, where a New Zealand company (Lion Nathan), is the largest player in both countries, and has recently established a brewery in southern China. On the other hand, New Zealand subsidiaries are often allowed substantial local autonomy, given the quality of local managers and the low risk from possible mistakes.

## Conclusions

New Zealand markets can provide some attractive opportunities for MNCs, but cost-effective in-country activities are limited to importing, distribution, marketing, and customer service. Marketing strategies from offshore are highly transferable. Thus New Zealand, often in association with Australia, will continue to provide profitable markets for MNCs without contributing significantly to their scale or locational advantages. The opportunity for technology-based MNCs to use New Zealand markets as test sites will remain. This strategy could be developed by linking domestic small industries, such as specialized software and radio communications systems, to the core MNC activities. The major opportunities for MNC involvement in the New Zealand economy is through investment in resource-based value systems, both in New Zealand and offshore. The main possibilities are in forestry and wood fiber processes, fisheries, dairy, meat, and fruit. The key strategies required are to integrate production activities with strong offshore branding, product differentiation, and control over distribution. In some instances, the opportunities for foreign MNCs are as collaborative partners with New Zealand interests. For dairy products, apples, and kiwifruit, an appealing strategy is to establish transnational organizations by linking other country sources with New Zealand to meet the needs and expectations of offshore customers.

## NOTES

1. For further detail, see Simon Walker, ed., *Rogernomics Reshaping New Zealand's Economy* (Auckland: New Zealand Center for Independent Studies, 1989); and Economic Monitoring Group, "The Economy in Transition: Restructuring to 1989, New Zealand Planning Council, July 1989.

2. Increasing attention is being focused on the requirement to establish and maintain international competitive advantage with foresight about signals of change. See *Competing in the New Millenium,* TRADENZ (Wellington, 1997).

3. See Stuart Birks and Srikanta Chatterjee, eds., *The New Zealand Economy— Issues and Policies* (New Zealand: Dunmore Press, 1992).

# CHAPTER 16

# Regional Groupings— ASEAN, AFTA, APEC, Etc.

*Mari Kondo and George S. Yip*

REGIONAL TRADE GROUPINGS provide strong glue to the highly diverse Asia-Pacific region. In addition, these groupings play an increasingly large role in stimulating economic growth and easing the participation of multinational companies (MNCs) in individual countries and in the region as a whole. Lastly, the groupings strengthen the region's links and bargaining power with the rest of the world. Asia-Pacific's alphabet soup of ASEAN, AFTA, APEC, etc. will soon become as familiar to the world as the EC (now EU), OPEC, and NAFTA. For MNCs, these groupings offer many ways to bypass trade barriers and restrictions, and to benefit from government subsidies and favors. In terms of the framework of this book, these groupings play a role in government globalization drivers. In this chapter, we focus on the groupings themselves, while in the individual country chapters we have discussed the extent to which these arrangements are relevant for a particular country. Readers should note that many of the official policies described in this chapter constitute intentions rather than reality.

## The Major Groupings

Unlike Western Europe or North America, and more like South America, Asia-Pacific does not have one encompassing trade bloc but a wide variety of independent, overlapping arrangements. The most important single grouping is ASEAN (Association of South East Asian Nations) founded in 1967, by Indonesia, Malaysia, the Philippines, Singapore, and Thailand, as a political and ideological bloc. Brunei joined soon after 1967. Its member states believed that forming a regional bloc would set in place relevant mechanisms to encourage cooperation and unity among the members, and strengthen ASEAN's bargaining position in international negotiations. Vietnam was admitted to membership in 1995 and Myanmar and Laos in 1997. After the violent coup d'état in Cambodia in 1997, that country's admission was postponed. ASEAN has evolved to become a trade bloc through the mechanism of AFTA, the ASEAN Free Trade Area. Overlapping with ASEAN are a number of broader and looser arrangements: APEC (Asia-Pacific Economic Cooperation)—an enormous grouping that spans both sides of the Pacific Ocean from Canada to Australia and Chile; ARF (ASEAN Regional Forum)—includes ASEAN nations and Russia, Laos, and Cambodia; and ASEM (Asia-Europe Meeting)—a forum that includes the European Union, Japan, China, and South Korea. Figure 16.1 depicts these groupings. Several other smaller groupings exist, such as ANZCERTA (Australian New Zealand Closer Economic Relations Trade Agreement) and SAARC (South Asian Association for Regional Cooperation—India, Pakistan, Bangladesh, Nepal, Sri Lanka, and the Maldives). In addition, an increasingly important arrangement takes the form of "growth triangles" or "growth polygons"—these cover contiguous areas of two or more countries, a prime example being SIJORI (Singapore, Johor Baharu in Malaysia, and the Riau islands in Indonesia).

## ASEAN

ASEAN began with political cohesion against regional threats as its primary objective. Economic objectives have since developed. After its founding, ASEAN made several attempts at regional economic cooperation. The earliest was the 1976 Bali Summit whose efforts were formalized in the Kuala Lumpur Summit in 1977, through a meeting of the

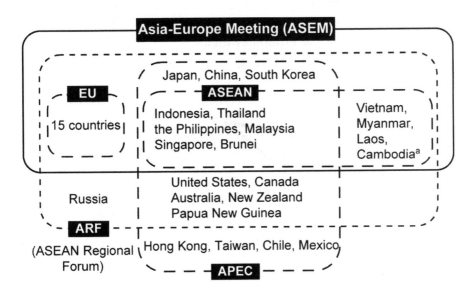

**Figure 16.1**  Trade Groupings—Asia and the Rest of the World. *Source:* Yukifumi Takeuchi, correspondent for *Asahi Shimbun*, Asian General Bureau, Bangkok, reported in "Europe Again Finds Asia Important," *Bangkok Post*, November 10, 1995, 4A
[a]Cambodia's membership in ASEAN has been temporarily postponed.

ASEAN Economic Ministers. During this time five special committees were formed, namely the Committee on Trade and Tourism; the Committee on Industry, Minerals, and Energy; the Committee on Food Agriculture and Forestry; the Committee on Transportation and Communication, and the Committee on Finance and Banking. The committees had the mission to start easing trade restrictions in their sectors. These efforts were reinforced by the implementation of the Preferential Trading Arrangement in 1977, ASEAN Industrial Projects in 1980, the ASEAN Industrial Complementation Scheme in 1981, and the ASEAN Joint Venture Scheme in 1983.

## Preferential Trading Arrangement (PTA)

The formulation of the PTA marked ASEAN's very first attempt at preferential trade liberalization, but has not been successful. Signed in 1977, by the ASEAN member foreign ministers, the PTA was unlike other regional trading arrangements because it did not specify any intention to become a customs union or free trade area. Instead, the PTA provided a mechanism whereby all the participating countries could choose the pace of intra-ASEAN trade liberalization. Under the PTA, member states can choose to utilize several instruments or transactions, including long-term quantity contracts, at preferential interest or financing rates, preference in procurement by Government entities, extension of tariff preferences; liberalization of nontariff measures on a preferential basis, and other measures. Very few products were approved for preferential tariff reductions at the outset of PTA. The situation did not improve much as its implementation lengthened. Three years after its implementation, the nature of the PTA was changed from voluntary to an across-the-board approach—a 20% preferential tariff cut applied to all intraregional imports falling under a certain ceiling value. This ceiling was continually elevated until it was eliminated in 1984.

Several factors contributed to the pale performance of the PTA. Foremost of these was the ability of the countries to grant preferences on goods not traded in the region or on goods that already had zero tariffs. Another factor was the high ASEAN content requirement of at least 50%. A significant factor that hindered the success of PTA was the long exclusions list submitted by participating countries. Member countries preferred to exclude heavily traded goods and products that were efficiently produced by other member countries. Although ASEAN tried to incorporate more changes to the PTA framework during the third ASEAN summit in Manila in 1987, the changes did not in any way improve the performance of PTA.

## ASEAN Industrial Projects (AIP)

The Basic Agreement on ASEAN Industrial Projects was formulated to facilitate the assigning of large-scale, government-initiated projects to the different member countries, but has also essentially failed. It gave priority to projects that utilized available resources in member states and that contributed to the increase in food production and foreign exchange earnings, or that saved foreign exchange and created employment.

Under the Agreement it was expected that each member would take charge of hosting at least one project that would benefit the entire ASEAN market. The host would hold 60% of the project's equity with the balance shared by the other states. Originally, five projects were designated. These included the urea fertilizer project for Indonesia and Malaysia, a copper fabrication project for the Philippines, a hepatitis-B vaccination program for Singapore, and a rock soda ash project for Thailand. Unfortunately the AIP was not successful in its objectives. Only two out of these five AIP projects were ever implemented.

## ASEAN Industrial Complementation (AIC)

The ASEAN Industrial Complementation Scheme constitutes the group's first successful trade liberalization program. The main objective of AIC is to divide different production stages of an industry among ASEAN countries so that companies in each can increase economies of scale. In 1983, the first stage of the AIC concerning the production and distribution of automotive parts and components was launched. The initial effects were not substantial due to the differences in ASEAN production facilities. As a response to the deficiencies of the first attempt, the second attempt employed a new strategy called Brand-to-Brand Complementation (BBC), specifically addressed to the production of particular automobile brands. The BBC scheme is an arrangement whereby specified parts or components of a specific vehicle model are traded and used by the brand owners and brand-related original equipment manufacturers. In other words, producers of a particular component can ship to other ASEAN countries tariff-free provided they take the equivalent value of other components of the same brand in return. Three countries chose not to join the BBC program—Singapore and Brunei had no automotive sector, while Indonesia had placed its automotive industry and market under protection.

Compared to the first attempt, the BBC scheme is more successful. At least eight companies have participated, namely Mitsubishi, Volvo, Mercedes Benz, Nissan, Toyota, DAF, and Renault. (In Chapter 9 on Thailand, we discussed how Toyota uses this scheme—see also Figure 9.1.) In 1991, the BBC scheme was amended to apply not only to automotive parts but also to non-automotive. Recently, Indonesia decided to join the scheme along with the original participating members: Malaysia, the Philippines, and Thailand.

## ASEAN Free Trade Area (AFTA)

AFTA constitutes ASEAN's most extensive effort at trade liberalization, and is meeting with increasing success. Motivations for forming AFTA were the need to respond to other regions' trade groupings and to the emergence of new markets such as China and Vietnam. Other factors included the need to globalize production networks due to the growing interdependence of countries in resources and MNC activities. With Vietnam's entry in 1995, AFTA became a market of 400 million consumers with immense purchasing capability.

AFTA was formalized in the 4th ASEAN Summit in Singapore in January 1992. All six ASEAN members joined AFTA, as has Vietnam since it joined ASEAN. AFTA is based on the principle of liberal protectionism where there will be free trade between the members of the trade bloc. The principles of AFTA are embodied in three different documents:

*Singapore Declaration of 1992.* This document contains the details concerning political and security cooperation, directions in ASEAN economic cooperation, external relations, functional cooperation, and restructuring of ASEAN institutions.

*Framework Agreement on Enhancing ASEAN Economic Cooperation.* This framework agreement contains the principles for strengthening economic cooperation between member states. Furthermore, this document defines the principles and areas of economic cooperation and acknowledges the importance of subregional economic arrangements, extra-ASEAN economic cooperation, and sector participation. It also identifies the monitoring, review, and arbitration body for provisions contained in the agreement.

*Agreement on the Common Effective Preferential Tariff (CEPT) Scheme for the AFTA.* This document provides for the different mechanisms of AFTA. The general provisions of the agreement, product coverage, schedule of tariff reductions, quantitative restrictions and nontariff barriers, foreign exchange restrictions, other areas of cooperation, maintenance of concessions, emergency measures, institutional arrangements, consultations, and general exceptions are also defined in this document.

The mechanism used to implement AFTA is the Common Effective Preferential Tariff (CEPT) scheme, the most important part of AFTA. CEPT is a cooperative arrangement among the ASEAN member states to reduce regional tariffs from their current levels to the 0–5% level, and remove nontariff barriers over a fifteen-year period starting in 1993. The goods that are included in this scheme are all manufactured products and processed agricultural goods. Figure 16.2 presents the average CEPT rates for each member country for the periods 1992–2003.

There are three instances when products may be excluded from the conditions set under CEPT: (1) general exceptions for products that relate to the protection of national security, morals, human, animal or plant life, and protection of articles with artistic, historical or archaeological value; (2) a temporary list subject to review after eight years—products that are considered sensitive and that need more time for development and innovation in order to withstand competition from products of other member economies; and (3) unprocessed agricultural products, defined as agricultural raw materials and products that have undergone simple processing with minimal change in form from other original products.

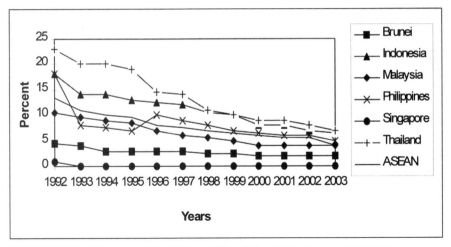

**Figure 16.2** Average CEPT Rates in AFTA 1992—2003. *Source:* ASEAN Secretariat.

To qualify for CEPT, a product must fulfill the 40% ASEAN content requirement. The local content rule can be taken in the context of content coming from one or more ASEAN countries. Figure 16.3 shows the formula for computing the 40% ASEAN content requirement.

There are fifteen commodity groups under the "fast-track program" by which products that have tariffs above 20% must be reduced to 20% by 1998, and then gradually to 0–5% by 2000. Meanwhile, for products with a tariff rate of 20% or below, tariffs must be reduced to 0–5% by 1998. Under the "normal track program" the tariff on specified products are being reduced to 0–5% within a period of seven to ten years beginning in 1993. Products with tariff rates above 20% must be reduced to 20% by 2000 while products with tariff rates of 20% or below must go down to 0–5% by 2003.

Many significant changes have been introduced to the AFTA document. First, the original timetable was accelerated to ten years instead of fifteen years (i.e., AFTA is expected to be fully implemented by 2003,

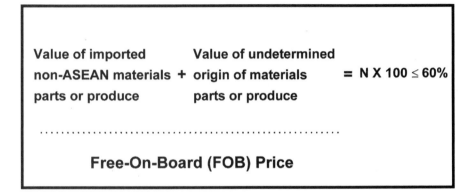

**Figure 16.3** Formula for 40% ASEAN Content

rather than the original target date of 2008). The implication of this is that by the year 2000, 90% of tariff lines included in the CEPT will have tariff rates of 5% or even less. In the new timetable, both the fast and normal track schedules were accelerated (Table 16.1).

Another change that was implemented concerns the inclusion of unprocessed agricultural products under the CEPT scheme. By 1996, nearly 1,358 tariff lines representing 68% of all unprocessed agricultural items were included in the CEPT scheme.

During its seventh meeting in Indonesia, the AFTA Council approved the transfer of products from the temporary exclusion list (TEL) of the CEPT to the inclusion list. The AFTA Council approved that products under the temporary exclusion list will be integrated in five equal installments starting January 1995, and concluding in January 2000. A total of 682 tariff lines were transferred from the TEL into the inclusion list, such as inorganic and organic chemicals and plastics, which are among the fastest growing traded commodities within the ASEAN region.

The AFTA Council has started discussion concerning the elimination of nontariff barriers (NTBs) in ASEAN. The deadline of November 1995 was issued by the AFTA Council concerning the schedule of reduction of priority barriers. The AFTA Council observed that most NTBs affecting intra-ASEAN trade were technical standards and customs surcharges.

The inclusion of services in AFTA was proposed during the September 1994 AEM and an ASEAN Framework Agreement on Services has been signed. The Agreement aims to strengthen and enhance trade in services among the ASEAN member countries through improving efficiency and competitiveness, diversifying production capacity, and supplying and facilitating distribution of services within and outside the region. Participating countries have identified seven priority sectors for this agreement: financial services, tourism, telecommunications, maritime transport, air

*Table 16.1*
**AFTA/CEPT Accelerated Tariff Reduction Schedule**

|  | Old Timetable | Accelerated Timetable |
| --- | --- | --- |
| *Normal Track* |  |  |
| Tariffs > 20% | 20% by 2001 | 20% by 1998 |
|  | 15% by 2003 | 0–5% by 2003 |
|  | 10% by 2007 |  |
|  | 0–5% by 2007 |  |
| Tariffs ≤ 20% | 15% by 2003 | 0–5% by 2000 |
|  | 10% by 2005 |  |
|  | 0–5% by 2007 |  |
|  |  |  |
| *Fast Track* |  |  |
| Tariffs > 20% | 0–5% by 2003 | 0–5% by 2000 |
| Tariffs < 20% | 0–5% by 2000 | 0–5% by 1998 |

*Source:* ASEAN Secretariat.

transport, construction services, and business services. Presently meetings are already being held at the official level to establish the format, guidelines for the conduct of negotiations, plans, schedules of future negotiation meetings, and exchange of information on the service regimes of the participating countries.

ASEAN is likewise looking into other frameworks aimed at further strengthening and deepening ASEAN economic cooperation to help ASEAN move toward greater integration. One of these is the ASEAN Industrial Cooperation Scheme (AICO). AICO provides the guidelines and institutional framework within which the private sector may collaborate on the basis of mutual and equitable benefits to increase industrial production for the region as a whole. Products within the scope of AICO are final products and intermediate and raw materials to be used by participating companies in the production of final products. Each of the participating companies must submit documentary evidence on resource sharing or industrial cooperation activities such as joint ventures, joint manufacturing, technology transfer, training, licensing, consolidated purchasing and procurement, management services, sales and marketing agreements, and other areas of cooperation.

Products to be included should be at the HS eight-digit level and above and must meet the Rules of Origin of the CEPT scheme. Participating companies will enjoy various privileges. For instance, approved AICO products traded between participating companies shall enjoy preferential trading rates of 0% to 5%, to be forfeited when the tariff rate of the product reaches the final CEPT rate. Another privilege is that local content accreditation shall be accorded where applicable to products manufactured by participating companies. There are also some nontariff incentives offered by the respective national authorities.

Some progress has been achieved in nonborder measures of facilitation. These include harmonization of tariff nomenclatures in ASEAN at the eight-digit level by 1997. The need for harmonization of common custom procedures, import and export procedures, and other common procedures has also been recognized. The elimination of nontariff barriers related to technical standards is likewise being given attention by the ASEAN Committee on Standards and Quality.

The AFTA document has undergone major changes in the very short span of four years. Many factors have contributed to its evolution such as the Uruguay Round negotiations, ratification of the new World Trade Organization (WTO), developments in APEC, and other economic activities in the region and in the world.

## APEC

Asia-Pacific Economic Cooperation (APEC) is a grouping of all the significant economies on both sides of the Pacific and was created in 1989. Its current eighteen members comprise Japan, South Korea, China, Chinese Taipei (Taiwan), Hong Kong, the Philippines, Indonesia, Brunei

Darussalam, Papua New Guinea, Malaysia, Thailand, Singapore, Australia, New Zealand, Canada, the United States, Mexico, and Chile. It has the strengths and weaknesses of such a large group. To date it has provided more bold declarations, such as the dramatic one in 1994 announcing totally free trade by 2020, than concrete actions. The United States, its largest member, has gone back and forth in its commitment to using APEC as a vehicle for collective trade liberalization. In contrast, the United States currently seems to prefer bilateral bargaining, for example, with Japan and China; or unilateral actions, such as the secondary boycotts of Cuba, Libya, and Iran.

The specific objectives of APEC include the promotion of free and open trade and investment in Asia-Pacific by 2010, for industrialized economies, and by 2020, for developing economies. APEC aims to reduce barriers to trade in goods, services, and investment among member economies in a manner consistent with GATT principles. It seeks to sustain the growth and development of the region by encouraging economic interdependence among its members.

The APEC meeting at Bogor, Indonesia, in 1994 adopted the major provisions of the Declaration of Common Resolve:

- the strengthening of open multilateral systems by accelerating the implementation of the Uruguay Round agreements, working for the deepening and broadening of the Uruguay Round outcomes, and continuing the process of unilateral trade and investment liberalization;
- the adoption of a long-term goal of free and open trade and investment in Asia-Pacific, the completion of which will be by the year 2010 for industrialized economies and 2020 for developing economies;
- the expansion and acceleration of APEC's trade and investment facilitation programs;
- the development of human and natural resources to ensure sustainable growth, equitable development, reduction of economic disparities, and improvement of the economic and social well-being of the people of the Asia-Pacific region.

It should be noted that none of the heads of state making the Bogor declaration of free trade in APEC by 2010 and 2020, expect to still be in office by those years! So they face no specific pressures for implementation.

Some APEC member economies have already implemented steps to liberalize unilateral trade. For example, Australia has reduced tariffs of 15% or 10% in four stages so that, by 1996, most of its industries had tariff rates between 0–5%. Average tariffs in Indonesia also fell from 27% to 20% by 1993. In May 1995, average tariffs in Indonesia were brought to as low as 15%, and a time-bound schedule of tariff reductions had also been announced. Other member economies are following the trend in tariff reduction.

Trade in services has been increasing among the member economies. The annual growth of traded services over the period of 1980–93 was nearly at 8%, compared with just 5% for trade in merchandise. The service sector has also been attracting foreign direct investment. As foreign direct investment increases, the transactions concerning the provision of long-distance services, including the movement of skilled personnel, also expand. Many member economies of the APEC region have engaged in the production and trade of commercial services.

After each annual APEC ministerial meeting, member economies develop respective Action Plans that contain specific and concrete details of how they will implement and realize the Action Agenda from the meeting. These Action Programs are then submitted during the next year's APEC Ministerial Meeting.

## Pacific Economic Cooperation Council

A prime mover of APEC is a nongovernment, tripartite organization called the Pacific Economic Cooperation Council (PECC). PECC brings together people from three separate fields: scholars, businesspeople, and government officials in their private capacities. Founded in 1980, PECC now comprises twenty-two Member Committees representing the economies of Australia, Brunei, Canada, Chile, China, Colombia, Hong Kong, Indonesia, Japan, Korea, Malaysia, Mexico, New Zealand, Peru, the Philippines, Russia, Singapore, Chinese Taipei, Thailand, the United States, Vietnam, and the Pacific Island Nations. PECC has defined the roles that it intends to perform for the Pacific Arena. It seeks to promote greater economic cooperation by encouraging regional consultation, coordinating information, addressing economic problems, reducing friction, promoting Pacific interests in global discussions, and promoting public awareness.

Aside from member committees coming from different countries, PECC has two other members that are nongovernment organizations (NGOs) in the same area. One of these NGOs is the Pacific Basin Economic Council (PBEC), while the other is Pacific Trade and Development (PFTAD). Founded in 1967, the Pacific Basin Economic Council (PBEC) is an association of business leaders from all over Asia-Pacific. It is basically a forum through which regional business leaders pursue common objectives. PBEC is composed of one thousand one hundred corporate members coming from nineteen developed and developing economies, namely Australia, Canada, Chile, the People's Republic of China, Colombia, Fiji, Hong Kong, Indonesia, Japan, Korea, Malaysia, Mexico, New Zealand, Peru, the Philippines, Russia, Chinese Taipei, Thailand, and the United States.

The other NGO that is also an active member of PECC is Pacific Trade and Development (PFTAD). It is a regionwide organization in the Pacific that is regarded as the intellectual force behind the cooperation movement. Its leadership is composed of liberal- and market-oriented economists from Japan, Australia, New Zealand, and the United States.

## Australia-New Zealand Closer Economic Relations Trade Agreement (ANZCERTA)

In 1983, the Australia-New Zealand Closer Economic Relations Trade Agreement (ANZCERTA) was formally established. Both countries felt that forging such an agreement would be beneficial to their trade relations in general. The main goal of the agreement was to gradually but progressively eliminate barriers to trade between the two countries based on an agreed schedule. Five years after its creation, ANZCERTA was subjected to a general review and acceleration. Further refining of its provisions was also implemented during the reviews done in 1992 and 1995. Before 1983, 80% of the value of trade between the two countries was already duty free. ANZCERTA was specifically aimed at the highly protected manufacturing industries of both countries.

When ANZCERTA was forged in 1983, it set the deadline of 1995 to achieve its goal of free trade in goods, especially those of the highly protected manufacturing industries. But this schedule was accelerated by five years during the 1988 review when the business sector saw the benefits that ANZCERTA was producing, such as a better trading environment brought about by industrial rationalization and harmonization.

ANZCERTA took a major step when it included services in the free trade arrangement, the very first international trade agreement to initiate such an action. It came up with the Trade in Services Protocol which provides for free trade in services applying the concept of national treatment. Some service sectors were excluded such as telecommunications, broadcasting, maritime transport, postal services, banking, and insurance. New Zealand and Australia removed broadcasting and banking respectively in the 1992 review. At present, some service sectors are still exempt from certain provisions of the protocol although the principle of free trade is applicable to all new service industries.

In 1995, plans began to link ANZCERTA with other regional groupings such as AFTA and Mercosur (in South America). During the AFTA-CER meeting in Brunei in 1995, it was agreed by the participants that both regions should work for information exchange, human resource development, customs matters, standards and conformance, trade and investment facilitation and promotion, competition policy, and industrial cooperation. ANZCERTA and Mercosur have likewise held discussions focusing on trade policy and trade facilitation with the objective of strengthening commercial linkages between the two regions.

## Asia-Europe Initiatives

The leaders of the European Union and key East Asian countries held a meeting in 1996 to improve economic relationships between the two re-

## Southern China Growth Triangle

The Southern China growth area is currently composed of Hong Kong, Macau, Taipei, China, and the four special economic zones (SEZs) in South China: Shenzhen, Zhuhai, Shantou in Guangdong, and Xiamen in Fujian. (These four economic zones were specially chosen due to their proximity to the capital abundant economies of Hong Kong and Taiwan. Most of the Chinese in Taiwan and Hong Kong can trace their ancestral origins to these provinces in southern China.) The growth triangle was established during the mid-1980s as a reaction to the changing economic climate within the region. Special rights and privileges were given to Guangdong and Fujian in 1979 to attract foreign investors to the area: tax concessions, lowering of land use fees, land exploitation fees, and road tolls, and lower charges for water, electricity, and telephone service. The local government of Guangdong and Fujian also made simplified investor procedures and requirements.

Each of the territories located at the Pearl River Delta growth area (around Guangzhou) has some factor endowments complementary to those of the other territories. Hong Kong, Macau, and Taipei possess financial resources, technology, managerial capability, and marketing skills. Hong Kong is abundant in entrepreneurs, excellent infrastructure, communications facilities, and electric supply systems. Taiwanese capital is readily available due to its huge trade surpluses. Guangdong and Fujian have manpower and land. They are rich in natural resources and are near markets or corporate bases. Furthermore, the central government invested substantial amounts over the past two decades to transform these special economic zones into a haven for investors. Among the participants of this growth area, Hong Kong and Guangdong province within the Pearl River Delta have enjoyed the longest interaction. Hong Kong investors were attracted to Guangdong's special economic zones and invested mainly in labor-intensive export-oriented manufacturing industries.

Most of the companies in these special economic zones operate in labor-intensive and light industries: toys, plastic products, electrical appliances, hardware, and machinery. Small and medium enterprise investors from Hong Kong and Macau employ an average of five hundred workers each. Most production in this area is exported to other countries because of government restrictions in marketing the products in the domestic market. Finished or semifinished products are shipped back to their base, such as Hong Kong or Macau, where final touches are made depending on the tastes and preferences of the export markets. The marketing of the product is done from the home base of the company outside the special economic zones.

Guangzhou, the capital city of Guangdong, is now veering away from manufacturing and other labor-intensive industries. It is instead gearing toward becoming a center for wholesalers and retailers. It is also competing with other cities to become a major service hub. In Zhongshan, more than one thousand joint ventures have been announced. Most of the industries in these joint ventures specialize in footwear, garments, electronic components and other light industries.

Xiamen is the special economic zone in the province of Fujian, covering 131 square kilometers. Due to the proximity of Fujian to Taiwan, most of the investors in Xiamen are Taiwanese. Light industries account for more than 50% of the total industrial output value of Xiamen. With the rapid development of Xiamen, certain infrastructure improvements have to be constructed in order to accommodate the demands of economic development. Several projects have been initiated in Xiamen: construction of four new deep water berths, a bridge or tunnel to connect Xiamen to the mainland, and a motorway linking Fuzhou, Xiamen, and Zhongzhou. Facilities are also being improved with the electrification of Ying-Xia, and installation of a digital telephone exchange and a microwave telecommunications system.

Policy makers in China see the importance of well-developed infrastructure facilities. China has agreed to create a high-level coordinating group with Hong Kong to hasten infrastructure development in the Pearl River Delta. This group will coordinate the use of airspace by the new airports in Shenzhen, Hong Kong, Macau, and Zhuhai, streamline and improve border checkpoints, and solve problems concerning the proposed new crossborder rail links.

A joint venture has been identified by China and Hong Kong to transport railway freight containers between the colony and Zhengzhou. A comprehensive range of services will be provided by the joint venture of Kowloon Canton Railway Corporation and China Railway Container Transport Center. The services include trucking, storage, transshipment, and container rental and repair.

Many factors contributed to the success of the South China growth triangle. First of all, the common cultural background of the members contributed to the establishment of the growth triangle. A large proportion of the Hong Kong population traces its roots to the province of Guangdong. The similarity in language and cultural practices enhances understanding between the players. Another contributing factor to the success of the growth triangle is the government support that each territory extended to the project. Through the initiative of the People's Republic of China to implement its open-door policy, many foreign investors were attracted to invest in the area, hastening the development of infrastructure and leading to rapid growth.

To ensure the continued growth and further expansion of the southern China growth area certain issues must be addressed by the participating members. First, the dwindling supply of quality or skilled labor. There is a surplus of eight million laborers in Guangdong province alone, but most of these laborers are unskilled and unfamiliar with technical details of production. At present, the Pearl River Delta area is going into heavy and high-technology industries, increasing the demand for skilled laborers. Policies must be implemented to attract skilled workers into these industries and to encourage companies to conduct training programs to address the problem of a dwindling supply of skilled laborers. Second, there is a need for coordination among participating members as the southern China growth area continues to expand to other municipalities within the Pearl River Delta. Members of the southern China growth area must coordinate their industrial policies so as to simplify business transactions and other procedures in the growth area.

## SIJORI Growth Triangle

One of the ASEAN growth triangles that is looked upon as a successful model of economic cooperation in the region is the SIJORI growth triangle, composed of Singapore, the Malaysian state of Johor Baharu, and the Riau islands in Indonesia, all located along a strategic route—the Straits of Malacca. SIJORI essentially combines Singaporean money, management, and technology with Malaysian and Indonesian labor, land, and markets. Singapore has an area of only 626 square kilometers, with no spare land, and is situated between Johor and Riau. Johor is the fourth largest state of Malaysia just above Singapore, with a land area of 18,961 square kilometers. Johor is fertile and crops are planted all year round in its many plantations. The province of Riau has several islands: Batam, Bintan, Bulan, and other small islands within the archipelago of Indonesia. The islands have abundant idle land, natural resources, and manpower.

SIJORI is attractive to foreign investors because of several factors. First, rules and regulations on foreign trade and investments in the participating regions complement each other. Investors suffer less delay and bureaucratic red tape. Second, the participating countries offer attractive incentive packages. Third, SIJORI boasts of a large market base—the Indonesian and Malaysian markets. Fourth, SIJORI offers lower production costs. Finally, well-built infrastructure makes relocation less problematic.

Six years after the creation of SIJORI in 1990, Johor and the islands of Riau still enjoy unparalleled growth. Many industries have relocated to Johor: textiles, electronics, rubber products, food, and wood products. For the last three years, some thirty thousand jobs have been created annually. Johor continues to have ambitious plans for the future. It hopes to increase the number of industrial estates from fourteen to twenty-one by 2001. Johor is attracting other investors, especially chemical, metal, and electronics industries. Johor puts a premium on technology. Its policy makers believe that technology will spell the difference in the development of the province and of the growth triangle in general. To realize this belief, the state government has approved the development of the Johor Technology Park.

The islands of Riau have benefitted from the creation of SIJORI, rapidly transforming into industrial centers and tourist destination spots from mere idle agricultural lands. Due to economic development, Batam island has experienced a rapid increase in population growth, from six thousand to one hundred twenty thousand people. Tourism is thriving. Hotels, resorts, golf courses, restaurants, and other facilities and services are being provided by the islands, creating more job opportunities for its people. The Salim Group, Wah Chang International, and Keppel Corporation are drawing up plans for the construction of a world-class resort with complete facilities and services. Batam is improving its infrastructure by expanding its airport and port to accommodate bigger aircraft and ships. Both Bintan and Bulan islands are enjoying a developing agribusiness industry which is turning into a major economic activity in these islands. Some industries thriving in the islands are hog raising, orchid cultivation, and crocodile and poultry farming.

The success of SIJORI can be attributed to several factors. First is political will. The governments of Singapore, Malaysia, and Indonesia displayed high levels of political commitment to the development of the growth triangle. They supported the undertakings of the different investors with complementary government policies. Second is the complementary factor endowments of each participating region. Johor has large tracts of available land, skilled and semiskilled labor, and physical infrastructure. Singapore has sophisticated financial marketing and service industries, excellent supporting infrastructure, and highly skilled human capital. Riau has land and manpower. Third, geographical proximity. The distance between Singapore and Johor is only 1.2 kilometers and the islands of Batam and Bitan are an hour's ferry ride from Singapore.

## BIMP-East ASEAN Growth Area

The Brunei-Indonesia-Malaysia-Philippines East ASEAN Growth Area (BIMP-EAGA) was established during the inaugural ministerial meeting in Davao, Philippines in 1994. Initiated by the President of the Philippines, Fidel V. Ramos, as a counterpart to the other growth areas in the region, BIMP-EAGA is composed of several provinces: East and West Kalimantan and North Sulawesi in Indonesia; Sabah, Sarawak, and Labuan in Malaysia; Brunei; and Mindanao and Palawan in the Philippines.

The growth area covers six hundred ninety-five thousand square kilometers and has a total population of twenty-eight million. It aims to take advantage of the different factor endowments of the region to foster the growth of trade, tourism, and investment. It aims to facilitate the movement of people, goods, and services, to share infrastructure facilities, and promote industrial complementation. There are numerous and varied areas of cooperation that the participants of the BIMP-EAGA are currently exploring. Four areas of cooperation have been identified for immediate attention and implementation: the expansion of air and sea linkages, expansion of transport and shipping facilities, joint development of the tourism industry, and expansion of the cooperation on fisheries. Other areas of cooperation that have likewise been identified by the different working groups are energy, forestry, agribusiness, people mobility, telecommunications, human resource development, construction and construction materials, capital formation and financial services, and environmental protection and management.

Since the formation of BIMP-EAGA, the participants have signed a memorandum of understanding granting landing rights to designated airlines. Air linkages already exist between Davao and Manado, Zamboanga and Labuan, and Cebu and Kota Kinabalu. More frequent flights are also plying the Brunei, Sarawak, and Sabah routes. In 1995, Brunei was granted landing rights to four areas in the Philippines. New sea routes have been opened up between Sandakan and Zamboanga, and General Santos and Bitung (Indonesia). New sea routes are being proposed between Davao City (Philippines) and Bitung, and between Davao City and Muara (Brunei). The travel tax on visitors traveling from the Philippines to the BIMP-EAGA region has likewise been lifted.

Most of the EAGA working groups have held at least two or three meetings to discuss their action agenda. Some of the agreements that have been reached at the level of working groups relative to the EAGA are the following:

- acceleration of free trade in the BIMP-EAGA on selected fishery products;
- harmonization of policies, rules, and regulations on forestry;
- establishment of a joint Maritime Training Center Network in the BIMP-EAGA;
- negotiation of new service agreements with member countries to ensure that the frequency and capacity will be available to facilitate the movement of tourists to and within the region;
- setting up of a BIMP-EAGA fund for development and commercial purposes;
- reduction or elimination of crossborder regulations on tariffs, trade, and access to market for construction and construction materials.

As of October 31, 1995, a total of U.S.$2.35 billion worth of joint venture agreements had been signed by the members of the EAGA business community. Some of these agreements include

- a $20 million joint venture between Sarawak Economic Development Corporation of Malaysia and Nova Vista Management and Development;
- a Philippines company to establish a coconut processing factory in Southern Mindanao;
- PT Bintang Utara Bumibahari Manado of Indonesia and South Star Telecom of the Philippines to carry out a joint study on communications systems, design, installation, and commissioning for marine, air, and land applications, committing an investment of $15 million;
- R. D. Fishing Industry of the Philippines and PT Asa Engineering Pertama Jakarta of Indonesia have jointly invested a total of $8 million for the construction of a hotel in General Santos City, Davao, Philippines;

- a joint shipping service by PT Prima Comexindo of Indonesia and Southern Ship Handlers Inc., of the Philippines;
- a joint telecommunications investment by Marbel Telephone System Inc.. of the Philippines and Sun Moon Star of Taiwan;
- a joint venture by Agro Hope Sdn Bhd, a subsidiary of Shalimar Development Sdn Bhd and PT Bohindas Permai of Indonesia to develop an eighteen thousand hectare oil palm plantation in Kalimantan, Indonesia.

A private sector counterpart of the BIMP-EAGA government sector has been formed, called the EAGA Business Council. At present it is in the process of establishing a full-time secretariat to assist in the promotion of the economic activities of the EAGA.

### IMT-North ASEAN Growth Area

The newest growth triangle in the ASEAN region is the Indonesia-Malaysia-Thailand (IMT) growth triangle, or the North ASEAN growth area. The territories included are North Sumatra and the Special Territory of Aceh in Indonesia; the northern states of Kedah, Perak, Penang, and Perlis in Peninsular Malaysia; and the southern provinces of Satun, Songkhla, Yala, Narathiwat, and Pattani in Thailand. The total population of these areas amounts to twenty-one million and the total area is two hundred thousand square kilometers.

The Asian Development Bank conducted a year-long study upon the request of the governments of Indonesia, Malaysia, and Thailand about the feasibility of a growth triangle among the three countries. The initial findings of the study revealed strong complementarities among the participating areas of the growth triangle. The study listed five priority sectors where the three countries can initiate cooperation: trade, investment and labor mobility, agriculture and fisheries, industry and energy, and tourism.

The formation of the North ASEAN growth triangle is expected to bring complementary benefits to the participating provinces. The fast development of the growth triangle is needed to further boost intra-ASEAN trade and investment. The successful economic integration of these provinces is expected to result in a borderless network of production processes.

The three countries have agreed to jointly promote certain industries and economic activities. Among the agreements are

- joint promotion of the tourism industry within the participating provinces;
- promotion of agroprocessing and fruit cultivation industries;
- relocation of labor-intensive sectors of the electronics industry from Penang (Malaysia) to southern Thailand and northern Sumatra (Indonesia);
- construction of rubberwood processing mills in southern Thailand;

- development of export-oriented industrial estates in northern Sumatra and southern Thailand.

A total of U.S.$15–$20 billion over a ten-year period will be required to finance the high- and medium-priority development projects of the growth triangle. The funding of the numerous projects and programs will have to be sourced from both the public and private sector. The private sector is expected to benefit from the investments coming into the North ASEAN growth triangle. The private sector can finance many projects, especially infrastructure. The creation of the North ASEAN growth triangle is expected to create opportunities for trade, investment, finance, and labor movement, supported by government policies and programs. As the growth triangle becomes more established, high economic growth will be experienced in these areas, which would enhance the purchasing power of the population and enlarge the market for goods and services.

Several issues and programs need attention under the different sectors of trade, investment, and labor mobility, according to the Asian Development Bank. There is a need to mobilize financial resources to finance crossborder investments. Several international development agencies and private investment groups have pledged a total amount of U.S.$30–$50 million. Two special economic zones (SPEZs) need to be established. One is along the Thai-Malaysian border; the other zone integrates northern Sumatra with the northern states of Malaysia. Investment and trade initiatives are needed in southern Thailand and northern Malaysia.

A number of Memoranda of Understanding (MOU) for the investment projects were signed in Penang in December 1994. A total of U.S.$1.3 billion was committed by companies for different investment and infrastructure projects within the North ASEAN growth area. Industries being established in the growth area include export processing zones in southern Thailand, factories in northern Sumatra, and haulage services in northern Malaysia. Several projects have been identified since the Penang MOUs. One of these projects is the proposed construction of a land bridge linking Penang and Songkhla in Thailand. The project, estimated to cost $2 billion, includes a road, a rail link, a crude oil pipeline, and a gas pipeline. East West Bridge Corporation (EWBC), a member of Malaysia's Sikap Group, was reported to have a stake in all four consortia.

A proposal to the Thai government outlines a plan to construct a power plant at Satun, south Thailand, by a consortium consisting of Sikap Project Management Services of Malaysia, Shinawatra Group of Thailand, and PT Bukaka Teknik Utara of Indonesia. Another joint venture in the North ASEAN growth area is BT Engineering Sdn Bhd, a subsidiary of Perak State Development Corporation, and Citra Muda of Indonesia. The joint venture deals with the manufacture of agricultural motorcycles at Ipoh in Malaysia's Perak state.

One recommendation during the January 1994 ministerial meeting was the establishment of a regional TV broadcasting station. A consortium has submitted its application to the governments of the three countries. Included in the consortium are Shinawatra Group, Medan Mas Sdn Bhd, PT Medanmas Andalas, PT Indomatha Inti Media, and a Japanese company, Nissho Iwai-NHK Itec.

## Business Response to Asia-Pacific's Integration Drivers

With the establishment of growth polygons and the emergence of an integrated market, the business sector must identify and exploit these events. How can this be done? Take the example of Nippon Denso, a Japanese producer of air conditioners and other automobile parts. Nippon Denso, once a subcontractor of Toyota, started its internationalization by exporting parts to the United States and other countries where Toyota had sales offices. Eventually, Toyota shifted its production to other countries. In order to support Toyota's overseas plants, Nippon Denso also started to establish their presence in the same countries or regions where Toyota plants were located. The company started as a subcontractor and then proceeded to internationalize.

Faced with the trend of an integrating Asia, Nippon Denso has a vision to create complementary networks of production (Figure 16.5). Nippon Denso has operated in Thailand since the mid-1970s. The company hopes to develop Thailand-Nippon Denso as its central plant for electronic parts, producing for both local and export markets. Thailand-Nippon Denso specializes in the production of starters, alternators, and wiper motors. Meanwhile, Malaysia has a highly developed electronics industry. Therefore, the company aims to make Malaysia-Nippon Denso the production and supply center of electronic automobile parts in the Asia-Pacific region. Nippon Denso has also decided to take advantage of the invigoration of the Philippine automobile market by constructing a local plant that manufactures meters. Indonesia has an ample supply of inexpensive labor resources. The company envisions Indonesia-Nippon Denso becoming the production center for labor-intensive products as well as products requiring high-precision technology. Therefore, its production center will specialize in the production of compressors and spark plugs. It should be noted that Nippon Denso's ASEAN network will be further complemented by its network beyond the ASEAN region, mainly in Taiwan and Australia.

### From Scale Economies to Network Economies

The example of Nippon Denso illustrates the increasing shift of MNC strategies from "scale economies" to "network economies,"[1] or a combination of both. The latter constitutes the savings achieved by spreading various stages of value-chain activities across regions or countries.[2] On the other hand, scale economies try to achieve cost and quality merit by

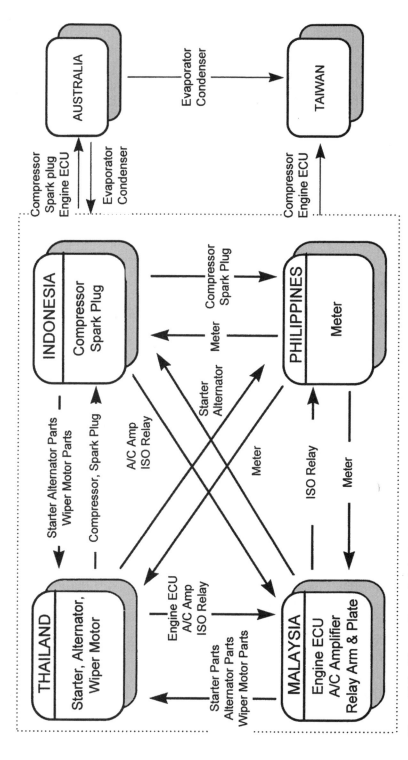

**Figure 16.5** Nippon Denso's Asia-Pacific Production Network for Automobile Parts, Vision for 1998, as of 1995.
*Source:* Nippon Denso.

centralizing production in one country. It is likely that scale economies will remain important. Between the two strategies, however, network economies will become increasingly more important in MNC strategies.

The need to establish a competitive network will continue to increase with the development of growth polygons in Asia and the realization of the AFTA and APEC visions. This will emerge as the key strategy in this period of growth polygons. What are the implications of shifting key strategies from scale economies to network economies? It requires a paradigm shift from "center" to "periphery." Economies of scale were attained by centralized production. Strengthening the center was the key for success. Subcontractors were scattered around the central production unit, so they could serve and support them anytime. Innovative products and goods always come from the headquarters. People from headquarters were regarded highly over the people working in the region. Under the paradigm of network economies, there is now no distinction between the center and the periphery. For example, Nippon Denso-Thailand is equally important as Nippon Denso-Australia or even Nippon Denso production units in Japan. It is not the center that produces the value, but the total work result of the network which creates values for the global market. Each unit in the network is indispensable. To support the network, logistics management will be more important than ever. If a company cannot create a network by itself, it can create a network by strategic alliances.

## Emergence of Growth Corridors

What is the effect of these numerous networks? If growth polygons are developed further, and national policy coordination on trade and investment-related matters by AFTA and APEC materialize, what will Asia look like? "Growth corridors" will likely emerge. Growth corridors contain several growth polygons and other regional centers linked closely by numerous networks in the private sector. In ASEAN, AFTA countries will constitute a Southeast Asia Growth Corridor. The Southern China Growth Triangle will be the merging point for the Northeast Asia Growth Corridor. A company will create networks within a corridor, and then, link to different corridors. Coming back to the vision of Nippon Denso, its network in the ASEAN region cannot be completed without ties to Australia and Taiwan. In other words, by centering on the Southeast Asia Corridor, Nippon Denso is trying to link with the Northeast Asia and Oceania Corridors. In the future, therefore, all these corridors can be connected as one (Figure 16.6).

## Conclusion

Regional groupings in Asia-Pacific are spreading and growing rapidly, with the strong support of most governments in the region. Many MNCs

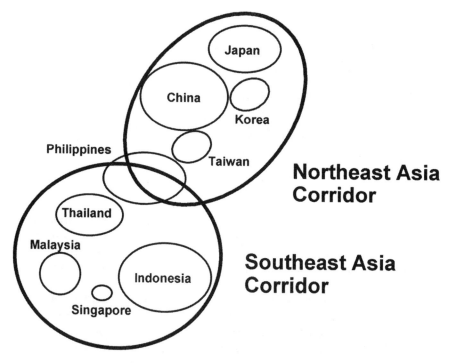

**Figure 16.6** Growth Corridors in Asia

are availing themselves of the benefits of these arrangements. Alignment of a company's global and regional strategies with these institutions and forces will greatly enhance success.

## NOTES

1. For a discussion of global networks, see Bruce Kogut, "Designing Global Strategies: Profiting from Operational Flexibility," *Sloan Management Review* (Fall 1985): 22–38; Christopher A. Bartlett and Sumantra Ghoshal, *Managing Across Borders: The Transnational Solution* (Boston: Harvard Business School Press, 1989); Christopher A. Bartlett and Sumantra Ghoshal, "Evolution of the Transnational," in *Current Issues in International Business*, W. F. Shepherd and Y. Islam, eds. (Cheltenham, U.K.: Edward Elgar Publishing Ltd., 1997); and Dennis S. Tachiki, "Corporation Investment Strategies for the Pacific Region: Some Evolving Changes in Japanese FDI," discussion paper, November 1995.

2. Although Nippon Denso is investing to complete its vision, the materialization of the network is still subject to the development of the ASEAN Industrial Cooperation Scheme, which is currently being discussed by ASEAN officials.

# CHAPTER 17

# Conclusions—Go East, Multinational Company

THIS BOOK HAS FOCUSED on what the Asia-Pacific region means for multinational companies (MNCs), instead of on the usual economic analyses about the great prospects for this region. In the process, we have also confirmed the economic analyses. MNCs have found, and should continue to find, Asia-Pacific to be highly attractive as a source of both markets and production, as well as for other value-adding activities. Continued and increasing MNC involvement will be one of the most important engines for continued economic growth and national prosperity.

We have demonstrated that our methodology can provide valuable insights into the current and potential roles of the countries and economies in the global and regional strategies of MNCs. In one sense, this book has applied a new approach to the analysis of country attractiveness. The traditional approach views countries while examining markets, cost, governments, and competitive conditions primarily on a stand-alone basis, with little regard for crosscountry implications.[1] In contrast, we have looked beyond these stand-alone factors to also examine the roles that countries can play in the multicountry regional and global strategies of MNCs. So, for example, while Hong Kong is today of only moderate attractiveness either as a market or as a production location, it is of great strategic attractiveness because of its role as a gateway to China and as a management base for this greatest market opportunity of the next twenty or so years. Malaysia is also of moderate importance on a stand-alone basis. But MNCs have played such a large role in involving that country in their activities that Malaysia has become a role model for both developing countries and MNCs in how the two can work together. On the other hand, our analysis finds that Japan is not only a tough market whose difficulties often exceed the achievable rewards (as we already knew), but that Japan can play only very limited roles on the supply side in the value chains of MNCs.

In this chapter, we first provide quantitative ratings of each economy in terms of the globalization drivers, strategies, and organizational approaches discussed qualitatively in each chapter. Second, we discuss how MNC managers can use these ratings to develop strategies and approaches for their own companies.

## Country Ratings

In this section we provide a summary and overview of the analyses reported in the individual country chapters. In particular, we present here seven tables that provide quantitative comparisons across each of the fourteen countries and economies on each of the individual globalization drivers, strategies, and organizational elements that we have examined. In each table we designate an overall rating on a five-point scale (illustrated by the number of stars). The economies are scored relative to the United States and major, affluent Western European countries, which would typically rate scores of five (the highest) on each measure. These ratings come from the collective judgment of all co-authors. They also report the situation as of 1997. In almost every case, the ratings will become more favorable for globalization in the foreseeable future. We have discussed these likely changes in the country chapters.

Providing quantitative ratings of fourteen economies across forty-nine measures requires a significant amount of judgment and daring or *chutzpah.* Nevertheless, we have chosen to take this risk so as to provide the maximum help to our readers. Methodologically, these ratings are the findings of our team of fifteen researchers, all of whom have significant expertise in analyzing the region. Using a quasi-Delphi technique, we reviewed these ratings through a number of rounds, including one face-to-face meeting of most of the group (during our second, concluding workshop).

Managers should use these ratings as an initial screen for where they should devote their own analytical efforts, and as a base reference for developing ratings for particular industries and businesses. Managers can always find exceptions. We hope that our ratings will give pause for thought and spur a search for reasons why the rating for a particular industry or business should be different. For example, we give China only two stars for common customer needs, primarily because of low income levels and, secondarily, because of deep-seated, unique Chinese tastes in this ancient civilization. That assessment should apply to most products and services and implies a need to adapt an MNC's offering in China. An exception might apply, though, for example, to luxury automobiles, where Chinese buyers may demand virtually the same vehicle as does most of the global market. But, clearly, there are far fewer potential customers in China than in, say, Japan, and there are likely to be local peculiarities.

### Ratings of Globalization Drivers

Table 17.1 summarizes market globalization drivers. It shows that, in general, the most developed and most Westernized economies—Hong Kong, Singapore, Australia, New Zealand, and Japan—have the most favorable market globalization drivers (i.e., those encouraging market participation by MNCs). In contrast, the least developed countries, particularly Vietnam and India, offer the fewest attractions. But it is these latter

### Table 17.1
### Summary of MARKET Globalization Drivers as of 1997

| | Common Customer Needs | Global Customers | Global Channels | Regional Customers | Regional Channels | Transferable Marketing | Lead Countries |
|---|---|---|---|---|---|---|---|
| Japan | **** | ***** | ** | ***** | *** | **** | ***** |
| South Korea | **** | *** | *** | *** | ** | **** | **** |
| China | ** | **** | * | ***** | ** | ** | ** |
| Taiwan | **** | **** | ** | **** | *** | **** | *** |
| Hong Kong | ***** | **** | **** | ***** | ***** | ***** | *** |
| Singapore | ***** | ***** | **** | ***** | ***** | ***** | *** |
| Malaysia | *** | *** | * | *** | *** | *** | *** |
| Thailand | *** | ** | * | *** | *** | *** | ** |
| Indonesia | ** | ** | * | ** | ** | *** | ** |
| Philippines | *** | ** | * | ** | ** | **** | ** |
| India | ** | ** | * | ** | ** | *** | ** |
| Vietnam | * | * | * | ** | ** | * | * |
| Australia | ***** | *** | *** | *** | *** | ***** | ** |
| New Zealand | ***** | ** | ** | ** | ** | ***** | ** |

* = very low, ***** = very high

*Source:* Based on country analyses. See definitions in Appendix.

*Note:* Ratings will vary somewhat by industry.

countries that see their market globalization drivers strengthening the fastest.

Table 17.2 summarizes cost globalization drivers. Here we have a much more mixed assessment. No countries are uniformly favorable. Japan's many favorable drivers are offset by having the least favorable country costs. In contrast, Vietnam's highly favorable country costs are offset by many unfavorable drivers. In general, MNCs will have to evaluate these ratings in regard to individual value-chain activities (we provide an overall assessment of these value chain elements in Table 17.6).

Table 17.3 summarizes government globalization drivers. Singapore, Hong Kong, New Zealand, Australia, Malaysia, Thailand, and the Philippines all rate at least moderately well on all counts, and in many cases rate highly favorably. The Hong Kong ratings allow for some expected deterioration after the 1997 return to China. Not surprisingly, Vietnam has the least favorable government drivers, with China and India also rating poorly. In particular, despite strong denials by Hong Kong's leaders, there will probably be more government intervention, more state-owned enterprises (in the form of mainland state enterprises participating in Hong Kong, and some decline in legal protection of business contracts and the like). On the other hand, these government drivers are probably the only ones that will be adversely affected by Hong Kong's change in status.

Table 17.4 summarizes competitive globalization drivers. Japan, China, and South Korea all rate strongly. Interestingly, both Hong Kong and Singapore also rate highly, particularly because of the critical regional roles that each plays. Again, Vietnam rates the least compellingly for MNC participation and activity.

## Ratings of Recommended MNC Strategies

Table 17.5 summarizes recommended MNC strategies. All countries, except for New Zealand and Vietnam, rate at least one star in being recommended for market participation. Only China rates above three stars. Many countries rate highly in their suitability for global, as opposed to local, products and services. No country achieves the maximum rating for activity location, mainly because the lowest-cost countries have weak infrastructures (and vice versa), as well as variations in the ability to support global and regional economies of scale and the other cost drivers. Location recommendations are more clear-cut when we examine individual elements of the value chain (below). Many countries rate very highly in their suitability for global marketing, particularly those with Westernized, English-speaking populations. (While many MNCs come from non-English-speaking nations, knowledge of English has become a nearly essential means of access to global consumer culture). Lastly, most countries also rate highly in their need for global competitive moves.

Providing more detail, Table 17.6 summarizes recommended MNC location strategies for individual elements of the value chain. For locating

## Table 17.2
## Summary of COST Globalization Drivers as of 1997

| | Global Scale Economies | Regional Scale Economies | Sourcing Efficiencies | Favorable Logistics | Good Infrastructure | Favorable Country Costs | Technology Role |
|---|---|---|---|---|---|---|---|
| Japan | ***** | ***** | *** | *** | **** | * | ***** |
| South Korea | **** | ***** | *** | *** | **** | ** | **** |
| China | *** | **** | *** | ** | * | **** | * |
| Taiwan | ** | *** | ** | ***** | *** | *** | ** |
| Hong Kong | ** | *** | ** | ***** | ***** | ** | ** |
| Singapore | ** | *** | ** | ***** | ***** | ** | *** |
| Malaysia | ** | *** | ** | ***** | *** | *** | ** |
| Thailand | ** | *** | *** | *** | ** | *** | * |
| Indonesia | *** | *** | **** | ** | ** | **** | * |
| Philippines | ** | ** | ** | ** | ** | *** | * |
| India | ** | *** | ** | * | * | **** | ** |
| Vietnam | * | ** | * | ** | * | **** | * |
| Australia | ** | *** | **** | ** | **** | ** | *** |
| New Zealand | * | ** | *** | * | **** | ** | ** |

* = very low, ***** = very high

*Source:* Based on country analyses. See definitions in Appendix.

*Note:* Ratings will vary somewhat by industry.

**Table 17.3**

**Summary of GOVERNMENT Globalization Drivers as of 1997**

| | Favorable Trade Policies | Favorable Investment Rules | Participation in Trade Blocs | Freedom from Government Intervention | Absence of State-Owned Competitors | Reliable Legal Protection | Compatible Technical Standards | Common Marketing Regulations |
|---|---|---|---|---|---|---|---|---|
| Japan | * | ** | ** | *** | ***** | **** | ***** | **** |
| South Korea | ** | ** | ** | *** | ***** | *** | ***** | *** |
| China | ** | ** | ** | * | * | * | *** | ** |
| Taiwan | **** | ***** | * | *** | *** | *** | ***** | **** |
| Hong Kong | ***** | ***** | * | **** | **** | **** | ***** | ***** |
| Singapore | ***** | ***** | ***** | **** | *** | ***** | ***** | ***** |
| Malaysia | **** | ****** | **** | **** | *** | ***** | ***** | *** |
| Thailand | **** | ****** | **** | *** | **** | *** | ***** | ***** |
| Indonesia | *** | ** | *** | ** | ** | ** | *** | *** |
| Philippines | *** | *** | **** | *** | **** | *** | ***** | ***** |
| India | ** | ** | * | ** | ** | *** | *** | *** |
| Vietnam | * | * | ** | * | * | * | ** | * |
| Australia | **** | ***** | ** | **** | **** | ***** | ***** | ***** |
| New Zealand | ***** | ***** | ** | ***** | ***** | ***** | ***** | ***** |

\* = very low, \*\*\*\*\* = very high

*Source:* Based on country analyses. See definitions in Appendix.

*Note:* Ratings will vary somewhat by industry.

## Table 17.4
### Summary of COMPETITIVE Globalization Drivers as of 1997

| | Global Strategic Importance | Regional Strategic Importance | Internationalized Domestic Competitors | Presence of Foreign Competitors | Interdependence via MNC Value Chains |
|---|---|---|---|---|---|
| Japan | ***** | **** | **** | *** | ***** |
| South Korea | *** | **** | **** | *** | *** |
| China | **** | ***** | ** | **** | **** |
| Taiwan | ** | *** | *** | *** | ** |
| Hong Kong | *** | ***** | ***** | *** | *** |
| Singapore | *** | ***** | ***** | ***** | **** |
| Malaysia | ** | *** | *** | *** | **** |
| Thailand | ** | *** | ** | *** | *** |
| Indonesia | *** | **** | ** | ** | *** |
| Philippines | ** | *** | ** | ** | * |
| India | *** | *** | ** | ** | * |
| Vietnam | * | ** | * | * | |
| Australia | ** | *** | *** | *** | ** |
| New Zealand | * | * | ** | ** | * |

* = very low, ***** = very high

*Source:* Based on country analyses. See definitions in Appendix.

*Note:* Ratings will vary somewhat by industry.

## Table 17.5
## Summary of Recommended MNC OVERALL Strategies as of 1997

| | Market Participation | Global Products/Services | Activity Location | Global Marketing | Global Competitive Moves |
|---|---|---|---|---|---|
| Japan | *** | **** | ** | **** | ***** |
| South Korea | *** | **** | *** | **** | ***** |
| China | **** | ** | **** | ** | ***** |
| Taiwan | ** | **** | **** | **** | *** |
| Hong Kong | *** | ***** | *** | ***** | *** |
| Singapore | *** | ***** | *** | ***** | *** |
| Malaysia | *** | *** | ***** | *** | *** |
| Thailand | *** | *** | ***** | *** | **** |
| Indonesia | *** | *** | ***** | *** | *** |
| Philippines | ** | **** | **** | ***** | *** |
| India | *** | ** | *** | ** | *** |
| Vietnam | * | * | ** | * | * |
| Australia | ** | ***** | ** | ***** | ** |
| New Zealand | * | ***** | * | ***** | * |

* = very low, ***** = very high
*Source:* Based on country analyses. See definitions in Appendix.
*Note:* Ratings will vary somewhat by industry.

Table 17.6

**Summary of Recommended MNC ACTIVITY LOCATION Strategies as of 1997**

| | Research | Development | Procurement Office | Production Operations | Regional Marketing Team | Regional Sales Force | Regional Distribution Center | Regional Customer Service | Regional HQ |
|---|---|---|---|---|---|---|---|---|---|
| Japan | ***** | ***** | *** | * | *** | ** | * | * | ** |
| South Korea | **** | **** | *** | *** | ** | * | ** | * | * |
| China | ** | ** | **** | ***** | * | * | * | * | * |
| Taiwan | *** | **** | *** | *** | ** | *** | *** | ** | ** |
| Hong Kong | *** | *** | **** | * | ***** | **** | *** | ***** | *** |
| Singapore | *** | *** | ***** | ** | **** | *** | **** | ***** | ***** |
| Malaysia | *** | *** | **** | *** | *** | ** | ** | *** | *** |
| Thailand | * | ** | *** | **** | ** | ** | *** | ** | ** |
| Indonesia | * | * | *** | **** | * | * | * | * | * |
| Philippines | ** | *** | ** | *** | *** | **** | ** | *** | *** |
| India | *** | *** | ** | **** | ** | * | * | ** | * |
| Vietnam | * | * | * | * | * | * | * | * | * |
| Australia | *** | *** | ** | * | *** | *** | * | *** | ** |
| New Zealand | ** | ** | * | * | ** | * | * | * | * |

* = very low, ***** = very high

*Source:* Based on country analyses. See definitions in Appendix.

*Note:* Ratings will vary somewhat by industry.

research, both high technological expertise and low cost of technicians and scientists are important, but seldom coincide in one country. Despite its high costs, Japan's high levels of technology allow it to receive the maximum rating, at least for those industries in which it plays a significant role. South Korea also rates highly. While still relatively low today, India and China both have potential to greatly increase their roles in MNC research and development activities. Readers can see for themselves the ratings on the other elements of the value chain. The last item, Regional HQ, is worth noting. The economies with the most favorable ratings are Hong Kong and Singapore. We dropped Hong Kong's rating by one star to four because of the uncertainties and likely changes brought by the return to China. MNCs probably will find it at least more difficult to get work permits for expatriates.[2]

## Ratings of Organization Approaches

Lastly, Table 17.7 summarizes recommended MNC organizational approaches. Hong Kong and Singapore clearly win out in their ability to operate independently (both of the need for local partners and home office supervision) and to participate in MNCs' global processes and culture. Vietnam is clearly worst, with China also presenting many problems.

# How Managers Can Apply the Findings

Managers in MNCs can use the evaluations in Tables 17.1–17.7 to help develop their global, regional, and country strategies (recalling the geographic levels of strategy depicted in Figure 1.1 in Chapter 1). This section will discuss the implications of each rating in turn. The discussion of the globalization drivers rated in Tables 17.1–17.4 will show implications also for many of the strategies and organizational approaches rated in Tables 17.5–17.7. In developing their individual strategies, managers should look back to the conceptual framework that we laid out in Figure 1.3 in Chapter 1.

## Market Globalization Drivers

Managers should use Table 17.1 to help them understand the extent to which each economy has market globalization drivers that (1) favor participating in the market, and (2) indicate the kinds of marketing strategies that should be followed (which is also discussed for Table 17. 5).

Companies looking for markets where *customer needs* are the most similar to those of developed Western countries should look first to Australia, New Zealand, Hong Kong, and Singapore. These markets typically show the fewest differences from American/Western European needs and tastes. Japan, South Korea, and Taiwan also rate highly, although more because of the effect of their high per capita incomes and somewhat less because of the Westernization of their cultures. In contrast, companies

#### Table 17.7
#### Summary of Recommended MNC ORGANIZATION APPROACHES as of 1997

| | Do Not Need Local Partners | Give Significant Autonomy | Use Global Management Processes | Participate in Global Processes | Can Use Local Managers | Can Use Nonlocal Managers | Source Global Managers | Instill Global Culture |
|---|---|---|---|---|---|---|---|---|
| Japan | *** | ***** | *** | ***** | ***** | * | **** | ** |
| South Korea | *** | ***** | *** | ***** | ***** | * | **** | *** |
| China | * | ** | * | *** | ** | **** | * | ** |
| Taiwan | ** | ***** | **** | ***** | ***** | ** | **** | **** |
| Hong Kong | ***** | ***** | ***** | ***** | ***** | ***** | ***** | ***** |
| Singapore | ***** | ***** | ***** | ***** | ***** | ***** | **** | ***** |
| Malaysia | *** | *** | *** | *** | **** | **** | *** | *** |
| Thailand | *** | *** | *** | *** | *** | *** | ** | ** |
| Indonesia | * | ** | *** | ** | ** | *** | ** | **** |
| Philippines | *** | *** | ***** | **** | **** | **** | **** | **** |
| India | ** | ** | *** | ** | *** | *** | **** | *** |
| Vietnam | * | * | * | * | * | **** | * | * |
| Australia | ***** | ***** | **** | **** | ***** | ***** | ***** | ***** |
| New Zealand | **** | ***** | *** | **** | ***** | ***** | ***** | **** |

* = very low, ***** = very high
Source: Based on country analyses. See definitions in Appendix.
Note: Ratings will vary somewhat by industry.

venturing to Vietnam, India, China or Indonesia can expect the greatest differences. These ratings have implications not just for product design and selection (further discussed below under Recommended MNC Overall Strategies) but also for the amount of market research needed. So the fewer the number of stars, the more time and money should be budgeted for market investigation.

Companies, particularly those in industrial or business-to-business activities with large customer accounts, need to be very aware of where they are likely to find *global customers.* Such global customers require not only more attention but more coordination across geographies. A common response is to use global account management programs.[3] These global customers are most likely to have regional or global headquarters or other significant operations in Japan, Singapore, and, to a somewhat lesser extent, Hong Kong, Taiwan, and China. Building a presence in these and other countries with high scores for global customers will create opportunities to deepen relationships with these very important accounts. On the other hand, presence in these countries will also increase the pressures for customer service and coordination. So managers should be prepared to deliver. The same arguments apply for the ratings on regional customers.

Similarly, countries with high ratings for *global channels* and *regional channels* pose greater opportunities and demands for customer service. Here, Hong Kong and Singapore stand out as having the most effective global and regional channels of distribution. Companies wishing to build extensive and sophisticated distribution systems in the Asia-Pacific region should, clearly, select these locations, with all other locations being second best.

Companies seeking *transferable marketing,* (i.e., the ability to use marketing approaches from the United States or Western Europe), should look to the same economies as those with the highest ratings on common customer needs—Australia, New Zealand, Hong Kong, and Singapore. An important difference between the ratings for common customer needs and transferable marketing apply to the Philippines and India. Because of these countries' widespread knowledge of English, their ratings on transferable marketing (at least for marketers from English-speaking home countries) are higher than those for common customer needs.

Lastly, managers need to consider the importance of participating in *lead countries,* with the attendant benefits of early exposure to market and customer innovations. At the same time, such participation requires the ability to serve typically highly demanding customers. In this regard, Japan clearly rates highest in the region, and indeed the world, for many product categories (e.g., consumer electronics and automobiles). Because of the rapidly increasing sophistication of its technology and markets, South Korea probably constitutes the second-best lead country in the region. Conversely, despite their high incomes, but because of their similar cultures, Australia and New Zealand offer few prospects to Western MNCs for generating market innovations. But Japanese MNCs, such as Fujitsu in computers, have found Australia to be a useful test market to prepare for entering the U.S. market.

## Cost Globalization Drivers

Managers can use Table 17.2 to help evaluate cost-related globalization drivers in the region. In particular, the country ratings significantly affect what types of activity location strategies will provide the most success.

Companies seeking markets that can contribute sales volume to achieve *global scale economies* or *regional scale economies* should look first to Japan, then Korea, provided they can get into these markets. As discussed in the next section, these two countries also pose some of the highest trade and investment barriers. China and Indonesia also provide significant potential to achieve economies of scale with somewhat lower import and investment barriers. Several other countries—Taiwan, Malaysia, Thailand, India, and Australia—also offer the potential of moderate economies of scale.

Some economies in the region are particularly attractive for their *sourcing efficiencies*. Managers can look particularly to Indonesia and Australia as the sources for many raw materials. Thailand and New Zealand also offer their distinct prospects, particularly in forest products and, in the case of New Zealand, dairy products. China does not offer much in the way of raw materials, other than some oil and gas, but it does, of course, offer the world's largest pool of labor. Japan and Korea have neither raw materials nor cheap labor, but do offer technical skills, as does Taiwan.

Nearly all producers of goods, and some of services also, do better in countries with *favorable logistics* either as a production site, a market, or both. As centrally located economies with among the best port facilities in the world, Hong Kong and Singapore clearly stand out. The other developed economies—Japan, Korea, Australia, and New Zealand—also score well. In contrast, the less-developed economies all have mostly unfavorable logistics.

Some companies may especially need to operate in countries with *good infrastructure*—roads (e.g., for producers of difficult-to-transport items), power (e.g., for heavy users of energy), communications (e.g., for information-based companies), and the like. In this regard, the developed economies clearly rank high, especially Hong Kong and Singapore.

Many companies seek *favorable country costs* for economical production, taking into account not just labor wage costs, but also overhead costs and productivity. The very low-labor costs in China, Indonesia, India, and Vietnam allow these countries to score highly in this regard, particularly for companies for which low-skilled cheap labor is critical (e.g., companies like Nike). Firms seeking a better balance between wages and productivity would do well to look to the partially industrialized countries such as Malaysia and Thailand. The Philippines, as a formerly prosperous nation and now with a rapidly improving economy, also offers attractive prospects.

For companies seeking economies that can play a *technology role,* Japan and South Korea clearly offer the best prospects. Singapore and Australia can also play significant roles for MNCs. In these four countries, local companies have developed significant technological expertise of their own. MNCs can acquire technology by working with these companies or by hiring locally. In contrast, other countries, particularly India, offer the prospect for MNCs to develop technology on their own by employing local scientists and engineers.

## Government Globalization Drivers

The ratings of government globalization drivers in Table 17.3 can help managers to evaluate the kind of roles that governments play in each country in the region, and the types of strategies that companies should pursue to deal with government intervention. Here we will focus on the countries with the lowest ratings as these are the ones that require the most thought and action on the part of managers.

Japan has the lowest ratings on *favorable trade policies.* As discussed in Chapter 3 (and also Table 1.5), Japan has easily the lowest ratio of imports to GNP in the region, despite ongoing efforts to open its economy. Furthermore, Japan mostly imports goods and services for which there is little domestic production (e.g., oil, jet aircraft, timber, and food). There are now serious pressures, both internal and external, on Japan to open its economy. Most foreign MNCs will have to decide whether to invest time and resources into entry efforts that may still easily fail. South Korea, China, India, and Vietnam all pose significant trade barriers. In contrast, many other economies in the region offer fairly open markets.

An alternative to, or along with, trade companies may choose to invest directly in these economies. In terms of *favorable investment rules,* the ratings are similar to those for favorable trade policies. The difference for managers lies in the relationships they will have to build with governments—typically much more long term for investment. Furthermore, unofficial rules, such as "have a government official or his relative as a partner," become more important. India and Vietnam pose the most stringent investment rules. India has multiple parties and layers of government, and only one party at the Federal level strongly favors foreign direct investment, while many at the local level oppose it. Vietnam, as a decidedly Communist state, continues to view foreign investment with suspicion.

An economy's *participation in trade blocs* can ease the paths of MNCs already active in other areas of a bloc. As discussed in Chapter 16, only ASEAN constitutes a really serious trade bloc that offers significant benefits to MNCs. So companies seeking such benefits should particularly look to Singapore, Malaysia, Thailand, the Philippines, and, to a lesser extent, Indonesia (the last not fully practicing the principles of AFTA, as evidenced by its slow reduction of tariff rates and its current "national car" behavior).

Three government globalization drivers—*freedom from government intervention, absence of state-owned competitors,* and *reliable legal protection*—have similar implications for MNCs. In particular, poor ratings within these dimensions require MNCs to have excellent skills, experience, and connections for coping with uneven and shifting playing fields. There are clear differences by national origin in this regard. On average, Asian MNCs have the greatest capability, European MNCs the next, and American MNCs the least. On the other hand, having the right local partners or employing the right local staff can particularly help to improve the ability to cope with government problems. There are also differences by industry. Companies in industries that rely on patents, proprietary knowledge, or intellectual capital need to think hard about participating in countries with poor legal protection. If they do participate, they need clear strategies for minimizing their risks of loss. Clearly, China and Vietnam, with their lack of Western-style legal systems, pose the greatest problems.

Most countries in the region have highly *compatible technical standards,* making it relatively easy for MNCs to market their products and technologies. Vietnam probably poses the most difficulties.

Lastly, some countries do pose problems in *common marketing regulations.* Vietnam and China can pose the biggest headaches for marketers. Both countries have weakly developed rules that many MNCs perceive as being arbitrary. Furthermore, while no one government agency or media outlet can authorize, say, an advertisement or television commercial, many bodies can reject them, even after production expenses have been incurred. The countries with strong religions—India, Indonesia, and Malaysia—can also impose restrictions, particularly in the depiction of relations between men and women.

## Competitive Globalization Drivers

Understanding competitive dynamics is particularly important in the Asia-Pacific region. Companies can use the ratings of the competitive globalization drivers in Table 17.4 to help diagnose the competitive strategies they should develop.

*Global strategic importance* and *regional strategic importance* of countries concern the extent to which an MNC's activities have strategic consequences beyond those countries. Japan continues to be, overall, the most globally strategic country in the region. MNCs need to make the tough decision as to whether to bypass Japan or make a minimal effort, thereby giving up much potential strategic advantage. But as argued in Chapter 2, the rise of non-Japan Asia, the current troubles of Japan, and its continued closure make the "bypass Japan" option increasingly viable. China holds a strong second place in global strategic importance. Nearly every MNC needs some kind of China strategy. China, Hong Kong, and Singapore head the list for regional strategic importance, the latter two for obviously different reasons than China. Hong Kong and Singapore are the two ideal locations for monitoring regional trends and global and regional competitors.

Companies also need strategies for dealing with strong local companies, particularly *internationalized domestic competitors*. Such competitors are already widespread in Japan, Korea, Hong Kong, Singapore, Australia, and Taiwan. But managers also need to watch developments in Malaysia, Thailand, and Indonesia, among others.

The *presence of foreign competitors* poses another set of challenges for MNC managers. Singapore's open and prosperous economy has attracted a very large number of MNCs. The key task there is probably to use Singapore as a location to monitor and match global competitors. China has also attracted many global competitors. But here the task is different. First, MNCs may need to deny this huge potential market to their global rivals. Second, and somewhat in opposition, MNCs need to avoid being drawn into ruinous competition that gives too much in the way of concessions. Global automakers provide the most salient current example of such a risk.

Lastly, MNC managers need to be concerned about each country's global *interdependence via MNC value chains* (the extent to which MNCs have created strategic interdependence between a country and others through sharing of activities such as factories or other parts of the value chain). Many countries in the region have done so, particularly Japan, China, Taiwan, Malaysia, and Thailand. In consequence, both activities and competitive struggles in these markets have global repercussions. Managers need to extensively coordinate with other geographic units when developing and implementing plans for such countries.

## Recommended MNC Overall Strategies

The ratings of country globalization drivers have direct implications for recommended MNC strategies. We discussed some of the implications in the previous section. The ratings in Table 17.5 make direct recommendations. Again, we need to caution that this book's recommendations can only be the starting point for MNC managers. They need to customize our overall recommendations for their individual situations.

*Market participation* constitutes a first, critical decision for MNCs. Based on all the various globalization drivers, no one economy receives a maximum five-star rating. On the other hand, the Asia-Pacific region, as a whole, would certainly receive an unambiguous five-star rating. In contrast, we would not have such certainty about any other region in the world, except for the United States. Furthermore, an MNC should adopt a portfolio strategy, with participation in a number of regions (Asia-Pacific, Western Europe, etc.) and markets within each region. Standard portfolio theory says that firms should invest in a mix of high-risk/high-return and low-risk/low-return assets. The same applies to participation or investment in countries. Perhaps the two most relevant types of risk in terms of market participation are government risk and competitive risk. Government risk constitutes the extent to which government actions may prevent an MNC from achieving its business objectives. Competitive risk applies to competitor actions. Figure 17.1 summarizes our overall

**Competitive Risk**

**Figure 17.1**   Government and Competitive Risks Matrix

diagnoses of these risks. In this evaluation, China constitutes high government risk and moderate competitive risk, while Australia and New
Zealand pose low risk in both. For comparison, we show the United States
as having low government risk and moderate competitor risk.

These risk ratings, plus the evaluations of country globalization drivers, help determine Table 17.5's overall ratings for market participation.
China stands alone with a four-star rating, primarily because of its potential and its global strategic importance. As we said in Chapter 4, China is
a "must bet" for any MNC. The main choice lies in how big a bet and what
sort of bet. Many economies rate three stars. An MNC should participate
in at least some of these. Lastly, MNCs should consider the two- and one-
star economies on an opportunistic basis. They should participate if they
have some special advantages or objectives for that economy.

The extent to which MNCs should offer in each economy *global
products/services* relates particularly to the *common customer needs* driver that
we discussed earlier. The challenges lie in the countries with the low ratings: Vietnam, India, and China. Here, managers will have to pay extra attention to product and service adaptation needs.

Once an MNC has decided to participate in one or more of these
countries, another portfolio decision concerns where to locate which
value-adding activities. Applying global strategy means not reproducing
every activity in every country. The *activity location* column in Table 17.5
indicates the overall attractiveness of each economy for locating activities
in general. China, Taiwan, Malaysia, Indonesia, and the Philippines all
rate four stars. In the next section, Recommended MNC Activity Location Strategies, we will discuss each individual activity.

The extent to which MNCs should use *global marketing* depends particularly on the *transferable marketing* and *common marketing regulations* globalization drivers discussed earlier. Vietnam, China, and India pose the greatest difficulties. So MNC marketing managers for those countries need to pay even more attention to local advice.

Lastly, MNCs need to recognize when they need to make *global competitive moves* rather than just local ones. Because of their global strategic importance, strong local and/or foreign competitors, and extensive roles in MNC value chains, Japan, South Korea, and China all rate five stars in this regard. Because of its gateway role for Indochina, Thailand rates one star more than its other Southeast Asian neighbors. Managers need to particularly evaluate the broader implications of moves they make in these four countries.

## Recommended MNC Activity Location Strategies

The clear message of Table 17.6 is that no one country has favorable ratings for every one of the nine activities we evaluated. So a value chain portfolio strategy is clearly called for.

Recommended locations for *research* and *development* activities depend mostly on the *technology role* globalization driver discussed earlier. An MNC would do well to locate some R&D activities in Japan and/or South Korea. Several other economies also offer significant prospects.

The location of a regional or global *procurement office* depends on access or proximity to important sources of supply. At the geographic heart of Southeast Asia and with its superb infrastructure, Singapore gets the highest rating. Hong Kong, Malaysia, and China also rate highly.

Many MNCs' first interest in Asia is as a site for *production operations*. Despite its continuing problems with worker productivity, China's other advantages make it the overall leader in this category, with a full five stars. MNCs can also locate production in many other attractive sites, especially Thailand, Indonesia, and now India. Of course, nearly every one of these economies has some production activities from foreign MNCs (with the possible exceptions of New Zealand and Japan). Hong Kong has rapidly moved from being a production site in its own right to being a base for managing production activities in China, as has Singapore in regard to Malaysia and Indonesia. Nevertheless, MNCs may decide to continue to place high-skill production activities in high-cost sites. A portfolio approach would have more than one significant production site in Asia-Pacific, the number depending on logistics and supply considerations as well as risk factors. For example, the possible military threats currently facing both Taiwan and South Korea would argue against putting all production eggs in those two baskets.

Many MNCs may wish to set up *regional marketing* teams, instead of, or in addition to, national ones. Factors affecting the choice include communications and transportation infrastructure, and the ability to attract or hire talented and cosmopolitan marketing executives. As the most exciting city in Asia, Hong Kong clearly comes out ahead. Singapore and the Philippines also offer attractive prospects in this regard.

In some cases, MNCs can also use a *regional sales force*. Cost becomes more of a factor than for typically smaller regional marketing teams. Hong Kong still comes out ahead, but less clearly so. English-language capability enhances the attractiveness of the Philippines; Mandarin Chinese capability that of Taiwan.

The location of a *regional distribution center* depends primarily on the logistics needs of a company and on the infrastructure of a country. Given the large distances in the region, no one location gets the maximum possible rating. But Singapore does the best, followed by Hong Kong, Taiwan, and Thailand. Most other countries are much less attractive in this regard.

MNCs are increasingly setting up *regional customer service* operations to replace local ones in the region. Good communications infrastructure plus multilingual capability are key determinants for the optimal location. Hong Kong and Singapore, and Malaysia and the Philippines to a lesser extent, are the clear choices here.

Lastly, most MNCs need a *regional headquarters* in the region. Major considerations include communications and transportation infrastructure, proximity to key markets, and the quality of life. Historically, many MNCs have located their Asia-Pacific HQs either far north in Tokyo or far south in Sydney. With the rise of the economies in between, most MNCs are shifting their HQs toward the center of the region. Hong Kong used to be the favorite. But a declining quality of life and concerns about the return to China have reduced its attraction. A 1996 survey of regional executives showed that Singapore has become the dominant choice, well ahead of Hong Kong, even though Hong Kong today has far more regional HQs.[4] Singapore also has the added attraction of proximity to India, the next big Asia-Pacific opportunity. Other interesting possibilities are Kuala Lumpur and Manila. Some companies may choose dual centers, focusing on the northern and southern parts of the region.

## Recommended MNC Organization Approaches

Managers should use Table 17.7 to help develop the appropriate organization and management approaches in each country. Despite certain similarities in "Asian culture" there are still many differences among Asia-Pacific countries that affect MNC management.

MNCs can go alone and *do not need local partners* if the countries are easy to operate in. But many countries pose sufficient barriers and difficulties for foreigners that local partners are highly necessary. Vietnam, China, and Indonesia all stand out in this need. India and Taiwan also both require significant use of local partners. Furthermore, in these cases, MNCs also need to be aware of how changing political situations may change the usefulness of particular partners. National leader succession problems, especially in Indonesia, and to a lesser extent in China, particularly affect partner choices.

MNCs need to decide whether to *give significant autonomy* to subsidiaries. This decision depends on such factors as the likely business experience and sophistication of local managers. Half the countries or economies rate five stars—Japan, South Korea, Taiwan, Hong Kong, Singapore, Australia, and New Zealand. At the other extreme Vietnam, China, and Indonesia all rate low in this regard.

MNCs need to decide whether to *use global management processes* or local ones. This decision depends on the experience and sophistication of local managers but also on whether there are strong local practices. So, while Japanese and Korean managers have extensive experience, they also have strong homegrown approaches to management. Hence, these two countries rate only three stars here.

A different consideration is whether to have country managers *participate in global processes,* such as global strategic planning, global teams, and the like. Most countries score higher in this regard than for using global management processes. That is, an Asia-Pacific subsidiary's managers can participate in global processes even though they use more local management processes internally. So, for example, Japanese and South Korean executives can easily work in global teams even if they maintain their distinctively national approaches to management when dealing domestically. On the other hand, executives from Japan, South Korea, China, and Taiwan, may have significant problems with the global language of business, English.

Countries clearly differ in the extent to which MNCs *can use local managers.* The low scores merit attention: Vietnam, China, and Indonesia. China's local management capabilities will improve with the large numbers of Chinese studying overseas and with the beginnings of local business schools. Malaysian, Filipino, and Indonesian managers have a strong appetite for education and development courses. In some highly rated countries, the difficulty comes more in retaining local managers, particularly in job-hopping Hong Kong.

The complementary consideration is whether MNCs *can use nonlocal managers.* Here, the main issues are the local acceptance of foreigners combined with the distinctiveness of local management approaches. In this regard, Japan and South Korea both rate poorly in their acceptance of foreign managers. In contrast, while Vietnam has limited tolerance for foreigners, particularly because of its recent history, it does not have strong managerial traditions of its own. Hence, foreign executives are reasonably well accepted.

MNCs may also wish to *source global managers* from particular Asia-Pacific countries. Experience, adaptability, and willingness to travel all come into play. Australia and New Zealand have traditionally provided talented executives willing to leave home. Hong Kong's political change has vastly increased the willingness of its inhabitants to leave home. The relatively low incomes, but high education levels, of Filipino and Indian managers make many of them eager and qualified to adopt expatriate careers.

Lastly, MNCs need to decide how far they should seek to *instill global culture*. The distinctiveness of local culture relative to Western culture provides the key consideration. Vietnam, China, and Indonesia all rate low in this regard, the first two because of their communist heritage, and Indonesia because of unclear guidelines or application of the *Pancasila* way of management described in Chapter 10.

## Conclusion

Readers should recognize that our evaluations and recommendations concern the current situation, with allowance for future changes. For example, Vietnam now rates poorly on most items. MNCs entering that country will have to face many difficulties. On the other hand, such early entrants will have the potential to reap first-mover advantages in the future, should Vietnam's economy continue to grow and its globalization drivers improve. In contrast, for the more mature economies, such as Japan and Singapore, the benefits to MNCs are immediate, but will improve less. We particularly recommend that managers take a portfolio approach, both to Asia-Pacific as a whole and to areas within the region. First, the region is far too important to not have a role in the global strategies of MNCs. Second, the region offers many diverse economies that can play differing roles within a regional strategy. In conclusion, managers who develop strategies and organization approaches that exploit the specific globalization potentials of individual economies will build successful global strategies for the Pacific region and maximize their "Asian Advantage."

### NOTES

1. For a classic approach to country attractiveness analysis, see Franklin R. Root, *Entry Strategies for International Markets* Lexington, Mass.: D.C. Heath and Company, 1987.

2. The actual change is that United Kingdom citizens, after June 1997, have to get work permits and visas as all other nationals had to before.

3. See George S. Yip and Tammy L. Madsen, "Global Account Management: The New Frontier in Relationship Marketing," special issue on Global Marketing Implementation, *International Marketing Review* 13, no. 3 (1996): 24–42.

4. A study conducted by Survey Research Singapore, reported in Katherine Stephen and Murray Hiebert, "Singapore Steals the Crown," *Far Eastern Economic Review*, December 26, 1996, and January 2, 1997, 50–52.

# APPENDIX

# Globalization Measures

THIS SECTION SUMMARIZES the globalization measures used in this book.

## Country Globalization Drivers

We used four sets of country globalization drivers, diagnosing the *current* and *potential* situation of each.

### Market Globalization Drivers

- Common customer needs
  —extent to which customer needs are common with the rest of the region and the world
  —extent to which economic growth and social changes have moved the country toward the consumption patterns of developed Western economies
- Global customers
  —extent to which corporations who behave as global customers have regional headquarters or other significant operations in the country
  —extent to which corporations who behave as global customers purchase/source from the country
- Global channels
  —extent to which global channels of distribution have regional headquarters or other significant operations in the country
  —extent to which corporations who behave as global channels of distribution purchase/source from the country
- Regional customers
  —extent to which corporations who behave as regional customers have regional headquarters or other significant operations in the country
  —extent to which corporations who behave as regional customers purchase/source from the country
- Regional channels
  —extent to which regional channels of distribution have regional headquarters or other significant operations in the country

   —extent to which corporations who behave as regional channels
   of distribution purchase/source from the country
- Transferable marketing
   —extent to which marketing approaches need to be adapted in
   this country
   —extent to which the country is generally amenable to marketing
   strategies and approaches used in other countries (e.g., acceptance of foreign brand names, packaging and advertising);
   availability of media.
- Lead countries
   —extent to which the country accounts for major product or market innovations

## Cost Globalization Drivers

- Global and regional scale economies
   —extent to which the country has markets that can contribute
   sales volume to MNCs needing to achieve global or regional
   scale economies. (Is the local market large enough to support a
   minimum efficient scale plant? If not, are there sufficient exports to support a minimum efficient scale plant?)
- Sourcing efficiencies
   —extent to which the country can provide critical factors of production in efficient volumes
- Favorable logistics
   —extent to which the country has favorable logistics (transporting goods and services to and within the country) as either a
   production site or a market or both
- Good infrastructure
   —quality of a country's infrastructure—roads, power, communications, etc.
- Favorable country costs (including exchange rates)
   —extent to which the country offers low production and other
   operating costs, taking into account not just labor wage costs,
   but also overhead costs
- Technology role
   —extent to which the country can be used as a base for developing technology

## Government Globalization Drivers

- Favorable trade policies
   —extent to which the country has favorable trade policies, including both tariff and nontariff barriers and how these are changing
   —role of regional "growth triangles"
- Favorable foreign direct investment rules
   —extent to which the country has rules that favor foreign direct
   investment, including currency regulations, repatriation of capital, and foreign ownership

- Role of Regional Trade Blocs
  - —how the country's participation in ASEAN, APEC, and other trade blocs affects opportunities for multinational companies
- Freedom from government intervention
  - —sensitivity of the country's government to foreign dominance of key industries, and response via intervention
- Absence of state-owned competitors
  - —extent to which industries of interest to foreign MNCs are dominated by government-owned competitors or customers
- Reliable legal protection of contracts, trademarks, and intellectual property
  - —extent to which contracts, trademarks, and intellectual property are protected from imitation
- Compatible technical standards
  - —extent to which the country uses global technical standards
- Common marketing regulations
  - —extent to which the country has marketing regulations similar to the rest of the world (e.g., rules on television advertising)

## Competitive Globalization Drivers

- Global/Regional Strategic Importance
  - —extent to which the country has global or regional strategic importance, and the role it should play in the market portfolio of a multinational company. Global or regional strategic importance is defined in terms of
    - · large source of revenues or profits
    - · home market of global or regional customers
    - · home market of global or regional competitors
    - · significant market of global or regional competitors
    - · major source of industry innovation
- Internationalized domestic competitors
  - —extent to which the largest local companies in the country are themselves globalized in terms of international revenues
- Presence of foreign competitors
  - —extent to which foreign competitors participate in business activity
  - —concerns about competitors based in other countries in the region
- Interdependence via MNC value chains
  - —extent to which MNCs create strategic interdependence between this country and others through sharing of activities such as factories or other parts of the value chain

## Global and Regional Strategy Levers

To analyze companies we focused on five dimensions of global and regional strategy.

## Market Participation

- Extent to which MNCs do, and should, participate in the country's markets

## Global Products and Services

- Extent to which MNCs do, and should, market in the country globally standardized products and services, and the extent to which they do, and should, make local adaptations.

## Activity Location

- Actual and potential use of the country as a location for different value chain activities:
    —research
    —development
    —procurement office
    —production operations
    —regional marketing team
    —regional sales force
    —regional distribution center
    —regional customer service
    —regional HQ
- Significance of the country's activities in the overall regional and global value chains of the MNCs.
- Actual and potential evolution of value chain role.

## Global Marketing

- Extent to which MNCs do, or should, adapt their marketing in the country, evaluated by each element of the marketing mix: positioning, brand names, packaging, labeling, advertising, promotion, distribution and selling methods, sales representatives, and service personnel.
- Extent to which price levels in this country differ from the rest of the region and the world.
- Special aspects of marketing success factors needed in this country.

## Global Competitive Moves

- Extent to which MNCs do, or should, include the country when they make global or regional competitive moves, as opposed to making competitive moves in this country independent of moves in other countries.

## Global Organization and Management

To analyze the global organization and management approaches of MNCs, we used several measures:

- Do not need local partners
    - —extent to which a foreign MNC does not need to have local partners
- Give significant autonomy
    - —way in which MNCs typically organize operations in the country (e.g., as autonomous subsidiaries or as tightly controlled extensions of units outside the country)
- Use global management processes
    - —extent to which MNCs can use global management processes or need to adapt management processes for the country: particularly strategic planning, budgeting, motivation, performance review and compensation, human resource management (including career planning and employment terms—e.g., lifetime employment), and information systems
- Participate in global processes
    - —extent to which MNCs can expect subsidiaries/partners in the country to participate in global management processes
- Can use local managers
    - —extent to which local managers are qualified to work in MNCs
- Can use non-local managers
    - —extent to which foreign or expatriate managers are acceptable in the country
- Source global managers
    - —potential of local managers for transfer to other countries
- Instill global culture
    - —extent to which global strategies of MNCs need to take account of local culture and the extent to which they can instill their global corporate culture

# Bibliography

Abdullah, Fadil Hisham. *RIS Backgrounder: Growth Triangles in ASEAN.* NSTP Research and Information Services. Vol. 2, no. 5, 1994.

Abegglen, James C. *Sea Change: Pacific Asia as the New World Industrial Center.* New York: The Free Press, 1994.

Abegglen, James C., and George Stalk Jr., *Kaisha: The Japanese Corporation.* New York: Basic Books, 1985.

*Advertising Age.* Various issues.

AMCOR. Annual company report and interviews with senior company personnel, 1995.

Arthur Andersen. *Doing Business in Vietnam.* Ho Chi Minh City: Arthur Andersen, 1995.

Ashwood, Neil. *Vietnam: A Business Handbook.* London: Graham & Trotman, 1995.

*Asian Business.* Various issues.

*Asian Wall Street Journal.* Various issues.

*Asiaweek.* Various issues.

A. T. Kearney. "Japan in Revolution: An Assessment of Investment Performance by Foreign Firms in Japan, 1995." Tokyo and Chicago.

*Australian Chamber of Commerce and Industry Report of Business Expectations.* November 1995.

*Australian Financial Review.* Various issues.

*B & T.* Various issues.

*Bangkok Post.* Various issues.

Bank of Japan. *Comparative Economic and Financial Statistics,* Tokoyo 1995.

Bartlett, Christopher A., and Sumantra Ghoshal. *Managing across Borders: The Transnational Solution.* Boston: Harvard Business School Press, 1989.

Bartlett, Christopher A., and Sumantra Ghoshal. "Evolution of the Transnational." In *Current Issues in International Business.* Edited by W. F. Shepherd and Y. Islam. Cheltenham, United Kingdom: Edward Elgar, 1997, 108–131.

Becknall, Bob. Cited in *Singapore: Your Global Business Architect.* 1992, Singapore: Economic Development Board, 1992, p. 8.

Birks, Stuart, and Srikanta Chatterjee (eds.). *The New Zealand Economy—Issues and Policies.* Dunmore Press, 1992.

Bloomberg News Service. "San Miguel Buys Two Food Brands from Manila Unit of P&G." April 19, 1995.

Budde, P. *Telecommunications Strategies, Featuring Superhighway Developments 1995/96.* Bucketty, NSW: Paul Budde Communication Pty. Ltd., 1995.

*Business News Indochina.* Various issues.

*Business Review Weekly.* Various issues.

*Business Week.* Various issues.

*Business Times* Various issues.

*Business Wire.* Various issues.

*Business World.* Various issues.

Centre for Monitoring Indian Economy. Various volumes, 1996.

Chakraborty, S. K. *Management Values: Towards Cultural Congruence.* New Delhi: Oxford University Press, 1991.

Chen, Min. *Asian Management Systems: Chinese, Japanese and Korean Style of Business.* London and New York: Routledge, 1995.

Cheung, Tak-Sing. *Confucianism and the Orderly Complex: A Sociological Interpretation of Chinese Thought.* Taipei: Great Waves Publisher, 1989. (In Chinese)

China Automotive Technology and Research Center and Ministry of Machinery—Automotive Industry (ed.). *China Automotive Industry Yearbook—1994,* Shandong: New China Publishers, 1994.

*Cho-sun* daily newspaper. Various issues.

Citibank. *Indonesia: An Investment Guide.* APEC edition. Jakarta: Citibank N.A. & Ida Sudoyo & Associates, 1994.

*South China Morning Post.* Various issues.

de Keijzer, Arne J. *China: Business Strategies for the '90s.* Berkeley, Calif.: Pacific View Press, 1992.

de Mesquita, Bruce Bueno, David Newman, and Alvin Rabushka. *Red Flag over Hong Kong.* Chatham, N.J.: Chatham House Publishers, 1996.

Department of Statistics Government of Malaysia. *Manufacturing Industries Survey.* Kuala Lumpur: Government Printers, 1995.

Dobbs-Higginson, M. S. *Asia-Pacific: Its Role in the New World Disorder.* Hong Kong: Longman Group (Far East), 1994; London: Mandarin Paperbacks, Reed Consumer Books, 1995.

*Doong-a* daily newspaper. Various issues.

Dun and Bradstreet Marketing Pty. Ltd. *Jobson's Year Book of Public Companies, 1996/97,* 1996.

Dunung, Sanjyot P. *Doing Business in Asia: The Complete Guide.* Lexington, Mass.: Lexington Books, 1995.

East Asia Analytical Unit. *ASEAN Free Trade Area: Trading Bloc or Building Block.* Australia Government Publishing Service, 1994.

Economic Monitoring Group. "The Economy in Transition: Restructing to 1989." New Zealand Planning Council, July 1989.

*Electronic Buyers' News.* Various issues.

Enright, Michael J., Edith E. Scott, and David Dodwell. *The Hong Kong Advantage.* Hong Kong: Oxford University Press (China) Ltd., 1997.

*Far Eastern Economic Review.* Various issues.

*Financial Times.* Various issues.

Foley, Sharon, and David B. Yoffie. "Internationalizing the Cola Wars: The Battle for China and Asian Markets." Harvard Business School Case 9-794-146, Boston: Harvard Business School, 1994.

*Fortune.* Various issues.

Hamel, Gary, Yves L. Doz, and C. K. Prahalad. "Collaborate with Your Competitors and Win." *Harvard Business Review,* January-February 1989, pp. 133–139.

Hamer, Andrew Marshall. "Cashing in on China's Burgeoning Middle Class." *Marketing Management* 4, no. 1 (1995): 9–21.

Harwit, Eric. *China's Automobile Industry, Policies, Problems, and Prospects.* Armonk, N.Y.: M. E. Sharpe, 1995.

Hee, Tan Jing, and You Poh Seng (eds.). *Developing Managers in Asia.* Singapore; Addison-Wesley, 1987.

Ho, Richard Yan-Ki, et al. (eds.). *The Hong Kong Financial System.* Hong Kong: Oxford University Press, 1991.

Hofstede, Geert. *Culture's Consequences: International Differences in Work Related Values.* Beverly Hills, Calif.: Sage, 1984.

*Hong Kong Economic Journal.* Various issues. (In Chinese)

Hsu, Ziangpin. "Reflection on the Development Strategies for Passenger Car Industry in China." *China Industrial Economics* 6 (1995): 41–45. (In Chinese)

*India Today.* Various issues.

Indonesian Central Business Data. *Information: Monthly Newsletter.* Various issues.

Inoue, Ryuichiro. "Motivations behind Direct Investment in Japan by Foreign MNCs." *Gaishikei Kigyo Soran 1995,* Toyo Keizai Shinposha.

Institute for Management Development and World Economic Forum. *World Competitiveness Report 1995,* Lausanne, Switzerland.

Institute of Southeast Asian Studies. *ASEAN Economic Cooperation.* Singapore: ISIS, 1991.

*International Business.* Various issues.

*International Herald Tribune.* Various issues.

Ip, Anita Mei Che. "Pepsi-Cola's Challenge in China and Its Strategic Moves into Equity Joint Venture." Hong Kong: The Chinese University of Hong Kong MBA Project, 1995.

*Japan Industrial Journal.* Various issues.

*Joong-ang* daily newspaper. Various issues.

Kakaw, Hiroshi. *Kokkyo-o koeru Asia Seicho-no Sankaku-chitai.* Toyo-Kerzai Shinpo-sha, June 1995.

Kamm, Henry. *Dragon Ascending.* Boston: Little Brown, 1996.

Kang, T. W. *Is Korea the Next Japan?* New York: The Free Press, 1989.

Kao, Xianchun, and Fulin Chi. *China: In Transition to a Market Economy.* Hainan, China: China (Hainan) Reform and Development Institute, 1995. (In Chinese)

Kogut, Bruce. "Designing Global Strategies: Profiting from Operational Flexibility." *Sloan Management Review,* Fall 1985, pp. 27–38.

Kondo, Mari. "Competitive Advantage. . . . AFTA: A Win-Win Game." *The Asian Manager,* November–December 1992.

Kondo, Mari. "AFTA: Agree First, Talk After? *The Asian Manager,* October–November 1994.

Kondo, Mari. "New AFTA and Beyond: Strategies for ASEAN Business for the Next Five Years." *The Asian Manager,* February–March 1995.

*Korea* daily newspaper. Various issues.

*Korea Economic Newspaper,* Various issues.

Krugman, Paul. "The Myth of Asia's Miracle." *Foreign Affairs,* 73, no. 6, (1994): 62–78,

Laothamatas, Anek. "From Clientelism to Partnership: Business-Government Relations in Thailand." *Business and Government in Industrializing Asia.* New York, Cornell University Press, 1994.

Lasserre, Philippe, and Helmut Schütte. *Strategies for Asia Pacific.* New York: New York University Press, 1995.

Lecraw, Donald J. "Outward Direct Investment by Indonesian Firms: Motivation and Effects." *Journal of International Business Studies,* 1993, pp. 589–600.

Levitt, Theodore. "The Globalization of Markets." *Harvard Business Review,* May–June 1983, pp. 92–102.

Lovelock, Christopher J., and George S. Yip. "Global Strategies for Service Businesses." *California Management Review* 38, no. 2 (1996): pp. 64–86.

Lueck, Harmut. Cited in *National Science and Technology Board, Annual Report 1994/1995*. Singapore: NTSB, 1995.

Luhulima, C. P. F. "A Strategic Overview of BIMP-EAGA." January 1995.

MacMurray, Trevor, and Jonathan Woetzel. "The Challenge Facing China's State-owned Enterprises." *The McKinsey Quarterly*, no. 2 (1994): 61–74.

*Maekung Business*. Various issues.

*Maeil* Daily newspaper. (South Korea) Various issues.

Malaysian Industrial Development Bank (MIDA). *Annual Report 1995*, Kuala Lumpur, 1996.

McKinsey and Company, and Australian Manufacturing Council. *Emerging Exporters: Australia's High Value-added Manufacturing Exporters*, June, 1993.

*Ming-Pao*. Various issues. (In Chinese)

Ministry of Finance, Government of Malaysia. *Economic Report 1996*. Kuala Lumpur.

Ministry of International Trade and Industry, Government of Japan. "Overseas Activities of Japanese Companies." Tokyo July 1995.

Ministry of International Trade and Industry. "Gaishikei Kigyo no Doko." August 1995.

Ministry of International Trade and Industry. "Status of FACs." August 1995.

Ministry of International Trade and Industry, Foreign Trade Statistics, Ministry of Finance, White Paper on International Trade Japan, 1995.

Ministry of Trade and Industry, Government of Singapore. *Economic Survey of Singapore, 1994*. Singapore, 1995.

Mohamed, Mahathir. *The Way Forward*. Kuala Lumpur: Government Printers, 1991.

Mohamed, Pengiran Ismail. "BIMP-EAGA Business Forum." November 1995.

Morrison, Allen J., and Paul Beamish. "Kentucky Fried Chicken in China (B)." London, Ontario: Western Business School, Case No. 9-90-G002, 1990.

Motorola Annual Report, Schaumburg, Illinois, 1995.

Naisbitt, John. *Megatrends Asia*. New York: Simon & Schuster, 1996.

Natarajan and Tan. *The Impact of MNC Investments in Malaysia, Singapore and Thailand*. Singapore: ISEAS, 1992.

*New York Times*. Various issues.

*Nihon Keizai Shimbun*. Various issues.

*Nikkei Business*. Various issues.

Ohbora, Tatsuo, Kanoko Oishi, and Hirokazu Yamanashi. "The Emperor's New Stores." *McKinsey Quarterly*, 2, 1994.

Ohmae, Kenichi. *Beyond National Borders*. Japan: Toppan Company, Ltd., 1987.

Ohmae, Kenichi. *The End of the Nation State*, McKinsey & Company Inc., 1995.

Overholt, William H. "Hong Kong after 1997, The Question of Sovereignty." *Columbia Journal of World Business*, 30 no. 2 (1995).

Pacific Economic Cooperation Council for APEC. *Milestones in APEC Liberalization: A Map of Market Opening Measures by APEC Economies*. 1995.

Pacific Economic Cooperation Council for APEC. *Survey of Impediments to Trade and Investment in the APEC Region*, 1995.

Pangestu, Mary. "Deregulation of Foreign Investment Policy." Paper presented at the seminar of World Bank and ISEI (Association of Indonesian Economists) on "Building on Success: Maximizing the Gains from Deregulation," Jakarta, April 26–28, 1995.

Perlmutter, Howard V. "The Tortuous Evolution of Multinational Corporation." *Columbia Journal of World Business*, January–February 1969.

Pernia, Ernesto M. "The Brunei Darussalam-Indonesia-Malaysia-Philippines East Asian Growth Area (BIMP-EAGA) Institutional Perspective." Jakarta: Bandar Seri Begawan, November 1995.

Philips, Annual Report, Eindhoven, Netherlands, 1994.

Pietrucha, Bill. *Journal of Business Strategy,* November 1995, p. 36.

Polsaram, Pussadee. *ISO 9000 in the EC: Are Thai Exporters Sufficiently Prepared.* Unpublished manuscript, Chulalongkorn University, 1995.

Porter, Michael E. *Competitive Advantage.* New York: The Free Press, 1985.

Porter, Michael E. "Changing Patterns of International Competition." *California Management Review,* 28, no. 2 (1986): 9–40.

Porter, Michael E. "The Competitive Advantage of Nations." *Harvard Business Review,* March–April 1990, pp. 73–93.

Porter, Michael E. *The Competitive Advantage of Nations.* New York: The Free Press, 1990.

Prahalad, C. K., and Yves L. Doz. *The Multinational Mission: Balancing Local Demands and Global Vision.* New York: The Free Press, 1987.

Prestowitz, Clyde V. *Trading Places.* New York: Basic Books, 1988.

Price Waterhouse. *Doing Business in Australia.* Sydney, 1993.

Price Waterhouse. *Doing Business in Indonesia.* Jakarta, 1990.

Putti, Joseph M. *Management: Asian Context.* Singapore: McGraw-Hill, 1991.

Putti, Joseph, Kulwant Singh, and William A. Stoever. "Autonomy and Localization of American, European and Japanese Subsidiaries in Singapore." In Carl L. Swanson, Abbass Alkhafaji, and Michael H. Ryans, eds., *International Research in the Business Disciplines,* Greenwich, Connecticut: JAI Press, Vol. 1, 1993, pp. 107–23.

Quinlan, Joseph P. *Vietnam: Business Opportunities and Risks.* Berkeley, Calif.: Pacific View Press, 1995.

Rahman, Yahia Abdul. *Lariba Bank: Islamic Banking.* Hiawatha, Iowa: Cedar Graphics, 1994.

Rau, Pradeep A., and John F. Preble. "Standardization of Marketing Strategy by Multinationals." *International Marketing Review,* Autumn 1987, pp. 18–28.

Ricks, David A. *Blunders in International Business.* Cambridge, Mass.: Blackwell, 1993.

Rohwer, Jim. *Asia Rising: Why America Will Prosper as Asia's Economies Boom.* New York: Simon & Schuster, 1995.

Root, Franklin R. *Entry Strategies for International Markets.* Lexington, Mass.: Heath, 1987.

Rugman, Alan M., and Joseph R. D'Cruz. "The Double Diamond Model of International Competitiveness: Canada's Experience." *Management International Review* 33 (2) (1993): 17–39.

SarDesai, D. R. *Southeast Asia: Past and Present.* 3rd ed. Boulder, Colo.: Westview, 1994.

Shaw, Stephen M., and Jonathan R. Woetzel. "A Fresh Look at China." *The McKinsey Quarterly,* no. 3 (1992) 37–51.

Shill, Walter E. "Japanese Mavericks." *McKinsey Quarterly,* no. 1 (1994).

*Singapore Unlimited.* Singapore: Economic Development Board, 1995.

Smith. Rodney, William Sullivan, and Lynn Wallace. "Malaysia: Moving From Public to Private." *Asian Century Business Report* 4, no. 1 (1995).

Sotojo, Heru. "A Report of Survey on Privatization: Indonesian Case." Faculty of Economics, University of Indonesia, Jakarta, 1995.

Spencer, Cisca, and Gitte Heij. *A Guide to Doing Business in Vietnam.* Perth, Australia: Asia Research Centre, Murdoch University, 1995.

*Standard and Poor's Industry Profiles—Tyres.* July 15, 1995.

Suehiro, A. *Capital Accumulation and Industrial Development in Thailand.* Bangkok: Chulalongkorn University Social Research Institute, 1985.

Sugarda, Yanti B. "Tinjuan Perilaku Konsumen di Indonesia." Paper presented for national discussion on "Power Marketing '95/'96. Organized by the Management Institute, Faculty of Economics, University of Indonesia, Jakarta, June 1, 1995.

Sun, Victor. *China Auto Sector: Putting It Together,* London: Peregrine Securities (U.K.) Ltd., 1995.

*Sunday Age* (Melbourne). Various issues.

Tachiki, Dennis S. "Corporate Investment Strategies for the Pacific Region: Some Evolving Changes in Japanese FDI" (Discussion Paper), November 1995.

Takuo, Kanaka. "Asia-Taiheiyo no Chiiki Kyoryoku." April 1994.

Thambipillai, Pushpa. "The East Asean Growth Area: Political and Economic Environment." (Discussion Paper), November 1995.

Thant, Myo, Min Tang, and Hiroshi Kakazu (eds.). *Growth Triangles in Asia: A New Approach to Regional Economic Cooperation.* ADB Publication. Hong Kong: Oxford University Press, 1994.

*The Australian Year Book,* Sydney, 1995.

*The Australian.* Various issues.

*The Bulletin.* Various issues.

*The Economic Times.* Various issues.

*The Economist.* Various issues.

The Economist Intelligence Unit. Various Reports.

*The Financial Review.* Various issues.

The World Bank. *World Development Report 1995.* Oxford University Press, 1995.

The World Bank, *Indonesia: Improving Efficiency and Equity Changes in the Public Sector Role.* Washington, 1995.

The World Bank. *Indonesia: Dimensions of Growth.* Country report, May 7, 1996.

*Time.* Various issues.

Tin Sin, Gregory Thong. "Managing Process in *Bumiputra* Society—Malaysia." In *Management: Asian Context.* Edited by Joseph M. Putti. Singapore: McGraw-Hill, 1991.

*Tokei Geppo.* Toyo Keizai Shinposha. Various issues.

TRADENZ. *Competing in the New Millenium.* Wellington, New Zealand, 1997.

UNCTAD Division on Transnational Corporations and Competitiveness. *World Investment Report 1995 (and 1996): Transnational Corporations and Competitiveness.* New York and Geneva.

United Nations. *Human Development Report 1994.* New York University Press, 1995. Sripaipan, Chatri. "Technology Upgrading in Thailand: A Strategic Perspective." In *The Emerging Technology Trajectory of the Pacific Rim.* Edited by Denis F. Simon. M. E. Sharpe, Inc., 1994.

Vanhonacker, Wilfried. "Entering China: An Unconventional Approach." *Harvard Business Review,* March—April 1997, pp. 130–40.

Vennewald, Werner. "Technocrats in the State Enterprise System of Singapore." Working paper no. 32. Asia Research Center. Murdoch University, 1994.

*Vietnam Investment Database.* Hanoi: Vietnam Investment Review, 1996.

Vogel, Ezra. *One Step Ahead in China, Guangdong under Reform.* Cambridge, Mass.: Harvard University Press, 1989.

Walker, Simon (ed.). *Rogernomics Reshaping New Zealand's Economy.* Auckland: New Zealand Center for Independent Studies, 1989.

Wang, N. T. *China's Modernization and Transnational Corporations.* Lexington, Mass.: Lexington Books, 1984.

Wie, Thee Kian. *Industrialisasi di Indonesia: Beberapa Kajian.* Jakarta: Pustaka LP3ES Indonesia, 1994.

World Economic Forum. *The World Competitiveness Report 1997.* Geneva, Switzerland.

World Trade Organization. *1995 International Trade: Trends and Statistics.* Geneva: WTO, 1995.

World Trade Organization. Information and Media Relations Division. World Trade Organization: Trading into the Future, Geneva: WTO, 1995.

Yip, George S. *Total Global Strategy: Managing for Worldwide Competitive Advantage.* Englewood Cliffs, N.J.: Prentice Hall, 1992; and Business School edition (paperback) 1995; Indonesian edition (Gramedia Pustaka Utama, Jakarta, 1998), Japanese edition (Japan Times, Tokyo, 1995), and Korean edition (Gimm Young, Seoul, 1994).

Yip, George S. "Global Strategy as a Factor in Japanese Success." *The International Executive,* Special Issue on Japan, 38, no. 1 (1996): 145–67.

Yip, George S., and Tammy L. Madsen. "Global Account Management: The New Frontier in Relationship Marketing. Special Issue of *International Marketing Review* 3, no. 13 (1996): 24–42.

Yoffie David B., and John Coleman. "Motorola and Japan (A), (A) Supplement, and (B)." Cases 9-388-056, 9-388-057, and 9-389-008. Boston: Harvard Business School Publishing, 1988 and 1989.

Yoshino, M. Y., and P. H. Stoneham. "Procter & Gamble in Japan (A), (B), (C), and (D)." Boston: Harvard Business School Publishing, cases 9-391-003, 9-391-005, 9-391-005, 9-391-054, 1991.

Yuan, Lee Tsao. *Growth Triangles in ASEAN.* Honolulu: East-West Center, University of Hawaii, Institute for Economic Development and Policy, Economic Brief No. 10, June 1992.

Yuan, Lee Tsao (ed.). *Growth Triangles: The Johor-Singapore-Riau Experience.* Institute of Southeast Asian Studies and Institute of Policy Studies, 1991.

# Index

# About the Authors

**Wayne Cartwright,** *Professor of Strategic Management, Department of International Business, University of Auckland,* and *Director, Prometheus Ltd., Auckland, New Zealand.* M.Agr.Sc. Massey University; Ph.D., Purdue University. Numerous articles and book chapters on international marketing and strategic management. Member, board of directors of three companies engaged in international business. Extensive consulting experience in the field.

**Peter T. FitzRoy,** *Professor and Head, Department of Marketing, Monash University, Melbourne, Australia.* M.Sc. Ind. Eng., Purdue University; Ph.D., Purdue University. Previous appointments include the Wharton School and Manchester Business School. Books include *Australian Marketing Management* and *Marketing in Australia.*

**Susan Freeman,** *Lecturer, Department of Marketing, Monash University, Melbourne, Australia.* Bachelor of Economics (Monash); Diploma of Education (Mercy); and Master of Educational Studies (Monash). Currently completing her doctorate at Monash University in a comparative history of trade between Austria and Australia. Business experience with Ansett (airline).

**Yoko Ishikura,** *Professor, School of International Politics, Economics, and Business, Aoyama Gakuin University, Tokyo, Japan.* M.B.A. Darden School, University of Virginia; D.B.A. Harvard, 1985, where she wrote cases with Michael Porter; senior manager at McKinsey & Co., Japan from 1985 to 1992, where she worked with Kenichi Ohmae. She has published two books in Japanese, one of them coauthored with Hirotaka Takeuchi.

**Yongwook Jun,** *Associate Professor, College of Business Administration, Chung-Ang University, Seoul, South Korea.* M.M., Kellogg School, Northwestern; Ph.D. International Business, M.I.T., 1985. Numerous articles and cases on South Korean business and companies; coauthoring a book on one of the South Korean *chaebols.* Cotranslator into Korean of *Total Global Strategy.* Member of Globalization Planning Committee, Ministry of Trade and Industry, Republic of South Korea.

**Siti Maimon Kamso,** *Professor and Dean, School of Business and Economics, Universiti Malaysia Sabah, Kota Kinabalu, Malaysia.* M.Sc. Industrial Admin., Aston University; Ph.D. Corporate Strategy, Bath University. She has written, edited, and translated eight books, three in English (e.g., *Corporate Turnaround, ISO-9000*) and five in Bahasa Malaysia (e.g., *Management in Malaysia: Global Competitive Challenge*). Numerous articles on corporate strategy, case writing, and global management.

**Mari Kondo,** *Professor, Asian Institute of Management, Manila, Philippines.* M.B.A., M.A., Stanford. Worked for various divisions of the World Bank and the International Finance Corporation. Product manager, Henkel Group-Japan. Research and publications on development economics, trade, and ASEAN/APEC.

**Joseph Putti,** *former Professor, National University of Singapore, Singapore.* Ph.D. Management, Michigan State University. Set up the M.B.A. Program and then the Human Resource Management Program at the National University of Singapore. Authored several books including *Business Strategy and Management: Text and Cases for Managers in Asia,* and edited *Management: Asian Context.* Articles in international journals such as *Human Relations, International Journal of Management,* and *Journal of International Administrative Sciences.*

**Kam-hon Lee,** *Professor and Dean of Business Administration, Chinese University of Hong Kong, Hong Kong.* M.Comm., Chinese University of Hong Kong; Ph.D., Northwestern. Numerous publications in international journals, including *Journal of Marketing, International Marketing Review,* and *European Journal of Marketing.* Active educator and consultant for companies in Hong Kong and China.

**Kavil Ramachandran,** *Professor, Indian Institute of Management, Ahmedabad, India.* Master of Commerce, University of Calicut; Ph.D., Cranfield Institute of Technology, 1986. Numerous case studies. Books include *Managing a New Business Successfully* and *Small Business Promotion: Case Studies from Developing Countries.* Numerous articles on strategic planning and entrepreneurship in *Journal of Business Venturing, Entrepreneurship & Regional Development,* and *Small Enterprise Development Journal.*

**Kulwant Singh,** *Senior Lecturer, Vice-Dean, Faculty of Business Administration and Co-Editor, Asia Pacific Journal of Management, National University of Singapore, Singapore.* M.B.A., National University of Singapore; Ph.D., University of Michigan, 1993. Papers in *Academy of Management Journal, Strategic Management Journal, Industrial and Corporate Change, Organization Science, Journal of Management, Journal of Economic Behavior and Organization, Journal of Southeast Asia Business,* and others on corporate and technology strategy, interfirm cooperation, and management of complexity in large organizations.

**Emanuel V. Soriano,** *Professor, Asian Institute of Management, Manila, Philippines.* Master of Industrial Management, University of Philippines; D.B.A., Harvard, 1972. Books include *Business Policy for Philippine Management, Business Policy in an Asian Context: Text and Cases, The Big Powers in Southeast Asia: Their Interests and Roles.* On board of directors of various companies.

**Kanoknart Visudtibhan,** *Visiting Assistant Professor, International Business, Chulalongkorn University, Bangkok, Thailand.* M.B.A., Australian Graduate School of Management; Ph.D., Wharton School, 1989. She has coedited *International Strategic Management: Opportunities and Challenges* with Franklin R. Root. Articles in *Journal of Operations Research* and *Chulalongkorn Business Review.* Consulting with Thailand Institute of Management Education and Training.

**Albert Widjaja,** *Lecturer, Master of Management Program, University of Indonesia, Jakarta, Indonesia.* M.B.A., University of Cincinnati; Ph.D., Claremont Graduate School, 1975. Books include *Political Culture and Economic Development in Indonesia.* Articles on strategic management, export strategy, and the Pacific Basin in various Indonesian journals. Prior experience as deputy general manager of a national newspaper in Indonesia.

**Ching-sung Wu,** *Professor, Graduate Institute of International Business, National Taiwan University, Taipei, Taiwan.* M.B.A., National Taiwan University; Ph.D., UCLA, 1987. Publications on strategic alliances and foreign direct investment in *Journal of Management Review, Management Science Review,* and *Journal of Economic Research.* Completing a book in Chinese with a Taiwanese perspective on international business management.

**George S. Yip,** *Adjunct Professor, Anderson Graduate School of Management, University of California, Los Angeles; and Visiting Fellow, Templeton College, Oxford.* M.A., Cambridge; M.B.A., Cranfield and Harvard; D.B.A., Harvard, 1980. Author of *Barriers to Entry* and *Total Global Strategy,* the latter having been published in ten languages. Articles in *California Management Review, Columbia Journal of World Business, Harvard Business Review, International Marketing Review, Sloan Management Review,* and *Strategic Management Journal.* Previous faculty positions at China-Europe International Business School, Georgetown, Harvard, and Stanford. Management experience with Price Waterhouse and Unilever.